Managerial Economics

Managerial Economics

KC Sankaranarayanan

Director
School of Computer Science and Management Studies
MES College, Marampally, Aluva, Kerala 683 107

Former Head, Department of Applied Economics, and
Dean, Faculty of Social Sciences
Cochin University of Science and Technology

CBS PUBLISHERS & DISTRIBUTORS PVT. LTD.
New Delhi • Bengaluru • Chennai • Kochi • Mumbai • Pune

ISBN: 978-81-239-1925-6

First Edition: 2011
Reprint: 2011, 2012, 2015

Published by:
Satish Kumar Jain for CBS Publishers & Distributors Pvt. Ltd.,
CBS Plaza, 4819/XI Prahlad Street, 24 Ansari Road,
Daryaganj, New Delhi – 110002, India
delhi@cbspd.com, cbspubs@airtelmail.in • www.cbspd.com
Ph.: 23289259, 23266861, 23266867 • Fax: 011-23243014

Branches:
• **Bengaluru:** Seema House, 2975, 17th Cross, K.R. Road,
  Bansankari 2nd Stage, Bengaluru - 560070
  Ph: +91-80-26771678/79 • Fax: +91-80-26771680
  E-mail: cbsbng@gmail.com, bangalore@cbspd.com
• **Chennai:** No. 7, Subbaraya Street, Shenoy Nagar, Chennai - 600030
  Ph: +91-44-26681266, 26680620 • Fax: +91-44-42032115
  E-mail: chennai@cbspd.com
• **Kochi:** 36/14, Kalluvilakam, Lissie Hospital Road, Kochi - 682018
  Ph: +91-484-4059061-65 • Fax: +91-484-4059065
  E-mail: cochin@cbspd.com
• **Mumbai:** 83-C, Dr. E. Moses Road, Worli, Mumbai - 400018
  Ph: +91-9833017933, 022-24902340/41 • E-mail: mumbai@cbspd.com
• **Pune:** Bhuruk Prestige, Sr. No. 52/12/2+1+3/2,
  Narhe, Haveli (Near Katraj-Dehu Road Bypass), Pune - 411041
  Ph: +91-20-64704058/59, 32342277 • E-mail: pune@cbspd.com

Printed at :
India Binding House, Noida (UP)

to
Neeraj Deepak (Kannan),
Niveditha Satheesh Shenoy (Ammu)
and
Mahya Deepak

Preface

Managerial economics is an infant subject. This subject was earlier known under different names such as business economics, economics for managers and so on. But now the title *Managerial Economics* is widely accepted. The first book on this subject was published only in 1951 by Joel Dean.

Managerial economics draws concepts and tools of analysis largely from microeconomics. It helps to develop critical thinking skills and provides students with a logical way of analyzing business decisions.

At present a number of books on managerial economics written by foreign as well as Indian authors are available. But some of these books are highly mathematical in nature and as such students find such books difficult to understand. This book avoids the use of any mathematics and as such will be easy to understand for the students.

This book is written according to the syllabus of Mahatma Gandhi University, Kottayam, Kerala, but will be useful to all the students who are undergoing MBA programme in various universities in India.

A textbook draws ideas from different authors who have contributed to the subject under reference. Being a textbook, this has drawn ideas from different books written by foreign as well as Indian authors. But wherever ideas are taken, they are properly acknowledged.

I am indebted to many personalities in shaping the book. First of all, I express my profound gratitude to Mr Sumesh Babu, Network Administrator, and Mr Rajeev Chandrasekhar, Technical Assistant, School of Computer Science and Management Studies, MES College, Marampally, for their assistance in preparing the diagrams and digitalizing the manuscript. My thanks are also due to my faculty colleagues in the Department of Business Administration, namely Mrs Elizabeth George, Head of the Department, Prof (Dr) CA Antony, Dr M Rajan, Mr Velayudhan Nair, Mr Sinosh PK,

Mr Vinu VG, Mr Dipu Varghese, and Mrs Viji Adarsh. My special thanks are due to Padmabhushan Prof (Dr) MV Pylee, National Professor and former Vice-Chancellor of Cochin University, and Prof (Dr) Jose T. Payappilly, former Director, School of Management Studies, Cochin University of Science and Technology and currently Dean, School of Communications and Management Studies, Muttom, who collaborated with me in writing an earlier version of this book. Last but not the least, I express my sincere gratitude to my wife Mrs Prameela Sankaranarayanan, my daughters Mrs Bobby Satheesh and Mrs Bindi Deepak, my sons-in-law Mr Satheesh and Mr Deepak. I also thank the publishers for publishing the book within a short span of time and in a beautiful manner.

Prof (Dr) KC Sankaranarayanan

Contents

7. Elasticity of Demand and Supply 94

8. Demand Forecasting 108

9. Cost Considerations 143

10. Cost–Output Relationship   160

11. Principles of Capital Budgeting   179

12. Cost of Capital 208

13. Techniques and Managerial Applications of Cost–Volume–Profit Analysis 230

14. Market Structure, Pricing and Output 254

Definition and Scope of Managerial Economics

A managerial economist is concerned with those aspects of economic theory and its applications which are directly involved in the decision-making process of a firm. He is not that much concerned with macroeconomic theory or economic policy, even though they are important enough to the understanding of the business situation. Therefore, in this book we give emphasis to microeconomic theory. From the area of macroeconomics we have included topics like national income calculation, fiscal and monetary policies.

For the sake of those who have not studied economics before, we have dedicated some chapters for explaining the basic concepts in economics. So we start from the very definition of economics.

What is economics? Different economists have defined economics differently at different times. But their definitions can broadly be classified into the following categories:

i. Classical or wealth definition
ii. Neo-classical or welfare definition
iii. Lionel Robbins' scarcity definition, and
iv. Samuelson's Growth Oriented Definition.

Classical or Wealth Definition

Adam Smith,[1] the father of modern economics, in his famous book *An Enquiry into the Nature and Causes of the Wealth of Nations* defined economics as the **Science of Wealth**. According to Smith, the main purpose of all economic activities is to amass as much wealth as possible. Therefore, he considered it necessary to study how wealth is produced and consumed. Other classical economists who supported wealth definition are JB Say, John Stuart Mill[2] and FA.Walker. According to Mill, economics is concerned with the study of the nature of wealth and the laws of its production and distribution. To Walker economics is that body of knowledge that relates to wealth.

Criticism of Wealth Definition

The wealth definition was criticised by philosophers as well as literary writers. Carlyle and Ruskin even dared to characterise economics as a dismal science or even as a bastard science. Teaching of economics was considered as the gospel of the devils. The other criticisms relate to selfish science, mundane science, a science of illth and not wealth.

The above criticisms of economics were largely due to the misunderstanding of the word wealth. Adam Smith used the term wealth as a means to an end and not an end by itself.

Neo-Classical or Welfare Definition

Alfred Marshall[3] in his famous book *Principles of Economics* clarified that wealth is needed not for its own sake, but for the sake of material welfare that it promotes. According to Marshall, Political economy or economics is a study of mankind in the ordinary business of life; it examines that part of individual and social action which is most closely connected with the attainment and with the use of the material requisites of well-being.

In the words of Beveridge[4] economics is the study of the general methods by which men cooperate to meet their material needs.

According to A.C. Pigou,[5] "The range of Economists' inquiry becomes restricted to that part of social welfare that can be brought directly or indirectly into relation with the measuring rod of money."

All the above definitions give importance to material welfare. So, one may conclude that this category of definitions considers the purpose of economics as the study of those human activities that are conducive to human welfare in its material aspect.

Lionel Robbins attacked the welfare definition of economics on several counts. According to him there are several economic activities that do not contribute to the material welfare, e.g. production and sale of alcoholic drinks. So also there are several activities that demand a price but have nothing material about such activities, e.g. the services of doctors and lawyers. The definition also ignores the scarcity of resources.

Scarcity Definition of Economics

Lionel Robbins[6] in his book *An Essay on the Nature and Significance of Economic Science* published in 1931 defined economics as the science which studies human behaviour as a relationship between ends and scarce means which have alternative uses.[7]

Robbins' definition highlights four important points. They are:

i. Ends (wants) are unlimited
ii. Means (resources) are scarce
iii. The scarce means have alternative uses
iv. Choice (decision) is to be made to obtain maximum satisfaction.

Economics is thus concerned with allocation of scarce resources among competing wants or activities for the attainment of maximum satisfaction or maximum profit.

Paul A Samuelson criticized Robbins' definition as static. Economics ceased to be 'scarcity centred' and has become 'growth centred'. According to Samuelson Economics is the study of how men and society choose, with or without the use of money to employ productive resources which could have alternative uses, to produce various commodities overtime and distribute them for consumption now and in the future among various people and groups of society.

Samuelson's definition deals with the problem of choice in its dynamic setting. It is also wider in scope. It encompasses changes, dynamism and growth.

We have seen that there are different definitions of economics given by different authors. But there are some economists who would do away with the definition of economics altogether. Auguste Comte[8], Jacob Viner[9] and the Nobel Prize winner Gunnar Myrdal[10] are some of such economists.

Definition and Scope of Managerial Economics

In the above paragraphs we were dealing with the definition of economics. Now we propose to discuss the nature and scope of managerial economics.

Nature of Managerial Economics

Managerial economics as a special branch of economics came into existence only in the early part of the 1950s. So the subject is in its infancy. Some authors use business economics as a synonym for managerial economics. Gradually, however, the term managerial economics has become more acceptable and seems to have displaced progressively the term business economics.

Managerial economics draws on economic analysis such concepts as cost, demand, profit and competition. It tries to bridge the gap between the purely analytical problems that intrigue many economic theorists and the day-to-day decisions that managers must face. It now offers powerful tools and approaches for managerial policy making.

Decision-Making and Forward Planning

Decision-making and forward planning are the two important functions of executives in a business organization. Decision-making is the process of selecting a particular course of action or a combination of the different courses of actions from a number of alternatives for accomplishing a particular target or targets. As applied to business a choice is made among alternative ways of allocating resources to accomplish predetermined objectives. Forward planning, on the other hand, means establishing plans for the future.

In many situations there may be more than two alternatives available to the business decision-maker. Hence choice and valuation is the central problem in decision-making. In reaching a decision, alternatives have to be weighed for rejection or acceptance by the decision-maker. Once a decision is made with respect to a goal to be achieved, plans as to production, pricing, capital, raw materials, labour, etc. are to be drawn out. Forward planning thus goes hand in hand with decision-making.

If the outcome of a course of action always could be predicted with certainty, decision-making would be a fairly simple process. But a prominent feature of the conditions under which business organizations work and take decisions is uncertainty. The conditions of an uncertain outcome place an added burden on the decision-maker. In addition to selecting from among alternative types of action, he must estimate the probable outcome of each of the alternatives. In substance, future alternatives are added to the decision-making process. These future alternatives lead to the following possibilities:

1. Complete realization of the objective,
2. Partial realization of the objective, or
3. Non-realization of the objective.

Risk and Uncertainty

Under the conditions of uncertainty of outcome, it can be realized that many business decisions involve risk. Risk is the chance that an objective or an end result that is sought may not be realized and a loss may occur.[11] Risk arises from uncertainty – uncertainty about the future and its effect upon a plan of action decided upon in the present.[12]

The areas of uncertainty are numerous. They include most phases of business operation as summarized below:

1. *Market demand:* Market demand influences revenues, production schedules and employment of resources.
2. *Production:* Production affects the amount and use of resources for different products and the allocation of resources over periods of time.
3. *Costs:* Costs influence the spending outlays of firms for the purchase and the use of needed resources.
4. *Pricing:* Uncertainties regarding market demand, production and costs create problems in the pricing of products to cover all costs and to yield a margin of profit.
5. *Financing:* Financing includes problems of raising adequate capital and credit in the right proportions at the right time for short- and long-term financial requirements.
6. *Environmental factors:* Environmental factors create problems in business management from changes in the

attitudes, policies or actions of government, labour, the public and other environmental agencies.

7. *Profit:* Uncertainties in each of the areas mentioned above cause variations in costs and market demand which in turn have a positive or negative effect on profits.

With full realization that knowledge of the future is uncertain, business executives must take decisions daily, and they must formulate plans for the future. In this process economic theory can be pressed into service with considerable advantage. Economic theory deals with a number of concepts and principles relating to profit, demand, cost, pricing, production, competition, business cycles, national income, etc. which aided by allied disciplines, like accounting, statistics, mathematics, can be used to solve or at least throw some light upon the problems of business management. The way economic analysis can be used to solving business problems of business management constitutes the subject matter of managerial economics.[13]

Definition of Managerial Economics

Managerial economics refers to those aspects of economics and its tools of analysis most relevant to the firm's decision-making process.[14] It focuses on the application of microeconomic theory to business problems. According to Mc Nair and Meriam, Managerial Economics[15] consists of the use of economic modes of thought to analyse business situations.[16] Some writers[17] consider managerial economics as the integration of economic theory with business practices for the purpose of facilitating decision-making and forward planning by management. The underlying idea of all these definitions is that managerial economics means economics applied in decision-making. So we may define managerial economics as a special branch of economics bridging the gap between abstract economic theory and managerial practice.

Using economic theory in many ways is analogous to using a road map. A road map abstracts away from nonessential characteristics and concentrates on what is relevant for the task at hand. Likewise the economic approach to understand economic decision-making reduces business problems to their most essential components. Understanding the fundamentals of business decision-making provides a way of thinking and analyzing problems that can be applied in a wide range of situations.

It may be pointed out that effective decision-making at the firm's level calls for a careful analysis and choice between alternative courses of action. In fact actual problem solving may require apart from knowledge of economic concepts some knowledge of accounting and of statistical concepts and methods that are not taught in economics. This is largely because the problems of industrial or business management do not neatly fall into any one academic discipline. Rather they cut across different disciplines.

Managerial economics is pragmatic; it is concerned with analytical tools that are useful, that have proven themselves in practice or that promise decision-making in future. In the attempt to be practical it cuts through many of the refinements of theory.[18]

Managerial economics differs from other disciplines in two important respects.[19] First, it is that portion of economics that has to do specially with managerial decision-making. Therefore, it makes a selection from among all the theoretical tools available and those that are directly applicable, empirically based, and thus testable. These qualifications do not mean that these tools are either easier to work with or to comprehend or that they do not require at least as high an order of economic know-how as the rest of economics.

Scope of Managerial Economics

The simplest way to clarify the scope of a field of study is to discuss its relation with other subjects. In this connection it is easy to see that managerial economics has close connection with economics, the theory of decision-making, operations research, statistics and accounting. The fully trained managerial economist integrates concepts and methods from all these disciplines, bringing them together to bear on managerial problems.

Managerial Economics and Economics

Managerial economics is defined as economics applied in decision-making. It is a special branch of economics bridging the gap between abstract economic theory and managerial practice. Both micro- and macroeconomics are used in business analysis and decision-making. The use of micro- and macro-economics depend on the purpose of analysis.

The areas of business issues to which economic theories can be directly applied may be broadly divided into two categories:

1. Operational or internal issues
2. Environmental or external issues.

Microeconomics Applied to Operational Issues

Operational issues are:

Choice of business and nature of the product
Choice of size of the firm
Choice of technology
Choice of price
How to promote sales
How to face price competition
How to decide on new investment
How to manage profit and capital
How to manage inventory?

Microeconomic theories that deal with most of these questions are:

Theory of demand (Consumer behaviour)
Theory of production and production decisions
Analysis of market structure and price theory
Profit analysis and profit management
Theory of capital and inventory management, etc.

Microeconomic concepts such as elasticity of demand, marginal cost, short and long runs, etc. are all of great significance to managerial economics. Well-known models in price theory such as the models for the monopoly price, the kinked demand theory and the model of price discrimination are also made use of in managerial economics. Even though some of the authorities on managerial economics[20] hold the view that the scope of managerial economics does not extend to macro- economics, macroeconomics is applied to business environment in the following areas:

- Economic systems
- General trends in production, employment, income, prices, saving and investment

- Structure and trends in the working of financial institutions
- Magnitude and trends in foreign trade
- Trends in labour and capital markets
- Government's economic policies
- Social factors like the value systems of the society, property rights, customs and habits
- Social organizations like trade unions, consumer's cooperatives, producers' unions
- Political environment
- The degree of openness of the economy.
- Forecasting. Post-Keynesian theory of income and employment has direct implications for forecasting general business conditions. Since the prospects of an individual firm often depend greatly on business in general, individual firm forecast depends on general business forecasts, which make use of models derived from theory.

A survey conducted in the United Kingdom showed that business economists have found economic concepts such as price elasticity of demand, opportunity costs the multiplier, propensity to consume, marginal revenue product, speculative motive, production function, balanced growth, liquidity preference, etc. quite useful of frequent application. They have also found the following main areas of economics as useful in their works.[21]

The demand theory

Theory of the firm—price and output

Business financing

Public finance and fiscal policy

Money and Banking

National income and social accounting

Theory of international trade, and

Economics of developing countries.

Some of the other areas that fall within the purview of managerial economics are:

1. Profit analysis
2. Cost determination

3. Production possibilities chart
4. Market penetration studies
5. Sales forecasting
6. Break-even analysis
7. Anti-trust studies
8. Plant location studies
9. Mergers and acquisitions
10. Labour cost studies
11. Inventory problem
12. Investment analysis
13. Capital budgeting
14. Cost of capital
15. Government regulations.

To quote Haynes, et al. "The relation of Managerial Economics to economic theory (either the micro or the macro varieties) is much like that of engineering to physics or of medicine to biology or bacteriology. It is the relation of an applied field to the more fundamental but more abstract basic discipline from which it borrows concepts and analytical tools. The fundamental theoretical fields will no doubt in the long run make the greater contribution to the extension of human knowledge. But the applied fields involve the development of skills that are worthy of respect in themselves and require specialized training. The practicing physician may not contribute much to the advance of biological theory, but he plays an essential role in producing the fruits of progress in theory. The managerial economist stands in a similar relation to theory, with perhaps the difference that the dichotomy between the "pure" and the "applied" is less clear in management than it is in medicine."[22]

Managerial Economics and the Theory of Decision-Making

The theory of decision-making has significance to managerial economics. Much of economic theory is based on the assumption of a single goal—maximization of utility for the individual or maximization of profit for the firm. It also rests on the assumption of certainty or perfect knowledge. The theory of decision-making, on the other hand, recognizes the multiplicity of goals and the existence of uncertainty in the realm of management. The theory of decision-making invariably replaces the notion of a single optimum solution with the view that the objective is to find solutions that "satisfy" rather than "maximize". It enquires into an analysis of motivation, of the relation of rewards and aspiration levels, of patterns of influence on human behaviour.

The theory of decision-making, in short, is a reminder of the complexities of decision-making and the frequent needs to compromise 'pure' models to make them useful in actual practice. Again, the theory of decision-making promises to contribute to the improvement of practice by focusing on new problems, and suggesting new lines of attack. Managerial economics must take note of these developments.

Managerial Economics and Operations Research

Operations Research is very closely related to managerial economics. Operations research is concerned with model building, i.e. the construction of theoretical models that aid decision-making. Managerial economics applies these models of decision-making. Operations research is often concerned with optimization; economics has long dealt with the consequences of maximization of profit or minimization of costs.[23]

Operations research as applied to business, generally is concerned with the broad, overall operation of a company rather than with details of any specific operation. Viewing the business in its entirety, studies are made of the inter-relationship and relative efficiencies of the various aspects of a business in combination, such as sales, production and financing. To find the most effective flow pattern, operations research may encompass the complete cycle of the flow of goods and services from suppliers to company plants and then to consumers. The primary purpose of operations research, as pointed out earlier, is to find the best (optimum) combination of factors to achieve a given objective, whether it is profit, reduction of cost, saving of time, or other objectives. The resulting solution serves as a guide to company policy and decision-making.[24]

It is the team approach that makes operations research distinctive. Operations research team is usually composed of persons from various disciplines and professions.

Because of the company-wide approach to problems, specialists in such disciplines as natural sciences, mathematics, economics, sociology, psychology, etc. are often included in the Operations research team. This type of pooling of diverse talents seems to be its distinctive feature. Operations research relies heavily on mathematics and statistics. Most of the best-known Operations research techniques are mathematical or statistical in character as opposed to the more subjective and qualitative techniques usually used by management. Thus mathematical or statistical techniques such as linear programming, game theory, queuing theory, and related methods are generally used by Operations researchers for analysis and evaluation of the problem.

As rightly pointed out by Haynes and others[25] it is not important to determine where managerial economics begins and operations research ends. But it is important to recognize the closer relation of the two subjects and the contribution that each makes to the other. The student who wants to do more advanced work in managerial economics should have a thorough training in mathematics and statistics, for the models which are likely to be important in the future will require considerable sophistication in the use of quantitative methods.

Managerial Economics and Statistics

Managerial economics and statistics are related in a number of ways. Firstly, it provides for the basis for empirical testing of theory. Generalization in economics, just like in any other science, is subject to empirical test. While deductive reasoning has made a central contribution to economics, the results of that reasoning can never be fully accepted until they are verified against data from the world of reality.

Secondly, statistics is important in providing the individual firm with measures of the appropriate functional relationship involved in decision-making.

Thirdly, the theory of probability, upon which many of the statistical studies are made, is also important in Managerial

Economics. Managers generally do not have all or exact information about the variables affecting decisions. So they must deal with the uncertainty of future events. Under such circumstances the theory of probability comes to the help of the managers in taking decisions.

Fourthly, linear programming which is an important statistical technique for treating problems is used by managerial economists to find the best solution or the best alternative. Linear programming is the answer to the dilemma of the business manager who may find it impossible to undertake personally the study of reports, figures, trends, and other data necessary in many decision programmes.

Managerial Economics and Accounting

Managerial economics is also related to accounting. Accounting is concerned with recording the financial operations of a business firm. Accounting information is one of the primary sources of data required by a managerial economist for the decision-making purpose. For example, the profit and loss statement of the firm indicates how well or ill the firm has done and the information it contained can be used by the managerial economist to throw some light on the future course of action—whether it should try to improve or close down.

Normative vs Descriptive Economics

Managerial Economics forms a part of normative economics. It tries to prescribe solutions. In other words, it is concerned with what decisions ought to be made. The main body of economic theory confines itself to descriptive hypotheses attempting to generalize about the relations among variables, without judgments about what is **desirable** or undesirable.[26] For instance, the law of diminishing returns is a generalization about what happens to output when variable inputs are added to fixed inputs, involving no judgments about whether the result is **good** or **bad.**

Normative economics encompasses those branches of economics that attempt to combine descriptive economics with value judgments to arrive at policy conclusions. Public policy or economic policy of the government is one form of normative economics and managerial economics is another.

There is one interesting feature of managerial economics that is of special significance to managerial economics. Some of the main propositions of managerial economics are heavily deductive. For instance, the statement that profits are at a maximum when marginal revenue is equal to marginal cost is entirely a matter of logic that do not require any check against the facts. A substantial part of economic analysis is of this character, providing a system of logic that is self-contained.[27] But it must be pointed out that it is necessary to fit the correct data into this logical framework to reach specific conclusions about what should be done. And the question whether a particular line of logic is useful is an empirical issue, requiring a check against the facts. Linear programming is an appropriate illustration.[28] The logic of linear programming is nothing but deduction in mathematical form. Given certain assumptions, linear programming denotes the logical consequences. But to use linear programming one must have the relevant data on items such as capacities, requirements, costs or whatever is involved.

Conclusion

Economics is the science which studies human behaviour as a relationship between ends and scarce means which have alternative uses. In other words, it is concerned with the study of the allocation of scarce resources among competing ends. Individuals, enterprises and nations constantly face problems of resource allocation. During the course of its development as a science, economics has developed a variety of concepts and analytical tools to deal with the resource allocation problems. The increasing use of mathematical reasoning and statistical methodology in recent years has introduced a great deal of sophistication in this field.

Managerial economics refers to those aspects of economics and its tools of analysis most relevant to firm's decision-making process. It provides a systematic, logical way of analyzing business decisions the focuses on the economic forces that shape both day-to-day decisions and long-run planning decisions.

Managerial economics applies microeconomic theory—the study of the behaviour of individual economic agents—to business problems in order to teach business decision makers how to use economic analysis to make decisions that will achieve the firm's goal: the maximization of profit.

Economic theory helps managers to understand real world business problems by using simplifying assumptions to abstract away from irrelevant ideas and information and turn complexity into relative simplicity. Like a roadmap, economic theory ignores everything irrelevant to the problem and reduces business problems to their essential components.

Managerial economics has been enriched by the growing influence of quantitative sciences especially through the medium of operations research. The influence of and advances in management theory has strengthened its applied bias and its ability to be an aid in solving practical problems enterprises face.

Review Questions

1. Define economics.
2. Define managerial economics.
3. Show in what respect or respects managerial economics differ from traditional economics.
4. Explain the scope of managerial economics.
5. "Managerial economics is the integration of economic theory with business practice for the purpose of facilitating decision-making and forward planning by management." Explain.

References

1. Adam Smith (1723-1790) was born in Scotland. After having education at universities of Glasgow and Oxford he became professor first of Logic and then of Moral Philosophy at Glasgow. As the tutor to the young Duke Buccleugh he had the opportunity to meet the leading thinkers of the day, including Voltaire, Quesnai, Turgot and Helvetius. He was the first Academic Economist. His famous works include The Theory of the Moral Sentiments (1759) and An Inquiry into the Nature and Causes of the Wealth of Nations (1776).
2. John Stuart Mill (1896-1873) is the author of Principles of Political Economy, that was the undisputed Bible of economic doctrines. He,

more than any English Economist, reflects the time in which early competitive capitalism—accompanied by English leadership in world markets-attained its zenith.

3. Alfred Marshall: The Principles of Economics, 6th Edition, p.1. Alfred Marshal (1842-1924). One of his most characteristic concepts was 'consumer surplus'. His special contribution to the problem of value and price lies in his analysis of the equilibrium between supply and demand. His chief work, *The Principles of Economics* appeared in 1890.

4. William Henry Beveridge (1879-1963) helped to shape Great Britain's post-World War 11 welfare state policies and institutions through his Social Insurance and Allied Services (1942), that is also known as the Beveridge Report. He directed the London School of Economics and Political Science from 1919 to 1937, when he was Elected as master of University College, Oxford. He worked out the blue prints of The new British Welfare State. His books include Full Employment in a Free Society (1944). Insurance for All (1924), British Food Control (1928), Planning Under Socialism (1936), Power and Influence (1953), Pillars of Security (1948) and a Defense of Free Learning (1959).

5. Pigou, A.C; The Economics of Welfare, 1920; p.11. A.C. Pigou (1877-1959) was Professor of Political Economy at the Cambridge University from 1908-1943. He is best known for his contributions to the theory of economic welfare. His other major works include Wealth and Welfare (1912), The Value of Money (1917), and The Theory of Unemployment (1933).

6. Lionel Robbins, An Essay on the Nature and Significance of Economic Science; London (1952), P.16. Lionel Robbins was Professor of Economic Science in the University of London. His main contribution is in the field of definition of economics.

7. Paul A Samuelson (1915-2009) was an American economist, and the first American to win the Nobel Prize in Economics.

8. Auguste Comte (1798-1857) was a French Philosopher and Sociologist.

9. Jacob Viner was professor of Economics at the University of Chicago. His main contribution is in the field of International Trade. His publications include Studies in the Theory of International Trade, "Angell's Theory of International Prices", *Journal of Political economics*, XXX1V (1926), Comparative Costs: A Rejoinder, *Quarterly Journal of Economics*, X111 (1928), "The Doctrine of Comparative Costs", *Weltwirtschaftliches Archive*, XXXV1 (1932,11).

10. Gunnar Myrdal was born in 1899. He was Professor of International Economics at the University of Stockholm and the Director of the Swedish Institute for International Economic Studies. He has served as an Advisor to the Swedish Government on Economic, Social and

Fiscal Policy and was Minister of Commerce. He won Nobel Prize for Economics in 1975. His works include Asian Drama, Economic Theory and Underdeveloped Regions, An International Economy, An American Dilemma, and The Political Elements in the Development of Economic Theory.

11. Wheeler, Bayard O; Business: An Introductory Analysis, New York, 1962, p.226
12. *Ibid p.230*
13. Varshney, R.L and Maheswari, K.L, *Managerial Economics, Delhi, p.*4.
14. Haynes, William Warren; Mote Vasant L and Paul, Samuel; *Managerial Economics: Analysis and Cases, Bombay, 1970, p.v*
15. The term used is Business Economics.
16. Mc Nair, Malcolm P and Meriam Richard S, *Problems in Business Economics*, New York, 1941, p.v
17. Spencer, M.H. and Siegel man, *Managerial Economics*, Illinois. 1959, p.1
18. Hynes, William Warren, et al. op.cit., p.1
19. Stokes, Charles J; Managerial Economics: A Casebook; New York, p.3
20. Haynes, William Warren et.al.
21. Alexander, K.J.W. and Kemp A.G., *The Economist in Business, A Survey, p.26*
22. *Haynes, William Warren, et al. op.cit. p.3*
23. *Ibid. p.4*
24. Wheeler, Bayard O; op.cit. p.233
25. Haynes, William Warren, et al. op.cit. p.5
26. Ibid. p.6
27. Ibid
28. Ibid.

2 Decision-Making and the Fundamental Concepts Affecting Business Decisions

"No war, no strike, no depression, can so completely destroy an established business or its profits, as new and better methods, equipment and materials in the hands of an enlightened competitor."

— *Society for the Advancement of Management*

What is enlightened business management? How can it be identified? What are the methods followed in such management? The answers to these questions lead us to the heart of the management function in business—decision-making. The quality of the decisions made by management is the central clue to business success or failure. It is the ultimate test of good (enlightened) management.[1]

Let us, therefore, examine the process of decision-making in some detail including the fundamental concepts affecting or facilitating decision-making.

Decision-Making Defined

Decision-making is the process of selecting a particular course of action or courses of actions from among a number of alternatives to accomplish a predetermined objective or objectives. As applied to business, a choice is made among alternative ways of using or allocating scarce resources to accomplish pre-determined objective or objectives.[2]

In many cases there may be more than two alternative courses of action available to the decision-maker. Under such situations the decision-maker should evaluate the alternatives before taking the decisions.

Steps in the Process of Decision-Making

The process of decision-making in its simplest form is given below:

Here we assume that four alternative courses of action are available to the decision-maker. The search for and identification of alternative courses of action for the accomplishment of a predetermined objective or objectives is the first step in decision-making. The alternatives available to the decision-maker in our case are listed below:

Alternatives available

Action   A

Action   B

Action   C

Action   D

The problem now is to select the appropriate course of action or courses of actions to accomplish the objective or objectives. The course of action or actions selected must be the most profitable one or ones. To ensure this, the decision-maker must evaluate the available courses of actions. So the second step in decision- making is the evaluation of the alternative courses of action.

Evaluation of the different courses of action.

Evaluation of Action   A

Evaluation of Action   B

Evaluation of Action   C

Evaluation of Action   D

The third step in decision-making is selection of the most profitable course or courses of action or actions to realize the goal. The course of action selected in our example is given below:

Course of action selected: Action D

The decision-making process is given below: in the form of a flow chart.

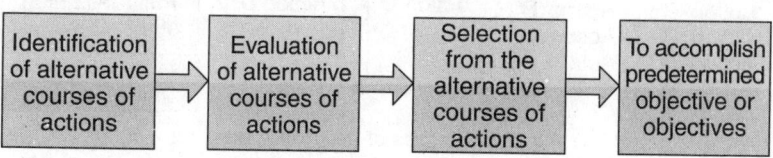

Variations in the Selection of Alternatives

The simplified model of decision-making given above assumes that only one course of action is selected. But in actual practice, the decision-maker may follow a multiple course of action. That is two out of four or more alternatives may be used, or two or more alternatives may be combined to form a combined course of action. But the variations in decision-making do not in any way modify the essential nature of the decision-making process. Only the alternatives are widened.

Uncertainty in Decision-Making

If everything could be predicted accurately, then decision-making would become a fairly simple process. But where the decision-maker cannot control the outcome of his decisions, an element of uncertainty is introduced. In business where people are involved and they can also affect the outcome of decisions, there are many circumstances under which the future may be wholly or partly unpredictable. Under such a situation an added burden is placed on the decision-maker. And this results in three possibilities:

1. Complete realisation of the objective,
2. Partial realization of the objective, or
3. Non-realization of the objective. These possibilities are illustrated in Fig. 2.1.

Because of the presence of uncertainty, the decision-maker must be extremely careful about each step in the process of decision-making. Under such conditions the decision-maker

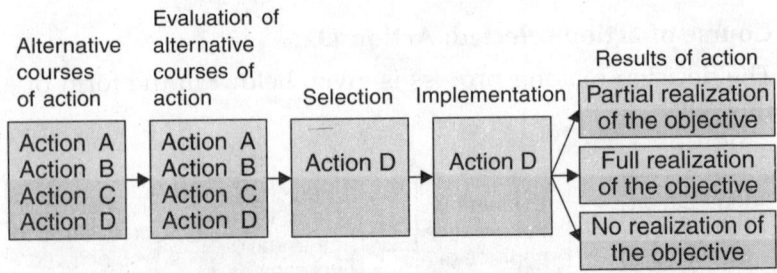

Fig. 2.1: Process of decision-making

has to rely on probability theory and feedback information systems. A simple model of the feedback information system is presented in Fig. 2.2.

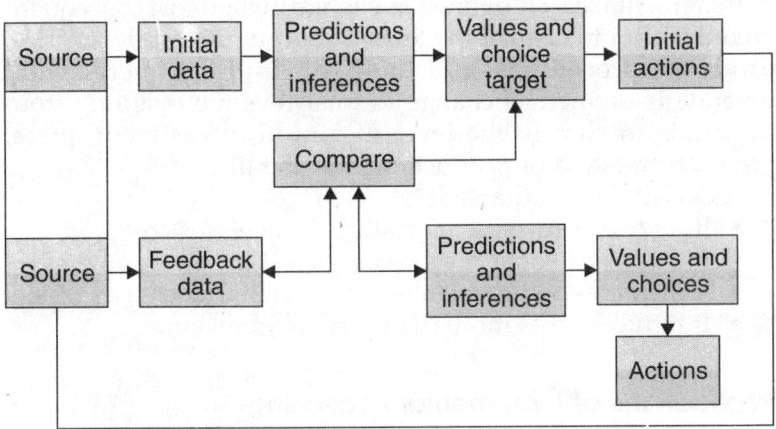

Fig. 2.2: Feedback information system for decision-making

Fundamental Concepts that Aid Decisions

In spite of the imperfections in knowledge and the presence of uncertainty management must, nevertheless, take decisions daily, and they must formulate plans for the future. There are various ways in which decisions can be made, ranging from "off the cuff" guesswork to fully informed conclusions combined with good judgment.[3] Experience has shown that the following five fundamental concepts, viz. the incremental concept, the discounting concept, the opportunity cost concept, the concept of time perspective and the equi-marginal concept help the management to make correct decisions. Here we propose to discuss each of these concepts in some detail.

Incremental Cost

Incremental reasoning involves estimating the impact of decision alternatives on costs and revenues, stressing the changes in total costs and total revenues that result from changes in prices, products, procedures, investments or

whatever may be at stake in the decision.[4] The two fundamental concepts in incremental analysis are:
- Incremental cost (IC), and
- Incremental revenue (IR).

Incremental cost is defined as change in total cost consequent on a decision to change the level of output, investment, price, products, procedures, and the like. Similarly, incremental revenue is defined as change in total revenue resulting from decisions to change the level of output, investment, price, products, method of production, and the like.

A decision is profitable if[5]
- It increases revenue more than it increases cost
- It decreases some costs more than it increases others
- It increases some revenues more than it decreases others
- It reduces costs more than it reduces revenue.

Implications of Incremental Reasoning

Some businessmen hold the view that to make an overall profit they 'must make profit on every job'. Consequently, they often reject orders that do not cover full cost (variable plus overhead) plus some provision for profit. But incremental reasoning shows that such action from the side of management is inconsistent with profit maximization in the short run. This can be seen from the following illustration.

Illustration

Let us assume that 'XYZ Ltd.' gets an order worth Rs. 100000. The full cost as estimated by the accountant of the company for meeting the order is given below:

Labour cost	Rs. 30000
Materials cost	Rs. 40000
Overhead (allocated at 120% of labour cost)	Rs. 36000
Selling and administrative expense (allocated at 20 % of material and labour cost)	Rs. 14000
Full cost	Rs. 120000

From the cost estimates made by the accountant, the above order appears to be unprofitable. But suppose there exists some idle capacity and that can be used for meeting this order. Also suppose that the acceptance of this order will add only Rs.10000 to overhead (the incremental overhead limited to the added use of heat, power, light, added wear and tear of machinery, added cost of supervision, etc.). Acceptance of the order doesn't require any selling or administrative expenses as the only requirement is the acceptance of the order. In addition only part of the labour cost is incremental since some idle workers already on the payroll can be put to work without any additional pay.

The incremental cost as estimated by the company economist is given below:

Labour cost	Rs. 20000
Materials cost	Rs. 40000
Overhead	Rs. 10000
Total incremental cost	Rs. 70000

From the accountant's estimate of costs it appears that the order, if accepted, will result in a loss of Rs. 20000. But from the Economist's version (based on incremental cost) the order is expected to contribute Rs. 30000 to profit.

It may be pointed out here that there is some misunderstanding about incremental reasoning. Incremental reasoning doesn't mean that the firm should price its products at cost or should accept all orders that cover merely their incremental costs. In fact "charging what the market will bear" is consistent with incremental reasoning, for it implies increasing rates as long as the resultant revenues increase.[6] The acceptance of the Rs. 100000 order in our example, depends upon.

- The existence of idle capacity which would otherwise go unused, and
- The absence of more profitable alternatives.

We would like to stress the fact that incremental reasoning never leads to acceptance of less profitable order in preference to one that is more profitable, in reality it leads to the opposite. In other words, what incremental principle wants to stress is that a decision is sound or valid if it increases revenue more than it increases cost or reduces costs more than it reduces revenue.

Incremental Reasoning and Marginal Reasoning

Those who know the elementary principles of economics will at once recognize the fact that incremental reasoning is very much related to the marginal costs and marginal revenues in economic analysis. But there are similarities and differences between incremental analysis and marginal analysis and that must be recognized.

Firstly, marginal costs and marginal revenues are always defined in terms of unit changes in output[7] whereas incremental costs and incremental revenues are not necessarily restricted to unit changes. For example, if one unit increase in output results in an increase in cost from Rs. 1000 to Rs. 1010 and an increase in revenue from Rs. 1200 to Rs. 1216 the marginal cost is Rs. 10 and marginal revenue Rs. 16. If the cost function is curvilinear, the marginal cost may change for each unit change in output. The marginal analysis (measurement of marginal revenues and marginal costs) enables one to have a microscopic picture about unit- by- unit changes. But in reality the decision-maker may not be interested in such a microscopic analysis of the situation. His interest may be limited to the sense that he wants to know only whether the decision as a whole is profitable or not. To know this he may be willing to look at the entire increase in revenues and costs. The defect of this approach is the possibility of some other changes in output within the range that might be even more profitable. but it is often pointed out that the cost of refinement is much more than the risk involved.

Secondly incremental concepts are more flexible than marginal concepts. As already noted, marginal costs and marginal revenues are restricted to the effects of unit changes in output. But decision-making may not be concerned with changes in output at all. For example, the problem may be one of substituting one process for another to produce the same output. The problem is then one of comparing the cost of the first process with that of the alternative. The marginal analysis is not particularly suited to this kind of decision.[8]

One method of comparing marginal and incremental reasoning is to draw a traditional cost diagram. In the diagram

(Fig. 2.3) marginal cost is depicted as a curve, rising over most of its range.

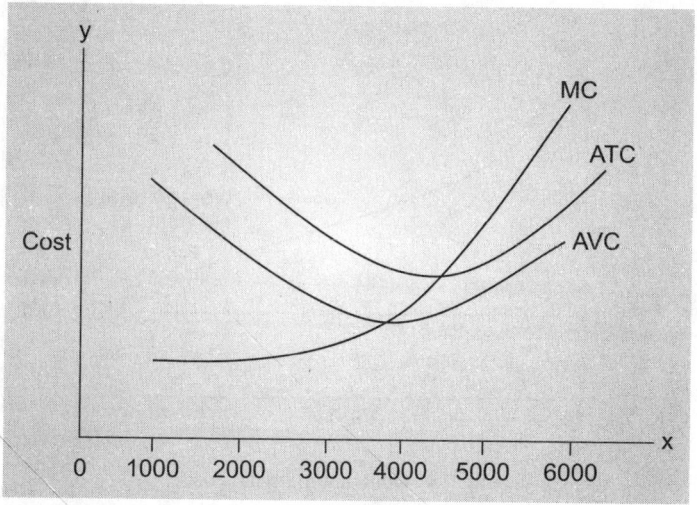

Fig. 2.3: Quantity

Let us consider increasing output from 4000 to 6000 units. What is the marginal cost of this change? It is dangerous to give any answer on the basis of the above diagram. In the range from 3000 to 4000 units the marginal cost is comparatively low, but it rises rapidly afterwards. Even to talk about anything like an average marginal cost over this range is to oversimplify and to ignore the dramatic change over the range of outputs.[9]

But many studies of cost functions[10] indicate the existence of constant marginal costs over a wide range of outputs. If that is the case, no error results from substituting a single marginal cost figure for the whole range.

Let us consider that the total fixed costs of the firm illustrated below are Rs. 6000 (per time period. The average available cost is Rs. 2 per unit. The marginal cost also is Rs. 2 per unit. Imagine that the decision involves a choice between an output of 3000 units and one of 6000 units. In the language of the marginal cost there is no doubt about how to express the change in cost—it is Rs. 2 per unit. In the incremental language it is perfectly valid to speak of an addition to total cost of Rs. 6000.

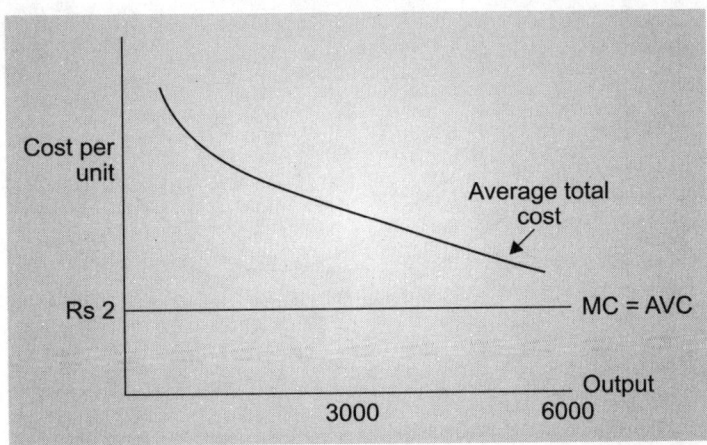

Fig. 2.4: Constant marginal costs

The question whether marginal costs are in fact constant may be asked at this juncture. If we could be certain of the universal linearity of short-run costs, then the problem of decision-making would be greatly simplified. But the difficulty is that there is no consensus of opinion on this point.

Studies conducted by Joel Dean,[11] Jonston[12] and Yntema[13] suggest that cost curves are linear and marginal costs are constant in the short-run. But studies conducted by Nordin[14] failed to validate the cost linearity hypothesis. So it seems rather dangerous to assume that the constancy of the marginal cost is universal. In the said context the validity of any decision can be judged on the basis of the following two theorems.

Theorem 1   : A course of action should be pursued up to the point where its incremental benefits equal its incremental costs.

Theorem 2   : Different courses of action should be pursued up to the point where all the courses provide equal marginal benefit per unit of cost.

Another point to be noted with marginal analysis is that marginal analysis assumes a single variable function, e.g. revenue depends on output, cost depends on output.

The decision rule in these cases will be:

- To maximize revenue, do not sell output beyond the point where MR = 0
- To maximize total product, do not employ any factor beyond a point where marginal product (MP) = 0
- To minimize cost produce till AC = MC.

Concept of Time Perspective

It was Professor Alfred Marshall who introduced the concept of time into economic analysis. Ever since short-run and long-run became widely used as economic concepts. Economists use these terms with a precision that is often missed in ordinary discussions.[15] In economics short-run refers to a period of time that is long enough to allow the variable factors of production to be used in different amounts in order to ensure that maximum profits are earned, but during which fixed factors cannot be altered in amount.[16] For example, the increase in output of a department requires variation in the quantity of labour and materials but not the area of floor-space or the number of machines. On the other hand, long-run refers to a period of time that is long enough to bring about possible variations in all inputs. Building a new plant is an example.

Managerial economists are concerned with the short-run and long-run effects of decisions on costs as well as revenues. The line between short-run and long-run revenue (or demand) is even fuzzier than that for costs. The crucial problem in decision-making is to maintain the right balance between the short-run, long-run and medium or intermediate run perspectives. In other words, the management should take a long-run view of effects on costs and revenues rather than merely a "short-sighted view".[17] A decision may be made on short-run considerations, but may, as time passes, have long-run repercussions that make it more or less profitable than at first seemed.[18] The following illustration may help to clarify this in a better way.

Assume a firm with some temporarily idle capacity. A possible order for 15000 units comes to management's attention.

The prospective customer is willing to pay Rs. 3 per unit, or Rs. 45000 for the whole lot. The short-run incremental cost (that ignores the fixed costs) is only Rs. 2. Therefore, the contribution to overhead and profit is Re. 1 per unit (or Rs. 15000 for the whole lot). In spite of this favourable position, before accepting this order, the management must take into consideration the long-run repercussions, viz.

- What will happen if the management commits itself to a series of repeat order at the same price?
- What will be the reaction of other customers if they come to know about the practice of accepting orders below full cost?
- Will this tarnish the image of the company?

The above questions lead to the following conclusion.

A decision should take into account the short-run and long-run effects on revenues and costs, consumers' reaction and company image, etc. giving appropriate weight to the most relevant time periods.

Discounting Principle

One of the fundamental principles in economics is that a rupee tomorrow is worth less than a rupee today. This means that a differentiation is to be made between cash received at different points of time. Even under conditions of certainty we cannot treat rupees received at different points in time as if they were equal since the earlier we receive a rupee, the earlier we can put it to use to earn additional money. The underlying assumption here is that, in an economy in which interest and opportunities for investment exist, a rupee received today can be invested to earn additional money immediately. A rupee to be received one year from hence could not be invested until it is received; therefore, it is less valuable than a rupee received today. In other words, there is a premium for waiting to receive benefits; the longer one has to wait, the more return one should expect on one's money. Stated in another way, where there is a time element there is a discounting problem. This demands the decision-maker in business to use interest theory in the solution of a specific problem with numerical examples.

It may be pointed out here that discounting is nothing but the inverse of compounding. Both methods seek to demonstrate the fact that a given sum of money in future differs in terms of purchasing power from an identical sum today. Compounding implies that interest accruing in any one year is added to capital outstanding at the beginning of that year and interest is then charged on the total sum (interest plus capital) during the ensuing year.

The following example will make clear the necessity of discounting. Suppose you are offered a choice between a gift of Rs. 100 today or Rs. 100 next year. Naturally you will prefer the Rs. 100 today. This is true even if there is certainty about the receipt of either gift, as today's Rs. 100 can be deposited and can accumulate interest during the year. Suppose that you can earn 10 percent interest on any money you have at your disposal. If so, by the end of the year the gift will accumulate interest to become a total of Rs. 110.

In other words, if a sum of Rs. X is invested at an interest rate of r percent per annum, the capital will have accrued by year end to Rs. $X(1+r)$. Interest on this amount is then charged during the second year at rate of r percent per annum so that at year end the capital has grown to $X(1+r)(1+r)$ or Rs. $X(1+r)^2$. To generalize, one can say that the future worth of Rs. X at r percent interest for n years is

$$\text{Rs. } X(1+r)^n$$

Another way of putting the matter that brings out the discounting principle more forcefully is to ask how much money today would be equivalent to Rs. 100 a year from now.[19] Again, assume a rate of interest of 10 percent. We must discount the Rs. 100 at 10 percent, which means that we divide the Rs. 100 by 1.10. Thus

$$Pv = \frac{\text{Rs. }100}{1+r} = \frac{\text{Rs. }100}{1+0.10} = \text{Rs. }90.90$$

Where Pv = present value

r = the rate of interest.

In other words, the present value of Rs. X, n years hence, at r percent interest is

$$\frac{X}{(1+r)^n}$$

The discounting concept is most relevant in investment decisions.[20]

Opportunity Cost Concept

We have already noted that decisions involve choices to be made among alternatives. When one alternative is chosen in preference to others, an alternative or opportunity cost of some sort is incurred. Thus the decision of company management to accept a strike of union workers rather than pay higher wages involves cost to the company, in this case the loss of income resulting from a shut down. On the other hand, the decision to pay higher wages also entails a cost in the form of increased wage bill.[21]

The principle involved here is that the benefit that can be gained from any course of action is offset in part by the benefits or gains that might come from the selection of alternative courses of action. In rejecting one alternative in favour of another, the potential benefits available from the rejected alternative are an offset or cost to the selected alternative. It can be seen, therefore, that a net loss may occur to the decision-maker if he chooses a course of action that have fewer benefits that a better course of action. This possibility points out the importance of careful study and evaluation of the comparative advantages of the various available alternatives. The skillful decision-maker recognizes this, so he attempts to fortify his decision by the collection and analysis of needed information to enable him to predict that course of action which will yield the best results in accomplishing the objective.[22]

According to Haynes and others opportunity cost of a decision means the sacrifice of alternatives required by that decision.[23] The following examples will clarify the meaning of the opportunity cost concept.

- The opportunity cost of the funds tied up in one's own business is the interest (or profits corrected for differences in risk) that could be earned on that funds in other ventures.

- The opportunity cost of time that a person puts into his own business is the salary he could earn in other occupations (with a correction for the relative psychic income in the two occupations).

- The opportunity cost of using a machine that is useless for any other purpose is nil, since its use requires no sacrifice of other opportunities.[24]

The opportunity costs, thus, are the "costs of sacrificed alternatives".

In any discussion of opportunity cost, it is useful to make a distinction between explicit and implicit costs. Explicit costs refer those costs that are recognized in the accounts. Examples are:

Payment for raw materials
Payment for labour
Payment for land

Implicit or imputed costs are not recognized in the accounts. Examples are:

- Interest on the owner's capital
- Rent to owner's land
- Salary to the owner.

In our definition of opportunity cost both explicit and implicit sacrifices are included.

It seems desirable to point out here that both incremental cost concept and discounting concept are special applications of opportunity cost concept. When excess capacity exists, it may be that the only sacrifice made in increasing a particular output is in employing variable inputs. Under such circumstances only part of the costs are reflected in incremental costs. Under conditions of full utilization of capacity or even full utilization of certain bottlenecks in production, the incremental cost of any alternative must reflect the sacrifice of other alternatives or opportunities. An estimate of incremental costs thus requires the application of opportunity cost reasoning.[26]

For example, in the simple problem outlined earlier (In the discussion on incremental concept) on accepting the order, materials cost of Rs. 40000, labour cost of Rs. 20000 and incremental overhead of Rs. 10000, etc. are all opportunity costs because all those require a sacrifice in the form of payment for these factors. The other costs are excluded as they require no such sacrifices in view of the existence of excess capacity. If the entire capacity had been used , the estimate of incremental costs would have included estimates of sacrifices of other alternatives and would have been much higher than Rs. 70000.[27]

Similarly the underlying reason for discounting is that when one ties his capital up in a particular project he sacrifices opportunities to earn profits on other alternatives.

Equimarginal Concept

An important proposition in economics is that an input should be allocated in such a way that the value added by the last unit is the same in all uses. This proposition is popularly known as the equi-marginal principle.

Imagine a case in which a firm has 100 units of labour at its command. Also assume this amount to be fixed so that the total payroll is fixed or predetermined. The firm is involved in four activities – activity A, activity B, activity C, and activity D. All these activities require the services of labour. The firm can increase any one of these activities by employing more labour, but only at the cost of other activities.

If it adds a unit of labour to activity A, an increase in output will result. The value of the added output may be termed as the marginal product of labour in activity A. Similarly the firm can estimate the value of the marginal product in activities B, C, and D. If the firm finds that the value of the marginal product is greater in one activity than another, the firm must realize the fact that an optimum has not been achieved. This means that it would be profitable to shift labour from the low marginal value activity to the high marginal value activity and thereby increase the total value of all products taken together. If for example, the value of marginal product of labour in activity A is Rs. 20 while that in activity B is Rs.30 then it is profitable to shift labour from activity A to activity B. The optimum will be attained when the value of the marginal product is equal in all activities. Symbolically this is achieved when

VMPLA = VMPLB = VMPLC = VMPLD

Where VMP = value of marginal product

L = Labour

A, B, C, and D are activities.

Clarification of the Principle

We are of the view that several aspects of the equi-marginal principle need clarifications.

1. The value of the marginal products in our formula is net of incremental costs. For instance, in activity A the addition of one unit of labour may result in an increase in physical output of 20 units. Each unit may sell @ Re.1 so that the 20 units will fetch Rs. 20. But the increased production may also be the result of additional raw materials, and/or other inputs and hence the variable costs in Activity A (not counting the labour cost) are higher. Let us assume that the incremental costs come to Rs. 10. This leaves a net addition of Rs. 10. The value of the marginal product that is relevant for our purpose is thus only Rs. 10.

2. If there is any disparity in time in the realization of revenues that result from the addition of labour, it is necessary to discount these revenues before comparisons in the alternative activities are made. For example, activity B might not produce revenue for two years while activity A will produce revenue almost immediately. In such a situation only the discounting of revenues will make them comparable.

3. It may be pointed out that the whole subject of capital budgeting discussed in Chapter 9 is based on the above principle. In capital budgeting the resources to be allocated consists of the funds available to the firm. The objective is to allocate the funds where the discounted values of the marginal products are the greatest, expanding the high value activities and reducing the low value activities until the equality of the marginal values is obtained.

4. The equi-marginal principle holds good only in cases where the law of diminishing returns operate.[28] This is depicted in Fig. 2.5.

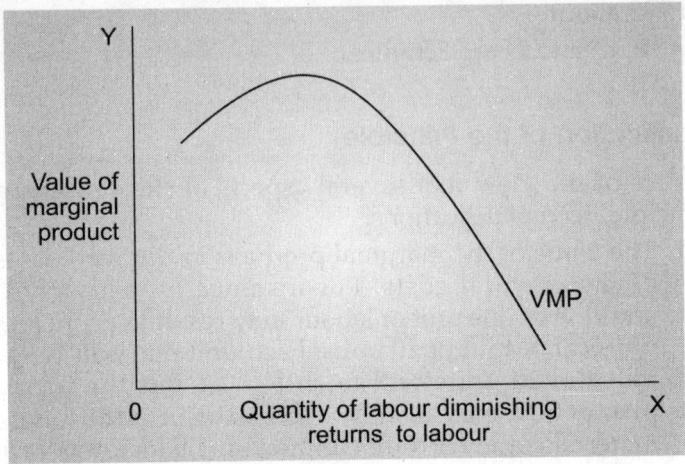

Fig. 2.5: Diminishing returns to labour

To return to our earlier example, as more labour is added to activity A, we expect the value of the marginal product of labour to decline as shown in Fig. 2.5.

We would also expect the operation of the law in other activities too in the same way, though each marginal product curve, depending on the technology and other relevant factors, will take different shape. Figure 2.6 shows four marginal product curves having different shapes.

Suppose that our firm allocates 25 units of labour to each activity as shown in Fig. 2.6. Clearly the firm has not equated the values of the marginal products. The value of marginal product in activity D is much higher than the marginal product in other activities. This means that this is profitable to transfer labour to activity D from activities A, B and C. By reshuffling labour in this way the firm can obtain optimum under the values of marginal products are equal in all activities. The optimum situation is represented in Fig. 2.7

But when the values of marginal products are constant (horizontal marginal value product curves) we need an alternative form of the principle, making use of inequalities rather than equalities.[29] This form of the principle may be stated as follows:

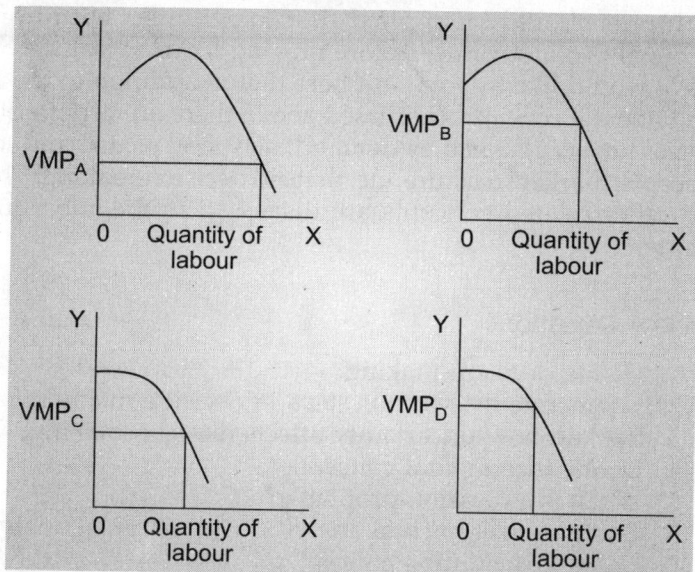

Fig. 2.6

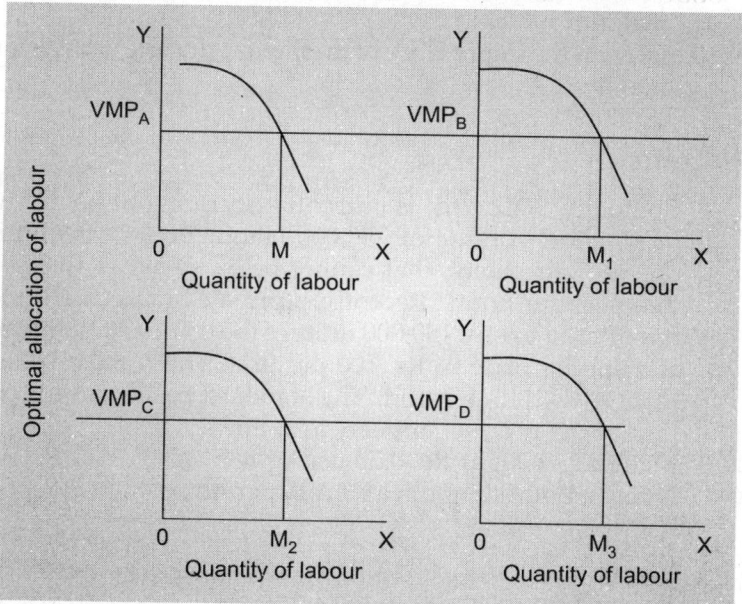

Fig. 2.7

"Inputs should be applied first to activities with higher marginal product values before moving to lower values."[30]

We would like to point out here that in addition to the five fundamental concepts discussed above there are certain other relevant concepts such as demand, elasticity of demand, cost concepts, market structure, etc. that aid decision-making. These and other related concepts are discussed in the subsequent chapters.

Review Questions

1. Define decision-making.
2. Enumerate the various steps in decision-making.
3. Explain how uncertainty affects decision-making.
4. Define incremental concept.
5. When is a decision profitable?
6. Compare incremental analysis with marginal analysis.
7. Define discounting concept.
8. What do you mean by opportunity cost?
9. What is the relevance of opportunity cost in decision-making?
10. Explain the importance of marginal principle in decision-making.

Problem

1. Company 'XYZ Ltd' is currently operating at an annual production volume of 750,000 labour hours. Its annual operating capacity, that cannot be exceeded is 10,00,000 direct labour hours. Recently, a private brand distributor has offered to buy 150,000 units of the company's product at a special price of Rs. 100 per unit. The regular selling price is Rs. 115 per unit. The standard cost sheet for one unit of the product appears as follows:

Material : 6 kg at Re. 0.50 per kg.	Rs. 3
Direct labour : 2 hours at Rs. 25 per hour	Rs. 50
Overhead	
Variable: 2 hours at Rs. 20 per hour	Rs. 40
Fixed : 2 hours at Rs. 10 per hour	Rs. 20
Total	Rs. 113

    a. Would it be profitable for the company to accept the offer?

    b. Would your answer be different if the offer called for is 270,000 units of the product in place of the original 150,000 units? Why?

2. A business executive who was drawing a salary of Rs. 400,000 per year resigns to start his business unit. He invests Rs. 600,000 the deposit he had in a bank which was earning him 10 percent interest per annum? He got evicted a building which was fetching him a monthly rent of Rs. 15000. Revenue during the year was Rs. 14,00,000. The other expenses were as follows:

Advertising	Rs. 40,000
Rent	Rs. 100,000
Taxes	Rs. 40,000
Employees' salaries	Rs. 350,000
Supplies	Rs. 35,000

Prepare two income statements, one using the Accountant's version and the other using Economist's version to calculate the profit.

References

1. Wheeler, Bayard O, op.cit., p.225
2. Ibid; p.226
3. Ibid; p.231
4. Haynes, W.W. et al. op.cit. p.15
5. Ibid
6. Ibid; p.17
7. For further information see discussion on marginal cost and marginal revenue.
8. Haynes, W.W. et al. pp. 22–23
9. Ibid; p.21
10. Dean, Joel: Statistical Cost Functions of Hosiery Mill, Chicago, University of Chicago press, 1941 and Johnston J. Statistical Cost Analysis (New York: McGraw Hill Book Company; Inc. 1960, Chapters 4 and 5).
11. and 12. See foot note under 10
13. United States Steel Corporation, T.N.E.C. papers, vol.11 (New York,1949) p.53. Please also see, Haynes, W.W, et al. op.cit., p.23
14. Nordin, J.A; Note on a Light Plants Cost Curves, *Econometrica*, July 1947, pp231–235

15. Haynes, W.W, et al. op.cit. p.23
16. Stonier, Alfred W & Hague, Doughlas C; *A Text-book of Economic Theory,* Longmans.
17. Haynes,W.W, et al. op.cit. p.25
18. Ibid
19. Haynes, W.W, et al. op.cit. pp. 28–29
20. See chapter on Capitalo Budgeting
21. Wheeler, Bayard O; Business, op.cit. p.228
22. Ibid; pp.228–229.
23. Haynes, W.W, et al. Managerial Economics; op.cit. p.30.
24. Ibid; pp.30–31.
25. Ibid.
26. Ibid; pp.31–32.
27. Ibid; p.32.
28. Law of Diminishing Returns states that as quantities of variable inputs are added to fixed quantities of other inputs, the marginal product eventually declines.
29. Haynes, W.W, et al. op.cit; p.38.
30. Ibid.

3 Case Method

The case method dates back to the 1880s when it was first used in the Harvard Law School. It has since been widely used in medical as well as business schools. Today there are numerous kinds of cases and varying concepts involving the case study method.

One of the basic objectives of the case method is to introduce a measure of realism in business education. The learning of economic analysis abstracted from actual decisions does not provide the skill required to bridge the gap between theory and practice. Each case is simply a written description of the facts surrounding a particular business situation and as such it reveals the complexity of the environment in which decisions are made. Again cases force the student to leave the ivory tower of abstract theory, to face up to the uncertainties of the real world, and to make the simplification required to create order out of the multitude of facts faced by management.

Benefit and Limitations of the Case Method

The case method becomes an effective teaching device when students are encouraged to analyse the data presented and formulate their own set of recommendations. Since there is no single 'correct' solution to a case and two students of equal standard and ability might select different alternatives doubts may be raised as to what students actually learn by working with business cases. One answer is that the preparation and discussion of case studies help students to improve their skills at oral as well as written expression. Secondly, the case method provides an easy way to students to learn about current business practices and methods. Thirdly, and perhaps important aspect of the case method is the experience it provides in thinking logically about different sets of data. In other words the development of students' analytical ability and judgment is the most valuable and lasting benefit derived from the case method.

How to Analyse a Case

There are a number of ways for students to approach the business cases. Each instructor may be having his own ideas on the number and nature of steps that are involved. We are of the opinion that the following four- step procedure is a logical and practical way to handle the case method:

Definition of the central issue or issues

Formulation of the alternatives

Evaluation of the alternatives

The decision or recommended solution.

Definition of the Central Issue or Issues

A case may contain a number of issues from the trivial to the significant. Once the student is familiar with the facts of the case, it is important that he isolates the key problem. Until this is done, it is usually difficult, if not impossible, to proceed with the effective analysis. The question at the end of the case need not necessarily always focus attention on the key issue. They are designed to facilitate the student to start with his analysis. Students should look at the questions as sign posts for action rather than as specific issues to be resolved. In no way are the questions designed to limit the scope or depth of the discussion.

Formulation of the Alternatives

In some cases the alternatives are clear, in others the student must formulate possible alternatives available to resolve the problem around which the case is organized.

Evaluation of the Alternatives

The most crucial aspect of the case method is the evaluation of the alternatives. To evaluate means to separate into parts so as to find out the nature, proportion, function and underlying relationship among a set of variables. Thus to evaluate is to dig into and work with the facts to unearth associations that may be used to judge the possible courses of action. The analysis should begin with a careful evaluation of the facts presented in the case. The student must be sensitive to the problem or sorting relevant material from that which is superfluous or irrelevant. In some cases, information designed to distract and confuse the imperative reader used to be included. In reviewing a case, the student must be extremely careful to distinguish between facts and opinion. It is also the responsibility of the student to make sure that the facts are consistent and reliable.

At times the most important facts in a case are obscurely buried in some chance remark or seemingly minor statistical exhibit. It is the responsibility of the student to carefully sift through the data to unearth all of the relationships that apply to the alternatives being considered. This invariability means that the quantitative information must be examined, using a variety of ratios, graphs, tables, or other forms of analysis. It is seldom that the data supplied in a case are presented in a form most suitable to finding a solution, and instructors expect the students to work out the numbers.

Often students will find gaps in the data given in the case. This entails that assumptions must be made if the analysis is to continue. Students should be aware of and able to defend the assumptions they make. It is also significant to realize that a complete analysis is not one sided. A review of a business situation is not dependable unless different aspects of important issues are examined.

Students are expected to base their analysis on the data given in the case. But his does not in any way mean that other information cannot be used. On the contrary, they must utilize facts that are available to the trade, and information that is general or public knowledge. It is also advisable to use relevant concept from other disciplines, such as accounting, statistics, marketing, psychology, and sociology. The only guiding principle in using the outside data or material is that it must be appropriate to the particular situation.

Decision

After carefully analyzing the data and the possible alternatives, the student must make his recommendations. In certain cases it is possible that more than one course of action will look attractive. This is not an unusual situation, as most cases do not have a single 'right' solution. Even under such situations the student must come up with a set of specific recommendations that seems best to him. He must be decisive. He should be aware of the limitations as well as strengths of his choice, and he should be bewaring of overstating his case. To arrive at a solution, the student must judge the relative risks and opportunities offered by the various alternatives. The optimum choice will be one that provides the best balance between profit opportunities and the risks and costs of failure.

Writing the Report

Reporting the solution of the case in a readable form is an important aspect of case method. True that writing a good report requires a certain skill. Here we propose to suggest a few ideas that may be of help to students for writing the report.

The student may follow the following order in writing the report.

    i. Statement of the problem
    ii. Analysis with dub-headings
    iii. Recommendations.

The problem statement must be brief. It may run to one or two sentences. The second section viz. the analysis part should form the bulk of the report and should include a number of sub-headings. The first sub-heading may deal with a statement of the possible alternatives. Some of the topics that may be considered in the analysis section are:

    i. Customer demand
    ii. Competition, type and possible reactions
    iii. Distribution channels
    iv. Product characteristics

v. Sales promotion and incentives

vi. Price and

vii. Effects on Company sales costs and profits.

The recommendations should be relatively short and concise. There is no optimum length for a written case analysis.

Review Questions

1. Enumerate the different steps in analyzing a case.
2. Mention the topics that may be considered in analyzing a case.

4 Some Basic Concepts

In this chapter we discuss certain basic concepts that are left out in Chapter 2.

They are:

i. **Functions:** Functions indicate the relationship between variables. Variables are things that change and can take a set of possible values within a given problem. For example, the revenue earned by a firm selling bicycles depends on the price of the bicycle and the number of bicycles that it sells. In this case total revenue is a variable of the number of bicycles (and that itself is a variable) and the price (that too is a variable) per unit. This shows that a function is not limited to the relation between two variables. A function may represent the relation between one or more independent variables and a dependent variable. The relationship in this case can be expressed as:

$$TR = f(PQ)$$

Where TR = Total revenue

P = Unit price, and

Q = Number of units sold.

A function can be represented in three different ways:

- Algebraic form
- Tabular form, and
- Graphic form

ii. **Parameter:** Parameter is a quantity that does not change in a given problem. In the equation given below, namely $Y = a + bx$; a and b are constants and x and y are variables.

x is the independent or exogenous variable while y is the dependent or endogenous variable. The values of x will be given from outside the system, while values of b will be determined from within the system.

Most of the variables of interest in economics can be studied in the form of three functions, total, average and marginal. The generalised form of these functions can be stated in the following forms:

- Total $Y = f(x)$
- Average $Y = f(x) / x$
- Marginal $Y = \Delta f(x) / \Delta x$

Differentiation can be used to derive marginal from the total function.

Optimisation

Optimisation is the act of choosing the best alternative out of all the available ones. It describes how decisions or choice among alternatives are taken or should be made. All optimization problems have three elements. They are:

- Decision variables
- The objective function, and
- The feasible set.

Decision Variables

These are variables whose optimal values have to be determined. For example a production manager wants to know at what level to set output in order to achieve maximum profit or maximum sales revenue. Here output is the choice variable.

Objective Function

It is a mathematical relationship between the choice variable and some variables whose values are to be maximized or minimized. For example the objective function could relate to profit to level of output or cost to amount of labour, machine time, raw materials, etc.

Feasible Set

The available set of alternatives is called a feasible set.

A solution to an optimization problem is that set of values of the choice of variables which is in the feasible set and which yields maximum or minimum of the objective function over the feasible set.

Utility

Utility means the capacity of goods and services to satisfy human wants.

Demand

Demand for a commodity implies

- Desire to acquire it
- Willingness to pay for it, and
- Ability to pay for it.

Demand for a commodity has to be stated with reference to time, place, price and the price of related commodities, consumer income and taste, etc.

Elasticity of Demand

The rate of change in the demand for a commodity as a result of a small change in its price is called the elasticity of demand.

Supply

Supply is the willingness and ability of producers to make a specific quantity of output available to consumers at a particular price over a given period of time.

Elasticity of Supply

The rate of change in the supply of a commodity as a result of a small change in its price is called the elasticity of supply.

Price

Price is the money value of goods and services traded.

Equilibrium

Equilibrium indicates a state of rest or evenly balanced situation.

Price Effect

Change in the equilibrium position of a consumer due to a change in the price of the commodity that he buys is known as price effect.

Income Effect

Change in the equilibrium of the consumer due to a change in his income is known as income effect.

Substitution Effect

Change in the equilibrium of the consumer due to relative change in the price of commodities that he buys is known as substitution effect.

Private Good

A private good is one that one buys and consumes, and for which the act of consumption affects no one else.

Public Good

A public good enables people to enjoy it without paying for it. For example, if you buy a public good other people can consume and enjoy it without paying for it. Similarly if some one else buys it, you can consume it without paying for it. Thus when public goods are involved, two issues have to be faced: how much of a public good should be bought and who should pay for it?

Externalities

Externalities occur when the action of an individual or firm, confer benefits or costs on individuals or firms not directly involved in those actions.

Economies of Scale

Economies of scale arise when the level of activity expands, the unit cost of producing output falls.

Break-even Point

Break-even point is no loss-no profit point where total cost equals total revenue.

Opportunity Cost

Opportunity cost is the value of what is given up to obtain something else or the benefits foregone from the next best alternative.

Theories and Principles

Economic theories and principles are statements about economic behaviour.

Ceteris Paribus

Ceteris Paribus or other-things being equal assumption is used by economists to construct their theories.

Micro and Macro Economics

Microeconomics looks at specific economic units while Macroeconomics examines either the economy as a whole or its basic subdivisions or aggregates such as the government, households, and business sectors.

Private and Public Good

A private good is one that you may buy and consume, and for which the act of consumption affects no one.

A public good is different from private good in the sense that even if you buy a public good other people can consume and enjoy it without paying for it. When public goods are involved, two issues have to be faced: how much of a given public good should be bought and who should pay for it. The price mechanism will not solve this problem. National defence, Police and Fire services, Light houses, etc. are examples of public goods.

5 Equilibrium of the Consumer

There are two approaches to consumer's equilibrium. The first one is the utility approach and the second, the indifference curve approach.

These two approaches are discussed in some detail in the following paragraphs.

Utility

Utility means the capacity of goods and services to satisfy human wants.

People demand goods and services because of their utility.

Assumptions

- Cardinal measure of utility
- Independent utilities
- Constant marginal utility of money.

Cardinal measure of utility: This means that utility is a **measurable** and **Quantifiable concept**. A person can specify how many units of utility that he gets **(say, 10 units)** by consuming one unit of good X.

Independent utilities: This means that utility is additive; the utilities derived from different independent goods can be added to get the measure of total utility.

Constant marginal utility of money: This means that the marginal utility of money remains constant for a particular consumer when he spends money on various goods.

Utility has the following characteristics. The more we have a thing the less is the marginal utility which we derive from it, *ceteris paribus*. In other words, when a consumer consumes more and more units of the same good the additional utility or satisfaction which he gets from every additional unit goes on diminishing, *ceteris paribus*. A law is formulated on the basis of this phenomenon and that law is known as the **law of diminishing marginal utility.** This is one of the fundamental laws of the consumption branch of economics. Gossen[1] and Bentham[2] were the pioneers of this law. In his discussion on 'Value' Jevons[3] also explains this law. Nevertheless, this law is mainly associated with Marshall.

According to Marshall **'the additional benefit which a person derives from a given increase of his stock of anything diminishes with every increase in the stock that he already has.'** Suppose a person eats apple one after the other **without any break** the first apple will give him more utility than the second **as the first apple** reduces the intensity of his appetite. The utility will go on diminishing with every successive apple and finally a stage comes when he does not need any more additional apple, i.e. the utility of apple will become zero. The implication of zero marginal utility is that the consumer has all that he wants of apples. If the consumer is compelled to consume more apples the utility may become negative. This can be illustrated with the help of Table 5.1.

Table 5.1

Units of apple consumed	Total utility	Marginal utility
1	10	10
2	17	7
3	22	5
4	25	3
5	25	0
6	22	- 3
7	20	- 5

From Table 5.1 we can see that as the consumer continues to eat apples the additional utility he derives from the consumption of every successive apple decreases till it becomes zero and then it becomes negative. The total utility increases till marginal utility becomes zero. This is graphically represented in Fig. 5.1.

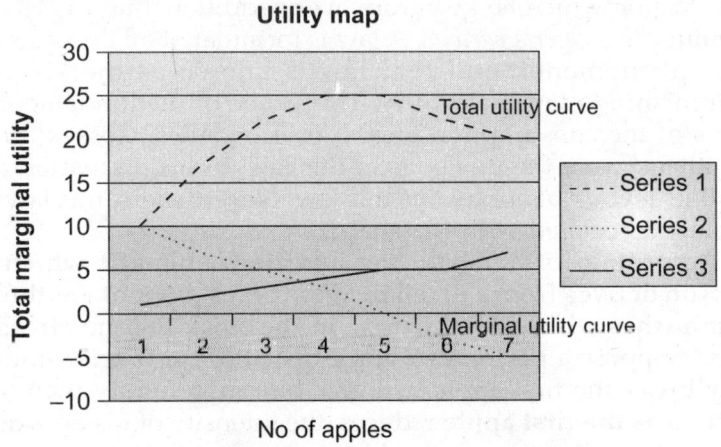

Fig. 5.1: Marginal and total utility

In Fig. 5.1 units of apples are measured along X-axis and units of utility along Y-axis. The units of utility from apples are represented by the rectangles. The more apples the consumer consumes the rectangles become smaller. The sixth and the seventh have disutility or negative utility.

Limitations of the Law

1. Utility is just a feeling of the mind, i.e. it is only a subjective idea and so the attempt to measure it in terms of money or numbers looks arbitrary.
2. The units of consumption should be reasonable and adequate. Suppose the units are small, then utility may increase instead of decreasing.
3. The commodity must be taken within a specified period of time. Otherwise the law will not hold.
4. Utility depends on fashion. So when fashion changes, utility may also change.
5. The law does not apply to rare collections, e.g. diamonds.

6. The character of the consumer should remain the same. If a consumer develops a craving for something the law will not apply.
7. According to Pigou the utility of certain commodities depends on the possession of the commodity by others, e.g. telephone.

Practical Importance of the Law

1. The law provides a basis for other laws of consumption, e.g. the law of demand is based on this law.
2. The reason behind the socialist argument for the redistribution of wealth is this law. The marginal utility a rich man loses when he loses some wealth is not as much as the marginal utility that a poor man gains by getting that wealth.
3. The law also forms the basis for a progressive system of taxation. Through progressive taxation the rich are made to pay higher rates of taxes. The argument behind this type of taxation is that by this method wealth can be shifted from the rich to the poor and thus the general welfare of the society can be increased.
4. The law also gives an explanation for the reduction of the value of a commodity when its supply increases. Thus this law forms the basis of the theory of value.

Law of Substitution

The Law of Substitution or Equi-marginal Utility has great importance in marginal utility analysis since consumer's equilibrium is explained with the help of this law.

We all know that human wants are unlimited in number and the resources to satisfy them are limited. Every consumer has a given income. The consumer being a rational person tries to maximize his utility when he spends his available income. If he finds that the utility that he gets by spending a rupee on one commodity is less than that from other commodity he spends less on the first and more on the second. After buying a few units of the second commodity if he feels that a third commodity would give greater utility he will purchase a few units of this third commodity, and so on. Now the question arises: how is he going to allocate his given money income among the different commodities that he proposes to buy? In other words when the consumer will reach equilibrium position with respect buying of these commodities? The answer depends on the marginal utility of each commodity that he proposes to buy. When the marginal utility of one commodity decreases he will go in for a second commodity. When the marginal utility of this commodity also decreases he will turn to a third commodity, i.e. he will substitute a low-utility commodity by a high-utility commodity. Finally he will reach a stage when the marginal utility of all the commodities that he bought are equal. Thus through a process of substitution he gets the maximum utility and satisfaction and that is why this is called the **law of substitution.** This law states that a consumer spends his available income in such a way that the marginal utilities of all the commodities are equal. Therefore, this is also called the **law of equi-marginal utility or equi-marginal returns.** Since the consumer maximizes his satisfaction through the substitution process, this law is also called the **law of maximum satisfaction.**

This law can be explained with the help of the following example:

Number of units	Marginal utility of consumed		
	X	Y	Z
1	30	27	24
2	27	24	21
3	24	21	18
4	21	18	15
5	18	15	12
6	15	12	9
7	12	9	6
8	9	6	3

Here the consumer distributes his available money income among the three commodities viz. X, Y and Z. Since his income is limited he has to decide how many units of X, Y and Z he should buy. If he has money only to buy 21 units of utility of each of the commodities, he will buy 4 units of X, 3 units of Y and 2 units of Z, since at this stage he can equate the marginal utilities of all the three commodities. Through this distribution he gets maximum satisfaction with his limited income. Any kind of change in his expenditure will result in less total utility. This kind of effort to get equal marginal utility from different commodities is seen in every branch of economic activity, let it be in the case of an individual, household, or firm.

The same law can be illustrated with the help of Fig. 5.2

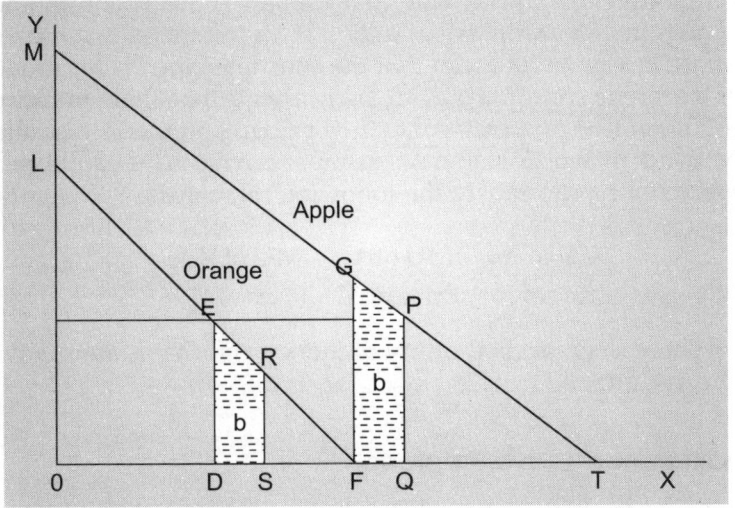

Fig. 5.2

Let there be only two commodities, oranges and apples and let LF and MT respectively the utility curves of oranges and apples. If our consumer spends OD on oranges and OQ on apples the marginal utilities that he derives from them will be equal, i.e. DE and QP. According to the **law of substitution**, through the distribution of money the consumer gets the maximum total utility, i.e. ODEL + OQPM. Suppose b stands for a small unit of money and b more is spend on orange and (b) less on apple. Then the marginal utility of apple increases by FG and orange decreases to RS. As the shaded areas prove there is more loss than gain of utility. In other words the total utility is less than what it was before. Therefore, we can conclude that the consumer gets maximum total utility when the marginal utilities of the commodities that he buys are equal.

Law of Proportionality

Marshall states the law in a different way: 'If a person has a thing which he can put to several uses, he will distribute it among these uses in such a way that it has the same marginal utility in all'. i.e. the consumer will distribute his expenditure on different commodities in such a way that the last rupee spent on each commodity gives him equal utility. If we put this statement in a different way it will mean that the consumer spends his money on different commodities in such a way that their marginal utilities will be proportional to their prices. And this law is called the law of proportionality. A consumer can reach his equilibrium position if he can satisfy the following relationship:

$$\frac{\text{MU of X}}{\text{Price of X}} = \frac{\text{MU of Y}}{\text{Price of Y}} = \frac{\text{MU of Z}}{\text{Price of Z}} = k$$

Where k is marginal utility of money and that is assumed to be constant.

Indifference Curve Approach

Utility approach is based on the assumption that utility is measurable and quantifiable. But utility indicates a state of mind it is argued that it is naïve to assume that utility is measurable and quantifiable. It is this line of thought that led to the development of indifference curve approach to determine the consumer's equilibrium. It was Professor FY Edgeworth who first made use of the indifference curve technique. Vilfredo Pareto put the indifference curve technique to extensive use. The other contributors in this area are RGD Allen, JR Hicks, Paul A Samuelson, Eugen Slutsky.

Definition of Indifference Curve

Indifference curve can be defined as the locus of points each of which represents a collection of two commodities that give equal satisfaction to the consumer and so the consumer is indifferent in selecting any combination of the two goods.

Assumptions of Indifference Curve Analysis

- **Rationality of the consumer:** Consumer aims maximizing satisfaction given the market price and the money income.
- **Ordinal utility:** Consumer can rank his preferences according to the level of satisfaction from the collection of different combinations of goods.
- **Consistency:** The consumer is consistent in his choice. If he prefers commodity A over commodity B in one period of time he will not prefer B over A in another period of time.
- **Transitivity:** If commodity A is preferred to B, and B is preferred to C, then A is preferred to C.
- Diminishing marginal rate of substitution.

Qualities of an Indifference Curve

1. Indifference curves slope downward from left to right.
2. Indifference curves are convex to the origin or concave upward.
3. No two indifference curves cut each other.

Indifference curves slope downward from left to right. If they did not slope downwards, they would either slope upwards or be horizontal. If an indifference curve were horizontal this would imply that the consumer would be equally satisfied with, say, 5 kilograms of apple and either 1, 2, 3, 4, 5 or 6 kilograms of grapes. This is against the principle of rationality. Nor is an indifference curve likely to slope upwards to the right, as this would mean that the consumer would regard a combination containing greater amount of both commodities as giving just the same satisfaction as one containing less of each.

Indifference curves are convex to the origin. This is an important quality. If one looks at any indifference curve, one can read off from it the marginal significance of one good in terms of the other. Marginal significance shows the rate at which the consumer is willing to sacrifice one good in order to gain one unit of the other good that he is interested to consume. The slope of an indifference curve at any point shows the marginal significance at that point. The quality that indifference curves are convex to the origin rules out the possibility, that there could be increasing marginal significance even at small ranges of indifference curves.

No two indifference curves cut each other. The basic assumption is that an indifference curve represents the different combination of two goods that give the same level of satisfaction to the consumer. If two indifference curves that represent different levels of satisfaction to the consumer cut each other, at the point of intersection unequal levels of satisfaction will become equal. And that is not acceptable.

Indifference Map

An indifference map may show all the indifference curves that rank the preferences of the consumer.

Equilibrium of the Consumer

The equilibrium position of the consumer is analysed by introducing money in to an indifference map. Money represents command over all goods. So by introducing money in to an indifference map we can show the consumer's tastes with respect to commodity X on the one hand and money representing general purchasing power, on the other. We can do this for money and any individual good, and we can do it making two assumptions, viz.

  i. the prices of all the other goods are given and constant and,

  ii. that the consumer spends all his money on one good or another and does not save any. On these assumptions we can draw an indifference map where the consumer is represented as choosing between, say, apple and other goods that his money can command.

Before going into the details how indifference curve analysis can be used to show how a consumer reaches equilibrium it will be useful to list all the assumptions connected with the indifference curve analysis, viz.

1. The consumer has an indifference map indicating his scale of preferences for combinations of the good in question and of money. This scale of preference remains unchanged throughout.
2. He has a fixed amount of money to spend and if he does not spend it on the good we are considering, he will spend all of it on the others.
3. He is one of many buyers and knows the prices of all goods. All prices are assumed to be given and constant, so that money can be treated as command over all goods other than the one that the consumer is buying.
4. All goods are homogeneous and divisible.
5. The consumer acts rationally and maximizes his satisfactions.

On the basis of the above assumptions we represent the equilibrium of the consumer in Fig. 5.3.

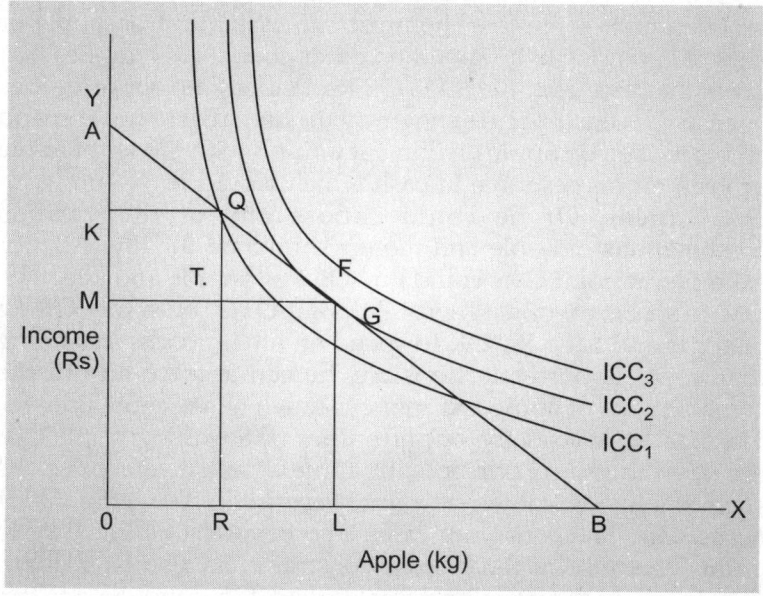

Fig. 5.3: Equilibrium of the consumer

In Fig. 5.3 three indifference curves, viz. 1, 2, 3 are shown. The consumer regards all the combinations of apples and money on indifference curve 1 in Fig. 5.3 as giving the same level of satisfaction as each other. Similarly all the combinations on indifference curve 2 give the same level of satisfactions but higher level compared with indifference curve 1.

Indifference curve 3 represents progressively higher level of satisfaction compared with indifference curves 1 and 2.

Line AB in Fig. 5.3 represents the size of consumer's income and the price of apple between them determines the consumer's purchases. The consumer has a fixed income, viz. Rs. OA (represented on Y-axis) which he can spend. The market price of apple is such that if he spends all his money on apple he can obtain OB kilograms. In other words, the price of a kilogram of apple is $\dfrac{OA}{OB}$ Rs and is shown by the slope of the line AB. The slope of such a line can be referred to as the slope of the price line.

As our assumption is that the consumer spends all his income on one good or another, he must either spend it on apple or keep it in money to be spend on other goods. This implies that given the price of apple (OA/OB Rs. Per kg.) the opportunities open to the consumer are shown by the line AB. He could spend all his money on apple arriving at point B with OB kg of apple or keep all his resource in cash which would leave him with OA Rupees. Or he could choose any of the various combinations of apple and money shown on the line AB. For example, at point G he could buy OL kg of apple and keep Rs. OM to spend on other goods. At point Q he could buy OR kg of apple and keep Rs. OK to spend on other goods. Assuming that apple is perfectly divisible, he can acquire any of the combinations of apple and money shown on the price line AB. The line AB shows the opportunities of acquiring apple that are open to the consumer with apple at its current price. As such this line is known as a *price-opportunity line, price line or budget line*. The consumer cannot go beyond this line, say to point F because of the income constraint. So also he will not remain inside the price line, say at point T, because he will not then be spending all his income, and our assumption is that he spends his income either on one good or another. The consumer reaches the equilibrium position when the price line becomes tangent to an indifference curve (Fig. 5.3). At point G the consumer is in equilibrium with OL kg, of apple and Rs. OM to spend on other goods. If we consider two consumer goods instead of one consumer good and money we have to assume that the consumer is paid an income in one of the goods and their prices in terms of each other are constant. Such a case is shown in Fig. 5.4. In the diagram units of good X are measured on the X-axis and units of good Y on the Y-axis. We still hold the assumption that the consumer's income, whether paid in terms of X or in terms of Y, is fixed. The consumer is able to buy OA of X if he spends all his income on X or OB of Y if he spends all his income on Y. The price line AB shows all the possible combinations of X and Y that the consumer can afford to buy with his available income. The steeper the slope of AB, the higher is the price of X in terms of Y that is the higher is the

relative price of X. We can write: $\dfrac{\text{Price of X}}{\text{Price of Y}} = \dfrac{\text{OB}}{\text{OA}}$. The slope of AB represents the ratio of the money prices of X and Y.

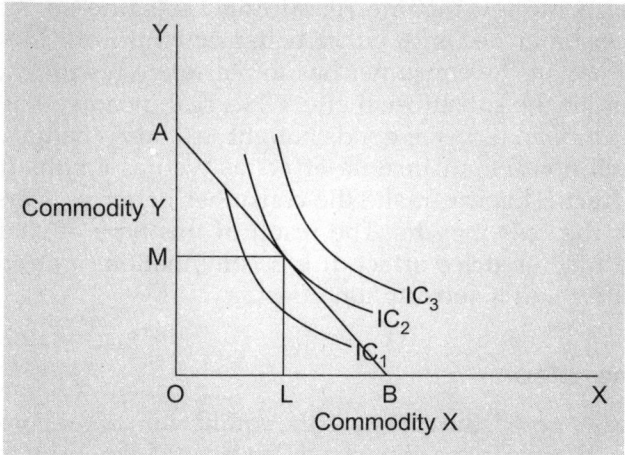

Fig. 5.4: Consumer's equilibrium

In Fig. 5.4, the highest indifference curve that the consumer can reach is IC_2. He is in equilibrium at point R with OL of X and OM of Y. At point R, the ratio of the prices of X and Y, namely OB/OA, is equal to the consumer's marginal significance of X in terms of Y.

Change in the Equilibrium of the Consumer

Three situations can change the equilibrium of the consumer. They are:

1. The income of the consumer changes but the prices of the commodities remain the same. The change in equilibrium of the consumer due to a change in the income of the consumer while the prices of the commodities remain the same is known as the income effect.

2. It is possible that prices may change, but that the consumer's money income changes at the same time in such a way that he is neither better nor worse off as a result. He will, however, find it worth his while to buy more of those goods whose relative price has fallen. He will substitute the relatively cheaper goods for the relatively dearer ones. The result of this type of change is termed as **substitution effect.**

3. It is possible that the price of one good may fall or rise with money income remaining the same so that the consumer becomes either better or worse off. In such a situation the consumer has to rearrange his purchase as under the substitution effect. His real income, that is his income in terms of goods bought will also change. There will now be **an income effect** as well as **a substitution effect**. This can make the consumer better or worse off, as the case may be. The result of this type of change is termed as **price effect.** It is a combination of an income effect and a substitution effect.

Income-Effect

As already noted, the change in the equilibrium of the consumer due to a change in his income while prices of commodities that the consumer buys remain the same is termed as the income effect. This can easily be represented with the help of an indifference curve map (Fig. 5.5).

Let us assume that the consumer considered in Fig. 5.5 starts with an income of OA in terms of X and OB in terms of Y. He will be in equilibrium at point R on IC_1. In this position he will have OM of X and OC of Y. If his income now rises to OA_1 in terms of X , or OB_1 in terms of Y, the consumer will move from point R (his old equilibrium position to R_1, the new equilibrium position. He will now be better off, being on IC_2 which lies at a higher level. At the new equilibrium position he will have OM_1 of X and OC_1 of Y. Similarly, the consumer will move to higher and higher indifference curves as his income increases.

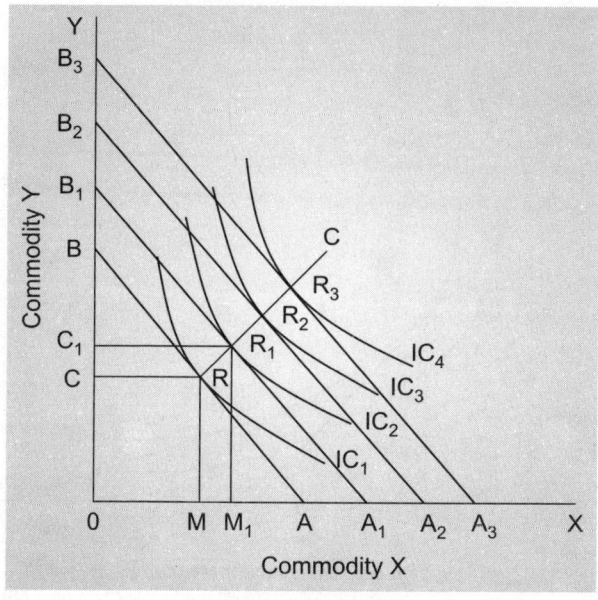

Fig. 5.5: Income effect

Income Consumption Curve

From the above analysis it is clear that there can be an indefinitely large number of equilibrium points such as R, R_1, R_2, R_3, etc. one for each possible level of income. If we join all the points namely, R, R_1, R_2, R_3, etc. we will get a curve which shows all possible positions of equilibrium of the consumer over the range of income between OA and OA_3 in terms of X and OB and OB_3 in terms of Y. Such a curve is termed as the Income Consumption Curve. This curve shows how the consumer's purchases of the two goods react to changing income when the prices of both goods are given and constant.

Substitution Effect

A substitution effect occurs when the relative prices of goods change but the consumer's money income is altered (or compensated for the change in real income) in such a way that he is neither better nor worse off than he was before. His real income remains exactly the same. However, he has to rearrange his purchases in accordance with the new relative prices. This is shown in Fig. 5.6.

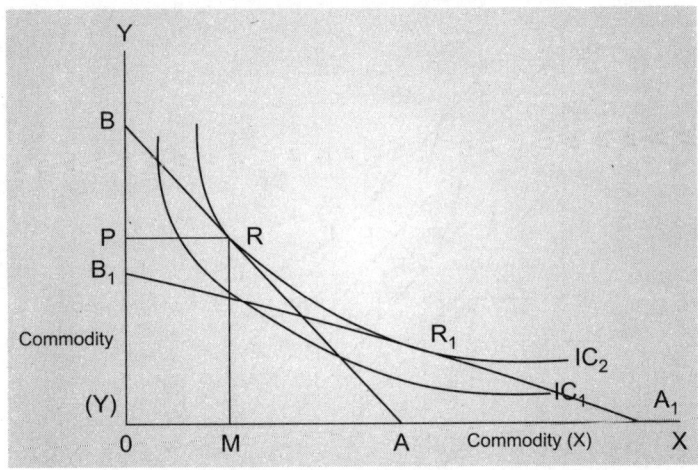

Fig. 5.6: Substitution effect

In Fig. 5.6 the consumer is initially in equilibrium at point R on IC_2 where his budget line is tangent to IC_2. At this point of equilibrium the consumer buys OM of commodity X and OP of commodity Y. Now suppose that the price of commodity Y increases and that of commodity X decreases. The rise in price of Y decreases the real income of the consumer while the decrease in the price of Y increases the real income of the consumer. The fall and rise in the real income of the consumer in terms of commodities Y and X respectively, is represented by the new budget line B_1A_1. Suppose that the rise in real income due to fall in the price of commodity X is just sufficient to compensate the loss in real income consequent on the rise in price of commodity Y, it is known as compensating variation in the consumer's income. As a result of this change we have a substitution effect. The consumer substitutes the relatively cheaper commodity (X) to the relatively dearer commodity (Y) and remains on the same indifference curve, but at a different point (R_1). Since he is on the same indifference curve he is neither better nor worse off than he was before. This was made possible because of the compensating variation in income. The move from point R to point R_1 on the same indifference curve represents a substitution effect. A substitution effect can therefore always be represented as a movement along the same indifference curve.

Price Effect

The change in the equilibrium position of the consumer due to changes in the prices of the commodities the consumer buys is known as the price effect. Here the relative prices of the commodities in question change but there is no compensating variation in income. The consumer's real income therefore either rises or falls. His money income gives him grater or lesser satisfaction than it did before, because prices have changed. The price effect is shown in Fig. 5.7.

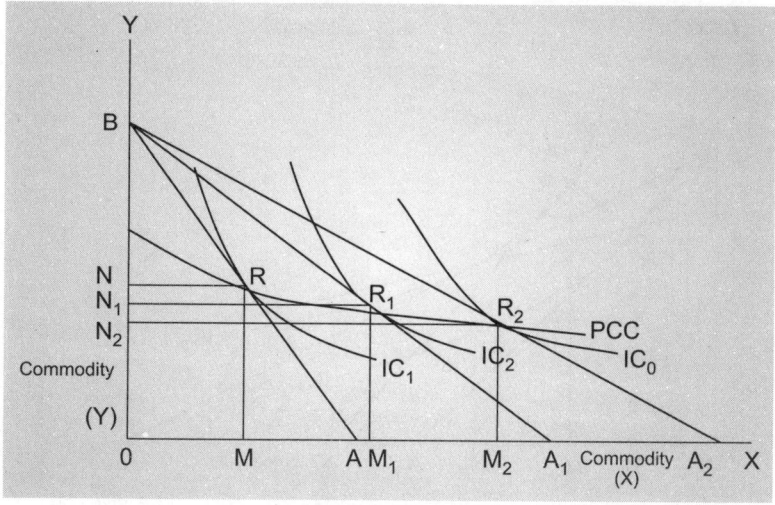

Fig. 5.7: Price effect

In Fig. 5.7 the original equilibrium position of the consumer is at point R where the consumer has OM of X and ON of Y. In this original situation, the price of X is such that the consumer could buy OA of X if he spends all his income on it. Let us now suppose that the consumer's money income remains the same, but that the price of X falls, so the same money income can buy OA_1 of X instead of OA. Since the price of Y remains the same, the consumer's income in terms of Y is OB all the time. The new equilibrium position is at point R_1 where the consumer can have OM_1 of X and ON_1 of Y. If the price of X falls again, the consumer can buy OA_2 of X if he spends all his given income on commodity X, the resulting equilibrium position will be at R_2. Each change in the price of X changes the slope of the price line by changing the ratio of prices of commodities X and Y. The cheaper X becomes compared with Y, the less steep is the slope of the price line and vice versa.

Price-Consumption Curve

If we connect all the points of equilibrium positions R, R_1, R_2, etc. in Fig. 5.8 then we will get a line which can be termed as the price-consumption curve (PCC).

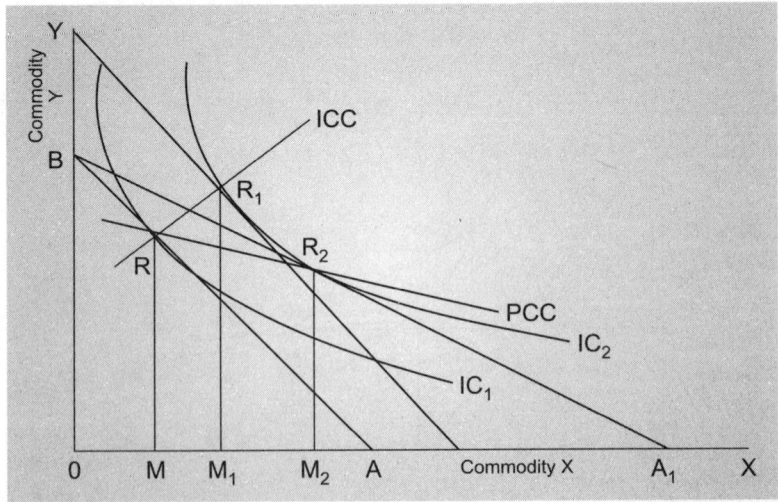

Fig. 5.8: Price effect as the sum of income effect and substitution effect

The effect of a price change can be looked at two levels. First there is an income effect which causes a movement along the income-consumption curve. This makes the consumer better off. As X becomes cheaper his real income increases. Second, there is a substitution effect which causes a movement along the indifference curve and enables the consumer to buy more of the commodity, X, whose price has fallen. X is now relatively cheap compared with Y. Since in the original equilibrium the relative prices of X and Y was equal to their marginal significance in terms of each other, this means that the marginal significance of X in terms of Y is now greater than its price in terms of Y. This prompts the consumer to substitute X for Y until once again the marginal significance of X in terms of Y equals the price of X in terms of Y. The consumer does this moving along the new, higher indifference curve. In Fig. 5.7 this means a move from R to R_1 as X is relatively cheap. If commodity Y were cheaper, the consumer would have moved above R on IC_2.

It is possible to show that the price effect is the combination of an income effect and a substitution effect (Fig. 5.8). In this figure the demand for X rises from OM to OM_2 as the consumer moves along the PCC from R to R_2. But one can consider a movement from R to R_2 as a movement initially from R to R_1 along ICC resulting an increase in demand of commodity X equal to MM_1 (this increase in demand as caused by an income effect), and then a movement from R_1 to R_2 resulting a further increase in demand of commodity X equal to M_1M_2 as a result of the substitution effect.

Hicks' and Slutsky's Approaches to Price-Effect—A Comparison

We have already noted that price effect is the sum total of a substitution effect and an income effect. But the decomposition of price-effect into a substitution effect and an income effect is done differently by J.R. Hicks and Slutsky. Their approaches to price effect are shown respectively in Figs 5.9 and 5.10

In Fig. 5.9 the consumer is at equilibrium at point R on IC_1 with his given income (Budget) represented by the line AB. **With a fall in the price of commodity X** the budget line moves

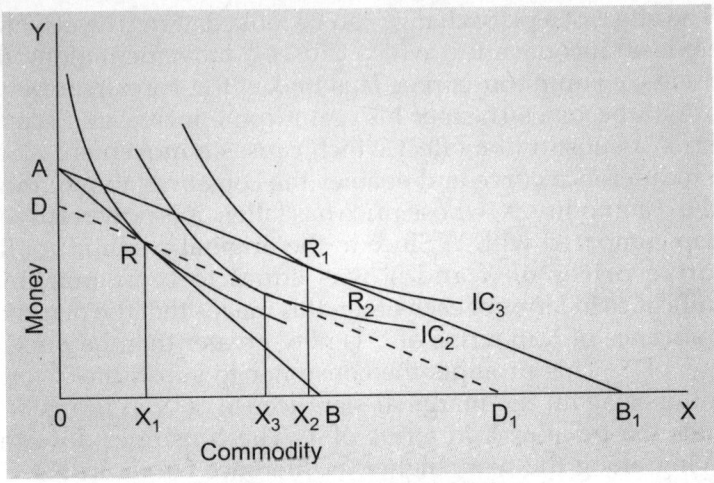

Fig. 5.9: Hick's approach to price effect

upwards and is represented by AB_1, and the new equilibrium of the consumer is at point R_1 on IC3. The total change in quantity demanded is from OX_1 (at **R**) to OX_2 (at R_1). i.e. OX_2—$OX_1 = X_1X_2$ and that is the price-effect. This can be decomposed into a substitution effect and an income effect.

We have defined substitution effect as the change in quantity demanded resulting from a change in relative price after compensating the consumer for the change in his real income. By the term, compensating the consumer for the change in his real income, what we mean is (a) the consumer has experienced a gain in his real income due to a fall in the price of commodity X and (b) we take away this gain from him by reducing his money income to a level so that he remains on the original indifference curve (IC_1).

Graphically we show this by drawing an imaginary budget line DD_1 which is placed at left and parallel to the new budget line AB_1 (the budget line after the fall in the price of X). The line DD_1 indicates the following:

- Had the consumer's real income not changed, consumer's equilibrium point would have shifted to R_2 because of a relative fall in the price of X in relation to the price of Y.
- At this equilibrium (at R_2) the consumer would have

increased his purchase of X from OX_1 to OX_3.
- OX_1, OX_3 can be regarded as the substitution effect.

We know the total effect is X_1X_2. Out of this X_1X_3 is accounted for the substitution effect. We are still left with X_3X_2.

Shift from the imaginary budget line DD_1 to the actual new budget line AB_1 represents an increase in real income. Since the price ratios at DD_1 and AB_1 are the same, change in quantity demanded (from OX_3 to OX_2) can be considered as the real income phenomenon. Thus OX_3 to OX_2 can be considered as the income effect of the price change.

Slutsky also decomposes the price effect into income effect and substitution effect holding the consumer's real income constant but in a slightly different way as shown in Fig. 5.10.

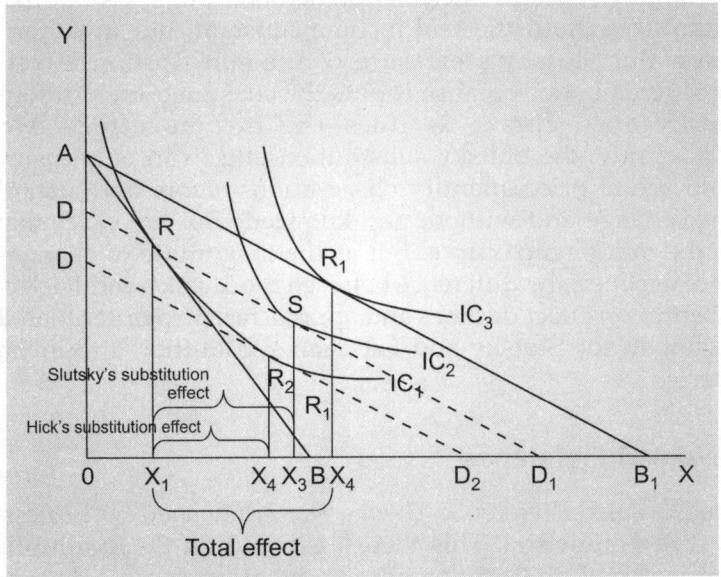

Fig. 5.10: Slutsky's approach to price effect

In Fig. 5.10 the original budget line is AB. As the price of X falls, the budget line shifts upward and is indicated by the line AB_1. The equilibrium position of the consumer shifts from point R on IC_1 to point R_1 on IC_3. Slutsky assumes that some one (government) takes away some nominal income from the consumer so that the consumer will have to go back to the original equilibrium point R. This is shown by drawing an imaginary income line DD_1 passing through point R and parallel to the budget line AB_1. But at DD_1 also we find the consumer doesn't like to go back to point R, instead he prefers S which is on a higher indifference curve. He likes to purchase OX_3 quantity of X.

This increased purchase of X, i.e. X_1X_3, owing to a fall in the relative price of X can be considered as the substitution effect.

Similarly, an increase in the quantity purchased of X from OX_3 to OX_2, i.e. X_3X_2 can be considered as the real income effect.

The difference in Hicks' approach and Slutsky's approach is that they hold the real income constant, but in different ways. But Slutsky's measure of the substitution effect is considered better because it puts the consumer on a different indifference curve, as does the income effect. Most importantly, the Slutsky substitution effect can be measured from actual price-quantity observations before and after the price change and without any knowledge of the exact shape on the indifference curve. But as the magnitude of change in price declines, the difference between the Slutsky and Hicksian substitution effect declines and approaches zero faster than the decline in the Slutsky and Hicksian substitution and income effects.

Revealed Preference

The Revealed Preference Theory was enunciated by Professor Paul A. Samuelson. This theory is based on the assumption that it would be better to observe what consumers do when they make their purchases, rather than suggest the unlikely idea that they operate with complete scales of preference set out in the form of indifference curves. What is done in the revealed preference analysis is that the consumer is asked to reveal the nature of his preferences by showing which goods he prefers in any set of circumstances.

The major advantage of the revealed preference analysis is that in this case one need not assume that the consumer can define or describe his/her indifference maps. Another major advantage of revealed preference theory according to Sir John Hicks is that it is explicitly designed to allow econometricians to make use of it.

In revealed preference analysis also we are dealing with an ideal consumer. But the analysis makes a distinction between strong ordering and weak ordering.

Strong ordering means that if a set of items is strongly ordered, then each has its own place in that order which is not shared by any other item. Weak ordering, on the other hand, accepts the possibility that it may not be possible to rank some items in a list ahead or behind each other.

In revealed preference analysis we need not assume that the consumer can order all the conceivable combinations of commodities with which he is faced with as in the case of indifference curve analysis. What is required in the revealed preference analysis is that we simply need to assume that the consumers can order (and choose between) those alternative combinations which they actually have to consider in making purchases.

The revealed preference theory is also based on the notion of two term consistency and transitivity. Two term consistency ensures that any two elements in a ranking are consistently placed to each other. For example, if A is above B, then B cannot also be above A. Then two term consistency is a necessary condition for consistent consumer choice. But it is not a sufficient condition. Consistent ordering also requires transitivity. This means that if a consumer prefers a combination of commodities A to a combination of commodities B and B to a combination of commodities C, then C cannot be preferred to A. The assumption of transitivity rules out circular relationships.

With the above mentioned assumptions we can proceed to explain the revealed preference theory. As in the case of indifference curve analysis we consider two goods. We assume prices of all goods except the one the consumer is considering (X) to be constant. So we can treat money as representing all other goods, but X. This is represented in Fig. 5.11.

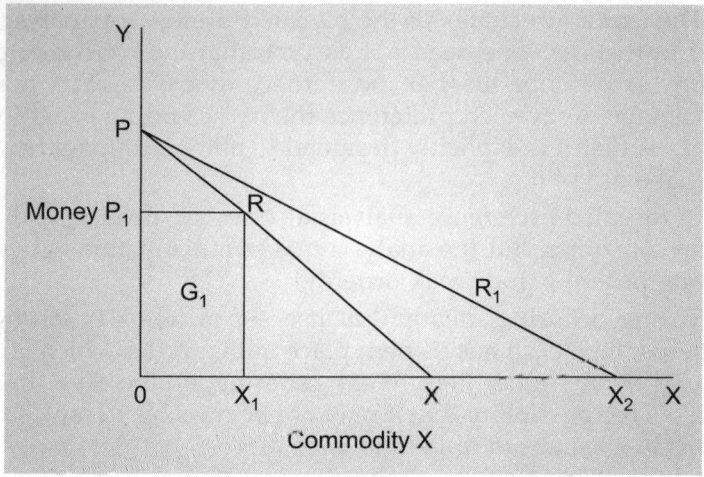

Fig. 5.11

In Fig. 5.11 good X is shown on the X-axis and money (representing all other goods) on the Y-axis. Initially the consumer's income is OP. He can, therefore, choose any of the combinations of Commodity X and money shown on the line PX. In fact, he chooses point R, buying OX_1 of X and keeping OP_1 of money. This amount OP_1 is available for spending on other goods. Point R is thus revealed as preferred to all other points on or within the triangle OPX.

However, if the 'ideal' consumer seeks to maximize his satisfaction, he is bound to choose some point along PX. If he does not, he is deliberately taking less of atleast one commodity than he might. For example, if he chooses a point like G, he could always increase his satisfaction by moving out towards the price line PX. But we cannot say where along PX point R will be. That will depend upon the consumer's tastes.

Now suppose that the price of commodity X falls. This will enable the consumer to buy OX_2 of X if he spends all his income on X. Let us further suppose that the consumer moves to point R1. Point R could lie anywhere in or on the triangle OPX_2. If the consumer is 'rational', it will lie on PX_2. As in the earlier case we have a move from R to R_1 which is the result of price effect.

Inferior Goods

We have already noted income effect and substitution effect. While substitution effect is invariably positive, income effect need not be so. In the case of certain commodities the income effect is really negative. Commodities whose income effect is negative are termed as inferior or Giffen goods. The name is derived from Sir Robert Giffen. For Giffen goods or inferior goods demand will decrease when consumer's income increases.

New Developments in Utility Theory

Certain advances have been made to the utility theory on the following lines:
  1. Making choices when there are risks as in gambling, insurance and investments; and
  2. Considering commodities on the basis of their attributes or characteristics, e.g. colour, texture, flavour, etc.

Making Choices when there are Risks

Modern utility theory holds that rational decisions look to expected or potential utility, not expected money value when risks are involved. Modern theory has been developed on the following two streams:
  i. Neuman-Morgenstern Method, and
  ii. The Friedman-Savage Hypothesis.

The Neuman-Morgenstern method of measuring the utility of money to a person is to find the probabilities the person will accept in deciding whether to put a sum of money to risk, e.g. in gambling. If the person insists on favourable odds, then for him the marginal utility of money declines or diminishes. If even odds are accepted, the marginal utility of money is constant, at least over some range. On the other hand, if a person willingly accepts unfavourable odds, the marginal utility of money increases, over some range.

The Friedman-Savage hypothesis holds the view that the marginal utility of money to many persons does indeed increase over some range of income, as otherwise such behaviour could not be explained.

Modern utility theory is widely used in methods of formal decision-making by modern business enterprises.

Seeing Commodities Based on their Characteristics

Kelvin Lancaster developed his demand theory by disaggregating individual commodities into separate characteristics. Each commodity is a unique bundle of different characteristics. But different commodities may share one or more characteristics. Commodities provide utility to consumers through their characteristics rather than directly. For example take toilet soaps. When choosing between different makes of soaps, consumers do not just consider their relative prices only, but consider their attributes such as colour, smell, shape. Hence consumer's choice can be examined, holds Lancaster, in terms of the characteristic of commodities.

Kelvin Lancaster developed his theory on the basis of the following assumptions:

    i. Goods possess different or various characteristics.

    ii. Different brands possess these characteristics in different proportions.

    iii. The characteristics are measurable and they are 'objective'.

    iv. The characteristics (along with price and income) determine consumer choice.

Let us illustrate this theory with the help of an example. Suppose one has to choose one among the three soaps, viz; Lux, Rexona and Jai. Each one has a different combination of two characteristics (e.g. colour and smell). Consumer's choice can be shown graphically as in Fig. 5.12.

In Fig. 5.12 the indifference curve map shows the different combinations of the two characteristics that give particular levels of utility. Thus any combination of the two characteristics on IC_3 gives a higher level of utility than those on IC_2 and so on.

The amounts of the two characteristics of the three soaps are shown by the three rays. The more is consumed of each will make the ray further up the respective ray to the consumer. Thus at point Q_1, the consumer is gaining OA of characteristic X and OY_1 of characteristic Y. Suppose that for the same money,

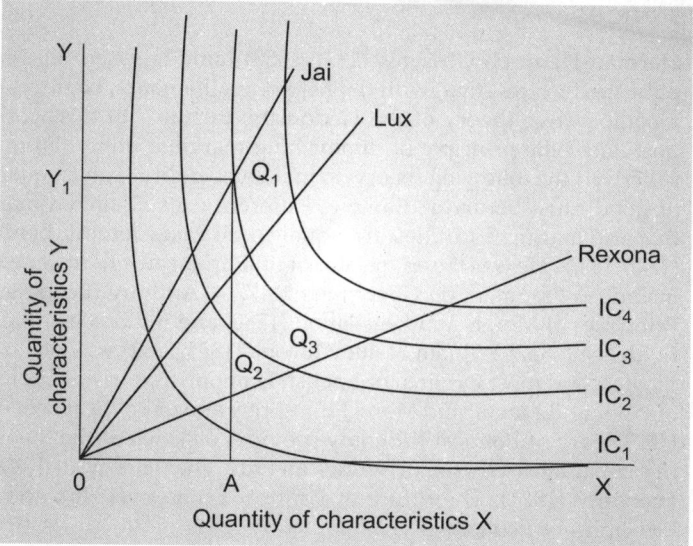

Fig. 5.12

the consumer could consume at Q_1, Jai and at Q_5, Rexona. The consumer will consume Jai as Q_1 is on a higher indifference curve than Q_2 and Q_3.

The Kelvin Lancaster theory has certain advantages compared with conventional indifference curve analysis in explaining consumer behaviour.

Some of the advantages are:

i. It helps to explain brand loyalty. When price changes slightly people will not shift to other brands, rather they will stick with the brand until a critical price is reached.

ii. Several goods can be shown on the diagram. Each good or brand will have its own ray.

iii. The theory helps to explain the nature of substitute goods. The closer the sub statutes, the closer will be their characteristics and hence closer will be their rays. The closer the rays, the more likely will be the shift in consumption to one good when the price of the other changes.

iv. Change in quality of a good can be indicated by rotating its ray.

References

1. Herman Heinrich Gossen's (1810-1858) fame is based on a book published in 1854 that, with the help of mathematics, he developed a comparative theory of the Hedonistic calculus. In this work he postulated the principle of diminishing marginal utility. From this is derived the following theory: to maximize utility, a given quantity of good must be divided among different uses in such a manner that the marginal utilities are equal in all cases Jeremy Bentham (1748-1832). He was the enunciator of utilitarianism. His major works include A Fragment on Government (1776), An Introduction to the Principles of Morals and Legislation (1780) and Rationale of Judicial Evidence (1827) William Stanley Jevons (1835-1882) was one of the greatest and most Original of English Economists. He was Professor of Logic and Mental and Moral Philosophy and of Political Economy. His Theory of Political Economy provides a sketch of the theory of the consumer. His major works include The Theory of Political Economy (1871), The future of Political Economy(1876), and The Principles of Economics (1905).

Demand, Supply, and Market Equilibrium

There is an old joke that says that if one teaches a parrot to say demand and supply to questions related to market one would have a good economist.

Demand analysis seeks to search out and measure the forces that determine sales.[1] There are different kinds of demand analyses that differ in purposes, methods and degrees of refinement.

In this chapter we confine our analysis to the theory and measurement of demand from a management viewpoint, i.e. in terms of the executive decisions that call for demand analysis and the kinds of estimates that are relevant for industrial products.

Purposes of Demand Analysis

From the point of view of managerial decision-making demand analysis has two objectives. They are:

- Demand forecasting, and
- Demand manipulation.

Forecasting Demand

Forecasting is by far the most common use of demand studies. Since demand forecast is the foundation for planning all phases of firm's operations, it follows that purchasing commitments, production schedules, inventory plans, cash budgets and capital expenditure programmes all hinge on the demand forecast.

Demand analysis can be used as a potential guide for manipulating demand. To do so the management must know the factors that affect demand. In other words, the management must have some understanding of the demand theory. Hence here we propose to discuss briefly the determinants of demand or the demand theory.

Demand

The demand for a commodity signifies a functional relationship between a dependent variable (i.e. the quantity bought) and several independent variables (i.e. price of the product, prices of substitutes, income of the buyers, mode of payment, population, quantity of the product, people's expectations about the future, the effectiveness of advertisement and sales force effort, etc.). Mathematically this can be represented as

$$Qd = f\ (x_1,\ x_2,\ x_3,\ldots\ldots x_n)$$

Where Q_d = the quantity demanded

$x_1,\ x_2,\ x_3\ldots x_n$ are influences such as price of the product prices of the substitutes, income of the buyers, the tastes of the consumers, population.

Among these various demand determinants, the economists single out one factor, viz. price, for special attention in economic analysis.

Demand for a commodity in simple terms implies:

- Desire to acquire it
- Willingness to pay for it, and
- Ability to pay for it.

Demand for a commodity must be stated with reference to time, its price and that of related commodities, consumer's income and tastes, etc.

Law of Demand

The law of demand states that the quantity demanded for a commodity, *ceteris paribus*, is inversely related to its price. This means that, other things remaining the same, more will be demanded at a low price and vice versa.

Demand Schedule

The price-quantity relationship can be represented in the form of a table. Such a table is known as the demand schedule (Table 6.1).

Table 6.1: Demand schedule

Price	Quantity demanded
Rs. 1000	10 Radios
Rs. 800	20 Radios
Rs. 600	50 Radios
Rs. 500	100 Radios

Demand Curve

The diagrammatic representation of a demand schedule is called the demand curve. It can also be defined as a curve that indicates the price quantity relationship. Figure 6.1 represents a demand curve.

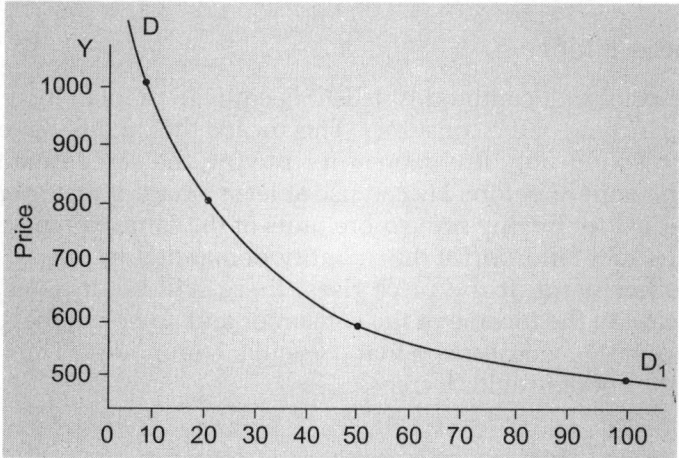

Fig. 6.1: Quantity marketed (demanded)

In Fig. 6.1 quantity demanded at various prices are shown on the X-axis and the prices of the commodity is represented on the Y-axis. Perpendiculars can be drawn from points indicating quantities on the X-axis and prices on the Y-axis. When we join the meeting points we get the individual demand curve for radios. The diagram shows that the demand curve slopes downwards from left to right which means that when price falls, the quantity demanded increases and, on the other hand, when price rises the quantity demanded falls.

Why do demand curves slope downwards?

The following reasons can be attributed to the inverse relationship between prices and demand.
1. Law of diminishing marginal utility
2. Income effect
3. Substitution effect

Law of Diminishing Marginal Utility

As indicated earlier the utility of a commodity diminishes as the stock of the commodity increases, *ceteris paribus*. Therefore a consumer will not buy more and more of a commodity if its price is not low.

Income Effect

If the price of a commodity falls it is equivalent to an increase in the income of the consumer. This means that at this stage he has to spend only less money for buying the same quantity that he bought before. He can use at least a part of that money so gained for buying some more units of the same commodity. So due to a fall in price the quantity demanded increases. On the other hand, if the price rises, there will be, in effect, a decrease in the income of the consumer and so he will have to reduce his expenditure on that particular commodity. Thus the quantity bought will decrease.

Substitution Effect

When a commodity becomes cheaper it will be substituted for costlier commodities. This is because the consumer can gain through this substitution. On the other hand, when a commodity becomes dearer that will be substituted by other goods, at least to a certain extent. Thus the reduction in price of a commodity results in increase in demand of that commodity and an increase in its price reduces its demand.

Assumptions of the Law of Demand

Following are the assumptions of the law of demand:
1. Consumer's taste remains the same
2. Consumer's income remains the same
3. Other commodities prices remain the same
4. New substitutes are not available.

Exceptions to the Law of Demand

Following are the exceptions to the law of demand:
1. **When price changes are anticipated:** There are occasions when increases in prices resulting in larger purchases and reduction in price results in less purchases. In such cases when price falls, consumers expect further fall and stop buying. When the price increases they expect further rises and rush to buy.
2. **Prestige goods:** There are commodities like diamonds that have prestige value. In their cases the demand curve may go upwards. People buy diamonds because of their high pieces. If the prices come down diamonds will lose their prestige value and so the rich people will reduce the purchase of diamonds. On the other hand, if the price falls steeply the poor people will be in a position to afford them and so they will buy them as they would like to satisfy their wish to wear them. Hence the demand for diamonds will increase.
3. **Inferior goods:** Inferior goods also form another example where the demand curve slopes upwards. Only when a commodity satisfies the following conditions it can be considered as inferior good:
   a. The commodity must be usually consumed at low levels of income and not one's income increases beyond a certain level.

b. A major part of a poor man's income should be spent on that commodity, and

c. The commodity should not have any substitute or near substitute available in market.

When the price of an inferior good decreases a considerable part of a person's income becomes released. Due to the reduction in the prices of inferior goods the consumer becomes in effect richer. And as the first condition laid down the commodity must be consumed at low levels of income. Since the consumer becomes richer due to a decrease in the price of inferior good he does not buy them. Thus the indirect result in the decrease in the price of inferior good is the reduction in its demand. Only when the income effect is substantial this takes place. However, in practice only very few goods satisfy the above-mentioned conditions that make them inferior good.

Market Demand

Market demand is the summation of demand for a good by all individual buyers in the market.

Autonomous and Derived Demand

If the demand for a commodity is not tied with the demand for any other commodity the demand is said to be autonomous and when the demand for a commodity is tied with any other commodity then demand is said to be derived demand.

Firm and Industry Demand

In normal situation more than one firm produce a particular product and so there is a difference between the demands facing an individual firm and that facing an industry. All firms producing a particular commodity constitute the industry demand curve while the demand for the product of a particular firm is known as firm's demand curve. For example the demand for Benz car alone is a firm's demand while cars produced by different firms form industry demand.

Shift in Demand

If demand changes due to any other factor than price then it is termed as shift in demand. The shift can be either forward or backward.

The demand curve shifts forward or upward or to the right when changes occur in any one or more of the factors such as income of the consumer, taste of the consumer, prices of substitute or complimentary commodities, etc. An upward or forward rightward movement in the demand curve due to changes in factors other than the price of the commodity concerned is known as increase in demand. Similarly a downward or backward or a leftward movement of the demand curve due to changes in factors other than price is known as decrease in demand.

Change in Demand *vs* Shift in Demand

It is important to distinguish between a movement along a given demand curve (due to change in price of the commodity in question) from a shift in demand (due to change in the determinants of demand other than the price of the commodity in question). The first situation is known as a change in quantity demanded while the second one is known as a shift in demand.

Figures 6.2 to 6.5 respectively show increase in demand, decrease in demand, and increase in quantity demanded and decrease in quantity demanded.

Figure 6.2 shows that when price increases from OP to OP_1 demand increases from OM to OM_1 this happens because consumers? Expect further rise in prices.

Changes in Demand

A change in one or more of the determinants of demand will change demand and therefore the location of the demand curve. A change in demand may result because of any one or a combination of the following factors, viz. consumer's taste, increase or decrease in the number of buyers, change in consumer's income, change in the prices of related goods (substitute or complementary), changes in expected prices, etc.

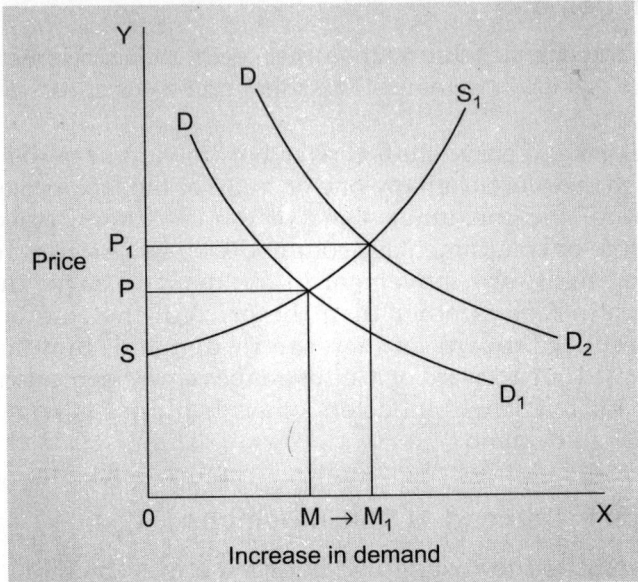

Fig. 6.2

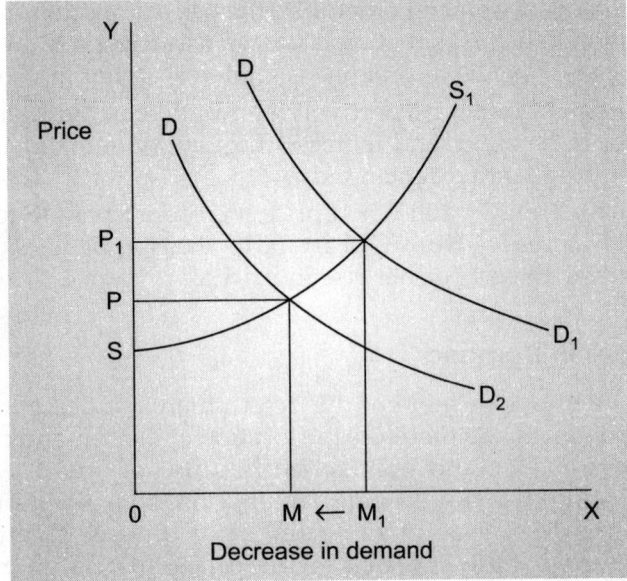

Fig. 6.3

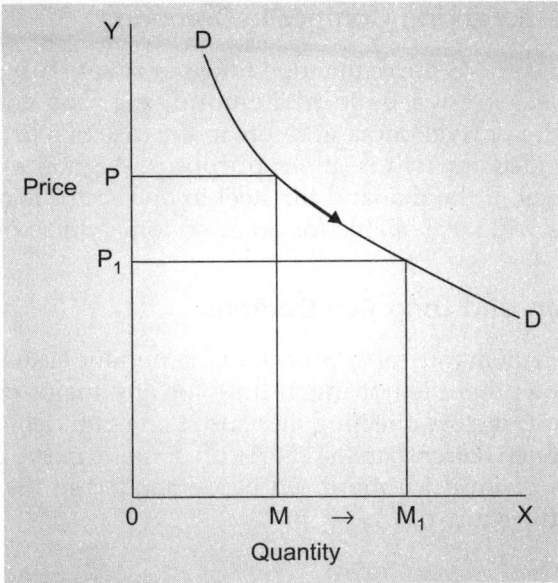

Fig. 6.4

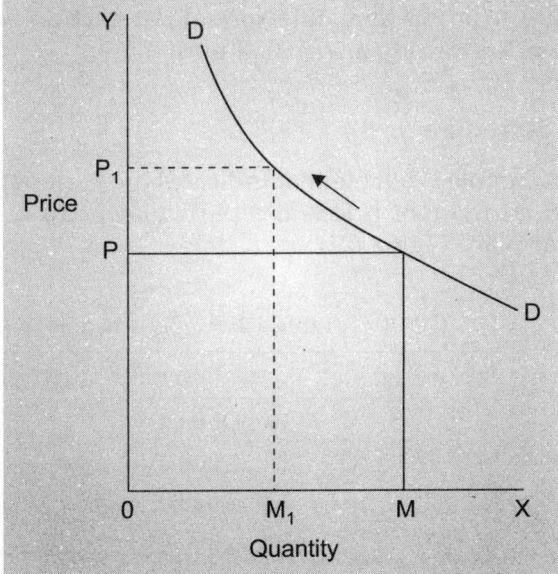

Fig. 6.5

Joint Demand and Composite Demand

When two goods are demanded together to satisfy a particular want, it is known as joint demand, e.g. car and petrol. Composite or rival demand refers to the case of a product that is demanded for two or more purposes. A good example of this is steel. If the demand for steel in one sector is more than only less will be available for other sectors, and so on.

Short-Run and Long-Run Demand

Short-run demand for a product is generally assumed to be constant as there is not much time for any major changes in the various factors affecting demand. Long-run demand curve will be much flatter than the short-run demand curve indicating that at a given price more can be demanded in the long-run than in the short-run.

Supply

Supply means the amounts of a product that producers will be willing to make available for sale at each of a series of possible prices during a specified period.

Supply Schedule

Supply schedule is a table that indicates the various quantities supplied at different prices at a particular point of time at a particular place (Table 6.2).

Table 6.2: Supply schedule

Price per kg.	Quantity supplied (apple)
Rs. 50	100 Quintal
Rs. 100	150 Quintal
Rs. 150	200 Quintal
Rs. 200	300 Quintal
Rs. 250	400 Quintal

Supply Curve

The graphical representation of a supply schedule is known as the supply curve (Fig. 6.6).

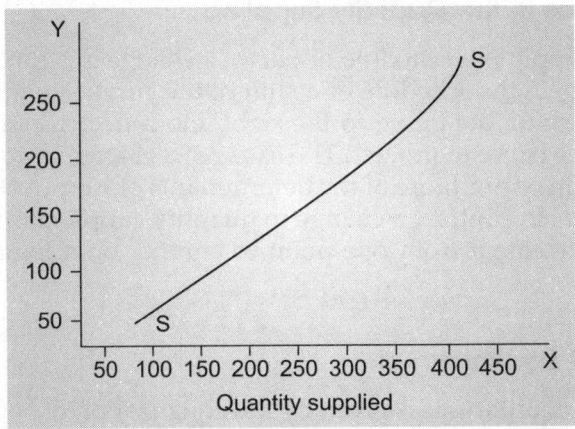

Fig. 6.6

Law of Supply

The law of supply explains the relationship between the price and the quantity supplied. A supply schedule or curve reveals that firms will offer for sale more of their products at a high price than at a low price.

Market Supply

Market supply is derived from individual supply in exactly the same way that market demand is derived from individual demand.

Determinants of Supply

Price is the most important determinant of supply. The other determinants of supply are:
- Resource prices
- Technology
- Taxes and subsidies

- Prices of other goods
- Expected price, and
- The number of sellers in the market.

Changes in the Quantity Supplied

Since supply is a schedule or curve, a change in supply means a change in the schedule or a shift of the curve. An increase in supply shifts the curve to the right and a decrease in supply shifts the curve to the left. The cause of a change in supply is a change in one or more of the determinants of supply other than the price. In contrast a change in quantity supplied is reflected by a movement from one point to another on a fixed supply curve.

Market Equilibrium

Market equilibrium is given by the equalization of supply and demand in the market. This is shown in Fig. 6.7.

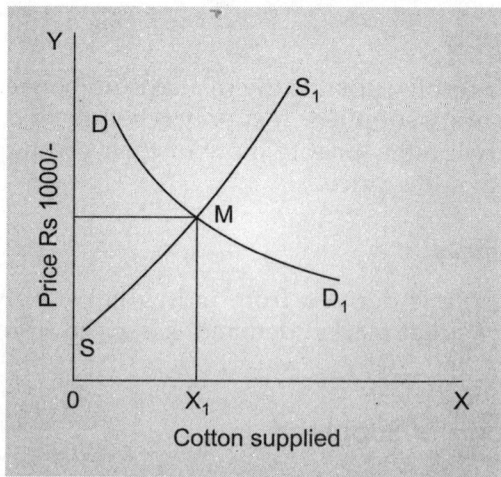

Fig. 6.7

Figure 6.7 shows that the market is in equilibrium at point M at which the quantity of cotton supplied is exactly equal to the quantity demanded at Rs. 1000 per bale of cotton.

Equilibrium Price and Quantity

The equilibrium price is the price at which the intention of buyers and sellers match. It is the price at which the quantity supplied match the quantity demanded.

Rationing Function of Prices

The ability of the competitive forces of supply and demand to establish a price at which selling and buying decisions are consistent is called the rationing function of prices.

Changes in Demand, Supply, and Equilibrium

It is a well-known fact that prices can and do change in markets. The changes may be due to various reasons. Suppose that the supply of commodity X is as represented by supply curves and the demand for the same increases as shown in Fig. 6.8. As a result the new intersection of the supply and demand curves is at higher values on both the price and the quantity axes. An increase in demand raises both the equilibrium price and the equilibrium quantity. In the same way, a decrease in demand, such as that shown in Fig. 6.9 reduces both the equilibrium price and the equilibrium quantity.

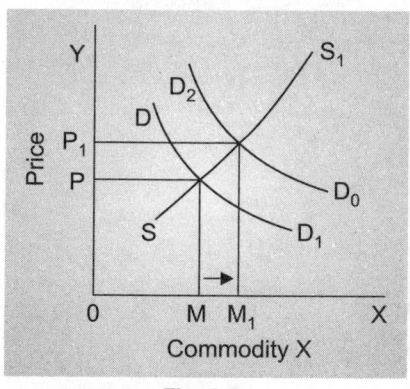

Fig. 6.8

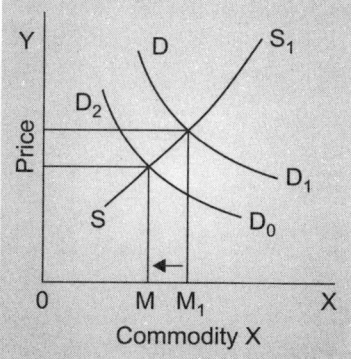

Fig. 6.9

Changes in Supply

What happens if the demand for X remains constant but the supply of the same increases? This situation is shown in Fig. 6.10.

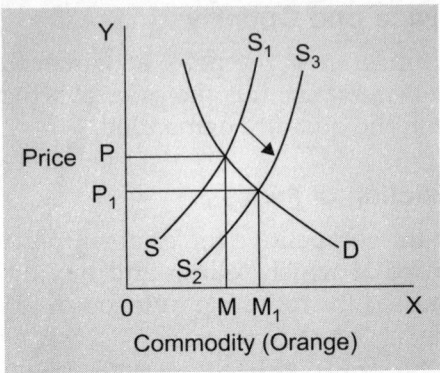

Fig. 6.10

Figure 6.10 indicates the new intersection of supply and demand. The intersection is at a lower equilibrium price OP_1 but at a higher equilibrium quantity OM_1. An increase in supply reduces the equilibrium price but increases equilibrium quantity. In contrast, the supply decreases as is shown in Fig. 6.11 the equilibrium price rises from (OP to OP_1) and the equilibrium quantity declines (OM to OM_1).

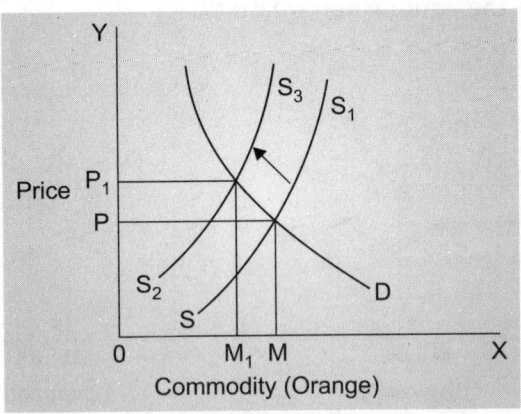

Fig. 6.11

What does happen when both demand and supply change? The effect will be a combination of the individual effects. Figure 6.12 highlights the situation.

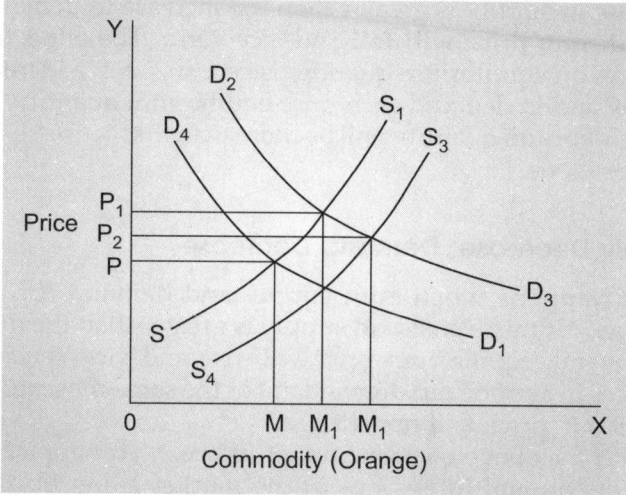

Fig. 6.12

Supply Increase; Demand Decrease

What happens when the supply of a commodity increases while the demand for the same decreases. This will result in a decrease in price. If the increase in supply is larger than the decrease in demand, the equilibrium quantity will increase and vice versa.

Supply Decrease; Demand Increase

A decrease in supply and an increase in demand, say for orange, will result in an increase in price. The combined effect of these will be an increase in equilibrium price more than that caused by either change separately. But the effect of such changes on equilibrium quantity depends on the relative sizes of the changes in supply and demand. If the decrease in supply is larger than the increase in demand, the equilibrium quantity will decrease and vice versa.

Supply Increase; Demand Increase

Suppose that both supply and demand for orange increases. What will happen then? Normally a supply increase decreases the price while a demand increase will raise the price. If the increase in supply is greater than the increase in demand, **the equilibrium price will fall** and vice versa. The effect of such changes on equilibrium quantity is certain, i.e. the increases in supply and in demand each raise equilibrium quantity. Hence the equilibrium quantity will be more than that caused by either change alone.

Supply Decrease; Demand Decrease

What happens when both supply and demand for orange decrease? If the decrease in supply is greater than the decrease in demand, equilibrium price will rise and vice versa. If the changes in supply and demand are of the same magnitude and cancel out, price will not change.

With the above background let us see what happens when the government intervenes in the market either by fixing a ceiling or a floor price for products. The **Ceiling price** is the maximum price a seller can charge for the product or service. A price at or below is legal, but above is illegal. **A floor price,** on the other hand, is the minimum price fixed by the government. A price at or above the floor price is legal and a price below it is not. The two situations are represented in Figs 6.13 and 6.14 respectively.

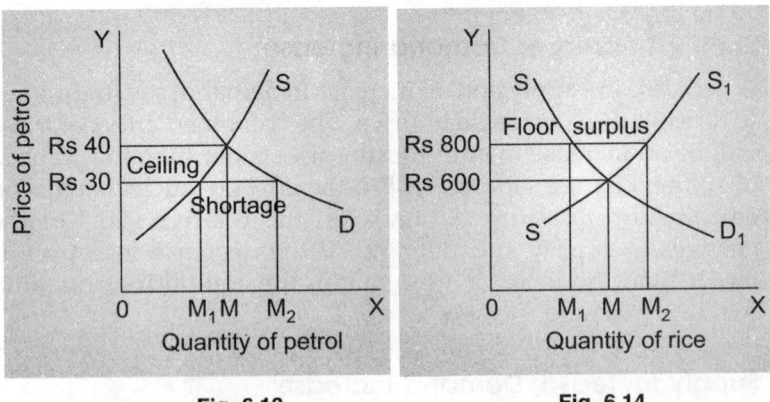

Fig. 6.13   Fig. 6.14

Figure 6.13 shows the effects of price ceilings. Suppose increase in income of the people boost the demand for automobiles. This will increase the demand for petrol. Suppose the equilibrium price for petrol is Rs. 40 per litre. Suppose this price burdens the moderate income group, there will pressure from this group on government to do something to reduce the price. Suppose on the basis of such pressure, the government fix a ceiling price of Rs. 30 per litre. This will adversely affect the rationing ability of the free market. The quantity of Petrol demanded increases to OM_2 while supply remains at OM_1. This results in a shortage of $M_1 M_2$ quantity of petrol.

Figure 6.14 represents a case where government fixes a floor price higher than the market equilibrium price. This will result in excess of supply than the equilibrium quantity that can be handled by the market.

From the above analysis it is easy to understand why economists "sound the alarm" when policy makers advocate either ceiling price or floor price for commodities or services.

7 Elasticity of Demand and Supply

Managers generally agree that the toughest decision they face is the decision whether to raise or lower the price of their company's product. When managers lower price to attract more buyers, total revenue may either rise or fall depending upon how responsive the consumers are to a price reduction. Obviously, managers need to know how a price increase or decrease is going to affect the quantity sold and the revenue of the firm.

Managers recognize that quantity demanded and price is inversely related. This is from their awareness of the law of demand. But the law of demand indicate only the direction of change when price of the commodity in question changes. But it doesn't indicate the extent of change in demand due to a change in the price of the commodity in question. It is the concept of elasticity that provides managers, economists and policy makers with a framework for understanding why consumers in some markets are extremely responsive to changes in price while consumers in other markets are not. This understanding is useful in many types of managerial decisions.

It is the concept of elasticity of demand that helps the managers to know the extent of change in demand or supply due to a slight change in price of the commodity. Elasticity of demand is a technical term used by economists to describe the degree of responsiveness in the demand for a good to a fall in its price (strictly speaking, elasticity of demand refers to the way in which the demand for a commodity responds to its change in price; whether a rise or fall). It was Alfred Marshall who introduced the concept of elasticity of demand into economic theory. According to him 'the elasticity (or responsiveness) of demand in a market is great or small according as the amount demanded increases much or little for a given fall in price, and diminishes much or little for a given rise in price.[1]

Price Elasticity of Demand

The responsiveness demand of consumers to a price change of a product is known as **price elasticity of demand.** The price elasticity or inelasticity of demand at a point is measured as follows:

$$Ed = \frac{\text{Change quantity demanded of X}}{\text{Original quantity demanded of X}} \Big/ \frac{\text{Change in price of X}}{\text{Original price of X}}$$

It is also measured as percentage change in quantity demanded of the commodity divided by percentage change in price of the commodity. So we can restate the formula as

$$Ed = \frac{\text{Percentage change in the quantity demanded of X}}{\text{Percentage change in price of X}}$$

Using Averages

There is some annoying problem that arises in computing the price-elasticity coefficient. A price change from, say, Rs. 4 to Rs. 5 along a demand curve is 25 percent (= Re.1/Rs. 4) increase, but the opposite price change from Rs. 5 to Rs. 4 along the same curve is a 20 percent (Re.1/Rs. 5) decrease. Which percentage change in price should we use in the denominator to compute the price- elasticity coefficient? And when quantity changes, for example from 2 to 4, it is a 100 percent (= 2/2) increase. But when quantity falls from 4 to 2 along the identical demand curve, it is a 50 percent (= 2/4) decrease. Should we use 100 percent or 50 percent in the numerator of the elasticity formula? Elasticity should be the same whether price rises or falls!

The simplest solution to the problem is to use the averages of the two prices and the two quantities as the reference points for computing the percentages. That is

$$Ed = \frac{\text{Change in quantity}}{\text{Sum of quantities}/2} \Big/ \frac{\text{Change of price}}{\text{Sum of prices}/2}$$

Or

$$\frac{\dfrac{Qi - Qo}{Qi + Qo}}{2} \Big/ \frac{\dfrac{Pi - Po}{Pi + Po}}{2}$$

For the same Rs. 5 – Rs. 4 price range, the price reference is Rs. 4.50 (Rs. 5 + Rs. 4)/2 and for the same 2–4 quantity range the quantity reference is 3 units (= 2 +4)/2. The percentage change in price is now Re.1/Rs. 4.50, or about 22 percent, and the percentage change in quantity is 4/3, or 75 percent. So Ed is about 3.41 percent. This solution eliminates the "up versus down" problem.

Strictly, elasticity of demand should be represented by a negative number. This is because demand curves slope downwards, changes in price and quantity demanded will be in the opposite directions. However, for convenience we denote elasticity by positive numbers.

Arc Elasticity

If we want to measure the elasticity over a range of the curve instead of at a point we use what is known as **arc** elasticity. The formula for arc elasticity is:

$$\frac{q_i - q_o}{q_i + q_o} \times \frac{p_i + p_o}{p_i - p_o} = \frac{\text{Change in demand}}{\text{Sum of quantities}} \times \frac{\text{Sum of prices}}{\text{Change in price}}$$

$$= \frac{\partial q}{\partial P} \times \frac{p_o + p_i}{q_o + q_i}$$

Here, po is the original price, and pi the new price. Similarly, qo is the quantity demanded at the original price, and qi the amount demanded at the new price.

Factors Affecting Price Elasticity of Demand

Price elasticity of demand is affected by
- Availability of substitutes
- Percentage of the consumer's budget that is spend on the commodity
- Time period of adjustment
- Nature of the commodity
- Extent of use
- Level of prices.

Availability of substitutes: There are commodities which have many substitutes. When their prices rise usually their consumption will be quickly reduced. Therefore their demand will be elastic. Commodities that do not have substitutes will have inelastic demand.

Percentage of the consumer's budget: Big items in a budget tend to have a more elastic demand than small items.

Time period of adjustment: The demand for a product becomes more elastic the longer the time period under consideration. It takes time to decide about another product before buying it before one develops a habit of using a particular product.

Nature of the commodity: The necessities of life usually will have inelastic demand. The reason is that the consumption of a necessary article does not undergo any great change as a result of changes in prices. On the other hand the demand for luxury articles changes much as a result of changes in price. Thus demand for luxury articles generally is inelastic.

Extent of use: The demand for those commodities that have different types of uses is generally elastic, e.g. Steel is a commodity which has many uses. When there is a slight fall in its price there will be great demand for it. So the demand for steel is generally elastic. On the contrary, commodities with limited uses have generally inelastic demand.

Level of prices: The level of price is also a factor that determines elasticity of demand. If the price of a commodity is already high and if the price increases once again that will result in quick reduction of consumption. On the other hand, if the price is low, small change in price will not affect demand much.

Thus it can be generalized that demand is generally elastic at higher levels of prices and generally inelastic at lower prices.

After discussing price elasticity we propose to discuss other elasticities viz. income elasticity, cross elasticity and advertising elasticity.

Income Elasticity

Income elasticity of demand is the rate of change in the demand for a commodity due to a change in the income of the consumer. The formula for calculating income elasticity is

$$E_L = \frac{\text{Percentage change in quantity demanded}}{\text{Percentage change in income}}$$

It is also defined as

$$\frac{\text{Proportionate change in demand}}{\text{Proportionate change in income}}$$

i.e. $\dfrac{\text{Change in demand}}{\text{Original demand}} \Big/ \dfrac{\text{Change in income}}{\text{Original income}}$

Types of Income Elasticity

There are different types of income elasticities.

1. **Zero income elasticity:** In this case a change in income will not result in any change in the quantity demanded. The demand for salt can be considered as an example for zero income elasticity.

2. **Negative income elasticity:** This is an exceptional case when an increase in income results in a reduction in the quantity of the commodity demanded. Suppose the income of a *Bidi* smoker increases. Then he might stop smoking *Bidis* and shift to cigarettes. This category of goods is called Giffen's goods or inferior goods.

3. **Positive income elasticity:** In this case an increase in income will lead to an increase in the quantity demanded. Positive income elasticity can be of three kinds: Unity elasticity, more than unity elasticity and less than unity elasticity. When a change in the income of a person results in exactly proportional to the quantity demanded it is

called unity elasticity. When the change in income of a person leads to a more than proportionate change in the quantity demanded it is called more than unity elasticity, and if a change in income results only in less than proportionate change in the quantity demand it is called less than unity elasticity. Luxury articles are examples for more than unity elasticity and articles of necessity are examples for less than unity elasticity.

Income Sensitivity

Income sensitivity of demand refers to the ratio of percentage in expenditure (in money terms) to percentage change in income. If an increase in income results in a more than proportionate increase in expenditure it is called positive income sensitivity. In case of inferior commodities such as coarse food grains and coarse cloth the income sensitivity can be negative.

Cross Elasticity

Here we consider the relationship between the demands for two different goods. When the demand for a commodity increases, the demand for its substitutes will naturally decrease. On the other hand the demand for its complements will increase. Cross elasticity is concerned with the changes in the quantity demanded of a particular commodity in response to a change in the price of some other related commodity. The formula for calculating cross elasticity is:

$$Cr = \frac{\% \text{ Change in quantity demanded of commodity X}}{\% \text{ Change in the price of commodity Y}}$$

$$\text{Or } Cr = \frac{\text{Proportionate change in the quantity of X bought}}{\text{Proportionate change in the price of Y}}$$

$$= \frac{\dfrac{QX_i - QX_o}{QX_o}}{\dfrac{PY_i - PY_o}{PY_o}}$$

Advertising Elasticity

Usually advertisement stimulates or expands demand. The expansion or stimulation of demand through advertisement or promotional activities can be measured with the help of advertising elasticity of demand or promotional elasticity of demand. The formula used to measure this type of elasticity is given below:

$$Ea = \frac{\text{Proportionate change in sales}}{\text{Proportionate change in advertisement expenditure}}$$

Or $$\frac{Q_i - Q_o}{Q_i + Q_o} / \frac{A_i - A_o}{A_i + A_o}$$

Where Q_i Stands for sales after additional advertisement expenditure.

Q_o Stands for sales before additional advertisement expenditure.

A_i Stands for new advertisement expenditure, and

A_o Stands for original advertisement expenditure.

Factors Affecting Advertising Elasticity

The stage of the product's market development, i.e. whether it is new product or a product with a growing market or with an established market.

The extent of reaction of the competitors to the company's advertisement by further advertising or by increasing the promotional or sales efforts.

Since variations in qualitative factors, say selection of advertising medium, or media may obscure the effects of quantitative variations in advertising outlays, the quality and quantity of the company's past and present advertising relative to that of competitors is also a factor that affects the advertising elasticity of demand.

The influence of non-advertising determinants of demand such as growth trends, prices, incomes, etc. and the extent to which these can be successfully determined for eliminating their effect in demand analysis.

The time interval that elapse between the advertisement expenditure and the response of sales to the advertisement expenditure. Since this depends on the type of the product, method of advertisement, etc. this is difficult to predict.

The delayed effect of company's past advertisement and its influence on current and future sales.

Methods for Determining Total Advertising Budget

There are several alternative methods for planning total advertising expenditures.[1]

1. **Percentage of sales approach:** Here the advertising budget is fixed as a fixed percentage of past or expected sales. The advantage of this method is that this is a convenient working formula. But this method is not very scientific as past or present sales may not have any relation with the cost of expanding sales further.

2. **All you-can-afford approach:** Under this approach the advertising budget is fixed as a fixed percentage of profits or cash funds. Accordingly advertisement expenditure gets enhanced when the business earns more profit or when the financial position of the business becomes more viable.

3. **Return on investment approach:** This approach is based on the following assumptions:

   a. Advertising increases immediate sales, and

   b. It contributes to the goodwill of the business by enhancing future earning power. If we discount the expected stream of future cash flows that result from the present advertising expenditure at an appropriate rate of interest we will be able to determine the present value of the future returns. The problems associated with this approach are:

      i. identifying which of the business cash flows are attributable to advertising and

      ii. separating the short-term effects of advertising from the long-term.

4. **Objective and task approach:** Under this approach one should take into consideration the pre-determined

objectives when one determines the budget for advertisement. Following are the three steps:

a. Define the objective, i.e. the sales target to be achieved,

b. Outline the tasks, i.e. the specific means and media of attaining the objective, and

c. Determining the cost accomplishing these tasks.

5. **Competitive parity approach:** Under this approach a firm decides its advertising expenditure by taking into consideration what other firms in the same industry spend. Under conditions of Oligopoly this method can help towards stabilizing market shares. This may also avoid competitive retaliation from other firms in the same industry.

6. **Marginal approach:** This is the application of marginal analysis. According to this approach it would be advantageous to increase expenditure on sales promotion so long as the additional gross profit is more than the additional cost of each increment of sales promotion expenditure.

Practical Applications of the Elasticity of Demand

The concept of elasticity of demand has got great practical importance not only in public finance, but also in the field of trade and commerce.

1. The principle of elasticity of demand is a very useful index for fixing the tax rate. To raise revenue for the State the Finance Minister should either introduces a fresh levy on certain commodities or he should raise existing tax rates. Before taking any such decision he makes a study of the elasticity of demand for the commodities in question; because if he taxes those items with elastic demand their consumption will be curtailed and thus defeat the very purpose of the levy.

2. When a businessman fixes the price for his commodity, he has to consider the nature of its demand. In case the commodity has inelastic demand, it will be better for him to charge a high price and sell a smaller quantity of his commodity. On the contrary, if the demand is elastic for

getting maximum revenue he should reduce the price and stimulate demand.

3. The term elasticity of demand also gives explanation to the paradox of poverty amidst plenty. Since food grains have inelastic demand, their bumper crop may bring only economic calamity and not prosperity to the producers. This is because a rich harvest will bring only less income to the producers.

4. Elasticity of demand also plays its role in determining the rewards of the factors of production. The efforts of the trade unions to increase the wages of workers will not succeed if the demand for workers is elastic. On the other hand, if the demand is relatively inelastic, the trade unions bargaining power will be much higher.

5. Also in fixing the prices of joint supply products elasticity is important. On the one hand, it is impossible to identify the separate marginal costs of joint products. On the other hand, his total receipts must cover at least the total costs. Therefore, he considers the elasticity of demand of the commodities as the guideline.

6. The concept of elasticity is also important for the government in the determination of industries as public utilities. Public utilities are vested with public interest. Therefore, if industries producing commodities with inelastic demand are controlled by monopoly interests they should be declared as public utilities and should be taken-over by the government.

Elasticity of Demand and Revenue Relationship

Before concluding this chapter we may point out the relationship between average revenue, marginal revenue, total revenue and the elasticity.

Average revenue (AR) is total revenue divided by output. Symbolically this can be stated as

$$AR = \frac{TR}{Q}$$

AR = Average revenue, TR = total revenue, and Q = total output.

The total sales proceeds is termed as total revenue. Marginal revenue (MR) at any Level of output is the revenue that would be earned by selling an additional unit of the firm's product., i.e. the difference in total revenue when one unit more or less is sold. Symbolically it is the addition to total revenue by selling 'n' units of a product instead of n – 1, where 'n' is any given number. Alternatively it means the addition to total revenue by selling n+ 1 unit instead of 'n' units.

Table 7.1 indicates the relationship between average revenue, marginal revenue, and total revenue.

Table 7.1

Quantity sold	Total revenue Price × Output	Average revenue	Marginal revenue change in total revenue
	Rs.	Rs.	Rs.
1	10	10	10
2	18	9	8
3	24	8	6
4	28	7	4
5	30	6	2
6	30	5	0
7	28	4	- 2

A careful analysis of Table 7.1 will reveal that

- So long as average revenue is falling, marginal revenue will be less than the average revenue.
- Marginal revenue falls more steeply than the average revenue.
- Total revenue will be rising so long as marginal revenue is positive.
- Where marginal revenue is negative, total revenue must be falling.
- Total revenue will be maximum at a point where marginal revenue is zero.

Now we show the relationship between price elasticity of demand, marginal revenue and total revenue.

1. When the price elasticity of demand is greater than one, the marginal revenue will be positive and the total revenue will rise as price falls.
2. When the price elasticity of demand is unitary, the marginal revenue will be zero and a change in price will not change the total revenue.
3. When the price elasticity of demand is less than one, the marginal revenue will be negative and the total revenue will fall as price falls.

The relationship between elasticity of demand and the firm's total revenue are given in Table 7.2.

Table 7.2: Elasticity of demand and total revenue

Change in price	Elasticity greater than one	Elasticity equal to one	Elasticity less than one
Price rises	Total revenue falls	Total revenue unchanged	Total revenue rises
Price falls	Total revenue Rises	Total revenue unchanged	Total revenue falls

Relationship between Average Revenue, Marginal Revenue and Price Elasticity of Demand

Mrs Joan Robinson shows the relationship between marginal revenue, average revenue and price elasticity with the help of the following formula.[2]

1. Average revenue = Marginal revenue $\times \dfrac{e}{e-1}$

   i.e. $AR = MR \times \dfrac{e-1}{e}$

2. Marginal revenue = Average revenue $\times \dfrac{e-1}{e}$

   i.e. $MR = AR \times \dfrac{e-1}{e}$

   Where e = point elasticity of demand on the average revenue curve.

Elasticity of Supply

The concept of price elasticity is equally applicable to supply. If producers or suppliers are responsive to price changes, supply becomes elastic. If they are insensitive then supply becomes inelastic.

The degree of price elasticity or inelasticity of supply is measured with the help of the Elasticity of Supply coefficient (Es) defined as percentage change in the quantity supplied divided by the percentage change in price.

i.e. $$Es = \frac{\text{Percentage change in quantity supplied of X}}{\text{Percentage change in price}}$$

Elasticity of supply can also be defined as proportionate change quantity divided by proportionate change in price.

i.e. $$Es = \frac{\text{Proportionate change in quantity supplied}}{\text{Proportionate change in price}}$$

$$Es = \frac{\text{Change in quantity supplied}}{\text{Original quantity}} \Big/ \frac{\text{Changer in price}}{\text{Original price}}$$

As in the case of price elasticity of demand there may be certain annoying problem in calculating elasticity coefficient of supply. That problem is solved, as in the calculation of price elasticity of demand by taking the averages or mid points, of the before and after quantities supplied and before and after prices as the reference points for the percentage changes. Suppose that an increase in the price of a good from Rs. 20 to Rs. 24 increases the quantity supplied from 100 to 150 units. The percentage change in price would be 4/22, or 18.182 percent and the percentage change in quantity would be 50/125 or 40 percent. So elasticity of supply equals

$$Es = \frac{18.182}{40} = 0.455$$

In the above case, supply is inelastic, as the piece elasticity coefficient is less than 1. If Es is greater than 1, supply will be elastic and if Es equals 1, supply will be unit elastic. Es is not negative as price and quantity supplied are directly related.

The degree of price elasticity of supply depends mainly on how quickly producers can shift resources between alternative uses to change production of a commodity. The easier and more rapid the transfers of resources, the greater would be the price elasticity of supply.

Review Questions

- List the different types of elasticity.
- Indicate the relationship between average revenue, marginal revenue and price elasticity of demand.
- Calculate price elasticity of demand if Q_i = 6000, Q_2 = 7500, P_i = Rs.10 and P_2 = Rs.9

Suppose the Management of Hindustan Liver Limited knows that the elasticity of demand for their product 'Lux' is minus 2.5. If the management wants to increase the sales of 'Lux' by 20 percent to what extent price of 'Lux' is to be reduced? How much increase in quantity of sales can be expected if price is reduced by 10 percent solution.

From the definition of price elasticity, it follows that

$$-2.5 = \frac{\text{Percentage change in quantity}}{\text{Percentage change in price}}$$

With a little bit of algebraic manipulation, the required percentage change in price equals 8 percent (= 20%/–2.5), i.e. The management must lower the price of 'Lux' by 8 percent in order to realize 20 percent increase in sales.

In the same way we can find out the increase in sales when price of 'Lux' is reduced by 10 percent.

i.e. $$-2.5 = \frac{\text{Percentage change in quantity}}{\text{Percentage change in price}}$$

$$-2.5 \times 10\% = 25\%$$

References

1. Dean, Joel; Managerial Economics, Prentice Hall of India Private Limited, New Delhi, 1976, p. 141.
2. Robinson, Joan; Economics of Imperfect Competition, Macmillan, 1969, p.36.

8 Demand Forecasting

Demand forecasting is like trying to drive a car blind-folded and following directions given by a person who is looking out of the back window.

— Philip Kotler

Information about demand is essential for making pricing and production decisions. Goods are to be produced in required quantities in advance at the appropriate time and they must be made available at the appropriate place and time and that too at appropriate prices. This means that the management must anticipate the future demand for the products and on this basis create the required production capacity. A knowledge of future demand conditions can also be extremely useful to managers of both price taking and price setting firms when they are planning production schedules, inventory controls, advertising campaigns, output in future periods, investments, etc.

The discussion on demand forecasting is divided into seven sections. The first describes the meaning, nature and the vital role played by demand forecasts in the operations of business. The second deals with the types of forecasting which arise out of the planning needs of business firms. The third explores the various approaches to demand forecasting. The fourth explains the major determinants of demand. The fifth deals with the major methods adopted in estimating future demand. The sixth explains the forecasting methods for new products. The last discusses how forecasts and forecasting methods can be evaluated in terms of their accuracy and costs.

Meaning, Nature and the Role Played by Demand Forecasts in the Operations of Business

Estimates of expected future conditions are called forecasts and estimates of expected future demand conditions are called demand forecasts.

Precise forecasts of future developments are clearly impossible. Expectations depend on the assumptions made. The reliability of the forecasts, hence, depends on the reliability of the assumptions.

The assumptions and methods employed in forecasting depend upon the nature of the planning required. There are two major types of planning which require the use of forecasts. They are:

i. short-term planning and

ii. long-term planning. In industrially well-developed countries these grow out of the need to predict short-term and long-term changes in demand conditions facing industries. This has been so because demand conditions were always more uncertain than supply in industrially advanced countries.

In recent times forecasting has come to play an important role in business decision-making. A company is in business to serve its customers' needs in some way or the other. Its survival and prosperity depends on its ability and willingness to adapt its operations to customers' needs to create or stimulate the need and serve it adequately and efficiently when the need arises. Demand forecast serves as the link between the evaluation of external factors in the economy which influence the business and the management of the company's internal affairs. The very term 'planning' is intimately connected with the future.

More often than not, one finds forecasting decisions which have an important influence on production planning operations being made by store-keepers or stockroom clerks with little or no procedural or policy guidance. Determination of the types of forecasts required and establishment of procedures governing generation of these forecasts are fundamental steps in the organization of a well-conceived production control system.

For production planning purposes it is particularly important to distinguish between forecasts of demand and forecasts of sales. While forecasts of sales may be important for estimating revenue, cash requirements and expenses, a production planning system is designed primarily to react to customer demand. Demand may differ from sales for a variety of reasons. For example, there may be substantial lag between customer orders and billings. Or sales may understate demand to the extent that the manufacturing and distribution system is unable to cope up with the volume of customer demand. The particular characteristics of demand forecasts which are pertinent to production and inventory control are the timing, detail and reliability of forecasts, and the assignment within the organization of the responsibility for making forecasts and controlling or improving the quality of forecasts.

Types of Demand Forecasting

From the point of view of the time span and from the planning requirements of business firms, demand forecasting can be classified under two headings:

  i. short-term demand forecasting, and
 ii. long-term demand forecasting

Short-Term Forecasting

Short-term forecasting is limited to short periods, usually not exceeding a year. It relates to policies regarding, sales, purchasing, pricing and finances. Here the reference is only to the existing production capacity of the firm.

In most companies, knowledge of conditions in the immediate future is essential for formulating a suitable sales policy. Production schedules have to be geared to expected rather than actual sales. Often by assuming that prevailing conditions will continue, a firm may find itself faced with a problem of overproduction or short supply. An understanding of near future prospects would make it possible to avoid some of the violent fluctuations which occur in production scheduling and sales planning.

Knowledge of future conditions is important in pricing. If prices of materials are expected to go up or shortages are expected, business men may take advantage of the rise by earlier buying. Proper price forecasting may, thus help the firm in reducing the costs of operation.

Demand forecasting is also useful to the businessmen in determining their price policy. An increase of prices is avoided when future market conditions are not expected to be good and lowering of prices is avoided when costs or sales levels are likely to rise considerably. Many companies use forecasting for setting sales targets and establishing controls and incentives. Sales targets will not accomplish their objectives if not geared meaningfully to the sales levels likely to be achieved. If set too high, the targets will be discouraging to those who have to meet them. If the targets are too low, they will be met very easily and incentives will prove meaningless.

Above all, demand forecasting of the type mentioned above will be of considerable assistance in short-term financial forecasting also. Cash requirements will depend upon the levels of sales and production levels. Some prior information is usually needed to procure additional funds on reasonable terms. Neglect of demand forecasting will complicate financial planning through its repercussions on production scheduling and inventory accumulation. In the preparation of budgets, therefore, short-term forecasts have come to play an important part.

Long-Term Forecasting

In short-term forecasting a company is concerned only about the use of its existing production capacity. But when questions of long-term planning are involved the businessman must know some thing about the long-term demand for his product. Thus the planning of a new production unit or the expansion of an existing unit must start with an analysis of the long-term demand potential of the products in question. A multi-product firm must ascertain not only the total demand situation, but also the demand for different items. This will involve the study of consumer preferences and trends, the economy and trends. Once the demand potential is assessed, it will be easier for the company to engage in long-term financial planning. Again, **manpower** planning for existing as well as new firms must be based on long-term forecasting of the company's growth.

When forecasts covering long periods are made, the probability of error will be high. Competent forecasts predict the conditions that are likely to prevail in the near future with comparative confidence, and with a relatively high degree of accuracy; the results are much less reliable when they attempt to forecasts conditions over longer periods. This is because; as the period becomes longer certain factors that forecasters take into account in making their estimates become more volatile. It is very difficult to predict over extended periods such items as the probable costs of production, the trend of prices and the changing nature of competition. Moreover, the longer the period covered by the prediction, the more likely it is that unanticipated events such as international conflicts including wars, periods of major depression and prosperity and inventions and technological advances will upset the calculations.

It is a function of the top management in each firm to make its own decision regarding the span of time to be covered by demand forecast. It is safer to forecast for longer periods, when the volume of demand held fairly constant from year to year. If demand has been erratic for reasons that are largely unexplainable, the forecasting period should be shorter.

Approach to Forecasting

The following four distinct steps must be kept in view in dealing with any forecasting demand problem.

  i. Identify and clearly state the objectives of the forecasting **problem**. In certain cases the required forecasts may be of a short-term nature. The approach needed here may be quite different from what long-term forecasts will call for. In certain other cases forecasts of market shares may be required which calls for an approach different from that needed for general industry forecast.

  ii. Ascertain the determinants of demand for the particular product or product group. The factors influencing demand differ widely depending on the product or products or industry or industries involved. Economists have a tendency to categorise goods and services into three broad groups for facilitating demand analysis. These three groups are:

a. Consumers' non-durable goods,
b. Consumers' durable goods, and
c. Capital goods.

We follow the same kind of categorization for purposes of demand analysis. The determinants of demand pertaining to these categories are different. They are discussed in detail in the next section.

iii. Select appropriate methods of forecasting. The method selected will depend upon the purpose or objective of the demand forecasts, the nature of the product or products involved, the types of data available, etc.

iv. Present the findings in a readable form. This is important because the management will be interested only in the actual forecast, its meaning and implications for policy.

Once a product forecast for the whole industry is available, it is easy for the company to estimate its share of the market. Analysis of past data can indicate the trends in market share among the competitors.

In preparing company forecasts the management may rely on two varying assumptions:

i. The ratio of company sales to total industry sales will continue as in the past, or

ii. The ratio of company sales to total industry sales will change.

Demand forecasts for the company may be made based on either of these assumptions. And often companies prepare alternative forecasts based on them.

Forecasting must be a continuing activity. Every forecast is based on a given set of data and assumptions and is relevant only as long as the underlying assumptions hold good. As additional or improved information becomes available, forecasts must be reviewed and revised so that the management is provided with better basis for decision making.

Determinants of Demand

Non-Durable Consumer Goods

There are at least three basic factors influencing the demand for non-durable consumer goods. They are: (a) Purchasing power (income), (b) Price, and (c) Demography.

   a. *Purchasing power:* One of the major determinants of demand is purchasing power of the consumer and this is determined by his income or rather disposable income. In India data on disposable income is not directly available. The Central Statistical Organisation has not yet started publication of data on disposable income. Indirect estimates can, however, be obtained from the published data.

   Use of disposable income for estimating demand has been criticized by some writers[1] on the plea that it does not constitute free purchasing power. Hence they prefer to use the concept 'discretionary income' in place of disposable income. Discretionary income can be estimated by deducting three items from disposable income, viz. imputed income and income in kind, major fixed outlay payments such as mortgage debt payment, insurance premium payments and rent and essential expenditures such as food and clothing. But here it may be pointed out that the disposable income concept is considered as equally satisfactory by many experts.[2]

   b. *Price:* The importance of price of a particular product and its substitutes in determining the demand has always been emphasised by economists. A measure of the price-demand relationship for a product is given by the concept 'elasticity of demand'. Concepts such as price elasticity, income elasticity, cross elasticity, etc. of demand are used in economic analysis.[3]

   c. *Demography:* Experience shows that the demand for a product is determined by certain population characteristics also. For example, a study of the demand for lipsticks must take into account the number of women by age. Again in a study of demand for tyres, the population consists of the number of cars, buses, trucks, and other motor vehicles in use. This shows that demography does not necessarily relate exclusively to human population. In fact its use is in differentiating between total market demands on the one hand and market segments on the other. The segments represent divisions of the total market into homogenous groups. The idea is to construct one or more segments that are considered to be important elements affecting demand for the product. Demographic or population groups can be defined in terms of educational background, sex, age, income, social status, geographic location, etc. The segment, if quantified, can be used as an independent variable affecting the demand for the product in question.

Purchasing power (Y), Price (P) and demography (D) can be combined in an additive relationship[4] in order to get a formula which can be used for predicting the demand (d) for a consumer good. The formula may take the form

$$D = Y + P + D$$

Durable Consumer Goods

Three different purchase characteristics can be distinguished in the case of durable consumer goods. They are:

- Time-use characteristics,
- Use-facilities characteristics, and
- Demographic characteristics.

Time-use characteristics. Consumer durables have got extended use and as such they are not used up in a single act as are match sticks or ice cream. This feature enables the consumers to go on using them by repairing if necessary, or to scrap them and get new ones. Experience shows that emergencies such as war or scarcity conditions force people to postpone replacement of durable goods and thereby lower the effective scrapping rate. The decisions to replace goods are influenced also by considerations such as social prestige and status, income and product obsolescence.

Use-facility characteristics. Generally durable goods require special facilities for their use. For example, to use a car, or a truck, one needs to have roads and petrol or diesel stations.

Again, to use a refrigerator or a radio, one needs electricity. Existence and growth of such facilities is an important variable in determining the volume of sales or quantity demanded of the products in question. Hence due consideration must be given in choosing the variables influencing the demand for durable consumer goods.

Demographic characteristics. The decision to purchase consumer durables is influenced also by factors such as size of families, income strata, price and other considerations. Demography here includes a study of populations other than human also. A study of the demand for commercial airlines has used the number of commercial airports as both as a use facility characteristic and as a demographic characteristic in deriving the forecasting equation. Hence three different purchase characteristics may be considered independently, or in combination, depending on the product and the economic judgment of the analyst.

The total demand for durable goods, in fact is the sum of two demands viz.

  i. a new owner demand and

 ii. a replacement demand. The new owner demand will increase the stock of the goods. Replacement demand tends to grow with the growth in the total stock with the consumers and at times it may even exceed the new demand. For certain well established products, life expectancy tables are made available in advanced countries in order to estimate the average or near average replacement rates.

The basic demand equation for durables may be stated as follows:

$$D = N + R$$

Where D represents total demand,
      N represents new owner demand, and
      R represents replacement demand.

Each of these independent variables may be forecast separately. It must be borne in mind that in the case of most durable goods there is an upper limit beyond which demand cannot grow. This upper limit refers to the 'saturation point'. For example, even if income goes up, there is limit to the number of TVs that people will buy. It is to this level towards which the actual volume of consumer stocks tends to gravitate. The difference between the 'saturation point' or the 'maximum ownership level' and the actual stock shows the growth potential of demand for durable goods.

Capital Goods

Capital goods are 'produced means of further production'. They are used to facilitate the production of other goods. Examples are machinery of all kinds, factory buildings, etc. The demand for capital goods is a case of 'derived demand'. Hence the demand for capital goods depends upon the profitability of the products of industries using the capital goods,[5] the ratio of production to capacity in user industries, the level of wage rates, the policy of the government, business prospects, etc. Where the wage rates go exceptionally high, the management will have an added tendency to go for labour saving equipment.

In the case of particular capital goods, demand will depend on the specific markets they serve and the end uses for which they are bought.[6] The demand for textile machinery, for instance, will be determined by the expansion of textile industry in terms of new units and replacement of existing machinery. Therefore, demand forecasts for capital goods will have to take into account new demand as well as replacement demand.

Two types of data are required for forecasting the demand for capital goods, intermediate or industrial goods. They are:

- the growth prospects of the user industries,[7] and
- the criteria or norm of consumption of the capital goods per unit of each end-use.[8]

The critical assumptions underlying the 'end-use approach' are:

1. The demand estimates for the 'end-use products' are available.
2. The norms of consumption (the technology of the industry) will remain unchanged during the period under consideration.
3. Norms based on present consumption patterns in industry, may, in part, reflect existing shortages and

import restrictions in the economy. In building bridges, for example, mild steel might be in use at present instead of construction steel (which is more suitable for the purpose). This may be due to the non-availability or high cost of construction steel. But as the pattern of availability changes, changing the norms of consumption in the process.

4. Forecasting methods: Several methods are employed for forecasting demand. However, the usual starting point is to have an idea of the general business forecasts relating to the economy for the period under consideration. Such macroeconomic or GNP forecasts enable an industry or firm to construct its own microeconomic demand forecasts. Macroeconomic forecasting is a highly developed technique in western countries especially in the United States of America; but in India it is only in its infancy. In India the Perspective Planning Division of the Planning Commission periodically prepares aggregative forecasts of national income and its components which can be made use of by industries and firms for their own individual purposes.

Here we propose to discuss the most commonly used methods by industries or firms for forecasting demand for established products.

Survey Methods

Opinion Surveys

The first method that we consider is called opinion surveys or survey of buyer intensions. Forecasting is essentially the art of anticipating what buyers are likely to do under a given set of conditions. This immediately suggests that a most useful source of information would be the buyers themselves. Ideally a list of all potential buyers could be drawn up; and each buyer is approached, preferably on a face-to-face basis, and asked how much he likes to buy the listed products in the stipulated future time period under the given conditions. He may also be asked to state what proportion of his total needs he intends to buy from the particular firm or at least what factors would influence his choice among suppliers. With this information, supposing that it is both obtainable and valid, the firm would seem to have an ideal basis for forecasting its demand.

This method is most useful when bulk of the sales is made to industrial producers. Here the burden of forecasting is shifted to the consumer (customer). But unfortunately, this method has a number of limitations in real situations. It would not be wise to depend wholly on the buyers estimates since the buyers are likely to exaggerate their requirements if shortages are expected. Again, this method is not very useful in the case of household consumers for several reasons, viz. irregularity in consumers' buying intensions, their inability to foresee what choice they will make when faced with multiple alternatives or choices, prohibitive costs, etc. A basic limitation of this method, according to Dufty, is that it is passive and does not expose and measure the variables under managements' control.

The favourite forecasting technique employed by industrial manufacturers appears to be the 'sales force composite method'. Under this method the company asks its salesmen to submit estimates of future sales in their respective territories. The sales force composite method is popular with industrial concerns because they have, under normal situations a limited number of customers and salesmen will be in a good position to assess the customer needs. Forecasts prepared by salesmen may be biased owing to the following reasons:

1. A salesman may be consistently pessimistic or optimistic or he may go to one extreme or another because of a recent sales setback or success.

2. Salesman may be often unaware of larger economic developments and company marketing plans that will shape future sales in his territory.

3. Salesman may understate demand so that the company may set a low sales quota.

4. Salesman may not have the time and concern to prepare careful estimates.

Because of the above defects, salesman's estimates are aggregated, reviewed and adjusted at higher management levels. In making the necessary adjustments the higher management takes into consideration such factors as expected salutary changes in product design, a plan for increased advertising, a proposed increase or decrease in selling prices, new production methods which will improve the product's quality, changes in competition, and changes in such economic forces as purchasing power, income distribution, credits, population and employment. This process of whetting the salesman's forecast is known as the 'jury of executive opinion method'.

An Evaluation of the Opinion Survey Method

The opinion survey method is relatively simple and straight forward. One of its advantages is that it makes use of the people in the organization who are directly involved in the activities which influence the level of sales, who are in a position to become acquainted with the forces and factors which will affect sales, and who probably have had the opportunity to acquire the experience and judgment which will enable them to evaluate the effects of these forces and factors. Another advantage of this method is that, unlike some of the other techniques discussed in this chapter, it requires no special technical skill. Finally, this method leads itself to use in the forecasting of sales of new products.

However, this method is subjected to severe criticisms. The most important among them is that it is almost completely subjective. This is of no consequence if the firm is fortunate enough to have personnel in its sales force and managerial ranks who have the inherent ability to make this type of subjective analysis. But unfortunately many organizations are not endowed with personnel of such calibre.

The appropriateness of the sales force opinion method increases to the extent that

   i. the salesmen are likely to be the most knowledgeable source of information;

  ii. the salesmen are cooperative;

 iii. the salesmen are unbiased or their biases can be corrected; and

 iv. there are some side benefits from the salesmen's participation in the procedure.[9]

Expert Opinion

Taking the opinion of well-informed persons other than consumers or company salesmen, such as distributors or outside experts is another method of forecasting.

In the United States of America, the automobile companies solicit estimates of sales directly from their dealers. But according to Philip Kotler these estimates are subject to the same strengths and weaknesses as salesmen estimates; like salesmen distributors may not give the necessary attention to careful estimating; their perspective about future business conditions may be too narrow; and they may supply biased estimates to gain some immediate advantage.

Firms in advanced countries also tap outside expertise for assessment of future demand. In effect, this happens when a firm uses or buys general economic forecasts or special industry forecasts prepared outside of the firm. In the United States of America, for example, various private and public agencies issue or sell periodic forecasts of short or long-term business conditions. While experts are supplying what amounts to opinion, this 'opinion' may be the joint outcome of jointly conducted surveys among buyers and suppliers as well as statistical/mathematical analysis of past data.

A related but a slightly variant of the expert opinion method is used by the Lockheed Aircraft Corporation. As a manufacturer of aircraft frames and missiles, the company deals with a relatively small number of customers each of which accounts for a relatively large percentage of sales. Therefore, Lockheed's forecasting problem is to predict or estimate what each customer will order during the forecast period. The marketing research group works up a preliminary forecast on the basis of surveys and statistical or mathematical techniques. Independently a group of Lockheed executives assume the different major customers and in a hard headed way they evaluate Lockheed's offering, in relation to its competitors' offerings. A decision on what and where to buy is made for each customer. The purchases from Lockheed are totalled and reconciled with the statistical forecast to become Lockheed's sales forecast.

An Evaluation on the Use of Expert Opinion

The use of expert opinion has a number of advantages and disadvantages. Its main advantages are:

- Forecasts can be made relatively quickly and cheaply.
- Different points of view are brought out and balanced in the process.
- There may be no alternative if basic data are lacking or difficult to collect, as in the case of new products.

The major disadvantages are:

- Opinions are generally less satisfactory than hard facts.
- Responsibility is dispersed and good and bad estimates are given equal weight.
- The method is more reliable for aggregate forecasting than for developing reliable breakdowns by territory, consumer group or even product.

Delphi Method

Delphi method[10] or technique is an extension of systematic analysis into the areas of opinion and value judgments. It counters the limitations of traditional quantitative methods. In areas where information is dispersed and scanty, judgments and expert opinions are valuable, historical data can lend itself to many interpretations. Delphi offers a scientific and systematic procedure for evaluation. In a way it is a sophisticated statistical method to arrive at a consensus. One of the drawbacks of any statistical or quantitative procedure is its inability to incorporate behavioural elements like personality, intuition and retrospection. Delphi has a built-in capacity to take into account of these variables.

Delphi technique was initially developed in Rand Corporation in the late 1940 by Helmer, Dalkey, and Gordon. Since then it had found its application in technological and environmental forecasting, selection of industrial targets in war, estimation of strength of bombardment and in futurology. In the business management area its relevance is in manpower planning, Bayesian probability estimation, and business forecasting and demand estimation. Other applications are in civil defence policy, computer applications, education, urban planning and other policy determinants, evaluation of research projects, foreign affairs and information processing. In fact, Delphi is the most applied of the technological forecasting methods and it has acquired a good standing among forecasters and long range planners.

An interesting feature of Delphi is the quick adaptability to both technological and social forecasting. Bayesian statistics is now an accepted process among decision makers for industrial forecasts. Delphi reinforces this procedure or converting judgments into probabilistic statements of value. In long-range planning Delphi provides a means of involvement and commitment when the panellists are drawn from the same organization. In policy forecasts, it enables to study the attitude and aspiration of the individuals. For analytical studies in management, it has better acceptance since Delphi is simple and easy to understand.

Delphi technique is designed to obtain the most reliable consensus opinion of interrogations of an individual, considered as an expert in the relevant area, through a number of rounds of 'interrogation, response and feedback'. Generally, in the first round inquiry, it is made on the type of information needed to arrive at the consensus eventually. In the second round specific questions are asked on the result variables after providing the needed information. If any additional information is needed indications are made and information provided to the individual only. In the third round the result variables are analysed for the response and the results are communicated along with the requested additional information. This feedback on response generally takes the form of inter quartile range, if the target variable is quantitative and key words or full statements for qualitative response. During this round each respondent is requested to reconsider his previous response in relation to the submitted inter quartile range. In case of a revision of an earlier response the reason for such an act is to be stated. At this stage too, a request for additional information is entertained. From the fourth round the process is repeated until convergence in terms of inter-quartile range or statements is obtained. At the right stage in the investigation process, all collected information at the request of all respondents (known as panellists). The information is provided to the entire group to enable reconsideration and convergence. Either through a statistical test for significance on the convergence or through judgment decision is taken to continue further rounds or to stop. The result at this final stage is taken as the consensus.

One variation of this process is to include few questions or statements to solicit data from the respondent in order to judge his 'claim for expertise'. These groups thus formed can also be used in the final response to contrast the estimated value by the experts. This variation suggests the first difficulty in applying this technique locating the expert group who are willing to go through the survey. The Delphi administrator will have to find his own ways of identifying this group. In the entire process until close to the last round, each individual's information is kept confidential except for the collated summary in the form of inter-quartile range, key words or statements. The identity is not revealed. Through this means of anonymity and secrecy the individualist behaviour is guaranteed. Delphi, contrasted to polling in an open meeting of experts in round table, precludes the possibility of:

1. group pressure
2. influence of dominant members
3. bandwagon effect of agreeing with majority opinion, and
4. taking the path of least resistance in terms of collecting information and interpreting.

This advantage may be lost if the panel is a closely knit group meeting frequently with opportunity to exchange ideas. The individualistic behaviour may suffer in such a situation and consensus may be forced. This is another difficulty in applying this technique. The prevention of direct confrontation is a distinct and important characteristic of Delphi. This situation supports the face validity for rationality of judgment by the respondents. The controlled feedback in every round and the provision for revising judgment after justification helps in clarifying new issues and factors which perhaps until then received little attention. If panellists are also implementers of the Delphi results then the feedback for consensus also could result in better commitment. Thus controlled feedback of collected results and information required is a distinctive feature of Delphi. A properly constructed class room Delphi exercise with emphasis on feedback can be used to highlight the value of information and to give numerical estimates to it. Sometimes Delphi may be used on multi-faceted problems of inquiry. In these situations, particularly when the inquiry is qualitative, it may not be possible to arrive at consensus. Then these responses can be used to construct a common frame of reference to promote a unified, collaborative effort. Thus it will provide a reasoning process to crystallize the issues. This is very much true for evaluating policies and to obtain guidelines for planning. Frequently the respondents are asked on their methods of usage of information. This results in consideration and clarity on the part of respondents. For the Delphi administrator, it is additional information.

Time Series Analysis

Time series analysis or trend projections rely on past data. In this approach, a company analyses its past sales to determine the nature of existing trend. This trend is then extrapolated into the future, and the resultant indicated sales are used as the basis for a forecast. The mechanics of this technique can be best illustrated by means of an example.

Suppose that the manufacturer of a TV decides to forecast the next year sales of his product by this method. He begins by collecting data on his sales for the past 5 years. When he does this he obtains the following results.

Year	Sales (in Lakh of Rs.)
2002	45
2003	52
2004	48
2005	55
2006	60

If we plot the sales against the years in which they take place, a graph representing the time series will be obtained. The graph for the data is shown in the Fig. 8.1

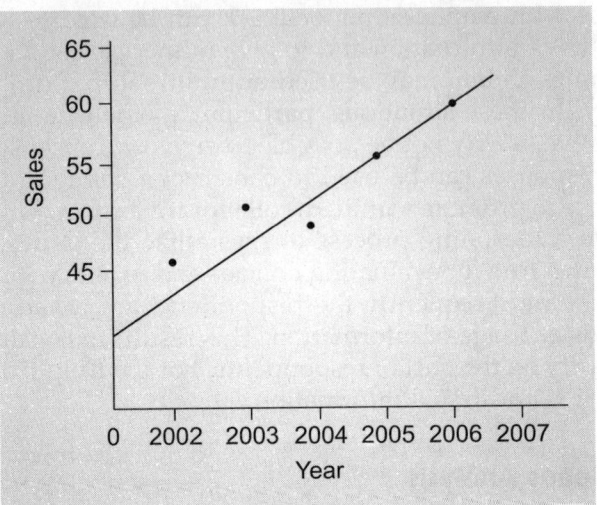

Fig. 8.1

An examination of Fig. 8.1 reveals that the sales are definitely showing an upward tend. The next step is to develop an equation which can give the nature and magnitude of this trend. This is done by fitting a so-called trend line to the points depicting the firm's sales. A number of ways for doing this exist, but a fairly common one is to construct the line of best fit by the method of least squares. Doing so means that the trend is assumed to be linear, but it may actually be curvilinear. If the latter is true, more complex methods of constructing the trend line must be used. However, we shall limit ourselves in this presentation to linear trends for purposes of simplicity.

In simple linear regression the relationship between the depended variable (Y) and some independent variable (x) can be represented by a straight line. The equation of this line is Y = a + bx, where 'a' is the intercept and 'b' shows the impact of the independent variable. The key step in deriving linear regression equation is finding values for the coefficients (a and b) that give the best fit to the data. One way to determine the coefficients is to plot the data on a graph and make a free hand estimate of the line that represents the relationship between the two variables.

Since in our case sales are to be forecast, they are considered to be the depended variable, Y. Also since sales will be assumed to vary with time, the time period (years) will be the independent variable, x. The 'y' intercept and the slope of the line are found by making the appropriate substitutions in the following 'normal' equations:

$$Y = a + bx$$
$$\Sigma Y = na + b\Sigma x \qquad \dots 1$$
$$\Sigma XY = a\Sigma x + b\Sigma x^2 \qquad \dots 2$$

Calculating the magnitude of the required quantities from our original data, we get the following:

1 Year	2 Sales in lakh (of rupees)	3	4	5
n	Y	x	x^2	xy
2002	45	1	1	45
2003	52	2	4	104
2004	48	3	9	144
2005	55	4	16	220
2006	60	5	25	300
$\Sigma n = 5$	$\Sigma y = 260$	$\Sigma x = 15$	$\Sigma x^2 = 55$	$\Sigma xy = 813$

When we substitute the values of Σx, Σx^2, Σxy, Σy and n in equations 1 and 2, we get

$$260 = 5a + 15b \qquad \dots 3$$
$$813 = 15a + 55b \qquad \dots 4$$

Solving equations 3 and 4, we get

$$780 = 15a + 45b$$
$$813 = 15a + 55b$$
$$780 = 15a + 45b$$
$$33 = 10b$$
$$b = 3.3$$

Substituting value of b in equation 3, we get value of a, as 42.1

$$260 = 5a + 15 (3.3)$$
$$260 = 5a + 49.5$$
$$260 - 49.5 = 5a.$$

210.5 = 5a

210.5/5 = a = 42.1

Therefore the equation for the line of best fit is equal to

$$Y = 42.1 + 3.3x$$

Using the above equation we can find the trend values for the previous years and estimate the sales for 2007. The trend values and estimates are given below:

Y 2002 = 42.1 + 3.3(1) = 45.4

Y 2003 = 42.1 + 3.3(2) = 48.7

Y 2004 = 42.1 + 3.3(3) = 52.0

Y 2005 = 42.1 + 3.3(4) = 55.3

Y 2006 = 42.1 + 3.3(5) = 58.6

Y 2007 = 42.1 + 3.3(6) = 61.9

The decomposition of time-series data is a useful analytical tool for understanding the nature of business fluctuations. But it is of limited value in actual business forecasting. This is because of the fact that the prediction of cycles is difficult as there is no regularity in the cyclical behaviour.

Moving Averages

Another method used to follow trends in demand data is the moving average. The forecaster simply computes the average volume achieved in several recent periods and uses it as a prediction of demand in the next period. This approach assumes that the future will be an average of the past achievements. Although moving averages can provide good forecasts when demand is stable, they are apt to lag behind when there is a strong trend in the data. A decisive issue in moving averages is determining the ideal number of periods (N) to include the average. With a large number of periods, forecasts tend to react slowly whereas low values lead to predictions that respond more quickly to changes in a series. For a better understanding of the assumptions underlying the technique of moving averages and some of its advantages and limitations it is necessary to look briefly at the mathematical representation of this method. In simple terms the techniques of forecasting with moving averages can be represented as follows:

$$St + 1 = \frac{X_t + X_{t-1} + \ldots + X_t - N + 1}{N}$$

$$\frac{1}{N} \sum_{1=t-n+1}^{t} X_1 \qquad \ldots 1.1$$

Where S_t = the forecast for time t,
X_t = the actual value at time t,
N = the number of values included in the average.

It can be seen from the above equation that the method of moving averages, equal weightage is given to each of the last N values observed before that time. It can also be seen from the equation that to compute the moving average we must have the values of the last N observations. A somewhat short form of the equation 1.1 for calculating the moving average can be developed. The moving average for period t is given by

$$St = 1 = \frac{X_t + X_{t-1} + \ldots + X_t - N + 1}{N}$$

Now it can be seen from equation 1.1 that St+1 is simply

$$St = \frac{X_{t-1} + X_{t-2} + \ldots X_{t-N}}{N} \qquad \ldots 1.2$$

Written in this form it is obvious that each new forecast based on moving average is an adjustment of the preceding moving averages to obtain historical data and then use either equation 1.1 or 1.2 to compute the forecast for the coming period. But it is necessary that he must also specify the number of periods to be used in the moving averages.

Exponential Smoothing

A feature of the moving averages that detracts from their ability to follow trends is that all time periods are weighted equally. This means that information from the oldest and the newest periods is treated the same way in making up the forecast. But a strong argument can be made that since the most recent observations contain the most recent information about what will happen in the future. They should be given relatively more weight than the older observations. What we should like is a weighting scheme that would apply the most weight to the most recent observed values and decreasing weights to the older values. Exponential smoothing satisfies this requirement and eliminates the need for storing the historical values of the variable.

In principle exponential smoothing operates in a manner akin to moving averages by 'smoothing' historical observations to eliminate randomness. The technique of exponential smoothing can be developed by using equation (1.2) for computing the moving average. Suppose we had only the most recent observed value and the forecast made for that same period. In such a situation equation (1.2) might be modified so that in place of the observed value in period (t-n) we could employ an approximate value. A reasonable estimate would be the forecast value from the preceding period. Thus equation (1.2) would be modified to give equation (1.3).

$$S_{t+1} = \frac{X_t}{N} - \frac{(St + St)}{N} \qquad \qquad ...1.3$$

Equation 1.3 can be written as

$$S_{t+1} = \frac{1}{N} X_t + (1\frac{1}{N}) S_t \qquad \qquad ...1.4$$

What we now have is a forecast that weights the most recent observation with weight of value $1/N$ and the most recent forecast with the value of $(1—1/N)$. If we substitute in place of $1/N$, we have

$$S_t = \infty X_t + (1- \infty) S_t \qquad \qquad ...1.5$$

Equation 1.5 is the general form used in computing a forecast by the method of exponential smoothing.[12]

The main decision with exponential forecasting is selecting an appropriate value for the smoothing constant (∞). Smoothing factors can range in value from zero to 1 (one) with low values providing stability and high values allowing a more rapid response to demand change.

Box-Jenkins Method

Perhaps the most common forecasting situation encountered in business is that of a time series in which a number of observations are taken over several periods of time and a forecast of some future time period is desired. As we have already seen all forecasting methods designed to handle such situations assume that there is a basic underlying pattern represented by the historical data and that in addition to that pattern some randomness has been exhibited. Thus the focus of the forecasting method is to isolate that basic pattern as far as possible and to use it as the basis for future forecasts. Although a method such as exponential smoothing may be suitable for short-term forecasting of time series in which there is not much fluctuations and the pattern is made up of combinations of trend, a seasonal factor, and a cyclical factor as well as the random fluctuations. In such situations a much more complex forecasting method is needed.

The Box-Jenkins method of forecasting is one that is particularly well suited to handling complex time series and other forecasting situations in which the basic pattern is readily apparent. The real power and attractiveness of this forecasting approach is that it can handle complex pattern with relatively little effort on the part of the forecaster. However, because it is dealing with much more complicated situations, it is much more difficult to understand the fundamentals of this technique and the limitations of its applications. In addition, the cost associated with the Box-Jenkins approach in a given situation is generally much greater than any of the other quantitative methods, but with this greater cost, much greater accuracy can be achieved.[13]

Barometric Techniques

We have noted that simple trend projections are incapable of forecasting turning points. Barometric techniques are based on the idea that certain events of the present can be used top predict the direction of change in future. This is accomplished with the help of relevant economic and statistical indicators which are selected time series related to the variables to be predicted. Here the key issue is finding indicators that have forecasting value for particular products. Some of the most commonly used indicators are listed below:

Construction contracts awarded

Personal income

New orders for durable goods

Employment

Agricultural income

Non-agricultural placements

Gross national income

Industrial materials prices

Wholesale commodity prices

Industrial production

Change in manufacturing and trade inventories

Bank deposits, etc.

Econometric Model Building

Econometric model building holds considerable promise as a method of forecasting demand. The best starting point toward an understanding of the basis of econometric forecasting is regression analysis. But the difficulty with respect to regression analysis is that it is used to forecast a single dependent variable based on the value and the relations between one or more independent variables. Each of these independent variables is assumed to be exogenous or outside the influence of the dependent variable. This may be true in many situations. But unfortunately, in most broad economic situations an assumption that each of the variables, with the exception of a single dependent variable, is independent is unrealistic. For example, let us assume that demand is a function of GNP, price and advertising. In regression terms we would assume that all three independent variables are exogenous to the system and hence are not influenced by the level of demand itself or by one another. This is a fairly correct assumption as GNP is concerned. If, however, we consider price and advertising, the same assumption may not hold good; for instance, if the per unit cost of some quadratic form, a different level of sales will result in a different level of cost. Again, advertising expenditures will often influence the price of the product, since the production and selling cost influence the per unit price. The price, in turn, is influenced by the magnitude of demand, which can also influence the level of advertising or promotional expenditure. All of these point to the independence of all four of the variables in our equation. When this interdependence is strong, regression analysis cannot be used. If we want to be accurate, we must express this demand relationship by developing a system of four simultaneous equations that can deal with the interdependence directly.

Thus in econometric form we can have

Demand $= f$ (GNP, Price, Advertising)
Cost $= f$ (Production and inventory levels)
Selling expenses $= f$ (Advertising and other selling expenses)
Price $= f$ (Cost and selling expenses)

That is, instead of one relationship, we now have four. As in regression analysis, we must (a) determine the functional form of each of the equations; (b) estimate in simultaneous manner the values of their parameters; and (c) test for the statistical significance of the results and validity of the assumptions. It should be realized that the advantages of econometric forecasting is that it provides the values of several of the independent variables from within the model itself, thus freeing the forecaster from having to estimate them exogenously.

The estimation of the equation parameters involves problems far more complex than those encountered in regression analysis. This makes the application of econometric forecasting difficult and expensive.

A number of mathematical techniques have been developed to help to solve econometric models. Some with which managers may be familiar are the method of least squares, the full information maximum likelihood method of estimation, two-stage least-squire methods and three-stage least-squire methods. The details of these techniques are beyond the scope of our discussion.

An econometric model includes a number of simultaneous equations that can be of different types and functional forms. The translation of econometric theory to the right type and form of equations and their developments into a set of functional relationships is termed as specification.

The accurate and the most appropriate specification of an econometric model is a key step in the use of this technique of forecasting.

A major part of specification is the identification of the exogenous and endogenous variables. One must arbitrarily decide on the degree of influence of the different factors and choose those that are least determined within the system as exogenous factors. This is akin to the distinction made in regression analysis between the independent and dependent variables. In an econometric model we will want to separate those factors that are most strongly influenced by one another into the exogenous group and those that can be assumed to be determined outside the system of simultaneous equations into the exogenous group.

Once the choice of endogenous and exogenous variables has been made one equation must be specified for each of the endogenous variables. When the number of the equations specified is equal to the exogenous variables, the model is said to be just specified. When the number of endogenous variables is less than the number of equations, the model is under specified and one or more of the variables has to be set arbitrarily to some initial value. These variables then become exogenous factors for the solution of the system of equations. Finally, if the number of endogenous variables is greater than the number of equations, the model is over simplified. It is the over simplified form of econometric models that is most often used for estimating the parameters of a set of simultaneous equations.

Econometric models are used most widely to forecast macro series of interrelated economic data such as income consumption and capital spending, and much less for business forecasts.

The great advantage of an econometric model is indirect. It can be used to predict the direction and extent of change of the overall economic activity or any of its components. This information then can become the input required to estimate the independent variables of a single equation forecasting model. Since this information can be obtained from outside sources, organizations do not have to develop their own models but can rely on outsiders to provide them with forecasts when they are required. Thus individual companies can forego all the high costs associated with developing, maintaining and running a large scale econometric model and obtain the information it offers through the third parties.

An additional experience is gained in the use of econometric models for forecasting, their application will undoubtedly become more wide-spread at both government and industry levels. These econometric models of the future should be substantially more accurate than they have been in the past and should provide the manager with additional information he can use in applying other forecasting techniques that are less costly and are more suitable for his purpose.

In addition to these most commonly methods, there are some other methods of forecasting which are used by certain companies in advanced countries. For the benefit of our readers we propose to discuss these methods very briefly in the following paragraphs.

Controlled Experiments

Under this method an attempt is made to vary separately certain important determinants of demand such as price, advertising, etc. which can be manipulated and conduct the experiments assuming that the other factors will remain constant. Thus the effect of price, advertisement, packaging, etc. on demand can be assessed by either varying them over different markets or by varying them over different time periods in the same market. For instance, different prices would be associated with different sales and basis the price-quantity relationship is estimated in the form of regression equation and used for forecasting purposes. It must be noted that the market division here must be homogenous with reference to the income, tasks, etc. In the US the Parker Pen Company used this method to find out the effect of a price rise on the demand for Quink Ink.

But this method is yet to establish itself as a viable one. This is due to a number of reasons. They are:

   i. such experiments are expensive and time consuming;

  ii. they are risky because they may lead to unfavourable reactions on dealers, consumers and competitors;

iii. there is great difficulty in planning the study so far as it is not always easy to determine what all factors should be taken to be constant and what factors should be considered as variable so as to segregate and measure their influence on demand;

iv. it is difficult to satisfy the condition of homogeneity of markets.

Input-Output Model

Industry sales potentials can also be derived from input-output tables for states and nations that show how business buy and sell goods from one another. Potentials can be extracted from input-output data by dividing sales to particular industries by the total sales made to all sectors of the economy.

The derivation of relative market potentials from input-output tables allows a firm to compare its own sales to particular market segments with the levels achieved by all firms in the industry. Although these comparisons look backward in time, they can reveal important market sectors that have been ignored by current marketing programmes. Input-output tables provide a useful way to construct relative sales potentials for areas based on current levels of sales achieved by different industries. Input-output tables also help in estimating the impact of some change within the market (an input-output table for a simplified economy is given below.).

Chain Ratio Method

Demand potential for individual products can be determined by applying a series of ratios or usage rates to an aggregate measure of demand. A firm may start with a total population figure for an area and then multiply by average annual per capita expenditure to give an estimate of maximum possible sales for a general product class (TVs). This number then could be reduced by multiplying by a percentage that reflected the sales of a particular size of TV and still by a percentage of customers that bought a particular type (Flat). The resulting estimate of total sales for flat TVs could then be divided among the firms in the industry.

Input-output table for a simplified economy

Purchases by Sales by	Primary industry	Manufacturing industry	Service industry	Final buyers			Total output
				Consumer	investment	government	
Primary industry	50 (0.125)	250 (0.167)	10 (0.020)	60	0	30	400
Manufacturing industry	100 (0.250)[2]	500 (0.333)	40 (0.080)	500	200	60	1500
Service industry	70 (0.175)	200 (0.133)	100 (0.200)	100	0	30	500
Primary inputs	180	550	350	Gross domestic product = 1800			
Total inputs	400	1500	500				2400

Computer-Assisted Forecasting

Computers are frequently used in demand forecasting as they are fast and can make predictions from masses of figures using complex procedures.

This allows the firm to make more frequent forecasts for much wider range of products. The computer can also be programmed to make adjustments in raw data, compare predictions generated by alternative methods and keep track of forecasting errors.

It may be pointed out here that no single method is foolproof. All are characterized by certain pitfalls into which the unwary analyst is prone to fall. Therefore, the forecaster should be beware of 'putting all his eggs in one basket.' It is better not to rely entirely upon a single method. The wiser course, and the one best for most forecasting situations, is to solve the problem from a number of different angles. If all individually constructed seem to point in the same direction, more confidence can be placed in the forecast that is finally transmitted to top management.

Demand Forecasting for New Products

Demand forecasts for new products call for more ingenuity and skill. Forecasting methods need to be tailored to the particular product. Joel Dean has suggested six possible approaches for forecasting demand for new products. They are:

1. *Evolutionary Approach*

Under this approach the demand for a new product is projected as an outgrowth and evolution of an existing product. For instance, the demand forecast for colour television sets starts with the assumption that colour television sets picks up from where black and white left off. But this approach is useful only when the new product is so close to being only an improvement of an existing product that its demand can be pretty a projection of the potential development of the underlying product.

2. *Substitute Approach*

Under this technique, the new product is analysed as a substitute for some existing product or service. This approach has great promise when applicable.

3. Growth Curve Approach

Here the rate of growth and the ultimate level of demand for the new product are estimated, on the basis of the pattern of growth of established products. For instance, analyze the growth curves of all established motor cars and try to establish an empirical law of market development applicable to a new brand of car. This method, even if it can be developed, has narrow applicability, and is useful primarily at the later stages of demand projection.

4. Opinion Polling Approach

Under this approach, demand for new products is estimated by making direct enquiries from the ultimate consumers, either by the use of samples or on a full scale. This method is widely used to explore the demand for new products. But this method encounters problems of sampling, probing real intentions, and conveying the complexity of multiple alternative choices, even for established products. For new products, these problems become more complicated. The forecaster has to clarify what a new product is and what it will do.

5. Sales Experience Approach

New product is offered in a sample market either by direct mail or through a chain-store and thus attempts to estimate the total demand for all channels and fully developed market. The main problem here lies in determining what allowance is to make for the immunity of the sample market and the peculiar characteristics.

6. Vicarious Approach

Under this technique consumer reactions to a new product are surveyed indirectly with the help of specialized dealers who are supposedly informed about consumers' needs and alternate opportunities. This method is temptingly easy and distressingly hard to quantify. Generally it is usable only as a cheap horse-back sally.

The various methods adopted for forecasting demand for new products are not mutually exclusive. A combination of several of them is often desirable when they can supplement and check each other.

Factors Affecting the Demand for New Producers' Durable Goods

Generally a producer will not purchase new durable producers' good unless he can reasonably expect that the return attributable to the new good over its 'life span' will be sufficient to cover all the costs (including a reasonable profit attributable to the purchase and use of the good, i.e. the purchase must be expected to be a profitable one.

According to Joel Dean the most important factors determining the profitability of such purchases are:[14]

The current demand and the future demand expected by the producer for his output of goods and services.

His present stock (number of units, age and efficiency of the units and the expected lifespan of the stock) of durable goods.

The purchase price of the new durable good, including financing charges.

The expected lifespan and efficiency of the new durable good, i.e. the expected life capacity of the new durable good.

The 'costs of using' the good, i.e. the labour, material, managerial costs, etc. involved in the use of the good.

The expected sales price per unit of the output of the good.

The current and the anticipated cost of (including the cost of using) substitutes, such as labour, for the new durable goods.

Criteria for a Good Forecasting Method

The ideal forecasting method, according to Joel Dean, is that one that yields returns over cost in accuracy, seems reasonable (consistent with existing knowledge), can be formalized for reasonably long periods, can meet new circumstances adeptly, and can give up-to-date results.

Summary

In recent times forecasting has come to play an important role in business decision-making. Determination of the types of forecasts required and establishment of procedures of those forecasts are fundamental steps in the organization of a well conceived production control system. From the point of view of time span and from the planning requirements, firms will be interested in estimating both short-term and long-term demand. For estimating long-term demand, the firm may use one or any combination of the following forecasting methods: Opinion surveys, expert opinion, chain ratio method, trend projections, barometric techniques, econometric models, input-output model, computer-assisted forecasting, etc. These models vary in their appropriateness with the purpose of the forecast, the type of product and the availability and reliability of data. Probably every firm can improve the accuracy of its forecasts by collecting more data and/or adopting a better methodology.

Demand forecasting for new products calls for more ingenuity and skill. Forecasting methods need to be tailored to the particular product.

The ideal forecasting method, according to Joel Dean, is one that yields returns over cost in accuracy, seems reasonable (consistent with existing knowledge), can be formalized for reasonably long periods, can meet new circumstances adeptly, and can give up-to-date results.

Review Questions

1. What is meant by demand forecast?
2. What are the uses of demand forecasts?
3. Enumerate the steps in demand forecasting.
4. What are the determinants of demand for
   a. Non-durable consumer goods?
   b. Durable consumer goods?
   c. Capital goods?
5. Explain the different forecasting methods:
   a. For existing products
   b. For new products.
6. Discuss briefly the various methods of forecasting demand and point out their limitations. What are the criteria of a good forecasting method?

Problem

The annual sales of 'XYZ Ltd.' for the last five years are given below:

(In thousands of Rs.)

Year	2002	2003	2004	2005	2006
Sales	50	60	75	55	80

By the method of least squares, find the trend values for each of the five years. Also estimate the annual sales for 2007.

References

1. The question whether demand forecasts are useful is not pertinent; the real problem is how to forecast demand as reliably as possible in order to cut planning costs.
2. **See** Haynes, et al. op.cit. p.160.
3. Spencer, Clark and Hoguest, etc.
4. These concepts have been discussed in detail in the chapter on National Income
5. **Some use a** multiplicative relationship. If such relationship is used the equation becomes d = YPD
6. The industries which use capital goods for producing goods are called user industries.
7. Haynes, et al. op.cit.; p.164
8. The analyst must forecast the demand trends in the different industries which use the particular capital goods.
9. The weight (tons) of steel castings required per railway wagon gives a consumption norm which is extremely useful. In estimating the demand for steel castings, provided the demand estimates for railway wagons are available. If the technology of an industry does not undergo any change during the period for which the forecast is made the consumption norms for intermediate goods will remain fairly stable. This method is often termed as 'end use method or end-use approach.
10. Philip Kotler, op.cit., p. 213
11. Srinivasan A.V; Executive Development Programmes in Late 80s. **A Delphi Forecast, Lok Udyog,** Vol.X1, No.4, July 1977.
12. For higher forms of smoothing see Wheelwright Steven C and **Spyros** Makidakis, Forecasting Methods For Management, John **Wiley &** Sons, Inc. 1973.
13. For the Mechanics of this method refer Wheelwright, et al. op.cit.
14. Dean Joel, op.cit. p.233

9   Cost Considerations

A business firm is an organization intended to make profits. And profits are the primary measure of the success of a firm. That means when the manager of a firm takes business decisions he should see to that the costs balance revenue in an optimal way.

COST CONCEPTS

While taking a business decision the successful manager has to identify which costs are relevant for that particular decision. Therefore, we shall, first of all, analyse the basic cost concepts that are relevant in business decision-making.

Opportunity Cost *vs* Outlay Costs

The point of distinction between outlay costs and opportunity costs is the nature of the sacrifice. Whereas outlay costs involve financial expenditure "opportunity costs take the form of benefits from alternative ventures that are foregone by using the limited facilities for a particular purpose". Since outlay costs involve financial expenditure, they are recorded in the books of account. But opportunity costs represent only sacrificed alternatives and so they are not recorded in the books of account. "In a cloth mill that spins its own yarn, for example, the cost of yarn is really the price at which the yarn could be sold if it were not woven into cloth. For the problem of measuring the profitability of the weaving operations in order to decide whether to expand them or abandon them, it is this opportunity cost – the foregone revenue from not selling the yarn – that is relevant".[1] The concept of opportunity cost is useful not only for short-run decisions but for long-run decisions also. In case of college education the cost includes not only the tuition fees and books, but also the income which is foregone since that candidate is not able to work on a fulltime basis.

In addition, opportunity cost plays its own role in sales strategy, in capital expenditure budgeting, etc. (for more details see chapter on capital budgeting). "In business problems the message of opportunity cost is that it is dangerous to confine cost knowledge to what the firm is doing. What the firm is not doing but could do is frequently the critical cost consideration which it is perilous, but easy to ignore."[2]

Past *vs* Future Costs

It is a matter of common knowledge that management decisions are forward-looking. This fact necessitates management decisions to require comparative conjunctures about future situations. Thus cost forecasting becomes inevitable. Following are the major managerial uses for which cost information is applied: expense control, projection of future income statements, pricing policy, etc. From this it is clear that future costs are the only costs which are necessary for most of the executive decisions. "The fact that the future is always uncertain does not detract from the necessity for making explicit forecasts of future costs. With crude implements and unsubstantial guesses, it is often possible to make a more accurate projection than that which is obtained when historical cost is used, because with historical costs, the implied though usually unrecognized assumption is that the future will be exactly like the particular period in the past when the costs were incurred. Rarely does this represent the best guess that can be made concerning the future."[3]

Short-Run *vs* Long-Run Costs

There is a difference in the pattern of behaviour between the short-run and long-run costs. "Roughly the short-run costs are those associated with variation in the utilisation of fixed plant when there is a perfect flexibility in the size of plant, labour force, executive talent, and so forth, long-run cost behaviour is involved. Anything short of perfect flexibility produces cost behaviour that can be changed with leeway, improved given time and investment resources. Such alterable costs are short-run."[4]

When a firm has to decide whether to produce more or not in the immediate future the short-run costs become relevant. In this case there is no question of erecting a new plant. The firm has to manage with the existing plant. Only when the firm has to decide as to the erection of a new plant the long-run costs become relevant.

Fixed *vs* Variable Costs

"A fixed cost is one relating to an item or service which has no direct relationship to the volume or type of trading, but which, as a result of the long-term plan, involves a certain amount of committed expenditure, the level of which is alterable only within narrow limits, thereby making the cost basically non-controllable by functional management either through volume of expenditure or effective usage."

A variable cost is one relating to an item or service which has some relationship to the volume or type of trading, and which is controllable by management through the amount expended or effectiveness of usage during the period.[5]

From the above-mentioned definitions of the fixed (also called constant) and variable costs it is clear that the distinction is according to the degree to which they change in total with changes in rate of output.

"Which cost items are fixed and which variable depends on the degree of adaptation of costs to output rate, i.e. the degree to which the adjustment is short-run as opposed to long-run. The distinction also depends on the size and the suddenness of the change in output, and on the amount of pressure put on management to increase efficiency and to defer postponable expenditures."[6]

Traceable *vs* Common Costs

Those costs which can be identified easily and indisputably with a unit of operation are called traceable costs. "Common costs are used broadly to cover costs that are not traceable to individual final products .... Common costs that are not traceable to individual products are, in economic analysis, further classified into joint-product costs and alternative-product costs."[7] Two products are joint when increasing the output of one product (e.g. coke) necessarily increases the output of the other product (e.g. gas). If increasing the output of coke should bring a decrease in the output of gas, then the products will be alternative. When multiple products which incur common cost differ considerably in production or marketing processes, and cost has significance in decisions on adding or subtracting from a product line, product pricing, or product merchandising the traceability or costs become important for management.

Out-of-Pocket *vs* Book Costs

Those costs which involve current payments to outsiders are called out-of-pocket costs. Electricity bill paid to the Electricity Board can be considered as an example of out-of-pocket-cost. Book costs do not involve any current cash payment (e.g. depreciation). To convert book costs into out-of-pocket-costs one can sell assets and lease them back from the buyer, thereby the rental payment replacing the depreciation charge and indirect cost of owned capital.

Incremental *vs* Sunk Costs

The added costs of a change in the level or nature of activity are called incremental costs. The change can be of different types: adding a new product, changing distribution channels, etc. There are also costs which are not affected by the change in question. Such costs are called sunk costs, e.g. Depreciation. Incremental costs are usually short-run, but not always.

Escapable *vs* Unavoidable Costs

Those costs which can be reduced by a contraction in the business activities of a firm are called escapable costs. These costs are avoided by a contemplated retrenchment. "It is the net effect on cost that is important, not just the costs directly avoidable by the contraction. Added costs elsewhere may partially be offset, since retrenchment often results in increase in activity in other parts of the organization. These additions to cost must be offset against the direct reductions in escapable costs in order to estimate the net impact of the change."[8] The unavoidable or sunk costs will be there whether an alternative is chosen or not.

Controllable *vs* Non-Controllable Costs

Those costs which can be regulated by the executive to whom it is assigned are controllable costs. The controllability of a cost depends on the level of management. A cost which is uncontrollable at some level may be controllable at some other higher level. This controllability distinction is primarily useful for expense and efficiency control.

Replacement *vs* Historical Costs

Historical cost is the cost of the plant and materials at their original price. Replacement cost, on the other hand, is the cost at the price that would have to be paid currently. Conventional financial accounts base their valuation on historical costs. But, during periods of changing price levels, historical valuation becomes only a poor projection of the future cost. And for managerial decisions it is future cost that has got relevance.

BEHAVIOUR OF COSTS

Fixed Costs and Variable Costs

Variations in output have generally no influence on fixed cost. The term fixed can however be interpreted as fixed in total amount or as fixed in relation to output changes. In the latter case fixed costs can change, but only reasons not associated with variations in output. Sizer accordingly breaks fixed costs into three categories.
  • Costs which are not susceptible to any substantial change within the short period, usually a year: for example certain types of depreciation and other such costs.

- Costs which are fixed for short periods in terms of providing the necessary facilities to produce, but which are liable to change if volume changes appear likely to continue in the future: for example supervision salaries, which, although may be fixed in relation to volume, may be affected by changes in wage rates.
- Costs which are fixed by the management and bear no functional relationship to the current volume of output: for example pure research and engineering costs.

Variable costs are costs which, in general, are directly affected by output changes. Thus, unlike fixed costs which are usually taken to be wholly incurred before any production is forthcoming, variable costs are incurred only when output is being produced.[9] Figures 9.1 to 9.6 show the behaviour of various costs.

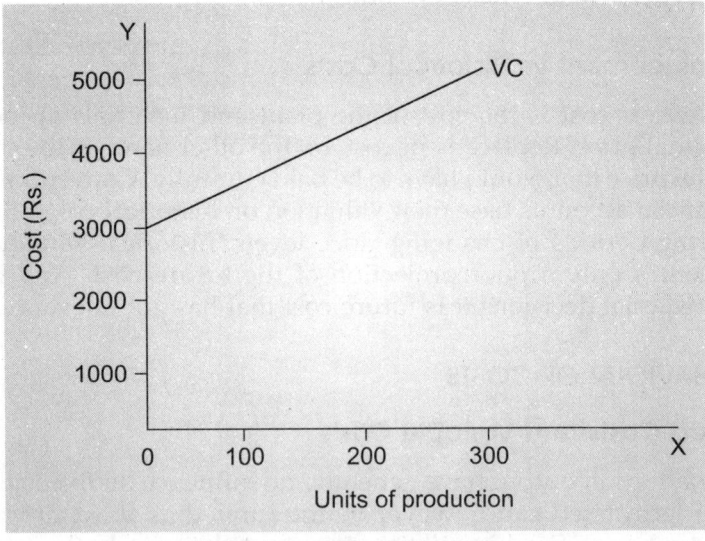

Fig. 9.1

Figure 9.1 shows that at zero production the cost is Rs. 3000. This is the fixed cost. At a production of 300 units the total costs are Rs. 5000. This means that the difference between Rs. 5000 and Rs. 3000 is the variable cost. This is illustrated with the help of Fig. 9.2

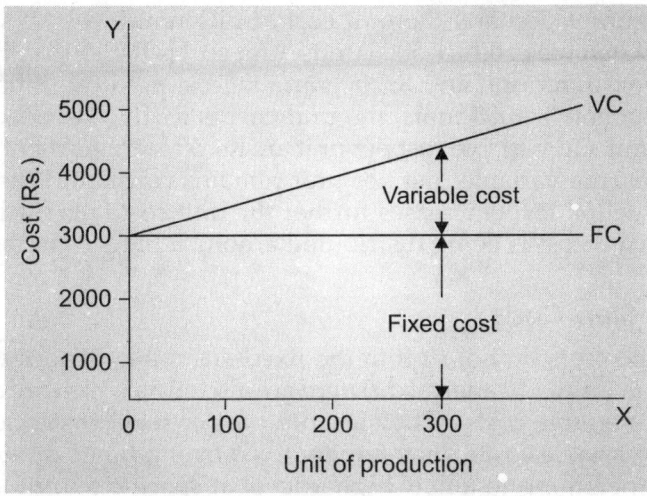

Fig. 9.2

When we calculate the cost of a single unit at different levels of production we can see that the variable cost or direct unit costs will be constant at any level of production. On the other hand, the fixed cost per unit varies according to the level of production. When the production is high the element of fixed cost per unit becomes smaller. This is illustrated in Fig. 9.3.

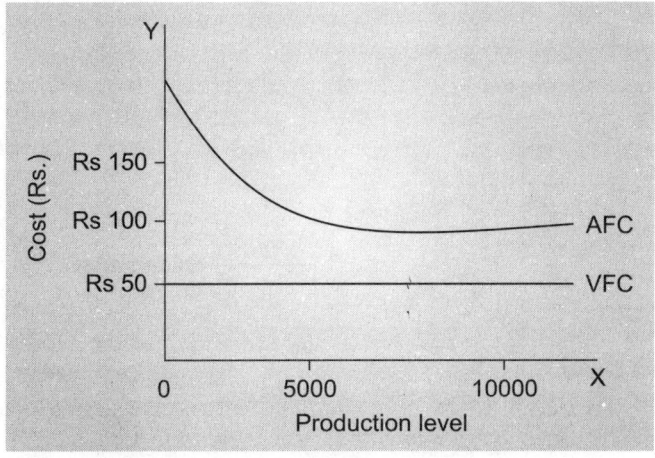

Fig. 9.3

Figure 9. 3 charts the unit cost at different levels. It shows that when we produce 5000 units, unit cost is Rs. 150, i.e. Rs.100 fixed cost per unit and Rs. 50 variable cost per unit. When the production is 1000 units, the unit cost is Rs.100, i.e. fixed cost per unit and variable cost per unit are Rs. 50 each. As mentioned earlier, the variable cost per unit remains constant. When the production level increases further the unit cost falls further as the fixed cost is being distributed among a bigger number.

Stair-Step Costs

All the costs do not fit into the fixed—variable pattern which we have already analysed. There are also costs which are called semi-variable costs. They are not part of fixed costs, nor are they variable costs. They remain fixed over a range of outputs and then jump to a new higher level at specific output levels. These are called stair-step costs. For example, usually the Foremen's salaries remain fixed till the output increases up to a certain level. Only beyond that level the management appoints an additional Foreman. At that stage the expenses of supervision increases in a single step. By changing the ratio between Foremen and labour and giving Foremen overtime work the management can avoid the sudden jumps in cost. Thus the stair-step costs are not very common in practice. Stair-step costs are represented in Fig. 9.4.

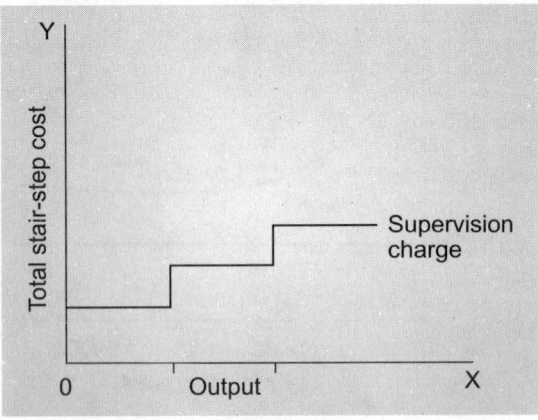

Fig. 9.4

Joint Costs and Common Costs

Since many firms produce more than one product they have to face the problem of common costs and joint costs. These costs which occur in relation to two or more products in fixed proportions are called joint costs. For example, we shall take the case of coke and gas. If, in order to produce one the other also has to be produced they are considered as joint products. The cost of production will depend on the quantity produced; but at any given level of production the proportion of coke and gas will be the same. There will be only one combination of outputs for any one level of cost. Of these two products one may be considered as the main product and the other the by-product. Even then, in principle they are joint costs. Figure 9.5 shows the relationship.

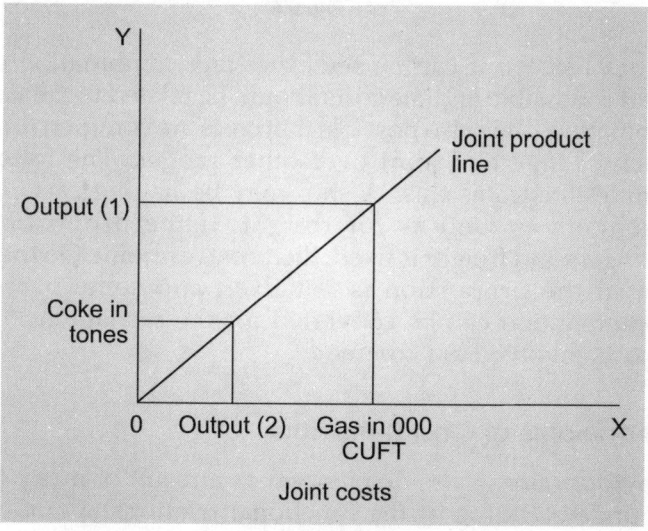

Fig. 9.5

The common costs also occur in relation to two or more products; but their proportion is not fixed. In other words, all combinations of the various products can be produced. Since the proportion is not fixed one level of cost may represent many possible combinations of outputs. Figure 9.6 presents this situation.

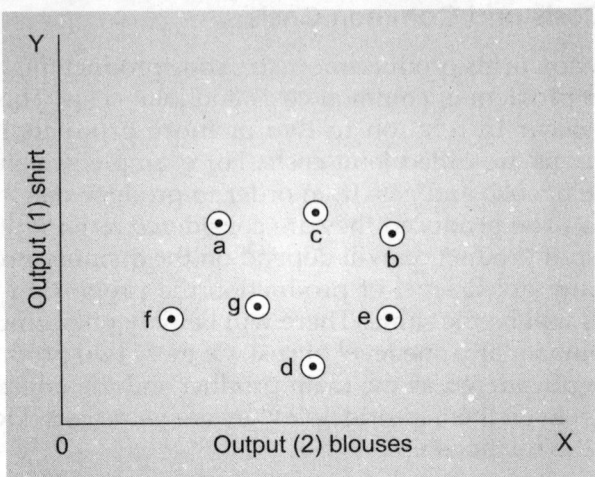

Fig. 9.6

From Fig. 9.6 it can be seen that any combination of the output is possible and the costs should be related to the varying combinations. It is also possible that costs are common for some capacity range and joint over other ranges. The following example illustrates this: A ship may be having capacity for passengers as well as for freight. If the proportion for passengers and freight is fixed, their costs are joint. On the other hand, if the proportion is not fixed and some passenger accommodation can be converted for the carriage of freight, the costs involved are common.

Determinants of Cost Behaviour

Behaviour of costs are determined as a result of many forces. The understanding of the functional relationships of cost to various forces will help us to provide the informational foundation for different cost forecasts. This will also make us estimates of the alternative costs of rival programmes. This is the characteristic feature of managerial economics.

What are the forces which play their role in determining the behaviour of costs? The cost determinants differ from firm to firm and problem to problem. Therefore a general rule which is applicable to all cannot be set. Still the following forces[10] are important enough to be considered as cost determinants in modern manufacturing enterprises:

    i. Rate of output (utilisation of fixed plant)
   ii. Size of plant
  iii. Prices of input factors (materials and labour)
  iv. Technology
    v. Size of lot
  vi. Stability of output
 vii. Efficiency (of management and labour)

Now we shall analyse these cost determinants one by one. Rate of output (*see* chapter on cost–output relationship)

Size of Plant

Following are the four methods of approach to the study of the problem of cost and size of plant.[11]

- Analysis of changes in actual cost which accompanied the growth of a single plant over a period of time.
- Analysis of differences in actual cost of plants of different sizes operated by different firms and observed at the same time.
- Engineering estimates of the alternative cost where the same technology of manufacturing is used in plants of different sizes.
- Analysis of differences in the actual costs of different-sized plants operated by one corporation.

Prices of Input Factors

When one chooses a programme from the alternative possibilities one should anticipate for the future the effect of changes in wage rates and material prices upon costs. The changes in price and wages affect the cost per unit of inputs as well as the minimum cost mix of labour, materials and capital. The effect of wage rates and material prices on production methods and on improve technology are usually insignificant for short-run problems and therefore may be ignored. But for the long-run cost forecasts one should remember that cheaper materials may be found. Moreover, there is also the possibility that technical advances stimulated by high wage rates will usually discover methods to displace man-hours.

Technology

To forecast the costs and plan the capital expenditures connected with technical advances one should know the relation of cost to technological progress *per se*. A change in the equipment generally changes the technology, the scale of the plant as well as its flexibility for changes in output. Replacement of equipment is one of the management problems which needs forecast of technology. Here one should determine the degree of obsolescence of the old machine to be replaced. For this, one should forecast the degree of obsolescence of the new machine also. From this it becomes clear that the projection of technical progress is essential for replacement decisions.

Lot Size

Even though the relation of cost to lot size—the size of a single production job – is easy to understand, methods of estimating savings and deciding upon the optimum lot size differ greatly. In situations where the erection cost of machinery is large, so that the economy of large lots is marketed, the information about the lot-size cost curve is absolutely essential for production planning.

Stability of Output

Stability of output also brings savings in different kinds of hidden costs of interruption and learning.

Efficiency

The above mentioned cost determinants do help for making the kinds of cost projections needed for decision-making. Still when human characteristics are involved cost functions must be treated sceptically. Usually it is necessary to choose a dimension of operation (from the different possibilities) to find

out the lowest cost operating pattern for a given output rate. For example, for increasing output one can increase:[12]
- Speed of machines
- Number of machine hours per day
- Number of operation days per month; and/or
- Number of machines operated.

Here we need not enquire whether a cost study can indicate the best method or not, since no firm has absolute flexibility in respect of each of the dimension mentioned above. Repair requirements, union attitude as well as the shift differentials affect the choice.

Approaches to Cost Functions

There are at least three possible ways for estimating cost functions. They are:

i. Accounting approach (Under this approach costs are classified into fixed, variable and semi-variable on the basis of judgment and inspection)

ii. Engineering approach (Cost–output relationships are estimated on the basis of engineering conjunctures)

iii. Statistical approach (Cost functions and degree of output variations are estimated on the basis of statistical analysis).

It may be stated here that the above mentioned approaches are not always mutually exclusive. So, any one of them can be used as the principal method and the other as supplements. Here we propose analyse which one deserves greater emphasis and why?

Accounting Approach

Accounting approach to cost can be beneficially used when:[13]

i. Experience with a wide range of fluctuations in output rate.

ii. A detailed breakdown of accounts kept on the same basis over a period of years.

iii. Relative constancy in wage rates, material prices, plant size, technology, and so forth.

For the success of this method it is not necessary that the output range is uniformly covered. Instead, it will suffice if one makes a group of observations at every extreme of the range. This approach is simpler and less expensive than the other two.

Engineering Approach

"In essence the engineering method consists of systematic conjunctures about what cost behaviour ought to be in the future on the basis of what is known about the rated capacity of equipment, modified by experience with man-power requisites and efficiency factors, and with past cost behaviour.

Hence it depends upon knowledge of physical relationships supplemented by pooled judgments of practical operators."[14] This approach is built up by way of physical units like man-hours, pounds of material, etc. Then they are converted into the current and prospective cost prices. When there is only little systematic historical basis to estimate cost behaviour this approach is the only possible one.

Statistical Approach

This approach uses multiple correlation analysis to find the functional relation between changes in costs and the cost determinants. This approach picks out the fixed cost elements in cost components and shows whether the marginal cost components and shows whether the marginal cost is constant or variable with changes in cost determinants.

This method deals with the problems of determining empirical cost relationships explicitly and therefore this is the most scientific method. However, if we apply this method in a thorough manner, this will become very expensive and time consuming.

Cost and Size of Plant

Here our aim is to find empirically the effect of changing the size of plant upon cost. For formulating a rational policy of plant size and plant location it is necessary to know the relation between cost and size. The term 'size' is used here to mean the volume of final product and not the amount of work done in the plant. Moreover, we assume that the plants of different sizes make the transformation of materials and labour into product.

Methods of Empirical Analysis

The following methods of approach for studying the problem of cost and size of plant are worthy of consideration.[15]

- Analysis of changes in actual cost which accompanied the growth of single plant over a period of time.
- Analysis of differences in actual cost of plants of different sizes operated by separate firms and observed at the same time.
- Engineering estimates of the alternative cost where the same technology of manufacturing is used in plants of different sizes.
- Analysis of differences in the actual cost of different-sized plants operated by one corporation.

Problems of Measurement

Measuring Size

Size can be measured either by the amount of fixed equipment or by input capacity as well as the output capacity. Usually the theoretical analysis is not made in these terms. But the same basic discrepancies between theoretical relationships are involved. To find an appropriate concept of size of plant, which will permit practical measurement, one can choose among the following several alternatives:[16]

Amount of fixed equipment in physical terms, e.g. number of spindles in value terms, e.g. total assets, physical assets, capital assets, tangible net worth.

- *Output capacity:* Maximum physical capacity, e.g. rated capacity of blast furnace, economic capacity, e.g. 'efficient' capacity throughput of a refinery.
- *Input capacity:* Physical capacity, e.g. size of 'change' of furnace, number of employees or man-hours.
- *Economic capacity:* For example 'efficient' capacity, 'normal' capacity.

Measuring Cost

Recorded cost is affected not only by the size of plant, but also by many other factors. For comparing the effect of size on cost one needs to remove these variables. This is the most difficult problem of methodology. Some of these irrelevant influences are the following.[17] Changes in:

- Rate of output
- State of the arts
- Accounting valuations and procedures
- Prices paid for input factors
- Managerial skill
- Location advantages
- Character of products.

Conclusion

When the manager of a firm takes business decisions it is important to see that the costs balance revenue in an optimal way. He should be able to identify which costs are relevant for that particular decision. For that he should have a fairly good idea about the cost concepts that affect or influence business decision-making.

The behaviour of costs is determined by many forces. Since the cost determinants differ from firm to firm and from problem to problem it is impossible to set a general rule which is applicable to all. Still there are some forces which can be considered as cost determinants in modern business enterprises.

There are several approaches to cost functions. Accounting approach, engineering approach and statistical approach are some of them.

For formulating a rational policy of plant size and plant location one should know the relation between cost and size. For this the methods of empirical analysis and the problem of measurement were dealt with.

Review Questions

1. Distinguish between
   a. Opportunity costs and outlay costs
   b. Past and future costs

    c. Short-run and long-run costs
    d. Fixed and variable costs
    e. Traceable and common costs
    f. Out of pocket costs and book costs
    g. Incremental and sunk costs
    h. Escapable and unavoidable costs
    i. Controllable and Uncontrollable costs
    j. Replacement and historical costs
2. What are the determinants of cost behaviour?
3. Enumerate the different approaches for estimating cost functions.

Problem

"Management is vitally concerned with future costs for the simple reason that they are the only costs over which managers can exercise any control. Hence historical costs are of no interest to management except as basis for evaluating past operations." Do you agree with the above statement? Why or why not?

References

1. Dean, Joel: Managerial Economics; op.cit.; p.259
2. Ibid; p.260
3. Ibid; pp 261–62
4. Ibid; p.262
5. Bishop E.B: The Effect of the Increasing Ratio of Fixed to Variable Costs; in Batty J: Development in Management Accountancy; London, 1968; p.204
6. Dean, Joel; op.cit. p.263
7. Ibid; p.264
8. Ibid; p.266
9. J. Sizer: An Insight into Management Accounting; 1969; pp.312–13 quoted from Curwen P.J.; Managerial Economics; London, 1974; pp.3-4
10. Dean, Joel; op.cit. p.253
11. Ibid; p.257
12. Ibid; p.280
13. Ibid
14. Ibid; p.299
15. Ibid; pp.303–304
16. Ibid; pp.306–307

10 Cost–Output Relationship

In Chapter 9 we have discussed in brief the different cost concepts. In this chapter we propose to discuss the Cost–Output relationship from the following different angles.
1. Cost–Output relationship in the short-run
2. Cost–Output relationship in the long-run
3. Economies and diseconomies of scale
4. Firm's cost curve and industry supply curve
5. Production function.

In economic theory short-run period means the period during which the physical capacity of the firm is fixed. During this period output can be increased only by using the existing capacity more intensively.[1] The long-run period does have sufficient time for the firm's physical capacity to be increased or reduced in size. Therefore to increase the output there are absolutely no limitations of the factors of production, since they can be changed.

Cost–Output Relationship in the Short-Run

This relationship may be analysed from the point of view of average fixed cost, average variable cost and average total cost.

Average Fixed Cost

Fixed costs do not change as output changes. These costs have to be met under all circumstances—whether the output of the firm is big or small. They remain the same irrespective of the volume of production. Therefore the fixed cost per unit of output (average fixed cost) will fall continuously as output increases. This is because as output increases, the total fixed cost spreads over more and more units and therefore, average fixed cost becomes less and less. When output becomes very large, average fixed cost approaches zero. The average fixed cost curve will generally be a rectangular hyperbola. Examples for fixed costs are insurance, cost of plant and machinery, etc. Figures 10.1 and 10.2 respectively are the diagrammatic representations of fixed cost and average fixed cost.

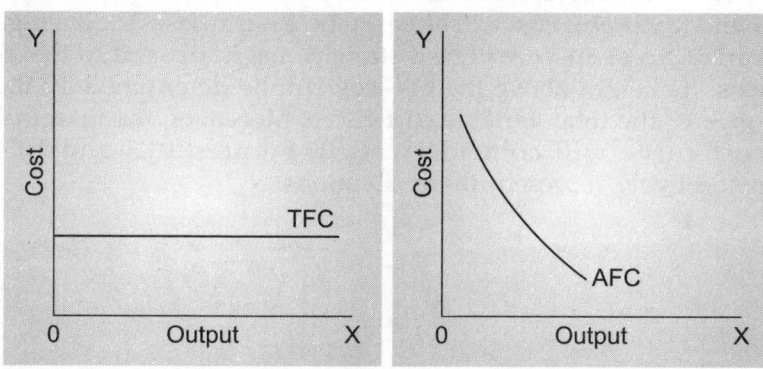

Fig. 10.1: Total fixed cost   **Fig. 10.2:** Average fixed cost

$$AFC = \frac{TFC}{Q}$$

Where Q, represents the number of units of output produced.

Average Variable Cost

Variable costs are those costs that change as output changes. For example, more raw materials, labour, power, etc. are required for increasing output and conversely only less raw materials, labour, etc. are required when output is reduced. Some variable costs change in exact proportion with output. In such cases the total variable cost curve (TVC) will be a straight line, whose slope represents the average variable cost. The steeper the variable cost curve, the higher the average variable cost.

Average variable cost (or variable cost per unit of output) is the total variable cost divided by the total number of units of output produced. Therefore,

$$AVC = \frac{TVC}{Q}$$

AVC = Average variable cost
TVC = Total variable cost
Q   = Total number of unit produced

In cases where the total variable cost is a straight line, the average variable cost will be constant. In such cases the average variable cost curve will be a straight line horizontal to the X-axis. Its height above the OX-axis will be determined by the slope of the total variable cost curve. Moreover, the marginal cost curve will coincide with it. Figures 10.3 and 10.4 respectively represent these situations.

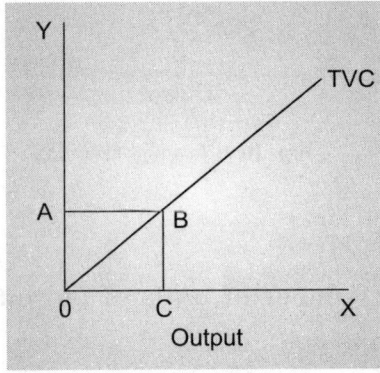

Fig. 10.3: Total variable cost

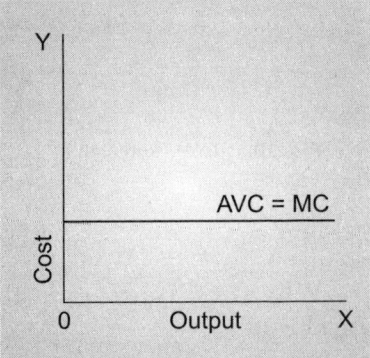

Fig. 10.4: Average variable cost

However in practice, the variable costs do not necessarily always change in exact proportion with output. Therefore the average variable cost is usually subjected to the law of variable proportions. An increase in output under normal situations will reduce the average variable cost till the maximum capacity is reached. When once the maximum capacity is reached any further increase in output will increase the average variable cost. This is because at this stage, the existing factors are used more intensively and thus the workers suffer from over strain. Moreover the frequency of machine breakdowns also increases. Therefore beyond the point of maximum capacity the average variable cost increases. That means, so long as the law of increasing returns operates, average variable cost reduces. In case of constant returns the average variable cost does not undergo any change. And when decreasing returns operate, average variable cost increases. Hence the shape of the average variable cost will normally be 'U' shaped. Figure 10.5 illustrates this.

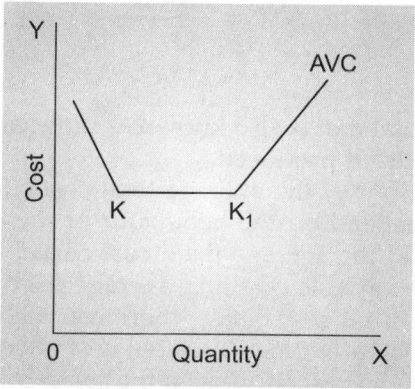

Fig. 10.5: Average variable cost

Figure 10.5 shows that up to the point 'K' the law of increasing returns operates, and between K and K_1 constant returns and beyond K_1 diminishing returns. In fact, there is only one law relevant in our illustration which is known as the law of variable proportions. Increasing returns, constant returns and diminishing returns are only different phases of this law.

Average Total Cost

The average total cost or what is simply called as average cost is the total cost divided by the number of units of output produced. So

$$ATC = \frac{TC}{Q}$$

Since total cost is the sum of total variable cost and total fixed cost, the average total cost is also the sum of average variable cost and average fixed cost. This can be proved in the following manner:

$$ATC = \frac{TC}{Q}$$

Since TC = TVC + TFC

$$ATC = \frac{TVC + TFC}{Q}$$

$$ATC = \frac{TVC}{Q} + \frac{TFC}{Q}$$

$$= AVC + AFC$$

Average total cost is also known as unit cost, as it is the cost per unit of output produced.

The behaviour of the average total cost curve (or unit cost curve) will depend on the behaviour of the average variable cost curve and the average fixed cost curve. In the beginning both average variable cost and average fixed cost curves fall. The average total cost curve, therefore, falls sharply in the beginning. When average variable cost curve begins to rise, but average fixed cost curve is falling steadily, the average total cost curve will continue to fall. But as output increases, there is a sharp rise in average variable cost that more than offsets the fall in average fixed cost. So, the average total cost curve or unit cost curve rises after a point. This is shown in Fig. 10.6.

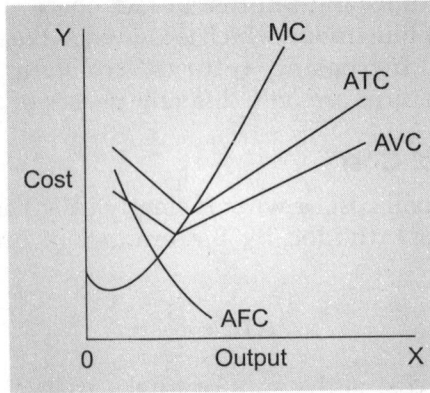

Fig. 10.6

We would like to add one more relevant point here, i.e. the marginal cost curve intersects both the average total cost curve and the average variable cost curve at their lowest points. The reasons are the following:

'If the marginal cost (MC) is less than the average cost (AC), it will pull AC down. If MC is greater than AC, it will pull AC up. If MC is equal to AC, it will neither pull AC up nor down. Hence MC curve tends to intersect the AC curve at its lowest point. Similar is the position about the average variable cost curve. It will not make a difference whether MC is going up or down.'[2]

The interrelationships among AVC, ATC and AFC are as follows:

1. If AFC and AVC fall, ATC falls
2. If AFC falls and AVC rises:
   a. ATC will fall where the fall in AFC is more than the rise in AVC.
   b. ATC will not fall where the fall in AFC is equal to the rise in AVC.
   c. ATC will rise when the fall in AFC is less than the rise in AVC.

Variability of Costs

Since the marginal cost approach is on the assumption that certain costs vary in sympathy with output we must analyse the variability of costs.

Edis[3] gives us the following result of the research study that was conducted regarding the behaviour of costs.

'Some time ago we did a little bit of research into the behaviour of costs which we classify as variable. Some examples of these are:

1. Direct materials
2. Consumable stores and tools
3. Direct labour
4. A good deal of indirect labour
5. Costs associated with these labour such as holiday pay, insurance, etc.
6. A proportion of power and similar costs

7. A proportion of maintenance costs

8. Carriage outwards.

The total actual cost of the items classified as variable costs was plotted on the Y-axis against the activity shown on the X-axis. If our interpretation were sound we should find a straight line varying directly with output.

First I should explain how we arrived at these figures. Actual variable cost represented the budgeted allowed cost minus variances. There was no special problem here as these figures are given in the departmental operating statements as a matter of routine. The output from our foundries could not be measured in weight, or numbers, because of the widely varying work content and weight of metal and cores, etc. of each item, so the workers activity percentage recorded in our system of budgetary control and standard costing was used. This was developed by aggregating the various standard units produced; labour hours, machine hours, weight of metal poured, etc. and in the case of general overheads the cost recovered to the common denominator of money by multiplying the units produced by the standard cost rates. The total was then expressed as a percentage of standard cost of the production normal.

This exercise covered several foundries were the type of production ranged from largely handwork to a highly mechanised modern foundry, and in all cases the type of product differed considerably. Space limits the examples but of the several available, I have selected three. Figure 10.7 is in respect of a highly mechanized foundry where the activity moved from 50 to 105 percent. Figure 10.8 is a foundry whose activity ranged from 70 percent of budget to 103 percent. Figure 10.8 is one where the piecework tempo is extremely high. Actual costs are shown by circles and the line of best fit has been calculated by the 'least squares' method. Standard costs are indicated by crosses (x) but these were the original unaltered standard costs and had been in force for three years. Seven costing periods are covered by the graphs and it was a time when, in the early part of the year, the Chancellor had his foot on the accelerator but by the end was stamping hard on the break! Such are the problems which beset many of us in practice.

My feeling was that this exercise confirmed for all practical
purposes that the costs we treat as variable are indeed marginal

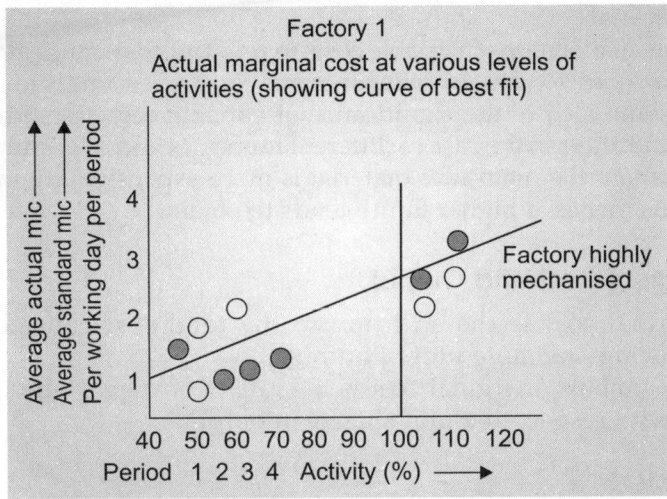

Fig. 10.7: Actual marginal cost at various levels of activities
(showing curve of best fit)

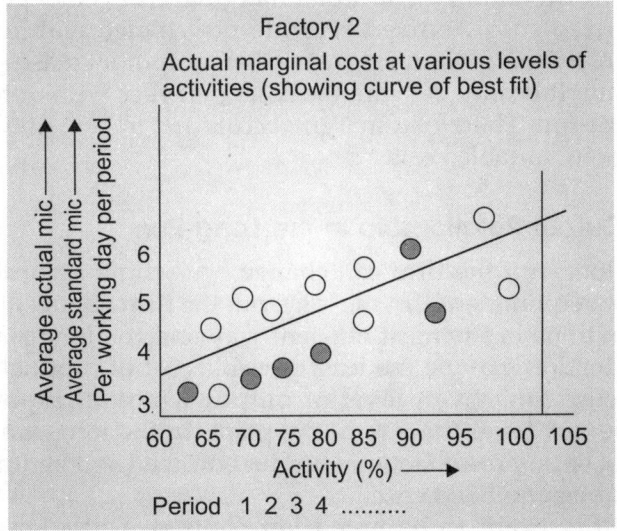

Fig. 10.8: Cost behavior with intensive piecework

costs as we British cost accountants understand this term. I say this advisedly because I am aware we have no proprietary rights to this expression and others may not accept that variable = marginal.

The relationship of variable costs to constant costs ranges from approximately 3:1 to 4:1 in most of our companies; this is to give you some idea of the significance of variable costs. Obviously the ratio alters in the case of different foundries and departments and where the main raw material is more expensive, e.g. non-ferrous metals, a higher figure tends to obtain.

Marginal Cost and Output

Marginal cost is the addition to the total cost caused by producing one more unit of output.

In symbols, marginal cost is the rate of change in the total cost with respect to a unit change in output.

i.e. $MC = \dfrac{d(TC)}{dQ}$

Where d, in the numerator as well as in the denominator indicates the change TC and Q respectively.

It is worth noting the fact that marginal cost is independent of the fixed cost. As fixed costs do not change with output, there are no marginal fixed costs when output increases in the short-run. It is only the variable costs that vary with output in the short-run. Therefore, marginal costs are, in fact, due to the changes in variable costs.

Cost–Output Relationship in the Long-Run

In the long-run the firm can change everything according to the new requirements. In the long-run the firm adapts its scale of operations in the most efficient way and the long-run cost of production may be the least possible cost of production of producing any given level of output when all inputs are variable including the size of the plant. In the long-run there may not be any fixed factor of production at all and hence there may not be any fixed cost.

Another point to be noted here is that in the long-run, variable costs will rise less sharply. This is because in the long-run, not only the size of the firm can be changed, but also overcrowding can be handled and the management has enough time to solve the problem of high output. In the long-run variable costs will not rise as sharply as in the short-run. To put it in other words, in the long-run, the indivisible factors of production can be used more efficiently or economically. This is because in the long-run, they are divisible to a certain extent. In the long-run capital can be changed and the management also can be arranged in different manner. i.e. in the long-run capital and management are divisible even though incompletely. It is unlikely that an entrepreneur produces an output twice as efficiently as he produces that output, however, long he is producing it. That means, even in the long-run, at some scales of output firms will produce cheaply than at other scales. That means the minimum points of the short-run average cost curves of the firm will be different.

The long-run **Cost–Output** relationship is shown graphically in Fig. 10.9.

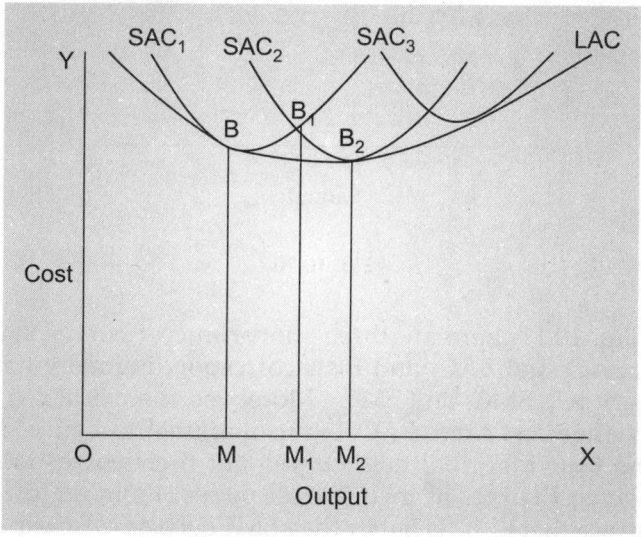

Fig. 10.9

Consider, for example, a firm is operating under the short-run average cost curve SACI and is producing the output OM.

Now suppose that an increase in the output is desired and the firm wants to produce OM_1. If the firm continues its production under the existing scale the average cost will be M_1B_1. Now suppose the scale (of production) is changed and there is a new short-run cost curve SAC_2. Under the new arrangement the average cost of producing the output OM_2 is only M_2B_2 which is smaller than M_1B_1. Thus in the long-run, the average cost, when the firm produces OM_2 quantity of output, is M_2B_2 and this is the long-run cost of producing OM_2 quantity of output. Figure 10.10 also helps us to understand the Cost–Output relationship in the long-run.

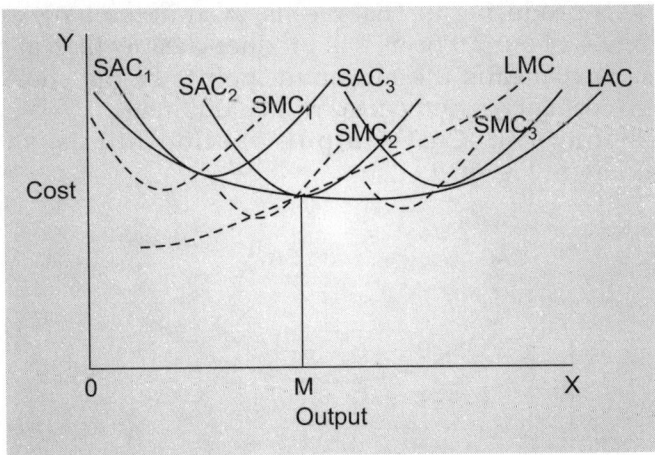

Fig. 10.10

In Fig. 10.11 there are three short-run cost curves, namely SAC_1, SAC_2 and SAC_3 and their corresponding marginal cost curves SMC_1, SMC_2 and SMC_3. Moreover, there is also a long-run average cost curve LAC and its marginal cost curve LMC. All the four marginal cost curves cut their corresponding average cost curves at their lowest points. From the diagram we can see that LMC is flatter than SMCs. This is also expected; because of the 'U' shape of the long-run average cost curve is less pronounced than that of the short-run average curves. "Thus if one starts from the long-run optimum point OM, and output increases, marginal costs rise more sharply in the short-run than in the long-run. Similarly, if output falls from OM, marginal cost fall more substantially in the short-run than in the long run."[4]

Why Long-run Average Cost Curves are U-Shaped?

The U-shape of the short-run average cost curve is explained with the law of variable proportions or the laws of returns. But in the case of long-run average cost curves the U-shape is due to the returns to scale. The returns to scale (or economies of scale) exist only up to a certain size of plant known as the 'optimum size of plant' where all possible economies of scale are fully exploited. So up to the point of optimum size of the plant average cost will decrease. Beyond the optimum plant size diseconomies of scale arise due to marginal inefficiencies and this makes the long-run average cost curve to rise upward. In Fig. 10.11 the point 'M' is the point of optimum output and at that level of output the average cost is the minimum.

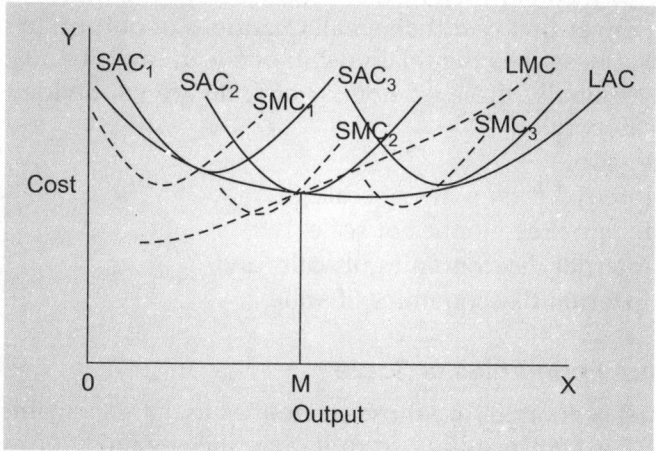

Fig. 10.11

What are the reasons that a firm first enjoys internal economies of scale and then beyond a certain point it has to suffer internal diseconomies of scale? Two major reasons are given for the economies of scale that accrue to the firm and due to which cost per unit falls. First, as the firm increases its scale of operations, it becomes possible to use more specialised and efficient form of all factors, especially capital equipment and machinery. Second, when the scale of operation is enlarged and the amount of labour and other factors become larger, introduction of a greater degree of division of labour or specialization becomes possible and as a result the long-run cost per unit declines.

According to Joan Robinson and Nicholas Kaldor economies of scale arise because of the imperfect divisibility of factors. Chamberlin, on the other hand, holds the view that with too large a scale of operation it becomes difficult for the top management to exercise control and to bring about proper co-ordination. This may result in diseconomies and consequently the average cost will rise.

Economies and Diseconomies of Scale

The term economies of scale is used to refer to any circum-stances which permit a firm to produce large quantities of out-put at lower unit cost than small quantities of output. In other words it describes the relationship between output and cost.[5]

Traditionally these economies of scale are subdivided into four categories.

They are:

1. Internal economies of scale
2. External economies of scale
3. Internal diseconomies of scale, and
4. External diseconomies of scale.

Internal Economies of Scale

Internal economies are those economies that are available to a particular firm resulting from its internal organization which enable the firm to produce more efficiently certain level of output than others.[6]

The types of internal economies available to a firm are:

1. Labour economies
2. Technical economies
3. Managerial economies
4. Marketing economies

5. Financial economies, and
6. Economies of risk spreading.

Labour Economies

When a firm expands its area of operation, it will be possible for it to reduce the labour cost per unit by introducing a policy of division of labour.

Economies of division of labour occur due to three different circumstances, first, to the increase in dexterity in every particular workman; secondly, to the saving of time which is commonly lost in passing from one species of work to another; and lastly, to the invention of a great number of machines which facilitate and abridge labour, and enable one man to do the work of many.[7]

Technical Economies

Technical economies arise from the use of big size machines and such scientific processes that are carried out in large production units.

Managerial Economies

As the size of the firm becomes large there is scope for utilizing specialized managerial personnel. This results in better co-ordination and higher efficiency which, in turn, may reduce cost per unit.

Marketing Economies

As the firm becomes large, its bargaining power increases. This will enable it to secure economies in its purchases and sales.

Financial Economies

A big firm will be in a better position to raise finance at a lower cost.

Economies of Risk Spreading

A big firm is in a better position to spread the risks through diversification. Diversification is possible on two accounts, viz. diversification of output and diversification of market.

External Economies of Scale

External Economies of scale arise when the price of inputs to the firm is reduced for any reason, thus enabling the firm to produce more cheaply for reasons external to the firm's own operations. For example, the construction of a railway line near the firm will enable the firm to reduce transportation cost and thereby produce more and sell cheaply than otherwise.

Internal Diseconomies of Scale

Internal diseconomies of scale result when a firm becomes progressively more inefficient as it expands. The quality of supervision or management may deteriorate or the workers may feel alienated in what used to be a family concern but which grows to become a large impersonal corporation.[8]

External Diseconomies of Scale

External diseconomies of scale arise where, for example, input prices go up for any reason when the firm purchases additional factors of production.[9]

Sargant Florence and Economies of Scale

Sargant Florence opines that the economies of scale can be attributed to the three principles that are in operation in a large sized business. They are the principle of bulk transactions, the principle of massed reserves and the principle of multiples.

Principle of Bulk Transactions

According to this principle the cost of dealing with large batch is often not greater than the cost of dealing with a small batch. In other words, the cost of placing an order, large or small, availability of discounts on bulk orders, or annual purchase contracts, economies in the use of large containers such as tanks or trucks of special design, for a container holding, say, twice as much as the other one does not cost double the amount.

Principle of Massed Reserves

Since a large firm has large number of departments its overall demand for services, e.g. transport services, will usually be large. But generally all departments will not make heavy demands of transport service at the same time. Thus the firm can own transport fleet and fully utilize it. The firm can thereby reduce its costs.

Principle of Multiples

This can be explained with the help of the following example. Imagine a case where a manufacturing operation involves three processes. Suppose in the first process a machine can make 30 units a week, in the second process an automatic machine can make 1000 units a week and in the third process a semi-automatic machine can make 400 units a week. If the output of the plant is not having some common multiple of 30, 1000 and 400 one or more of the processes will have unutilized capacity. Since their LCM is 6000 to utilize all the machines in the best possible way the plant size must be at least 6000 units or any of its multiples.

Economies of Scope

As the volume or scale of production increases a firm enjoys certain economies of scale. This may be on account of various factors. But if the same plant can produce multiple products simultaneously at a lower cost than they are produced separately it is a case of economies of scope. Broad banding often helps manufacturers to enjoy economies of scope.

Firm's Cost Curve and Industry Supply Curve

In the above discussion we have analysed the cost curves of the individual firms. From these cost curves we can derive the industry supply curve. This is done by adding the quantities supplied by all firms in the same industry at different prices.

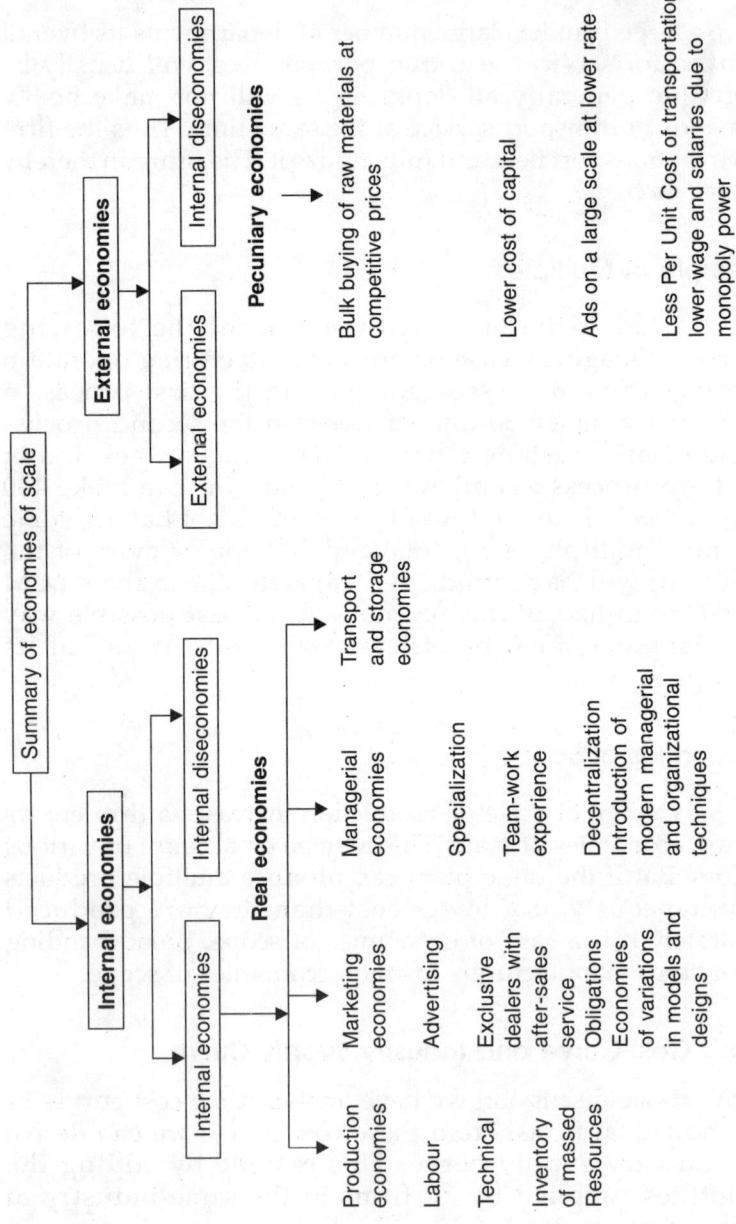

Summary of economies of scale

Internal economies

Internal economies

Internal diseconomies

Real economies

Production economies
- Labour
- Technical
- Inventory of massed Resources

Marketing economies
- Advertising
- Exclusive dealers with after-sales service
- Obligations Economies of variations in models and designs

Managerial economies
- Specialization
- Team-work experience
- Decentralization Introduction of modern managerial and organizational techniques

Transport and storage economies

External economies

External economies

Internal diseconomies

Pecuniary economies

Bulk buying of raw materials at competitive prices

Lower cost of capital

Ads on a large scale at lower rate

Less Per Unit Cost of transportation lower wage and salaries due to monopoly power

Supply–Definition

Supply may be defined as the amounts of a product that producers will make available for sale at each of a series of possible prices during a specific period. Mayers defines supply as a schedule of the amount of a good that would be offered for sale at all possible prices at any instant of time, or during any one period of time, for example, a day, a week, and so on, in which the conditions of supply remain the same.

The Law of Supply

The supply of a commodity depends upon the price which the producers get for it. "Other things remaining the same, as the price of a commodity rises its supply is extended, as the price falls its supply is contracted." i.e. as price rises, the quantity supplied rises; as price falls, the quantity supplied falls. We shall explain this with the help of the following imaginary supply schedule:

Price per kg (Rice)	Quantity supplied (Rice)
Rs. 10	100 kg
Rs. 15	150 kg
Rs. 20	250 kg
Rs. 25	300 kg

When the price of rice is Rs.10 per kg, 100 kg of rice is supplied. When price rises to Rs.15 per kg, quantity supplied increases to 150 kg. When price rises further to Rs. 20 and Rs. 25 per kg; the supply increases to 250 and 350 kg respectively.

Market Supply

Market supply is derived from individual supply in exactly the same way market demand is derived from individual demand. This is done by summing up the quantities supplied by each producer/seller at each price. In other words, we get the market supply curve by 'horizontally adding' the supply curves of the individual producers.

Determinants of Supply

Generally the supply schedule is constructed on the assumption, *ceteris paribus*. But other things do not remain the same. If any one of the factors which are assumed to be constant changes, a change in supply will occur meaning that the entire supply curve will shift.

The basic determinants of supply are:
1. Resource prices
2. Technology
3. Taxes and subsidies
4. Prices of other goods
5. Expected price, and
6. The number of sellers in the market.

Changes in Quantity Supplied

The distinction between a change in supply and a change in quantity supplied parallels the distinction between a change in demand and the change in quantity demanded. Because supply is a schedule or curve, a change in supply means a change in the schedule and a shift in the curve.

An increase in supply shifts the curve to the right; a decrease in the supply shifts it to the left. The cause of a change in supply is a change in one or more of the determinants of supply.

References

1. See Chapter 9 on Cost Considerations.
2. It is easy to understand that if the cost of an additional unit of output lowers the average cost, it must itself be less than the average cost.
3. Edis DC: Standard Marginal Costing in Action – A Case Study. Quoted in Batty J : *Development in Management Accountancy*, London, 1968, pp. 338–341
4. Stonier, Alfred W & Hague, Douglas C: *A Textbook of Economic Theory*; London, p.121.
5. Curwen, Peter J: *Managerial Economics*; Macmillan, London, p.10.
6. Stonier, Alfred W & Hague, Douglas C: op.cit., p.139.
7. Adam Smith: *The Wealth of Nations*; London, 1964 (Ed), p.7.
8. Curwen, Peter J: op.cit, p.11.
9. Ibid.

11 Principles of Capital Budgeting

Probably no other area of decision-making is as important to the success of the company (firm) as capital budgeting. Management is typically faced with an array of possible investments. The selection of the most profitable investment, giving regard to the availability of funds to finance the expenditures, can be considered the key function of management. Not only is capital budgeting of fundamental importance to the company, but it also is of great importance to the economy as a whole. Fluctuations in business investment in plant and equipment are greatly regarded as being one of the decisive factors causing business cycles.

The nature and impact of capital budgeting on the company's well-being can easily be seen from the following statement.[1]

Capital expenditures involve long-term commitment of resources to realize future benefits. Hence capital expenditures reflect basic company objectives and have a long-term and significant effect on the economic well-being of the firm.

Effective planning and controlling of such expenditures are particularly important because:

1. the long-term commitment increases financial risk;
2. the magnitude of expenditures is substantial and the penalties for unwise decisions are usually severe; and
3. the decisions made in the area provide the structure that supports the operating activities of the firm.

Meaning and Significance of Capital Budgeting

Capital budgeting involves current investment of considerable size (but not always) the benefits of which extend over a period of time extending one year. The key characteristic of capital expenditure is that at least a major part of the expenditure is made at one point of time and the benefits are realized at different points of time in the years to come. Since capital expenditure involves the commitment of large sums for long periods of time, any error in their evaluation may be very serious for the firm. Consequently capital budgeting usually involves specialized procedures and organization.

A number of investment techniques are developed so as to help in selecting the best investment proposals. However, there is no single technique which is universally acceptable as the most appropriate technique for selecting the best proposal/s in all circumstances. Our purpose here is to discuss the various investment criteria, examine their comparative advantages and limitations and to recommend the use of one over the other under different investment circumstances. But before doing that we propose to discuss the general procedures that are followed in preparing the capital budget for a company or firm.

General Procedures

Basically there are two levels in decision-making process of capital budgeting: the departmental level and the top management level. First each department head determines the various possible capital expenditures that he believes are necessary or worthwhile. Usually there are many alternatives available to meet a given need. These are called conflicting proposals, because they are mutually exclusive; that is, if one is adopted, the others cannot be carried out.

Second each department head must choose the best alternative from among the conflicting proposals for submission to the top management. Selection from among the conflicting proposals may require that the department head knows the overall cost of capital.[2]

Various proposals passed on by department heads will also be conflicting. For example, the personnel manager may request an addition to the employees' convenience. The production manager may ask for a new set of machinery to replace the existing ones or to introduce a new product. The proposals that are generated at various levels of authority may fall within one or more of the following categories of investments.

1. Essential investments
2. Replacement investments
3. Profit enhancing investments
4. Cost reducing investments
5. Product obsolescence investments
6. Expansion investments
7. New product investments
8. Welfare investments
9. Prestige enhancement investments
10. Strategic investments.

Most firms screen proposals at multiple levels of authority. How high a proposal must go before it is finally approved usually depends upon its size. The greater the capital outlay, the greater the number of screening required. Plant managers, for example, may be able to approve moderate sized projects on their own; but final approval for larger projects is received only at higher levels of authority. Where projects are approved at multiple levels, it is very important that the same acceptance criterion is applied objectively and consistently through out the organization. Otherwise capital is likely to be misallocated in the sense that one division might accept a project that another would reject.

The top management may consider the following five points when selecting the best project or proposal from the list of projects or proposals:

The amount and timing of each outflow(s) or investment.

The amounts and timings of cash inflows (benefits).

The discounted cash flow rate of return on the proposed investment.

The rate of return and the cost of capital, and

The qualitative aspects of the proposed investments.

The first point pertains to cash outlays or costs of the proposal. The second is related to estimating the benefits from the proposed investment. The third and fourth points pertain to measuring the profitability of an investment using the discounted cash flow rate of return method[3] and comparing the resulting rate with the cost of capital. The last point is important in emphasizing the non-monetary aspects of capital expenditure proposal.

Illustration

Suppose a firm is considering the introduction of a new product. In order to launch the product, it will need to spend Rs.1,50,000 for special equipment and initial advertising campaign. The marketing department considers the product life to be six years and expects incremental sales revenue to be as given in Table 11.1.

Table 11.1

Year 1	Year 2	Year 3	Year 4	Year 5	Year 6
Rs.	Rs.	Rs.	Rs.	Rs.	Rs.
60,000	1,20,000	1,60,000	1,80,000	1,10,000	50,000

Cash outflows include labour and maintenance cost, material costs, and various other expenses connected with the product. As with sales, these costs must be estimated on an incremental basis. In addition to these outflows, the firm will have to pay higher taxes if the new project generates higher profits; and this incremental outlay must be included. Suppose that on the basis of the above considerations the firm estimates total incremental cash outflows as indicated in Table 11.2.

Table 11. 2

Year 1	Year 2	Year 3	Year 4	Year 5	Year 6
Rs.	Rs.	Rs.	Rs.	Rs.	Rs.
40, 000	70,000	10,00,000	1,00,000	70,000	40,000

As depreciation is a non-cash expense it is not included in these outflows. The expected net cash flows from the project are as given in Table 11.3

Table 11. 3

	Initial cost	Year 1	Year 2	Year 3	Year 4	Year 5	Year 6
	Rs.	Rs.	Rs.	Rs.	Rs.	Rs.	Rs.
Cash inflows		60000	120000	160000	180000	110000	50000
Cash outflows	150000	40000	70000	100000	100000	70000	40000
Net cash flows	150000	20000	50000	60000	80000	40000	10000

Thus for an initial cash out flow of Rs. 1,50,000, the firm expects to generate net cash flows of Rs. 20,000, Rs. 50,000, Rs. Rs. 60,000, Rs. 80,000, Rs. 40,000 and Rs. 10,000 over the next six years. These cash flows represent the relevant information we need for evaluating the attractiveness of the project.

Evaluation of Projects

Once we have collected the needed information, we will be in a position to evaluate the attractiveness or profitability of the various investment proposals under consideration. Since our purpose in this chapter is to examine the basic principles or concepts of capital budgeting, we assume

1. that the risk or quality of all investment proposals under consideration does not differ from the risk of existing investment projects of the firm and that the acceptance of any proposal or group of investment proposals does not change the relative business risk of the firm,
2. all cash flows occur instantaneously, usually at the end or beginning of a period,
3. interest is compounded annually.

These assumptions may not always hold good. For instance, cash flows may not always occur daily, weekly, monthly, yearly or continuously. Cash may flow at one point of time while it may flow out at another point of time. Interest may be compounded daily, weekly, monthly, half-yearly or yearly. The cash flows of one project may have greater certainty than of another. However, the assumptions (2) and (3) are made only for simplicity and the investment criteria under discussion hold good even in the absence of these assumptions. Assumption (1) regarding identical degree of certainty to each project or proposal is crucial and in the absence of this assumption we have another set of investment techniques which will be discussed later. The investment decision will be either to accept or to reject the proposal.

Here we propose to discuss six approaches to capital budgeting viz. the Payback method, Accountant Rate of Return method, Discounted Cash Flow method, Net Present Value method, Net Terminal Value method and MAPI method.

Payback Period Method

The Payback Period Method is one of the simplest and apparently one of the most frequently used methods of capital investment analysis not only among the small and less efficiently managed firms, but also among the largest and most successful corporations in the western world.

What is Payback Period?

The Payback Period may be defined as the length of time required to receive benefits equivalent to the total investment. In other words, the Payback Period is the length of time required for the stream of cash proceeds by an investment to equal the original cash outlay required by the investment.

If an investment is expected to produce a stream of cash proceeds that is constant from year to year, then the payback period can be obtained simply by dividing the initial investment by the annual net return.

Symbolically $P = \dfrac{C}{R} = 1$ ...1

Where P = Payback period
C = Initial investment
R = Uniform annual net return before depreciation but after taxes.

Thus if an investment required an original outlay of Rs. 10,000 and is expected to produce a stream of uniform cash proceeds of Rs. 2500 a year for seven years, the payback period would be Rs. 10000 divided by 2500 or 4 years. If the stream of expected Rs. 2500 is not uniform (equal), then the payback period must be determined by adding up the expected proceeds in successive years until the total is equal to or greater than the original outlay. Symbolically the payback period equals t^*, where t^* is the lowest value of t for which the following condition holds good

$$C \le \sum_{T=1}^{t^*} Rt$$ ...2

t^* = Minimum value for t
Rt = Net return before depreciation and interest cost, but after taxes.

Suppose the cash inflows in our previous example are Rs. 2000 in the first year, Rs. 3000 in the second year, Rs. 5000 in the third year, Rs. 3000 in the fourth year, Rs. 2500 in the fifth year, Rs. 1500 in the sixth year and Rs. 1000 in the seventh year. Then the original investment of Rs. 10,000 would be realized in three years, i.e. Rs. 2000 + Rs. 3000 + Rs. 5000. Hence the payback period is three years. On the payback criterion a project will be selected if and only if its payback period is less than or equal to the firm' desired maximum payback period, which is normally stipulated by the management in screening investment proposals.

If the payback period is used to rank mutually exclusive investment projects, the project with the lowest payback period will be ranked first. To check the reasonableness of such ranking let us consider the following six hypothetical investments given in Table 11.4.

Table 11.4: Description of hypothetical investments

Projects	Initial cost (1) Rs.	Net proceeds (before depreciation and interest but after taxes)				
		Year 1 Rs.	Year 2 Rs.	Year 3 Rs.	Year 4 Rs.	Year 5 Rs.
A	20000	20000	5000	1000	1000	1000
B	20000	8000	10000	12000	5000	2000
C	20000	10000	10000	7000	6000	3000
D	20000	20000	6000	6000	2000	2000
E	20000	10000	8000	6000	5000	5000
F	20000	12000	12000	8000	5000	1000

Assume that each of these investments has zero salvage value. The application of formula (1) yields the payback periods for these investments, which together with the ranking are given in Table 11.5.

Table 11.5

Project	Payback Period (years)	Ranking
A	1	1*
B	2 1/6	4
C	2	3

Contd...

Table 11.5

Project	Payback Period (years)	Ranking
D	1	1*
E	2 1/3	5
F	1 2/3	2

From Table 11.5 it can be seen that investments A and B are both ranked as 1, because they both have shorter payback periods than any other investments, namely one year. But investment D earns total proceeds of Rs. 36,000 whereas investment A earns only 28,000. Obviously investment D is superior to A. A ranking procedure, such as the payback period, that fails to disclose this fact is deficient.

Characteristics of Payback Method

The payback period is a time concept. It does not measure profitability. Rather it is concerned only with how fast the investment will be recovered. The fact that one investment has a shorter payback period than another does not guarantee that the investment which has a shorter payback period is more profitable than the one which has a longer payback period. If any generalisation is to be made, it is more sensible to assume that long-lived investments could and should earn more than short-lived investments.

Since the primary purpose of economic evaluation is usually to measure profitability of a proposed investment, and payback does not measure profitability, the payback method should not be used exclusively for capital investment analysis. By its very nature, the payback method has a built-in bias against longer-lived investment with initially small but constantly increasing benefits. If carried to an extreme, use of the payback method could lead to investing capital in short-lived investments at the expense of more profitable long and intermediate-lived investments.

When is Payback Useful?

The payback period becomes an ideal measure of the desirability of an investment in situations in which the speed of recovering the investment is critical. These situations occur when a company has cash problems, when the product a company is selling usually lasts for a short period of time, when the proposed investment if known to have a high degree of obsolescence, when the company is working under a government contract that may be cancelled on short notice, or, in foreign investments, when the possibility of adverse governmental action exists. Payback is useful when used as supplementary method. For example it can be used as a quick screening device to identify very poor or very good investments. Also it can be used to indicate the cash return pattern of an investment and the effect of a proposal on the cash budget. It can help in evaluating the sensitivity of the returns of an investment to different estimates of its life. The payback method can be used for evaluating minor capital expenditure proposals when the investments are small and the cost of using more sophisticated methods of analysis exceeds the possible benefits from the refinement in such analysis. Finally, payback may be used if estimates of cash flows are unreliable and the life of the proposed investment is indeterminable.

Chief Advantages of the Payback Method

- Easy to understand
- Simple in use
- Well known
- Easy to sell to operating personnel
- Easy to sell to top management
- Low in cost
- Easy to post audit
- Requires few assumptions
- Can be used for evaluating different types of investment proposals.

A variant of the payback method is the payback period rate of return method. It is obtained simply by dividing 100 by the number of years in the pay off period. Larger the payback period rate of return for a project better is the project. Obviously, the payback period method and the payback period rate of return method will give the same ranking.

Accountant Rate of Return Method

Another approach to capital budgeting is Accountant Rate of Return Method. It is so called because the benefits are usually measured in terms of accounting concepts. Terms such as accounting method, the simple rate of return method, the initial year rate of return method, the average annual rate of return method, the unadjusted rate of return method, the financial statement method, the simple rate of return on investment method, the net return on investment method and the return on investment by financial statement method are also used to represent the accountant rate of return method. These variations are due to the wide differences in practices in computing the accountant rate of return. But two features are common in all these methods and they are:

    i. use of accounting concepts in determining the benefits and

    ii. making no adjustment for the time value of money. These two factors justify us in ignoring the variations and studying the accountant rate of return as one method.

Definition of Accountant Rate of Return

The accountant rate of return on investment may be defined as the percentage of annual net return before interest cost but after depreciation and taxes to the initial investment. The simplest way to compute the Accountant Rate of Return (ARR) is to add all the net returns[4] from the project during its life period and divide this sum by the number of years, and express the resulting figures as a percentage of the initial investment. Thus

$$ARR = \sum_{T=1}^{T} \frac{(Rt - Dt)}{T} \times \frac{100}{C}$$

Where the new notations are

Dt = depreciation in period t

T = Project's expected life

On the basis of the accountant rate of return criterion a project will be accepted if and only if it guarantees an average annual rate of return which is greater than or equal to the firm's or management's desired minimum rate of return, which would, of course, be greater than its cost of capital. Among the mutually exclusive alternative projects, the project with the highest ARR would rank the first and one with the lowest ARR would rank the last. When there is capital rationing, the number of selected projects will be constrained by the given capital stock.

The use of ARR method in investment decision is illustrated in Table 11.6.

Table 11.6

Project	Initial cost	Total net returns	Total depreciation	Total net return after depreciation	ARR	Rank
	Rs.	Rs.	Rs.	Rs.	%	
A	20000	28000	20000	8000	8	6
B	20000	37000	20000	17000	17	2
C	20000	36000	20000	16000	16	3*
D	20000	36000	20000	16000	16	3*
E	20000	34000	20000	14000	14	5
F	20000	38000	20000	18000	18	1

* Indicates tie between two investments.

On the basis of the ARR criterion, only project F will be selected (accepted) if the management stipulates a minimum return of 18 %. But if the minimum expected return is 16%, then projects B,C,D and F will be undertaken provided there is no capital constraint. If the total investible fund is Rs.20000 only, then project F alone will be undertaken even if the minimum required rate of return is, say 8%, and so on. Ranking of these projects is obvious from Table 11.6.

Advantages of ARR

- It is easy to understand
- It is simple in use
- It is well known
- It is easy to sell to operating personnel
- It is easy to sell to top management

- It is easy to post audit
- It is low in cost
- It can be used for evaluating different types of investment proposals, and
- It analyses future data.

Weaknesses

1. It ignores the time value of money
2. It depends exclusively on accounting concepts.

The ARR method is superior to payback method since it measures profitability and the analysis is usually extended over the entire life of the project. It allows ranking of proposals by rate of return and produces a rate that can be compared with a pre-determined cut off rate. But the ARR is considered, in theory, inferior to discounted cash flow method.

Discounted Cash Flow Method

Because of the various short comings in the accountant rate of return and payback method discussed above, it is generally felt that the discounted cash flow method provides a more objective basis for evaluating and selecting investment projects.

The most important feature of this method is that it takes into account the time value of money. This means that a differentiation is made between cash flows received in different points in time. Before adding cash flows to be received at different times, they are adjusted. This adjusting process is called discounting.

The concept of time value of money is explained by stating that a rupee received today is better than a rupee received tomorrow or any time later. We can not treat rupees received at different points in time as if they were equal since the earlier we receive a rupee, the earlier we can put it to use to earn additional money. Thus a rupee received today is worth more than a rupee to be received a year from now. The underlying assumption here is that, in an economy in which interest and opportunities for investment exist, a rupee received today could be invested to earn additional money immediately. A rupee to be received one year from hence can not be invested until it is received; therefore, it is less valuable than a rupee received today. In other words there is a premium for waiting for receiving benefits; the longer we have to wait, the more return we should expect on our money.

Present value is calculated on the same basis as compound interest. Compound interest takes a present value and look forward to see what sum that value will have grown at some time in the future. Present value takes a sum receivable in future and looks backwards to the present time to ascertain what the original sum would have had to be to grow to the future value.

If a business can earn 10 percent of the funds it employs in the business, then a number of years, the original sum of Rs.100 invested would grow in the way represented in Table 11.7.

Table 11.7

Initial investment	After one year	After two years	After three years	After four years	After n years
Rs. 100	Rs. 110	Rs. 121	Rs. 131.1	Rs. 146.41	$100(1+0.1)^n$

To say that Rs. 100 received now will become Rs.110 in one year's time is the same as saying that Rs. 110 received after one year has a present value of Rs. 100 only. Instead of looking forward from the present time to a time in the future as shown in Table 11.7, in Table 11. 8, we take a future time and relate it back to the present.

Table 11.8

Initial period (Rs.)		After one year (Rs.)
a. 100	$\longrightarrow$	110
b. 100	$\longleftarrow$	110
c. 100/110	$\longleftarrow$	100
d. 0.909	$\longrightarrow$	1

Now assume a range of years, continuing with a 10 percent rate of interest, we have already seen that the value of Rs. 100 would grow over a series of years. Using the same process as was used in Table 11. 4 we can now relate these sums to present values and arrive at a common basis for all calculations – the present value of Re.1. This is shown in Table 11. 9.

For a mathematical calculation of the present value of a future sum the following formula may be used:

$$\text{Present value (PV)} = \sum_{T=1}^{n} \left(\frac{Rn}{(1+i)^n} \right)$$

Where R = returns
i = interest rate
n = number of years.

Table 11. 9 gives present value of Re. 1 receivable at varying times in future discounted at the rate of 10 percent.

Table 11. 9

Year	Present value
1	Pisa 90.9
2	Pisa 82.6
3	Pisa 75.1
4	Pisa 68.3

Internal Rate of Return

One method of using the discounted cash flow (DCF) is known as the internal rate of return method (IRR). The IRR may be defined as that rate which when applied to discount the net returns (before depreciation and interest cost but after taxes) will make the discounted value of net returns equal to the initial project cost. Mathematically it can be defined as

$$C = \sum_{T=1}^{t} \frac{Rt}{(1+r)^t}$$

Where r = internal rate of return, and the other notations have the same meaning as before.

The acceptance criterion generally employed with the IRR method is to compare the IRR with a required rate of return known also as the cut off or hurdle rate. If the IRR exceeds the required rate, the project is accepted; if not it is rejected.

The several mutually exclusive projects will be ranked on the basis of their IRRs. The project with the highest IRR will be ranked first and the project with the lowest IRR will be ranked the last. In the presence of capital constraint, the project will be selected from the priority list until the capital constraint is not violated. The computations of IRR for six hypothetical projects are given in Table 11.10.

If the management's minimum required rate of return is say, 29 percent, then project A,B,C,D and F will be undertaken provided the capital constraint is not binding. However, if the investor has only Rs.20000, he will accept project D only. The ranking of the project is self explanatory in the table.

Net Present Value

The net present value method is another discounted cash flow approach to capital budgeting. It is similar to IRR method, but rather finding the rate of return that equals the cash inflows with the cash outflows at an assumed (required or desired) rate of return is rather difficult. Through the discounting process the present value of the benefits is determined. Then the initial investment is deducted from the present value of the investment to get the net present value. A positive NPV indicates that the proposed investment is profitable. The net present value of an investment is

$$NPV = \sum_{T=1}^{t} \left(\frac{Rt}{(1+r)^t} \right) - C$$

Where i = is the required rate of return (appropriate discount rate) and the other notations have the same meaning as before.

It is obvious from the formula that NPV is a negative function of the discount rate. That is lower the discount rate 1, ceteris paribus, higher will be the NPV.

On the basis of the profitability index or the benefit-cost-ratio, a project is acceptable if PI or BCR is greater than one. According to the EBCR technique, a project will be accepted if and only if it guarantees a positive EBCR. Like NPV, both BCR and EBCR are negative functions of the discount rate. The computation of BCR and EBCR for our hypothetical projects presented in Table 11.4 are illustrated in Tables 11.12 and 11.13 respectively.

Table 11.10: Internal rate of return

Project	Cost	IRR calculations	IRR%	Rank
A	Rs. 20000	$= \dfrac{20000}{(1+r)} + \dfrac{5000}{(1+r)^2} + \dfrac{1000}{(1+r)^3} + \dfrac{1000}{(1+r)^4} + \dfrac{1000}{(1+r)^5}$	29.60	4
B	Rs. 20000	$= \dfrac{8000}{(1+r)} + \dfrac{10000}{(1+r)^2} + \dfrac{12000}{(1+r)^3} + \dfrac{5000}{(1+r)^4} + \dfrac{2000}{(1+r)^5}$	29.75	3
C	Rs. 20000	$= \dfrac{10000}{(1+r)} + \dfrac{10000}{(1+r)^2} + \dfrac{7000}{(1+r)^3} + \dfrac{6000}{(1+r)^4} + \dfrac{3000}{(1+r)^5}$	29.00	5
D	Rs. 20000	$= \dfrac{20000}{(1+r)} + \dfrac{6000}{(1+r)^2} + \dfrac{6000}{(1+r)^3} + \dfrac{2000}{(1+r)^4} + \dfrac{2000}{(1+r)^5}$	42.00	1
E	Rs. 20000	$= \dfrac{10000}{(1+r)} + \dfrac{8000}{(1+r)^2} + \dfrac{6000}{(1+r)^3} + \dfrac{5000}{(1+r)^4} + \dfrac{5000}{(1+r)^5}$	24.66	6
F	Rs. 20000	$= \dfrac{12000}{(1+r)} + \dfrac{12000}{(1+r)^2} + \dfrac{8000}{(1+r)^3} + \dfrac{5000}{(1+r)^4} + \dfrac{1000}{(1+r)^5}$	36.60	2

Table 11.11

Project	Terminal value	Terminal va;ie at r* = 20 (Approx) Rs.	Computed initial investment At r* = 10 (Approx) Rs.	NTV	Rank
A	$20000(1+r^*)^4 + 5000(1+r^*)^3 + 1000 (1+r^*)^2 + 1000 (1+r^*) +$	$1000 = 52490$	32200	20290	6
B	$8000(1+r^*)^4 + 10000(1=R^*)^3 + 12000(1+R^*)^2 + 5000(1+R^*) +$	$2000 = 59140$	32200	26940	3
C	$10000 (1+R^*)^4 + 10000(1+R^*)^3 \ 7000(1+R^*)^2 + 6000(1+R^*) +$	$3000 = 58280$	32200	26080	4
D	$20000(1+r^*)^4 + 6000(1+r^*)^3 + 6000(1+r^*)^2 + 2000(1+r^*) +$	$2000 = 64820$	32200.	32620	1
E	$10000(1+r^*)^4 + 8000(1+r^*)^3 + 6000(1+r^*)^2 + 5000 (1+r^*) +$	$5000 = 54200$	32200	32000	5
F	$12000(1+r^*)^4 + 12000(1+r^*)^3 + 8000(1+r^*)^2 + 5000(1+r^*) +$	$1000 = 64100$	32200	31940	2

Table 11.12: PI or Benefit–cost ratio

Project	Present value at i=10%	Initial Cost	BCR at i=10 percent	Rank
A	Rs. 24368	Rs. 20000	1.218	5
B	Rs. 29209	Rs. 20000	1.460	3
C	Rs. 20545	Rs. 20000	1.027	6
D	Rs. 30256	Rs. 20000	1.513	2
E	Rs. 26801	Rs. 20000	1.340	4
F	Rs. 30872	Rs. 20000	1.544	1

Table 11.13: Excess benefit–cost ratio

Project	NPV at i=10%	Initial cost	BCR at i=10%	Rank
A	Rs. 4368	Rs. 20000	0.218	5
B	Rs. 9209	Rs. 20000	0.460	3
C	Rs. 546	Rs. 20000	0.027	6
D	Rs. 10256	Rs. 20000	0.513	2
E	Rs. 6801	Rs. 20000	0.340	4
F	Rs. 10872	Rs. 20000	0.544	1

It can also be seen from Tables 11.12 and 11.13 that the NPV, BCR and EBCR give the same ranking to the six hypothetical projects.

However, these slightly different methods do not always give consistent ranking. When different projects involve different amounts of initial investment, the BCR and EBCR criteria may sometimes give different rankings than the NPV method. For example, consider the following mutually exclusive projects given in Table 11.14.

Table 11.14

	Project A	Project B
Present value of net cash flows	Rs. 20000	Rs. 8000
Initial cash outlay	Rs. 15000	Rs. 5000
Net present value	Rs. 5000	Rs. 3000
Profitability index	1.33	1.60
EBCR	0.25	0.375

According to the net present value method, project A would be preferred, whereas according to profitability index and EBCR criteria, project B would be preferred. Nevertheless the three criteria will always give the identical accept–reject decisions. For all practical purposes they are essentially the same. But for ranking projects with different initial capital outlays, BCR and EBCR seem to be better than the NPV criterion.[5]

Present Value Method *vs* Internal Rate of Return Method

In general, the present value and internal rate of return methods lead to the same accept or reject decision. In Fig. 11.1 the two methods applied to a typical investment project is illustrated.

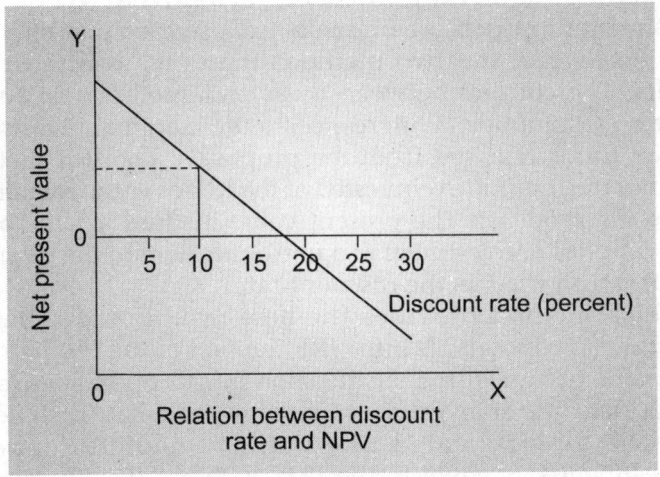

Fig. 11.1

Figure 11.1 shows the relationship between the NPV of a project and the discount rate employed. When the discount rate is zero, net present value is simply the total cash inflows less the total cash outlays of the project. Assuming that total inflows exceed total outflows and that outflows are followed by inflows, the typical project will have the highest net present value when the discount rate is zero. As the discount rate increases, the present value of future cash inflows decreases relative to the present value of cash outflows.

If the required rate of return is less than the internal rate of return, then the project would be accepted using either method. Assume that the required rate were 10 percent. As seen in Fig. 11.1, the net present value of the project then would be K. In as much as K is greater than zero, the project would be accepted by using the present value method. Similarly, the project would also be accepted by using the internal rate of return method as the internal rate exceeds the required rate. For required rates grater than IRR, the project would be rejected under either method. Thus it can be seen that the IRR and PV methods give identical answers with respect to the acceptance or rejection of an investment project.

However, important differences exist between the IRR and PV methods and they must be recognized. When two investment proposals are mutually exclusive, so that only one can be selected, the two methods may give contradictory results. The conflict between these two methods is due to different assumptions with respect to the marginal investment rate on funds released from the proposals. The IRR method assumes the funds are reinvested at the IRR over the remaining life of the proposal. The present value method, on the other hand, implies reinvestment at a rate equivalent to the required rate of return used as the discount rate.

Which method provides the best results in evaluating investment proposals? Is it the IRR method or the PV method? According to Van Horne the question hinges upon what is the appropriate rate of investment for the intermediate cash flows. We have already stated that the IRR method implies a reinvestment rate equal to the IRR, whereas the PV method implies a reinvestment rate equal to the required rate of return used as the discount factor. Perhaps the ideal solution would be, says Van Horne, to take the expected rate of investment for each period and calculate a terminal value.

If a choice is to be made, the present value method generally is considered theoretically superior. With the IRR method, the implied investment rate will differ depending upon the cash flow stream for each investment proposal under consideration.

For proposals with a high internal rate of return, a high reinvestment rate is assumed and for proposals with a low internal rate of return, a low reinvestment rate is assumed. Only in exceptional cases will the internal rate of return calculated represent the relevant rate for reinvestment of intermediate cash flows. With the present value method, on the other hand, the implied reinvestment rate represents the minimum return on opportunities available to the firm, given our assumptions. The reinvestment rate implied by the present value method may be conservative, but it has the advantage of being applied consistently to all investment proposals. To the extent that we can regard the required rate of return, as an approximate measure of the opportunity rate for reinvestment, the present value method is preferred to the internal rate of return method.

Net Terminal Value Method

The net terminal value (NTV) of an investment is the compounded value of its all net returns before depreciation and interest cost but after taxes less the compounded value of its initial investment, where the former compound rate is the reinvestment rate and the latter compound rate is the cost of capital. It can be computed with the aid of the following equation:

$$NTV = \sum_{t=1}^{T} Rt(1+r^*)^{T-t} - C(1+i^*)^T$$

Where r^* = reinvestment rate, and
$\quad\quad I^*$ = cost of capital

The above formula assumes the same reinvestment rate and the same cost of capital over the life of the project. Furthermore, it assumes that all loan (=C) is repaid at the project's termination. If it varies, the formula becomes more complicated. Instead of r^* and i^*, we will then have r^*t. If instead of net cash inflows, there is at any time of the project life net cash out flow, then that periods net returns be compounded by the expected capital cost in that period instead of by the reinvestment rate.

The NTV criterion work in the same way as does the NPV criterion in investment decisions. The projects which guarantee positive NTV are acceptable while the others are not economically viable. The project which promises a higher NTV is better than that gives a lower NTV. It should be noted here that in this criterion, NTV of each project is computed at the termination period of the project with the longest life for ranking of mutually exclusive projects. The use of the NTV criterion is illustrated in Table 11.15 for our hypothetical investment projects.

Since all projects in Table 11.15 guarantee positive NTV, all of them are acceptable. Their ranking is self-explanatory from the Table.

Advantages and Limitations of NTV

a. The NTV method takes into account all the cash proceeds during the life of the project.
b. It also take into account the timings of cash inflows and out flows over the life of the project.
c. It does not make any objectionable assumptions regarding the reinvestment rate. The reinvestment rate is assumed to be that rate at which net cash flows are expected to be invested.

An important limitation of the NTV method is that it requires the forecasts of reinvestment rates for future cash flows. Where these are not cash inflows this method requires expected capital costs in that future period. But in a world of uncertainty, forecasting of future reinvestment rates and capital costs encounters formidable problems.

MAPI Method

The Machinery and Allied Product Institute Method, popularly known as the MAPI method or MAPI formula, is one of the important methods of evaluating capital expenditure proposals. This method is associated with George Terborgh who developed it first in 1949. The MAPI method is fascinating and has some appealing characteristics that make it a theoretically acceptable method. But much confusion and misunderstanding surround the MAPI method in practice.

Table 11.15

Project	Terminal value	Terminal value at r* = 20 (Approx) Rs.	Computed initial investment At r* =10 (Approx) Rs.	NTV	Rank
A	$20000(1+r^*)^4 + 5000(1+r^*)^3 + 1000 (1+r^*)^2 + 1000(1+r^*) +$	$1000 = 52490$	32200	20290	6
B	$8000(1+r^*)^4 + 10000(1=R^*)^3 + 12000(1+R^*)^2 + 5000(1+R^*) +$	$2000 = 59140$	32200	26940	3
C	$10000 (1+R^*) +10000(1+R^*)^3 \; 7000(1+R^*)^2 + 6000(1+R^*) +$	$3000 = 58280$	32200	26080	4
D	$20000(1+r^*)^4 + 6000(1+r^*)^3 + 6000(1+r^*)^2 + 2000(1+r^*) +$	$2000 = 64820$	32200	32620	1
E	$10000(1+r^*)^4 + 8000(1+r^*)^3 + 6000(1+r^*)^2 + 5000(1+r^*) +$	$5000 = 54200$	32200	32000	5
F	$12000(1+r^*)^4 + 12000(1+r^*)^3 +8000(1+r^*)^2 + 5000(1+r^*) +$	$1000 = 64100$	32200	31940	2

The MAPI method can be considered as a sophisticated rate of return method. It achieves the computation of an after-tax return, called the MAPI rate of return. This after-tax return is a measure of profitability. It measures the return on average investment over the comparison period, generally one year. When a one year comparison period is used, it measures the after-tax return if the investment is undertaken now versus the alternative of waiting one more year before making the investment. Investment proposals may be ranked according to their rate of return. The rate of return may also be compared with the cost of capital to determine the profitability of a proposed investment.

The one year comparison period is generally used for calculating the MAPI rate of return or MAPIR. This is because the real choice is not, for example, between buying a new machine with a service life of, say 25 years and keeping a 25-year old machine for another 15 years, but by replacing the old machine now and replacing it later. (To base the analysis on a 15-year period is irrational as an old machine cannot or should not be kept for such a long period.) Effective management of capital expenditures requires a periodic review (if possible annually) of the facilities for determining the time that a replacement is required. In other words the management should ask itself once a year the question: is it advisable to replace each investment now or wait for another year and repeat the analysis then.

Another reason for using one year basis is that one year is the typical accounting period for financial reporting, and capital budgets are prepared annually. This means that if a different period is used by a company (for example, if capital expenditure is reviewed every two years that period could be used as the computation period for MAPI calculations).

When comparison periods longer than one year are used, the computation becomes more complicated. However, a shortcut method using simple averages can be thought of.

Like the ARR, the MAPI rate of return (which will be referred to as MAPIR) is found by dividing some form of benefits by an investment figure. Thus:

$$\text{MAPIR} = \frac{\text{Average benefits}}{\text{Average investment}}$$

Although the end result of using the latest (1967) MAPI method would be an after-tax of return on the average investment, more information could easily be derived. For example, it is easy to obtain from the form used the before-tax return and, with some manipulation, the payback period and the return on equity.

The MAPI method is used for evaluating minor capital expenditure projects or what may be called shop projects. It is not designed primarily for use in evaluating major capital expenditure projects (front office projects). However, it could be used, with some modifications, as a supplementary measure or as an initial screening device for major projects.

Computation of MAPI

The 1967 MAPI rate of return concept may be expressed as follows:

$$\text{After-tax return} = \frac{A + b - (c + d)}{X}$$

Where a = next-year or average operating advantage

b = next-year or average capital consumption avoided

c = next-year or average capital consumption incurred

d = next-year or average income tax adjusted

x = average net-investment.

For a one-year comparison period, the five components of the above formula may be described as follows:

a. Next-year operating advantage. This is the sum of the increase in revenue and the reduction in operating cost resulting from the project, as compared, of course, with the operating results that would be obtained in its absence.

b. Next-year capital consumption avoided. This is the difference between the initial investment (if, any) in the alternative and the amount remaining at the end of the year.

c. Next-year capital consumption incurred. Here we have the consumption of the project investment itself. It is the amount by which the remaining use-value (or as we shall call it, the 'retention value') of the project at the end of the year is below its cost. In other words, it is the amount by which this value runs off during the year (the cost of the project being taken as the initial value).

d. Next-year income-tax adjusted. It may be seen at the first glance that the after-tax return from a project is simply the pre-tax return reduced by the tax percentage. But the matter is not so simple, however. A more complex calculation is necessary. The adjustment itself is the net increase in income-tax resulting from the project.

e. Average net investment. This is the average of the net investment at the beginning and at the end of the year. The initial net investment is the installed cost of the project, less the initial investment in the alternative. The terminal net investment is the retention value of the project at the end of the year, less the disposable value of the alternative.

The Best Investment Criterion

In theory, the net terminal value method is the best technique for investment decisions. However, as usual, the best method is more complicated and its application requires more information which is rather difficult to come through than the other methods. Furthermore, the best method is not always the better method than the others. In fact, in the evaluation of normal investment projects, the best method gives the same decisions as some other methods. Thus for evaluating the economic worth of an investment proposal there may not be any unique best method and even if there is one, the same may not be practical. It is for these reasons that we discussed all the investment criteria in the previous sections.

Under conditions of complete certainty or equal degree of uncertainty about future cash flows from various projects, there is no justification for the use of either the pay back period method or the average annual rate of return method for any investment decision. The real choice, there fore, has to be made from the net present value (and its slight variants namely the benefit-cost-ratio and the excess benefit-cost–ration) internal rate of return and the net terminal value methods. Under ordinary circumstances all these discounted cash flow methods give identical results. However, under certain identical conditions these three methods may give different investment decisions.

Review Questions

1. Differentiate between capital expenditure and revenue expenditure.
2. List the general procedures for capital budgeting.
3. Mention the different types of investments.
4. List the principal methods of ranking alternate investment proposals.
5. Enumerate the merits and demerits of each method of evaluating capital investment proposals.

Problems

(1) *Niveditha & Company Ltd.*

Niveditha & Co.Ltd. is considering an investment in a new product developed by the company's R&D section. The investment required is Rs. 1 billion and the estimated gross return per annum is Rs. 0.1 billion. The cost of capital for the company is 15 percent. The life span of the product is 20 years. What is the expected profit or loss?

(2) *See Through (Private) Ltd.*

The management of See Through (Private) Limited is considering a set of investment projects. The net cashflows from each project are given below.

			Net cashflows				
Project	t1	t2	t3	t4	t5	t6	t7
A	Rs. 10000	Rs. 12000	Rs. 8000	Rs. 8000	Rs. 6000	Rs. 6000	Rs. 5000
B	Rs. 8000	Rs. 0000	Rs. 10000	Rs. 8000	Rs. 5000	Rs. 5000	Rs. 5000
C	Rs. 6000	Rs. 8000	Rs. 8000	Rs. 10000	Rs. 4000	Rs. 4000	Rs. 3000
D	Rs. 12000	Rs. 8000	Rs. 7000	Rs. 8000	Rs. 8000	Rs. 5000	Rs. 1000
E	Rs. 9000	Rs. 9000	Rs. 6000	Rs. 5000	Rs. 5000	Rs. 4000	Rs. 2000

Suppose the firm's cost of capital is 10 percent and each project will last for five years and there will be no scrap values. The net cash outflow for each project is Rs. 2000 Which of the above independent projects will be accepted (i) when a discount rate equal to the cost of capital is used to evaluate them? (ii) Will the ranking be different when you use Payback technique? Give reasons.

(3) Bindi Transport Corporation

Bindi Transport Company is a family concern owned by two sisters. Ramachandran, an MBA from Cochin University of Science And Technology has recently been appointed as the Financial Controller of the firm with specific responsibility of evaluating major capital investment projects. Ten major projects are under the consideration of the company. A brief description of each of these projects together with their costs and estimated cash flows (after tax plus depreciation) from each project over their estimated life are presented in the following table.

On the basis of the evaluation of the cash position of the company Ramachandran comes to the conclusion that Rs. 3 crore will be available for capital investments. The sisters believe that any project that does not generate less than 20 percent return is not worth undertaking.

Year	Expected Returns		
	Project A	Project B	Project C
1	Rs. 20,0000	Rs. 300,000	Rs. 400,000
2	Rs. 300,000	Rs. 500,000	Rs. 400,000
3	Rs. 500,000	Rs. 500,000	Rs. 600,000
4	Rs. 700,000	Rs. 800,000	Rs. 900,000
5	Rs. 900,000	Rs. 900,000	Rs. 900,000
6	Rs. 100,000	Rs. 110,000	Rs. 900,000
7	Rs. 120,000	Rs. 110,000	Rs. 140,000
8	Rs. 120,000	Rs. 140,000	Rs. 150,000
9	Rs. 100,000	Rs. 150,000	Rs. 80,0000
10	Rs. 500000	Rs. 100000	Rs. 50,000

1. The investment required for each project is Rs.20 lakh. Calculate the profitability of the each project.
2. If the company has only Rs. 20 lakh to invest, which project it should accept and why?

References

1. Abdel Samad, Mustafa H., *A Guide to Capital Expenditure Analysis*, Amacon, INC, 1973, p.9
2. Cost of capital is discussed in Chapter 12.
3. This technique is discussed in pp. 188–193.
4. The different ways of computing benefits using ARR, see Abdel Samad, Mustafa H, op.cit.,pp 45-65.
5. Van Horne prefers NPV to BCR in choosing mutually exclusive projects. According to him the NPV expresses in absolute terms the expected economic contribution of the project whereas the profitability index expresses only the relative profitability of the projects. See Van Horne James C, *Financial Management and Policy*; Third edition, Prentice Hall of India Pvt.Ltd., New Delhi, 1974, p.77.

12 Cost of Capital

Cost of capital plays a very predominant role in taking investment decisions. It has an important bearing on the acceptance or rejection of particular investments when the firm is a going concern. No matter what method is actually employed to judge the attractiveness or desirability of various investment proposals, the cost of capital must enter into the decisions. In chapter eleven we have seen that the discount rate is the vehicle through which investors judge the attractiveness of an investment opportunity. Now it can be stated that no project should be undertaken if its expected rate of return does not exceed the expected cost of capital. Alternatively,

  i. accept a project if its net present value is positive when all cash flows are discounted at the cost of capital rate and

 ii. accept a project if its internal rate of return is greater than the cost of capital.

In this chapter we propose to discuss the cost of capital—its definition and computation.

Definition of Cost of Capital

In pure economic theory, the cost of capital may be defined as the interest paid on borrowed money. But this is rather a simple definition because funds to finance an investment proposal may be obtained by a firm in a number of ways: by borrowing, by allowing short-term liabilities to expand, by selling marketable securities such as government bonds, by selling other assets or parts of its business, by issuing additional securities (either bonds, preferred stock, or common stock) or by committing funds generated by operations.

If an investment proposal is to be financed by borrowing, is the interest rate on the specific loan the relevant cost of capital for this investment? If this criterion is followed, the cost of capital would become an erratic quantity, fluctuating up or down as the firm obtains additional increments of capital from varying sources. Even though there are situations in which a particular investment can be related to a specific source of financing, more commonly there exists on the one hand a group of apparently desirable investment proposals and, on the other, a variety of sources of additional capital funds that taken together could supply the financing for the increased investments.

It is true that the determinants of the rate of interest provide much of the understanding necessary for the financial manager to interpret and/or forecast changes in the cost of capital in the economy. These are not; however, a sufficiently satisfactory explanation of the determinants of capital costs to the particular firm. In order for the financial manager to achieve the lowest cost of capital for his firm, he needs to be aware of the elements affecting the costs to his firm. The financial manager also finds it necessary to measure the cost to his firm if decisions are to be made concerning the proper amount of capital to employ relative to other factors of production, the total level of all factors to employ, and the allocation of capital in his firm.

Cost of Capital Calculations

In all cases of determining the cost of capital, whether the sources be permanent or temporary, debt or equity, common or preferred stock, we will note that the essential notion is that of opportunity cost. That is to say, the cost of capital sources to a firm is a matter of determining the alternative use to which capital can be put and the determining cost from the return in that use. But for simplicity, at this stage, expected outcome will be seen to consist of interest, discounts on debt, dividends, price appreciation, earnings per share, or some variation of these, whichever is the most appropriate to the case at hand.

The market values and/or book values are just that. In the discussion that follows we will be primarily concerned with the cost of capital determination of each of the several major sources of capital.

Cost of Equity Capital

The cost of equity capital **(common stock)** is the most difficult cost to measure. In theory it may be defined as the minimum yield that the firm must earn on the equity financed portion of its investments in order not to adversely affect the market price of the stock. In other words, it is rate at which an investment of a known equivalent risk sells in the market.

A number of valuation models have been formulated, but no one model has got universal acceptability. Some models emphasize dividends while some others emphasize earnings. A third group of formulations emphasize both. An accepted version is to regard the value of a stock as the present value of its future cash flows. One interpretation of common stock is that it is present value of all future cash dividends. The formula for evaluating such cash flows is given below:

$$PV = \sum_{t=1}^{t} \frac{Dt}{(1+Kc)t} \qquad \ldots 1$$

Where PV = The present market price per share of the stock
D = The cash dividends per share to be received
Kc = The cost of common stock capital
t = The number of relevant periods to take into account.

The cost can be found out by solving for Kc given that PV equals the current market price per share. The formula states that the cost of equity capital, Kc can be found out by finding that discount rate (d = Kc) which will make the right hand side of the equation equal to the left hand side. In other words, the present value of a share of stock (its current market price) is equal to the present value of all the dividends that will be forthcoming on that stock, taking into consideration the relevant timespan.

A slightly different version of the above formula is given below. This formula assumes that capital gains are realized cash flows and therefore must also be taken into consideration.

$$PVo = \sum_{t=1}^{t} \frac{Dt + (PVi - PVo)}{(1+Kc)^t} \qquad \ldots 2$$

Where PVo = The present value at the beginning of the period

PV = The present value at the end of the period and all other symbols are the same as they were in the first formula (1).

(PVi–PVo) i.e. the difference in share prices represents the capital gains from holding the shares. The formula explains that the present value of shares (current market price per share) is equal to the discounted sum to cash dividends and price appreciation. Alternatively, the cost of equity capital, when capital appreciation is taken into consideration, is that rate for Kc which equalizes both sides of the formula. As t approaches to infinity, the formula reduces to

$$PV = \frac{D}{Kc}$$

and $PVo = \dfrac{D + (PVi - PVo)}{Kc}$

By rearranging the formula, the cost of equity capital can be viewed in the following fashion:

$$Kc = \frac{D}{PV} = \frac{D}{mps} \text{ and}$$

$$Kc = \frac{D + (PVi - PVo)}{PVo} = \frac{D + (PVi - PVo)}{mps}$$

Where mps = the current market price per share.

Neither of the formulae given above is simple when it requires that the Financial Director estimates individual period-by-period cashflows either to perpetuity or at least for a period long enough to eliminate influences on the price of distant flows. These estimates, would in effect, be expected values of some subjective probability distribution for the investor and the Financial Director.

One way to simplify the analytical process is to assume that the cashflows increase at some constant rate, say g in perpetuity. Then $Kc = (D/PV)+g$.[1]

Equity stock valuation models based on earnings are also formulated. The simplest of them is $PV=E/Kc$, and the cost of capital becomes $Kc = E/PV$ where PV is current market price and E is earnings. E must be specified. It is current earnings, the validity of the model necessitates that investors expect no growth. If a new project is being considered, earnings would at least have to be adjusted for the project profit expectations, so that E becomes expected earnings. It is also assumed that the method of financing does not affect the risk of investment in the stock. According to some authors E should be regarded as earnings projected for years in the future in order to reflect growth.[2]

Because of the difficulty of using the complicated versions of the different formulations and because investor's in a firm's share may consider current earnings as a reasonable proxy for its future earnings or because current or expected earnings may be considered as reasonable proxies for dividends, the following simple formulation, viz.

$$Kc = \frac{E}{PV} \quad \frac{mps}{eps}$$

has found a prominent place in the investing community. This version is known as the earnings yield where Kc is the yield; E (eps) is the current market price per share. It is often used to determine the cost of equity capital. The inverse of the formula results in what is popularly known as the price-earnings ratio. If we redesignate $1/Kc$ as price-earnings ratio (PER), the formula for calculating the price-earnings ratio becomes

$$PER = \frac{mps}{eps}$$

Where PER = price-earnings ratio
      mps = the current price per share
      eps = the earnings per share, current or expected.

The above formulation is generally used by investors to place a value on a firm's share. The range of price-earnings ratios that is likely to be used in any given situation will depend on the risk class of the stock under consideration and the price-earnings ratio applicable to that class.

Whether earnings per share or dividends per share are the proper elements to be capitalized in determining the cost of equity capital is a mute point. The only factor common to those who argue either side of the matter is that they agree that some sort of 'benefit' ought to be capitalized. But the real question is what constitutes 'benefits'? The supporters of the earnings argue that the chief benefits received by a shareholder is the earnings of the firm and therefore that they should be capitalized. They hold the view that companies that pay no dividend or very low dividends can still have high common price. Since this is so, investors expect that the marginal productivity of the retained earnings will exceed the productivity of the capital already employed and that earnings expectations in the future will be even greater. Many investors in equity shares who employ the price-earnings ratio method apparently take this position.

The proponents of the dividend per share argue that dividends are the only benefits received by shareholders and that higher earnings per share are indicative only of higher dividends per share in the future and hence these cash benefits should be evaluated rather than earnings per share. But writers such as Miller and Modigliani are of the view that it does not make a great deal of difference whether earnings or dividends are capitalized.[3]

When computing the cost of equity capital, as in the case of other securities, the costs of flotation or sales of shares must be deducted from the price in the market.

Illustration

Assume that 'XYZ Ltd's shares sell at Rs.100 each. Rs.10 in cash dividends are expected indefinitely; capital appreciation is expected to be Rs.2 per share per year and flotation costs are Rs.5 per share. The cost of common stock to 'XYZ Ltd. would be:

$$Kc = \frac{Rs.\,10 + Rs.\,2}{Rs.\,100 - Rs.\,5} = \frac{12}{95} = 0.126 = 12.6\%$$

If under another model, the dividend growth rate in perpetuity were 2 percent and there where no capital appreciation, the cost would be

$$Kc = \frac{Rs.\,10}{Rs.\,95} + 0.2 = 0.105 + 0.02 = 12.5\%$$

If expected earnings were Rs. 12 and the price per share in the market less flotation costs were Rs. 95, the cost would be

$$Kc = \frac{Rs.\,12}{Rs.\,95} = 0.126 = 12.6\%$$

The above illustrations show that one could arrive at the same cost regardless of the model used. But in certain cases such a common result would be unlikely.

Cost of Long-Term Debt

The cost of long-term debt capital is the present effective interest rate for long-term securities of the firm.[4] It must be borne in mind that the indicated contractual interest rate of an outstanding debt security may not be the effective rate of interest because the security may be selling at a premium or discount. Generally bond tables are used to find out what the yield to maturity of the bonds would be in such cases. But the following formula can be used to make an approximate computation of yield when bonds are selling at a discount.

$$Kb = \frac{1 + D/n}{(p + MV)/2}$$

Where

Kb = Yield to maturity of bonds (Gross cost of debt issue)

1 = Interest income

D = the amount of the discount (Face value– market price)

n = the number of years to maturity

p = the current market price of the bond

MV = the maturity value of the bond.[5]

Illustration

If, for example, a Rs. 1000 face value bond with an interest of 10 percent is to mature in 10 years and were selling at Rs. 900, its yield to maturity according to our formula would be:

$$Kb = \frac{Rs.\,100 + Rs.\,100/10 \text{ years}}{(Rs.\,900 + Rs.\,1000)/2}$$

$$= \frac{Rs.\,100 + Rs.\,10}{Rs.\,1990/2} = \frac{Rs.\,110}{950} = 11.6\%$$

Cost of Short-Term Debt

The cost of short-term debt may not be easily recognized by the borrowing firm. This is because of the fact that lines of credit may require compensating balances of 10 to 20 percent of the line or the loan amount outstanding. This required deposit necessarily increases the cost of the source. Suppose a firm is given a credit of Rs. 100,000 at 6 percent interest. Also suppose that the firm is required to keep a demand deposit of at least 20 percent of the loan outstanding. In such a situation when the line is fully used the effective amount lent would only be Rs. 80000 but interest would have to be paid on Rs. 100,000. The effective or actual cost in this case would be 7.5 percent or 0.06 x Rs. 100,000/ Rs. 80000 rather than the quoted 6 percent.

The formula for calculating the effective rate when the firm is required to keep a compensating balance is

$$Kb = R.LO/EAL$$

Where

Kb = Effective cost of short-term capital
R = Quoted rate of interest
LO = Loan outstanding
EAL = Effective amount lent

The equation given below may be used to compute the amount a firm must borrow when a compensatory balance is a must to secure the loan.

$$X - AX = b$$

Where

$\quad\quad$ X = the amount borrowed

$\quad\quad$ A = percentage of compensating balance required, and

$\quad\quad$ b = the amount required by the firm.

Illustration

Suppose firm XYZ needs to borrow Rs. 100,000 and the bank insists the firm to maintain a deposit balance averaging 15 percent of the loan. If the firm normally carried no average balance, then the entire balance also must be borrowed. Then the entire amount of the loan thus would be

$\quad$ X – 0.15X = Rs. 100,000

$\quad$ 0.85X $\quad\quad$ = Rs. 100,000

$\quad$ X $\quad\quad\quad\quad$ = Rs. 117,647

If the firm normally carried a positive balance, the equation would be X –(AX—q) = b, where b is the average cash balance carried by the firm when not borrowing. For the above data, and assuming that the firm carried a Rs.10,000 average deposit balance, the amount that must be borrowed would be

$\quad$ X – (0.15X= Rs. 100,00) = Rs. 100,000

$\quad$ 0.85X $\quad\quad$ = Rs. 90000

$\quad$ X $\quad\quad\quad\quad$ = Rs. 105882.

If the loan were to be repaid in equal monthly installments, the actual cost would be approximately double the stated rate. The formula for calculating the actual rate in this case is

$$Kt = \frac{2mC}{A(n+1)}$$

Where $\;$ Kt = the effective cost of installment debt capital

$\quad\quad\quad$ m = Number of payments in one year

$\quad\quad\quad$ C = Rupee cost of the entire loan

$\quad\quad\quad$ A = Amount of the loan

Illustration

Suppose a one year Rs. 1000 loan at 5 percent were to be repaid in equal monthly installments, the effective amount lent would be a little over Rs. 500 and the total interest cost would be Rs. 50 (or 0.05x Rs. 1000). The effective or actual rate would be approximately 10 (Rs. 50/Rs. 500) percent. The application of the above formula in this case would give us an effective rate equal to 9.23 percent. Here n = 12, m =12, C = 0.05, and A = Rs. 1000

Therefore the effective rate of the installment loan is

$$Kt = \frac{2(12)\,(Rs.\,50)}{Rs.\,1000\,(12+1)} = 9.23\%$$

Cost of Preferred Stock

Computation of the cost of preferred stock is rather easy when compared to the computation of the cost of debt. The main difference between this computation and that for bonds is that dividends on preferred stock, although limited in nature (like interest on bonds), are presumed to be payable into perpetuity, for there is no maturity date for preferred stocks, even though the preferred stock may contain a sinking fund provision. Assuming that preferred dividends are not deductible for tax purposes, the formula for computing the cost of preferred stock is

$$Kp = \frac{EO}{P} = \frac{dps}{mps}$$

Where

    EO = dps = expected outcome (the dividend payment) per share

    P = mps = current market price per share

    Kp = cost of preferred stock

The cost of preferred stock is equal to the ratio of the actual dividend income per share to the current market price of the preferred stock. This ratio is popularly termed as the current dividend yield. Because dividends on stock are not generally deductible for tax purposes (now there is a tax in India), the yield (Kp) resulting from our calculation is not adjusted as it was in the case of bonds. But when there is a tax, that must be adjusted.

Illustration

Suppose a firm has 5 percent, Rs. 100 per value preferred stock outstanding. Assume that the market price of the preferred stock is Rs. 90 per share, the dividend yield on these preferred stocks and hence their cost is

$$Kp = \frac{EO}{P} = \frac{dps}{mps}$$

$$= \frac{Rs. 5}{Rs. 90} = (5\% \text{ of Rs. } 100 \text{ par})$$

$$Kp = 5.56\%$$

Cost of Retained Earnings

Computation of the cost of retained earnings is very much similar in nature to the computation of the Cost of other sources of funds. But many businessmen believe that there is no cost to the firm when earnings are retained. If what they mean by this is that there are no explicit or tangible costs for retained earnings, there can be no dispute. But nobody can deny the fact that opportunity costs are associated with retained earnings. In other words the cost of retained earnings is the investment opportunity (or opportunities) foregone by stockholders because of such retention. What kind of investment opportunity would be foregone? It should be an investment opportunity equal to the risk and expected return found in the firm itself. As there is, in fact, no investment opportunity to exactly the same kind and quality as the firm that retains the earnings, we use the firm itself to show the opportunity foregone. The retention of earnings by a firm is equivalent to a common stock, in the firm since it represents an ownership commitment. The cost of these retained earnings then is computed in the same manner as the cost of common stock. For example, if the expected earnings per share are Rs. 6 and the current market price is Rs. 50 per share, the cost of retained earnings will be Rs. 6/Rs. 50 or 12 percent (and there are no floatation costs).

But some argue that in computing the cost of retained earnings allowance should be given for the marginal tax rate on the common stockholders ordinary income. The argument runs as follows: the cost of retained earnings is measured by the opportunities foregone by the stockholders. Now if the retained earnings were paidout to stockholders for personal use, the additional income that they received would involve an increase in their tax. Because it is assumed that earnings received are reinvested in the common stock of the firm whose stock they already own, the investment of the disbursed earnings in these stocks should take into account the additional tax that the stockholders must pay. This calculation of the cost of retained earnings must account for this tax. For instance, assume that there are Rs. 6 earnings per share, all of which are paid out, and the marginal tax rate of all recipients is, say 25 percent. Then the amount available for reinvestment by the stockholders in this stock after taxes would be Rs. 4.50 or Rs. 6 – (Rs. 6 × 0.25). Since the stockholder still has to pay capital gains tax on the gains on price per share because of profitable reinvestment, the difference in taxability is perhaps only one half the marginal tax rate in as much as capital gains (long-term) are taxed at half the rate on ordinary income. For earnings per share for income taxes for the average stockholder at rate T overstates the tax saving because he pays a capital gains tax (eventually) and so the tax-saving by reinvestment is only about one half T (or T/2).

Relating this adjustment outcome to the current market price per share will bring a cost of retained earnings under one formulation to 10.5 percent (Rs. 5.25/Rs. 50). The formulations for this calculation is

$$Kr = \frac{eps(1 - T/2)}{mps}$$

Where T = the estimated average marginal tax rates of stock holders

mps = the current market price per share, and

Kr = the cost of retained earnings (the yield of disbursed earnings reinvested by stock-holders in the firm).

Weighted Average Cost of Capital

Once the cost of the constituent components of the capital structure has been computed, these costs may be weighed according to some standard and a weighted average cost of capital computed. As an illustration of only the mechanics of the computations, assume that 'XYZ Ltd' had the following capital structure at the end of the last financial year.

Items	Amount Rs.	Proportion (percent)
Debt	30,00000	30
Preferred stock	10,00000	10
Common stock	20,00000	20
Retained earnings	40,00000	40
	100,00000	100

Also suppose that the firm calculated the following explicit after tax costs for these component methods of financing.[6]

Items	Cost (percent)
Debt	8
Preferred stock	12
Common stock	15
Retained earnings	14

If the above weights are used, the weighted average cost of capital for our firm will be

Method of financing 1	Proportion percent 2	Cost percent 3	Weighted cost percent (2 × 3) 4
Debt	30	8	2.40
Preferred stock	10	12	1.20
Common stock	20	15	3.00
Retained earnings	40	14	5.60
Weighted average			
Cost of capital			12.20

In an operational sense, a firm's overall cost of capital is measured as the after tax current cost of the individual sources in the total mix of sources expected to be used in the future financing weighted by the expected long-run market proportions felt by the firm to minimize the cost of capital at the level of capital needs anticipated. This may be expressed symbolically as follows:

$$Wd \times Kd = Wd\ Kd$$
$$Wp \times Kp = Wp\ Kp$$
$$We \times Ke = We\ Ke$$
$$Wr \times Kr = Wr\ Kr$$

Where Wd = The expected proportion of debt

Wp = The expected proportion of preferred stock

We = The expected proportion of equity capital

Wr = The expected component of retained earnings

Kd = Cost of debt

Kp = Cost of preferred stock

Ke = Cost of equity capital

Kr = Cost of retained earnings.

Now the real question is whether 12.20 percent represents 'XYZ Ltd's real cost of capital to be used for evaluating investment projects. If the business risk is held constant, is 12.20 percent is the minimum rate of return that must be realized as an investment to leave the market price of the stock unchanged? The answer to this question depends upon how accurately the firm has measured the individual marginal costs upon the weighting system, and a number of other assumptions. Assume for the time being that the firm was able to measure accurately the marginal cost of the component sources of financing. Now let us examine the importance of the weighting system.

Weighting System

Marginal Weights: The underlying assumption in any weighting system is that the firm will in fact raise capital in the proportions specified. Because the firm raises capital marginally to make a marginal investment in new projects, we need to work with marginal cost of capital to the firm as a whole. The rate depends upon the mix of funds employed to finance investment projects. In other words, we are concerned with new or incremental capital and not with capital raised in the past. In order for the weighted average cost of capital to represent a marginal cost, the weights employed must be marginal. In other words, the weights must correspond to the proportions of financing inputs the firm intends to employ. If they do not, capital is raised on a marginal basis in proportions other than those used to calculate this cost. Consequently, the real weighted average cost of capital will differ from that calculated and used for capital investment decisions. An obvious bias results if the actual cost is greater than that which is measured, certain investment projects will be accepted that will leave investors worse of than before. On the other hand, if the actual cost is less than the measured cost, projects will be rejected that could increase shareholder wealth. Hence the 12.20 percent weighted average cost of capital calculated in our example is realistic only if the firm intends to finance in the same proportions as its existing capital structure.

It is an accepted fact that raising of capital is 'lumpy', and strict proportions cannot be maintained. For instance a firm might find it difficult to finance each project undertaken with say 30 percent debt, 15 percent convertible securities, 20 percent equity and 35 percent retained earnings. In practice, it may finance with debt in one instance and with equity or retained earnings in another. But over a long period of time, most firms may be in a position to finance in roughly a proportional manner. It is in this sense that we try to measure the marginal cost of capital for the package of the financing employed. Another problem is that retained earnings, a chief source of funds for most firms, are constrained by the absolute amount of earnings. If a firm's investment opportunities warrant expansion at a rate faster than the growth in earnings, financing by means of retained earnings must diminish relative to other means. Where the expansion is expected to be continuous for a number of years, the financing package of the firm is subject to the constraint with respect to the ability of the firm to retain earnings. This constraint must be recognized. Often, however, expansion is concentrated in a few years so that in the long-run the firm is able to finance with a roughly constant proportion of retained earnings.

Change in Capital Structure

A problem occurs as and when the firm wishes to change its capital structure. The costs of the component methods of financing usually are based upon the existing capital structure, and' these costs may vary from those that rule once the firm has achieved its desired capital structure. Because the firm cannot measure its costs directly at the desired capital structure, these costs must be estimated. During the period of transition from the present capital structure to one that is desired, the firm usually will rely upon one type of financing. It might, for example, finance with debt until the desired capital structure is achieved.

Modigliani–Miller Argument

F. Modigliani and M. Miller are of the opinion that the capital structure of a firm does not affect the cost of capital. In other words, any rational choice of debt and equity results in the same cost of capital. This proposition has been stated in the form of a theorem as follows:

The average cost of capital to any firm is completely independent of its capital structure and is equal to the capitalization rate of a pure equity stream of its (risk) class.[7]

Their argument was based on a number of assumptions. They are:

i. The average expected future net operating income (NOI) is represented by a subjective random variable and that all investors agree as the expected value of this probability distribution;

ii. All firms can be placed in equivalent risk classes so that all firms in a class can be termed as homogeneous;

iii. Capital markets are perfect. Information is perfect to all investors, investors are rational, and no transactions costs exist.

They support their arguments about the value of the firm being unaffected by the financial package under these assumptions by pleading that rational investors will use arbitrage in the market to prevent the existence of two assets in the same risk class and with equal expected returns from selling at different prices. For instance, the shares of two firms in the same risk class with equal expected returns cannot sell at different prices, simply because one has a larger proportion of debt than the other, as the investor can use personal leverage as a substitute for firm leverage to achieve identical results (Leverage means the ratio of preferred stock and bonds to total capitalization).

Imagine that we have two firms that fall in the same risk class and each has an expected value of Rs. 10 lakh of NOI. Also assume that one firm has Rs. 20 lakh of 5 percent debt outstanding and the other is an all-equity firm.

Under the NOI and MM models the value of their securities will be the same. If they were not, investors will use arbitrage to gain from this market imperfection.

Illustration

Assume that the market value of 'ABC Ltd.' is less than that of 'XYZ Ltd' as shown in Table 12.1. Assume further that the D/E ratio for 'ABC Ltd' is zero and for 'XYZ Ltd.' is Rs. 20 lakh/Rs. 40 lakh = 22 percent. In this model the return to shareholders of 'XYZ Ltd.' is 10 percent. But 'XYZ Ltd's share involves more risk because of the prior fixed interest claim.

Table 12.1

	ABC Ltd	XYZ Ltd
NOI	Rs.1,000,000	Rs. 1,000,000
Interest	..	Rs. 100,000
NI	Rs. 1,000,000	Rs. 900,000
Kc =10%	× 10	× 10
Equity	Rs. 10,000,000	Rs. 9,000,000
Debt	..	Rs.2,000,000
Total value of firm	Rs. 10,000,000	Rs.11,000,000

As we know that investors confronted with choice of investment outlets will prefer the investment that promises the greatest return, given that the risks are equal, or prefer the investments that possess less risk, provided that the returns are equal. Therefore, rational investors will sell 'XYZ Ltd's shares and buy 'ABC Ltd's shares until return for a given level of risk is equal. They will do this for all firms in a given risk class.

Criticism of the MM Theorem

The MM theorem is a truism but cannot stand the test of scientific scrutiny. Many points of criticism have been leveled against it. Firstly, it asserts that the leverage cannot influence the price of common stock, because the individual investor will neutralize any change in the leverage on corporate account by an equivalent and offsetting change in his leverage on personal account. But the fact remains that an individual corporate investor will not be able to make costless, effortless and frequent shifts as between common stock on the one side and preferred stocks and bonds on the other. Secondly, the MM theorem does not consider the tax aspect which is very important in the context of capital. Thirdly, the assertion of 'equal costs of funds from all sources' are not correct except under the highly artificial assumptions of perfect competition. Fourthly, the theorem signifies a static approach to the problem of cost of capital. The equilibrium position that it assumes as present at all conditions of capital mobilization for a firm, does not describe the real state of affairs, because the ral capital market is one which is characterized by disequilibrium.

Supply of Capital

Supposing that the firm has determined an appropriate capital structure, it faces the problem of having to raise capital in roughly in those proportions. The crucial question is that whether it can really raise this capital at an average real cost equal to the weighted average cost of capital. Writers such as Duesenberry, Robert Lindsey and Arnold postulate an upward sloping curve of capital. This means that the weighted average cost of capital rises with the total amount of capital raised.[8] According to them, in the short-run, the average cost curve rises in a manner similar, perhaps, to those shown in Fig. 12.1. The exact shape of the supply curve will vary according to the size of the firm and conditions in the capital market.

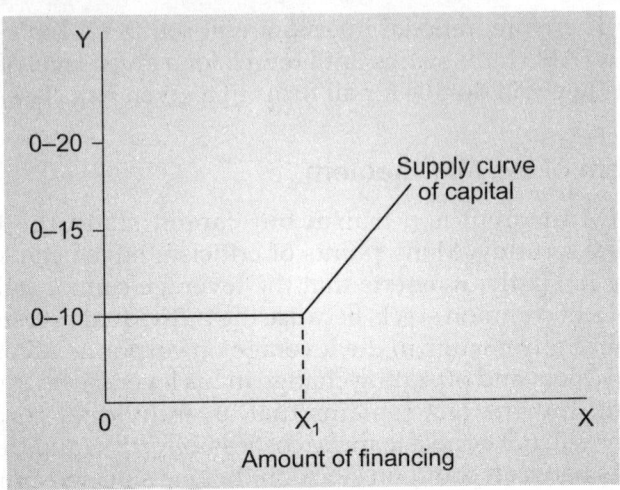

Fig. 12.1

An upward rising supply curve indicates that the firm cannot raise an unlimited amount of capital at one time at the same cost. Instead a digestion period is required during which the firm invests in projects and demonstrates to investors and creditors its ability to generate profits on those investments. Figure 12.1 implies that at a moment in time, the firm can raise capital at real cost of 10 percent up to an amount of OX rupees. After OX, the average cost of capital rises. Given a sufficient digestion period, the firm again will, however, be able to raise capital at a real cost of 10 percent.

The cost of capital approach described so far implies a horizontal supply curve. The assumption is that the company can raise any amount of capital at the measured-average real cost. But in the short-run, as pointed out earlier, this occurrence is unlikely or is only a very remote possibility. However, most companies are investing continuously in projects and financing these investments. If the amount of financing in one period does not differ much from the amounts on previous occasions, there is no reason to believe that the real cost of capital will fluctuate significantly from period to period. In each period, the firm would be raising capital in approximately the same area of the supply curve. In addition, the supply curve would not be sharply upward sloping in the initial stages. In spite of this, if the firm does have to undertake substantial financing in one period, and this amount is significantly out of line with amounts in previous periods, the firm's cost of capital may be higher. This would influence the investment decision. Certain projects yielding returns close to the measured cost of capital cut off rate no longer would be acceptable. The company may choose to postpone these projects until a time when the amount of capital investment, and financing, is not expected to be as large.

Thus an upward sloping supply curve for capital adds a new dimension to the investment and financing decisions. It indicates that the cost of capital cannot be determined independently of the amount of funds to be raised. However, the amount to be raised depends upon the investment opportunities available. Therefore, the investment and financing decisions of the firm are determined simultaneously. An illustration of this occurrence of this is shown in Fig. 12.2. The intersection of the marginal cost of capital line with the marginal rate of return as investment line determines the amount of funds to be invested and the amount of financing for the period.

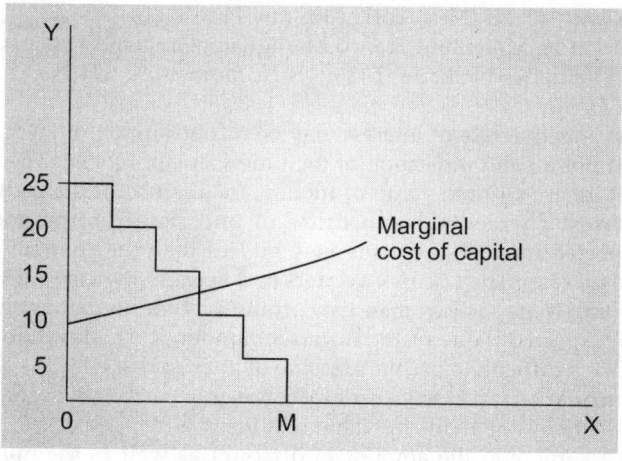

Fig. 12.2

It is evident from the discussion that the financial manager must be well informed of capital market conditions that would cause the marginal cost of capital of the firm to raise the amount of funds required. These conditions should be taken into account in formulating the capital budgets of companies.

Review Questions

1. What do you mean by cost of capital?
2. How do you calculate
   a. The cost of equity capital?
   b. The cost of debt capital?
   c. The cost of retained earnings?
3. What do you mean by weighted average cost of capital? Explain with the help of an example.
4. State the MM theorem.

References

1. For the derivation of this formula, see Myron J. Gordon and Eli Shapiro; Capital Requirement Analysis: The Required Rate of Profit, *Management Science*, 3:102 (October, 1956)
2. Benjamin Graham David L., Dodd and Sidney Cattle; *Security Analysis*, 4th Ed (New York: McGraw Hill, 1962)
3. Merton H. Miller and Franco Modigliani; Dividend Policy, Growth and Valuation of Shares; *The Journal of Business, 34: 411. No.4 (October, 1961).*
4. The effective rate of interest may be a contribution of three factors and not a valid indication of the time value of money. These three factors are (i) time value of money, (ii) the use of the contractual interest payments, but because of uncertainty of payment the expected interest payments may be less than the contractual, (iii) the investors may be risk averters and because the amount they are willing to pay is less than they would pay for an amount equal to the expected value of the uncertain amounts. The last two factors make it difficult to use the measure of interest cost which is obtained from market prices to take into account only the time value of money.
5. Usually by the maturity value of a bond will be assumed to be its face value and the amount of discount as well as the number of years to maturity will be based on that figure and the maturity date. In some cases a firm may anticipate retiring the bonds some time before maturity. It can ordinarily do this at its option but usually at a price above the face value. Under these circumstances the 'call

value' of the bond then becomes MV, and n will be measured from what it would otherwise be because the magnitude of n and MV changes.

6. The cost of retained earnings is less than the cost of common stock because of the absence of under pricing and floatation costs associated with a new stock issue.

7. Franco Modigliani and Merton H. Miller; 'The Cost of Capital, Corporation Finance and Theory of Investment', *The American Economic Review*, 48: 3, June 1958.

8. See, for example, James S Duesenberry; *Business Cycle and Economic Growth,(New York: McGraw* Hill Book Company, 1958) Chapter 5 and J Robert Lindsey and Arnold W Sametz, *Financial Management – An Analytical Approach* (Homewood Ill: Richard D. Irwin Inc, 1967), Chapters 19 and 20.

13 Techniques and Managerial Application of Cost–Volume–Profit Analysis (Break-even Analysis)

A picture is worth a thousand words. The break-even chart is a picture which sums up for management the characteristics of its profit structure as it was in the past or as it will appear in the future. This impression cannot be obtained from reports, tabulations or profit and loss statement.

The analysis of the impact of profits on changes in the volume of sales can be a useful tool for management. Decisions such as product pricing, level of production or introduction of new products can be made more effectively when volume-profit relationship is considered.

Generally the term break-even analysis is used to describe this activity. Since a reasonable prospect of revenues covering expenses might be an important constraint in evaluating new products or projects, the determination of break-even point is indeed an important element of this analysis. In most cases, however, it is useful to consider not only the point at which a product may be expected to break-even, but also the probable profit at various levels of activity. It is not enough for management to be concerned with breaking even; the maximization of profit must be considered as well.

Break-even Point Defined

The break-even point can be defined as that volume level (or sales) at which revenue exactly equals total cost. The firm neither makes a profit nor suffers a loss at this point. In other words the break-even point can be defined as that level of sales or production at which profit is zero or break-even point is a no profit no loss point.

The break-even analysis is directly concerned with the effect on profits of changes in:

  i. fixed costs;
  ii. variable costs;
  iii. sales quantities;
  iv. sales prices; and
  v. sales mix.

An analysis offering relevant insights into these effects and their interrelationships in the enterprise has obvious merit. The management must realize the importance of this aspect of break-even analysis.

Here we propose to emphasize (i) the basic concepts underlying the break-even analysis; (ii) indicate some of its applications; and (iii) consider its relationship with profit planning and control.

Before we can interpret a break-even chart we need to know something about costs. Costs are expenses necessarily incurred by an organization in producing its product.

Classification of costs according to the concept of cost variability requires three cost categories.[1]

  i. Fixed costs.
  ii. Variable costs.
  iii. Semi-variable (or semifixed) costs.

For simplicity we have classified costs into two categories—fixed and variable. These data are obtained from:

  i. Variable budget information, and
  ii. Analysis and classification of accounts.

In considering the variable budget concept, the following problem areas are important:

  i. Definition of costs when related to output or activity
  ii. Selection of an activity base that appropriately measures departmental output or activity
  iii. Methods of analyzing costs to identify separately the fixed and variable components of costs
  iv. Use and application of the variable budget concept.[2]

Usually the total cost function is drawn on the assumption of constant factor cost prices, plant scale, technology and efficiency. So also, the total revenue function assumes constant selling prices and unchanged product mix.[3] This enables us to plot total costs and total revenues as straight lines.

Construction of Break-even Chart

Revenue Function

Assuming that the price of the product being sold is set, the total revenue will be a function of the units sold. Symbolically this can be represented as

$$Y = bX$$

Where $Y =$ total revenue
$b =$ the price per unit
$X =$ the units sold.

At zero unit sold, total revenue will be zero. Hence the total revenue line will pass through the origin of the graph.

Cost Function

The cost function is formulated on the assumption that all expenses may be classified as either entirely fixed or entirely variable. By definition, there will be some fixed expense at zero sales but no variable expense. For every unit sold, the total expense will increase by an amount equal to b'. Symbolically, the cost function can be written as

$$Y' = a' + b'X$$

Where $Y' =$ total cost
$a' =$ fixed expenses
$b' =$ variable cost per unit
$X =$ number of units sold.

The following break-even charts are drawn based on the data given in Table 13.1.

Table 13.1

	Fixed cost	Variable cost	Total (Rs)
Budgeted sales			500000
(200000 units @ Rs. 25 per unit)			
Budgeted cost:			
Direct material		Rs. 900000	
Direct labour		Rs. 1000000	
Factory overhead	Rs. 700000	Rs. 300000	
Administrative expenses	Rs. 600000	Rs. 100000	
Distribution expenses	Rs. 500000	Rs. 300000	
Total	Rs. 1800000	Rs. 2600000	4000000
Budgeted profit			600000
Capacity of production 250,000 units			

From the information given in Table 13.1 let us calculate the break-even point of ABC Ltd. by using the above formula.

The equation for the total revenue curve is

$$Y = bX$$

Substituting Rs. 25 for b we get

$$Y = 25X$$

The equation for the total cost curve is

$$Y' = a' + b'X$$

Substituting for a' and b' the values we get

$$Y = 1800000 + 13X$$

At the break-even point, Y must be equal to Y'; thus

$$
\begin{aligned}
25X &= 1800000 + 13X \\
25X - 13X &= 1800000 \\
12X &= 1800000 \\
X &= 150000 \text{ units.}
\end{aligned}
$$

Let us plot the above information in the form of a graph (Fig. 13.1). The vertical axis in the graph represents revenue and cost in terms of rupees. The horizontal axis represents the activity base, the volume or output sold – in our case units sold. The three lines in the graph represent total revenue, total cost and variable cost. The point at which the revenue and total cost line intersect is the break-even point (Rs.3750000 or 150000 units). The area between the lines to the right of this point represents the profit potential.

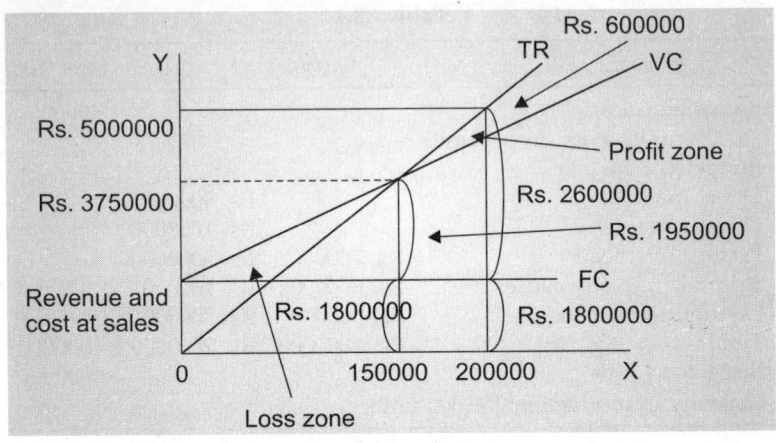

Fig. 13.1

The break-even charts may take different forms. The needs of the specific situation should dictate the choice of the form to be used.

When expenses are plotted, the fixed expenses are generally plotted first (i.e. below variable costs). This is done in Fig. 13.1. But another variation frequently used shows fixed costs plotted above variable costs. This is done in Fig. 13.2. This method has the advantage of indicating the recovery of fixed costs at various volume levels before profits are realized.

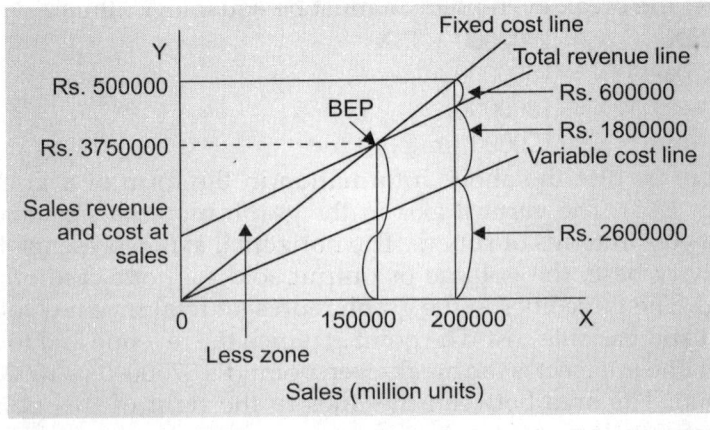

Fig. 13.2

A third method shows the various fixed and variable costs in particular sequence; for example, in the order found on the income statement for major classifications such as manufacturing, distribution, and administrative expenses. This is shown in Fig. 13.3.

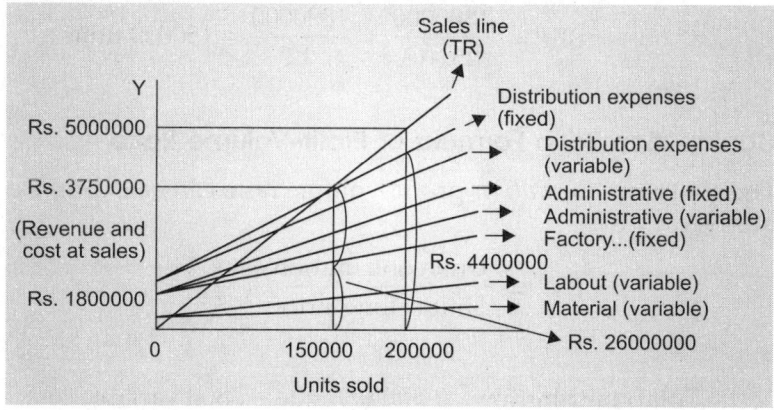

Fig. 13.3

Obviously, the break-even point is the same in each of the three methods explained above.

The break-even point as well as other important information may be determined through the use of simple mathematical procedures. There are a number of formulas that may be used for these computations; the important among them are given below:

1. **Break-even calculation based on unit contribution:** Unit contribution is the difference between selling price and the out of pocket or variable cost of one unit of production. To find the break-even point we find the level of production at which fixed costs are recovered by variable contribution. This is done by dividing the fixed costs by the unit contribution.

$$\text{Break-even point} = \frac{\text{Fixed cost}}{\text{Unit selling price} - \text{Variable cost per unit}}$$

Symbolically this can be written as $\dfrac{F}{C}$ or $\dfrac{F}{Sp - v}$

Where F = fixed cost

C = Unit contribution (Unit selling price – unit variable cost)

Using the above formula, let us compute the break-even point of company ABC Ltd.

$$BEP = \frac{1800000}{25-13} = \frac{1800000}{12} = 150000 \text{ units}$$

Contribution Ratio Formula or Profit–Volume Ratio

The contribution ratio or profit–volume ratio can be expressed in several ways:

$$PV = \frac{\text{Unit contribution}}{\text{Unit selling price}} = \frac{C}{Sp}$$

Or

$$PV = \frac{\text{Total contribution}}{\text{Total selling price}} = \frac{\text{Total revenue} - \text{Total variable cost}}{\text{Total revenue}}$$

$$PV = 1 - \frac{\text{Variable costs}}{\text{Corresponding sales}}$$

2. **Break-even sales using contribution ratio:** Basing company ABC Ltd's data we can find out the break-even sales using contribution ratio formula.

$$BES = \frac{\text{Fixed cost}}{PV}$$

Substituting company ABC Ltd's data we get

$$BES = \frac{\text{Rs. } 1800000}{\dfrac{25-13}{25}}$$

$$= \frac{\text{Rs. } 1800000}{12/25}$$

$$= \frac{\text{Rs. } 1800000}{0.48} = \text{Rs. } 3750000$$

$$\text{BEP in units} = \frac{\text{Rs. } 3750000}{25} = 150000 \text{ units}$$

Or

$$\text{BES} = \frac{\text{Fixed cost}}{1 - \dfrac{\text{Variable cost}}{\text{Corresponding sales}}}$$

Substituting the above data we get

BES = Rs. 1800000

$$= \frac{1 - \dfrac{\text{Rs. } 2600000}{\text{Rs. } 5000000}}{} = \frac{\text{Rs. } 18000000}{1 - 0.52} = \frac{\text{Rs. } 1800000}{0.48}$$

= Rs. 3750000   or

$$= \frac{\text{Rs. } 3750000}{25} = 150000 \text{ units}$$

The above formula provides an insight into the features of break-even analysis. That is when we divide variable costs by sales we get variable cost ratio. For instance, the 0.52 (that is Rs. 2600000/5000000) derived above show that variable cost is 52 percent of sales. In other words 0.52 paisa of every sales rupee is necessary to recover exactly the variable cost. Deducting the variable cost ratio from 1 (one) we get the profit-volume ratio. For instance, the 0.48 (that is 1 − 0.52) derived in the illustration above shows that 48 percent of sales are available to cover fixed costs (and generate profits). In other words 48 paisa of each sales rupee is available to cover fixed cost and to make some profit. Since profit at break-even is zero, dividing the fixed cost by the profit–volume ratio (0.48 also referred as PV) gives the number of rupees of sales revenue necessary to exactly recover fixed costs (Rs. 1800000/0.48 = Rs. 3750000).

Profit Formula

Profit at a given sales can be expressed in three different ways. Profit (P) = Sales (S) minus Fixed expenses (F) minus variable expenses (V)

$= S - F - V$

$= S - (F + V)$ ...1

or, the more usual way to express the formula for profit in cost–volume–profit analysis is:

$P = (S \times Pv) - F$ ...2

Instead of viewing profit as the difference between total sales and total expenses, the second interpretation is to be preferred (namely, that profit is the gross contribution of sales less the fixed expenses). Using the break-even chart, profit can be expressed in a third way also:

P = (Sales – Break-even sales) $\times$ PV

 $= (S - BE)PV$ ...3

This last formula separates the profitable range of sales (Sales – BES) from that portion of sales whose contributions pay for the fixed expenses. Since profit is developed above the break-even point at the PV rate, the range of profitable sales is multiplied by the PV to get the profit.

As an example let us compute present profit in a company with an annual fixed expense of Rs. 400000, a PV of 0.40 and present sales of Rs. 1500000 using formula 2 and 3.

Formula 2 does not require the BE calculation:

$P = (S \times PV) - F$

 $= (Rs.\ 1500000 \times 0.40) - Rs.\ 400000$

 $= Rs.\ 200000$

Formula 3 first requires that BES to be computed. Thus

$BES = F/PV$

  $= Rs.\ 400000/0.40$

  $= Rs.\ 100000$

$P = (S - BE)\ PV$

 $= (Rs.\ 1500000 - Rs.\ 100000)\ 0.40$

 $= Rs.\ 200000.$

Margin of Safety Formula

The margin of safety is the percentage drops in sales that can occur before any loss starts. This formula is a dramatic way of calling management's attention to how close their sales level is to their break-even point. It can be expressed in one of the two ways:

$$MS = \frac{Profit}{Contribution} \times 100$$

$$= \frac{P}{C} \times 100 \qquad \qquad ...4$$

$$MS = \frac{(Sales - BES)}{Sales} \times 100$$

$$= \frac{(S - BES)}{S} \times 100 \qquad \qquad ...5$$

Both formulae are used. Using the data from the above profit calculations, the total rupee contribution is Sales × PV. Or Rs. 1500000 × 0.40 = Rs. 600000 and

$$MS = \frac{P}{C} \times 100$$

$$= \frac{Rs.\ 200000}{Rs.\ 600000} \times 100$$

$$= 33.3\%$$

Or

$$MS = \frac{S - BES}{S} \times 100$$
$$= Rs.\ 1500000 - Rs.\ 1000000 / 1500000$$
$$= Rs.\ 500000 / Rs.\ 1500000$$
$$= 33.3\%$$

The MS percentages of 33.3 means that sales could drop 33.3% before losses develop. Another way of looking at the situation is that the company's break-even point is 66.7% of present sales.

Obviously if the company is selling at their BES rate their margin of safety is zero.

Sales Formula

Often it is desirable to know what level of sales is required to satisfy certain conditions of costs, contribution, etc. Sales can be expressed in various ways:

$$S = F + V + P \qquad \text{...6}$$
$$\text{Or } S = (P + F)/PV \qquad \text{...7}$$

The second one (7) is the better way of expressing sales for cost-volume-profit use. Again, using the above data, assume we want to know how much sales are required to earn Rs. 200000 profit.

$$S = (P + F)/PV$$
$$= \text{Rs. } 200000 + \text{Rs. } 400000/0.40$$
$$= \text{Rs. } 1500,000$$

Fixed Expense Formula

Often, management wishes to know how fixed expenses are affected by certain proposed actions, perhaps to justify an increase in variable expenses, etc. The formula is:

$$F = S - V - P$$
$$= S - (V + P) \qquad \text{...8}$$
$$F = (S \times PV) - P \qquad \text{...9}$$

Using the same data, we may wish to know how much fixed expenses should be to provide a profit of Rs. 200000.

$$F = (S \times PV) - P$$
$$= (1500000 \times 0.40) - \text{Rs. } 200000$$
$$= \text{Rs. } 600000 - \text{Rs. } 200000$$
$$= \text{Rs. } 400000.$$

Variable Expense Formula

In a manner similar to using the fixed expense formula, from solving for the variable expenses, management might want to know how much the variable cost would change with changes in prices, volume etc. The formula for this is:

$$V = S - (F + P) \qquad \text{...10}$$

To find the amount of variable expenses from these same data:

$$V = S - (F + P)$$
$$= \text{Rs. } 1500000 - (\text{Rs. } 400000 + \text{Rs. } 200000)$$
$$= \text{Rs. } 1500000 - \text{Rs. } 600000$$
$$= \text{Rs. } 900000.$$

Techniques and Managerial Applications

Summary of Break-even Terms and Formulae

Abbreviations and terms	Break-even formulae
PV = Profit volume ratio or Contribution ratio	$PV = C/Sp$
C = Contribution (Sp – V)	$PV = \dfrac{Sp - V}{Sp}$
Sp = Selling Price	
V = Variable cost.	$PV = (1 - V/S)$
BES = Break-even sales	$BES = F/PV$
F = Fixed cost	$P = S - (F + V)$
	$P = (S - BES)\, PV$
P = Profit	$P = (S + F)/PV$
MS = Margin of safety	$F = S - (V + P)$
	$F = (S \times PV) - P$
	$V = S - (F + P)$
	$PV = (P + F)/S$
MS = (S – BES)/S (100)	$S = V/(1 - PV)$
	$V = S\,(1 - PV)$
	$MS = S - BES$
	$MS = P/C \times 100$

Basic Assumptions Underlying Break-even Analysis

The basic assumptions underlying the break-even analysis (Cost–volume–profit analysis) are:

i. The concept of cost variability is valid and, therefore, costs can be classified realistically as fixed and variable.

ii. There is a relevant range of validity for all facets of the analysis that must be observed.

iii. Selling price does not change as physical volume of sales change.

iv. There is only one product, or, in case of multiple products, the sales-mix remains constant.

v. Basic management policies on operations remain more or less the same in the short run.

    vi. The general price level remains stable in the short run.

    vii. Sales and production levels are synchronized; in other words inventory remains zero.

    viii. Efficiency and productivity per person remains essentially unchanged in the short run.

Some of the Assumptions Relaxed

As we have already noted the break-even analysis or cost-volume- profit analysis is developed under the assumption that the concept of cost variability is valid and, further, that it is possible to identify fixed and variable components of cost. Many leading firms have shown that this concept and its applications are valid.

But it is likely that neither one will be a straight line. It is possible that as more variable factors of production are applied to the fixed factors, a point will be reached where there is a decrease in efficiency. This will cause the total expense curve to have an increasing slope. It is probable that, at low levels of production, efficiency was actually increasing; thus the slope of the total expense curve would be decreasing at that level of production. But this latter possibility can be ignored with no material consequence to the analysis, as the firm is more likely to be operating at a level where the marginal costs of successive units are either constant or increasing.

It is interesting to see that there are two break-even points in Fig. 13.4.

In Fig. 13.4 the first break-even point occurs at point B and the other at point K. This occurs because it is assumed that the total cost curve, instead of being a straight line, curves upward (reflecting decreasing efficiency). The firm will actually attempt to operate somewhere between sales of OQ and OR units. The point of maximum profitability will be where the vertical distance between the curve and the line is the greatest (where the difference between revenues and costs is the greatest), in this case at sales OS. The total revenue curve, when plotted as a straight line, assumes that no decrease in prices will be necessary to increase sales. It is assumed that in order to increase unit sales, it is necessary to reduce price, then the total revenue plot need

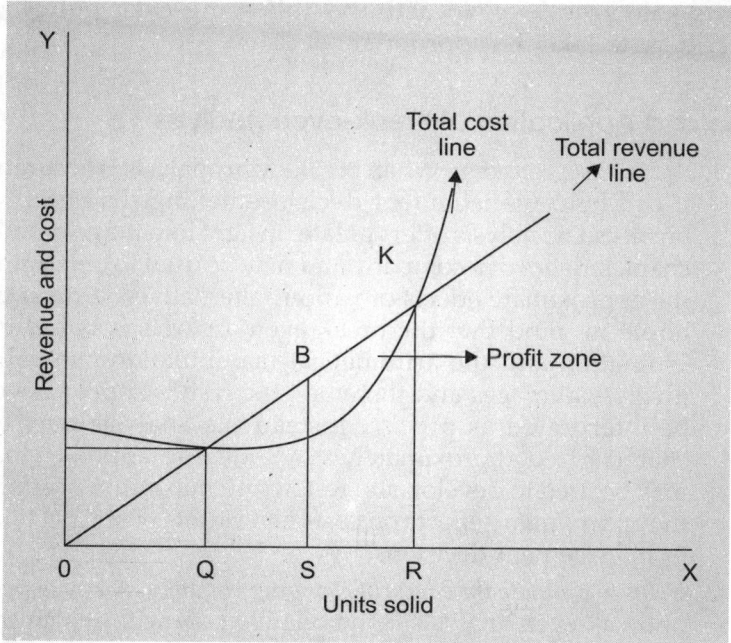

Fig. 13.4

not be a straight line. An effort to plot the different total revenues resulting from different unit sales, assuming different pricing policies, would complicate the analysis. A possible way to avoid such complications is to plot the total revenues and costs, assuming different pricing policies on different charts. It is likely that the total cost curves will also be different because of the necessity of changing marketing and sales promotion policies to correspond with pricing policies.

Figures 13.5a and b illustrate the type of analysis that may be 3 used to decide which of the pricing policies will be most profitable. Figure 13.5a shows the volume-profit-cost analysis with a price of Rs.10 per unit. Figure 13.5b is akin to Fig. 13.5a, except that the total revenue curve has a greater slope reflecting the higher price, and additional selling expenses are anticipated. Which will be the best course of action? The answer will depend upon some additional information which is not available in the figure. Information regarding what will be the number of units sold (the level of activity) following each policy is necessary to take the appropriate decision.

Use and Application of Break-even Analysis

1. *Aids decision-making*: When break-even analysis is accurate, it can help management decision-making. Essentially, break-even analysis offers greater insight into the economic characteristics of a company and may be used to determine the approximate effects of various alternatives. It must be borne in mind that the break-even analysis is based on estimation and the arithmetical manipulation generally involves averages and therefore, the results should never be interpreted as precise. Instead the analysis may be characterized approximately as a 'slide rule' approach that may be used to develop and test, with a maximum of effort, the approximate effects on costs and profits of several type of management decisions.

2. *Helps to evaluate the effects of changing variables*: A key aspect of break-even analysis is the relative ease with which the effect of a contemplated management decision can be evaluated even when more than one factor is changed. This is an important aspect of break-even analysis during the development of the annual profit plan, because it allows early and continuous testing to determine the probable overall effect of the alternatives under consideration.

Here we propose to evaluate the effect of changes in (i) fixed costs and (ii) variable costs.

Effect of change in fixed cost on break-even sales, sales necessary to achieve budgeted profit, margin of safety and contribution ratio.

To determine the effect of change in fixed cost on break-even sale, sales necessary to achieve the budgeted profit and margin of safety, let us return to the earlier illustration in this chapter concerning company ABC Ltd. Let us assume that the management of the company is contemplating 10 percent increase in fixed cost. The effect of this decision on break-even sales, sales necessary to achieve the budgeted profit, the margin of safety and contribution ratio are given below:

1. Effect on BES $= \dfrac{\text{Rs. 1.98 million}}{1 - \dfrac{\text{Rs. 2.6 million}}{\text{Rs. 5 million}}}$

$= \dfrac{\text{Rs. 1.98 million}}{0.48}$

$=$ Rs. 4.125 million

i.e. Break-even sales increases from Rs. 3.75 to Rs. 4.125 million. Figure 13.6a.

2. Sales necessary to earn the budgeted profit of Rs. 06 million.[4]

$= \dfrac{\text{Rs. 198 million} + \text{Rs. 0.6 million}}{1 - \dfrac{\text{Rs. 2.6 million}}{\text{Rs. 5 million}}}$

$= \dfrac{\text{Rs. 2.58 million}}{0.48}$

$=$ Rs. 5.375 million.

This means that in order to earn the budgeted profit of Rs. 0.6 million, the sales must increase from Rs. 5 million to Rs. 5.375 million.

3. Margin of safety

$MS = \dfrac{\text{Sales} - \text{Break-even sales}}{\text{Sales}} \times 100$

$= \dfrac{\text{Rs. 5 million} - \text{Rs. 4.125 million}}{\text{Rs. 5 million}} \times 100$

$= \dfrac{0.875}{5} \times 100$

$= 17.5\%$

Margin of safety declines from 25 to 17.5%.

4. Contribution ratio

$PV = \dfrac{\text{Selling price} - \text{Variable cost}}{\text{Selling price}}$

$$= \frac{\text{Rs. } 25 - \text{Rs. } 13}{\text{Rs. } 25}$$

$$= 0.48$$

Since there is no change in the selling price and the variable cost, PV remains the same.

Effect of changes in variable cost on break-even sales, sales necessary to achieve budgeted profit, margin of safety and contribution ratio.

Assume that the management is contemplating to increase the variable cost by 10 percent. Assume further that all other things remain the same. The effect of this decision on break-even sales, sales to achieve the budgeted profit, margin of safety and contribution ratio are indicated below:

1. $\text{BES} = \dfrac{\text{Rs. 1.8 million}}{1 - \dfrac{\text{Rs. 2.86 million}}{\text{Rs. 5 million}}}$

$$= \frac{\text{Rs. 1.8 million}}{0.428}$$

$$= \text{Rs. 4.206 million.}$$

Break-even sales increase from Rs. 3.75 million to Rs. 4.206 million (Fig. 13.6b).

2. Sales necessary to earn budgeted profit of Rs.0.6 million.

$$= \frac{\text{Rs. 1.8 million} + \text{Rs. 0.6 million}}{1 - \dfrac{\text{Rs. 2.86 million}}{\text{Rs. 5 million}}}$$

$$= \frac{\text{Rs. 2.4 million}}{1 - 0.572}$$

$$= \frac{\text{Rs. 2.4 million}}{0.428}$$

$$= \text{Rs. 5.608 million.}$$

This means that sales to earn the budgeted profit of Rs. 0.6 million increases from Rs. 5 million to Rs. 5.608 million.

3. Margin of safety

$$MS = \frac{\text{Sales} - \text{Break-even sales}}{\text{Sales}} \times 100$$

$$= \frac{\text{Rs. 5 million} - \text{Rs. 4.206 million}}{\text{Rs. 5 million}} \times 100$$

$$= 15.88\%$$

Margin of safety falls from 25 to 15.88%.

4. $$Pv = \frac{\text{Selling price} - \text{Variable cost}}{\text{Selling price}}$$

$$= \frac{\text{Rs. 25} - \text{Rs. 14.3}}{\text{Rs. 25}}$$

$$= 0.428$$

Pv falls from 0.48 to 0.428

These results can be illustrated in the form of graphs.

Break-even charts can be used to find out solution to the problem whether to close down a manufacturing unit or not. This is shown in Figs 13.5a to 13.6b

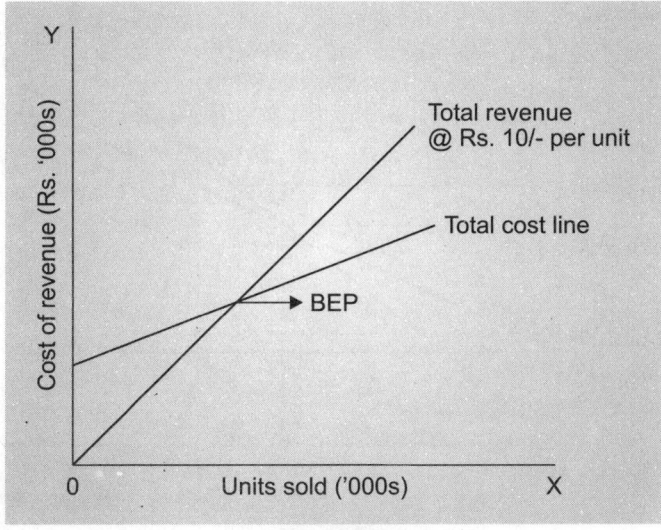

Fig. 13.5a

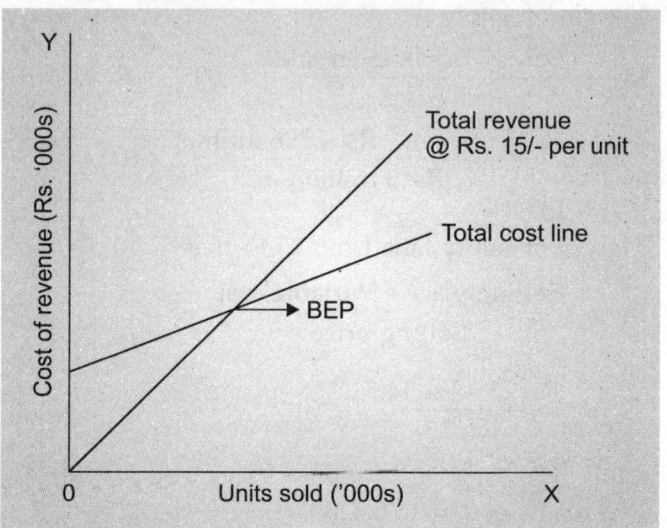

Fig. 13.5b

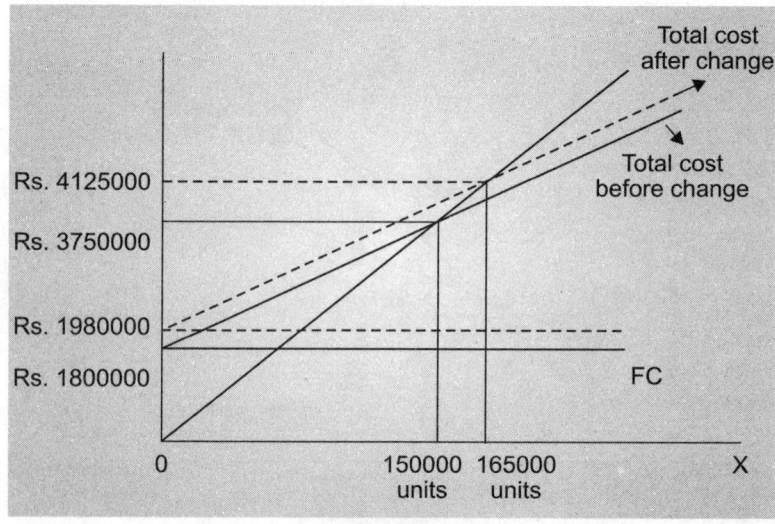

Fig. 13.6a

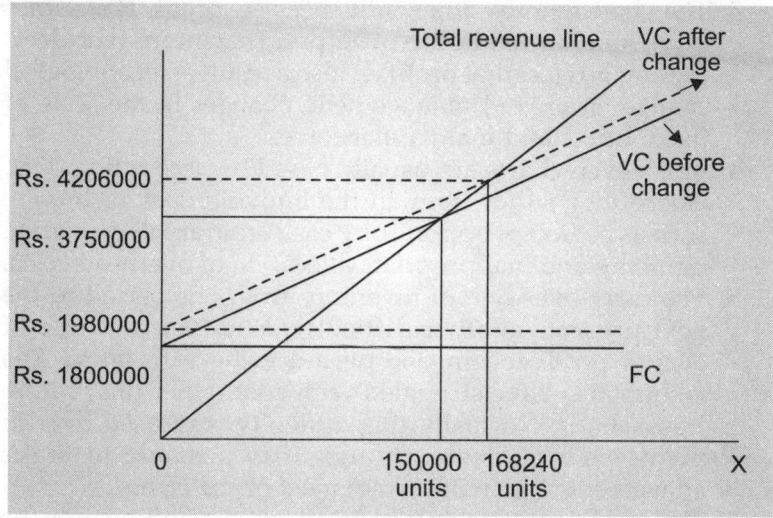

Fig. 13.6b

Limitations of Break-even Analysis

For profit forecasting the static break-even chart has serious limitations. These limitations, says Joel Dean, arise from four general sources. They are:

i. Errors of estimating cost function

ii. Oversimplification of the static revenue function

iii. Dynamic forces that shift and modify these static functions, and

iv. Managerial adaptation to altered environment.

According to Haynes, Mote and Paul, the break-even analysis contains the following defects:

1. The chart usually is not correct for changes in factor prices. If a break-even chart is based on past data, those data should be adjusted for changes in factor prices.

2. The chart usually assumes that the price of the output is given. In other words, it assumes a horizontal demand curve. But this assumption is valid only when there is perfect competition.

3. The chart ignores other influences on profit. It assumes that profits are a function of output. That means it neglects the obvious fact that profits is also a result of technological change, improved management, changes in the scale of fixed inputs and many other forces.

4. Break-even charts are usually based on accounting data. Hence they suffer from all the limitations of such data, such as neglect of opportunity cost; arbitrary depreciation estimates and inappropriate allocation of overhead costs.

5. The carry-over cost of inventory from one period to the next presents another difficulty. What is the value of output produced in one period to be sold later? The accountants have struggled with past rather than future transactions. Normally this difficulty is glossed over in break-even analysis, though it is possible to make adjustments that will correct most of the errors.

6. The inclusion of selling costs effects the accuracy of the estimate of total cost, and this makes profits production more unreliable. There is no functional relation between output and costs incurred to modify the firm's demand curve. Selling activity may remain substantially constant. Yet the demand curve may shift with fluctuations in national income and tastes. Moreover, there is much latitude for manipulating the amount and timing of many kinds of selling expenditures. Furthermore, the relationships into the future.

7. Costs in a particular period may not be a result exclusively of output in that period. Maintenance expenses, for example, are especially hard to attribute to a given time period, being a result of past output or a preparation for future output. Maintenance costs are usually not perfectly matched with output, resulting in an error of profit projections.

8. The use of sales (in properly weighted units) rather than production to measure output is satisfactory only if selling is the dominant activity of the firm or if the production and sales are closely synchronized. Otherwise serious error is introduced particularly if the analysis period is short. Normally, it is better, to measure activity by production, and to reconstruct any expenses that are a function of sales or orders, on the assumption that the output is sold in the period produced.

9. Break-even analysis is virtually useless for some firms. This is particularly likely when the predominant cost fluctuates because of fluctuations in materials cost. This is also true when the product mix varies greatly and profit margins differ among products or when advertising or sales promotion are important and highly shiftable, or when the product design or technology changes continuously over short periods.

10. The simple form of break-even chart shown so far makes no provision for taxes, particularly the corporate income tax. One may develop the chart to show part of the profit going to the government in taxes, and the remaining going to the share holders or retained for expansion.
    If the company suffers alternating years a profit and loss or if it falls into varying tax brackets the adjustment for taxes is somewhat difficult to show on the chart.

11. "Perhaps the most difficult problem," says Dean, 'for break-even analysis is to get a good index of output for a multiple product plant with variable product-mix.' A change in the sales mix may mean that the revenue–output relationship shown on the chart is no longer applicable. "Changes in the composition of demand," says Dean, "impair the accuracy of the static sales line and may vitiate the profit projection. Whenever products differ in contribution margin and there is variation in product mix from period to period, profits will vary at a given output rate. Under these circumstances, the constant price-sales line is inaccurate, even as a static function."

Conclusion

Even with all its limitations, the break-even chart is a simple and understandable method of picturing to management the effect of changes in volume on profits. Detailed analysis of break-even data will reveal to management the effect of decisions that converts costs from variable to fixed or vice versa; the effect of decisions which reduce or increase sales volume and income; and the effect of decisions to change unit selling prices. It is a device which portrays the effect of any type of forward planning by evaluating alternative courses of action.

Review Questions

1. Define break-even point.
2. What all data do you need to construct a break-even chart?
3. Enumerate the basic assumptions underlying the break-even analysis.
4. What do you mean by margin of safety?
5. What are the limitations of break-even analysis?
6. List the managerial uses of break-even analysis

Problems

1. Rajaram, the Financial Controller of XYZ Ltd. has been considering for some time setting up some profit control mechanism on which he can rely for profit planning. XYZ ltd. is a medium sized producer of razor blades. Its plants are located at Mysore. Sales in the latest fiscal year (2007) were Rs. 20 million with operating profit amounting to Rs. 4 million.

   After discussing his intention with the Chairman of the firm, Mr. Roberts, Rajaram has selected the break-even analysis and the break-even chart as a means of profit planning and control. From the latest fiscal year, he has obtained the following data:

Sales	Rs. 20,000,000
Direct materials	Rs. 6,500,000
Direct labour	Rs. 6,300,000
Factory overhead	Rs. 1,500,000
Administrative overhead	Rs. 1,000,000
Selling overhead	Rs. 700,000
Total operating expenses	Rs. 16,000,000
Operating profit	Rs. 4,000,000

   From the conversation with the HR Manager, Rajaram has learnt that wage rates will go up by 10 percent next fiscal year as the result of current wage negotiation with the labour union. In order to maintain a 20 percent operating profit margin, Rajaram is considering raising prices for the product. It is the company's policy to grant its clerical employees 90 percent of the pay rate hike received by the workers. Wages paid by the clerical employees in the 2007 fiscal year accounted for 33 percent of the factory overhead, 30 percent of the administrative overhead and 4 percent of the selling overhead.

What do you think Mr. Rajaram should do with respect to the following?

a. What percentage increase in price should the company decide upon to maintain the 20 percent operating profit margin goal?

b. Construct a break-even chart to illustrate your answer.

2. Firm XYZ produces 3 products. The fixed cost of the firm is Rs. 18 lakh, the details about variable cost per unit and the price per unit are as follows:

Product	Variable cost per unit	Price per unit
A	Rs. 150	Rs. 210
B	Rs. 200	Rs. 300
C	Rs. 230	Rs. 350

Calculate the overall break-even point. How many units of each product are produced at the break-even point? How much the firm has to produce if it wants to earn a profit of Rs.7 lakh?

References

1. For definition, see chapter on cost concepts.
2. For detailed understanding of this, see Welsh, Glenn A; *Budgeting: Project planning and control(fourth edition)*, Prentice Hall of India, Private Limited, New Delhi, 1976, Chapter 10.
3. But these are not necessary conditions. Break-even analysis can be used to test the alternative variations in cost, volume, profit, prices and product mix under future conditions and in various activity segments of the business. Thus by exposing the effects of various future proposals under these multiple conditions, the system becomes a powerful tool for product planning and profit making.
4. The desired profit figure is merely added to the fixed costs because the contribution of sales above variable costs is to cover fixed costs and profits.

Market Structure, Pricing and Output

The nature of the price and output decision is strongly influenced by the structure of the market in which the firm sells its products. The market structure determines whether a firm is a price-maker or a price-taker. There exists a large body of literature which discusses various types of competitive conditions running the range from perfect competition to pure monopoly, and which seeks to analyze their effects on prices and output.[1] It is convenient to start our discussion by listing some of the important market situations. Let us first start with perfect competition.

Perfect Competition

The theoretical market structure in which the firms take the market price as given is called perfect competition.

Features of Perfect Competition

An industry is said to be operating under perfect competition when the following conditions are satisfied.

1. **Large number of sellers and buyers:** There must be large number of sellers (firms) and buyers. Each individual firm, however large it may be, supplies only a small part of the total quantity offered in the market so that any action (addition to or removal from the market) on its own part will have no effect on the price and output of the industry. The same holds good in the case of buyers.
2. **Homogenous product:** Each firm in the industry produces a product which is accepted by buyers as being identical

or homogenous with that made by all the other producers in the industry. This ensures that no producer can put his price up above the general level.

3. **Free entry and exit of firms:** There is no barrier to entry to or exit from the industry. Entry and exit is largely determined by the possibility of earning profit.

4. **Independent decision making:** Firms take independent decisions. There should not be any collusion or agreement between or among firms in decision-making.

5. **Perfect mobility of factors of production:** The factors of production are free to move from one firm to another or from one occupation to another through out the economy in response to pecuniary signals and transport costs are ignored.

6. **Perfect knowledge:** It is assumed that all the producers (sellers) and buyers have perfect or complete knowledge regarding the conditions prevailing in the market. Information is free.

If only the first three conditions are present then competition is said to be pure.

Now let us examine some of the implications of the assumptions of perfect competition. Under perfect competition, firms will be price takers rather than price makers and as such the demand curve (AR curve) of the firm will always be a horizontal straight line. In other words the demand curve of the firm will be perfectly elastic to price. The assumptions further imply that a particular relationship exists between the firm and its market.

The total demand curve for a product shows the total amount of the product demanded by consumers at different prices. It will be a normal downward sloping demand curve showing that for the industry as a whole quantity demanded increases as price falls. This is shown in Fig. 14.1.

Figure 14.2 shows the firm's perceived demand curve which is horizontal, i.e. it is perfectly elastic demand curve with respect to price. It hits the vertical axis at the current market price OP. If a higher price is charged buyers will leave the firm as they know that they can buy the same product from others

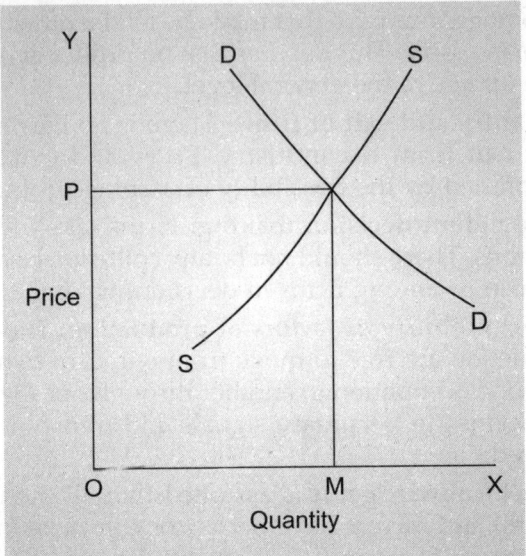

Fig. 14.1

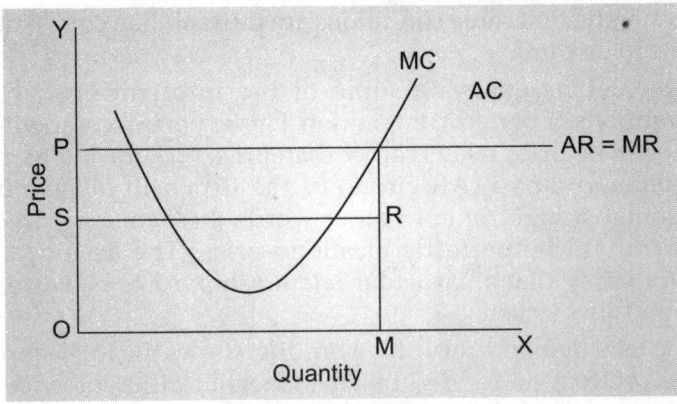

Fig. 14.2

at a lower price. The firm also will not undercut the price as the firm can sell all its output at the prevailing market price.

Equilibrium of the Firm and the Industry

Firms aim at maximizing profit and they can be in equilibrium only when they achieve this. Firms achieve maximum profit when they equate their marginal cost (MC) with their marginal revenue (MR). If MR is greater than MC, the firm adds more to its revenue than it adds to cost by increasing output and sales. When this happens profits will increase. Similarly, if MR is less than MC, the firm adds more to costs than it adds to revenue by increasing output and sales. When this happens profits will decrease. This follows that the firm will be in equilibrium when it equates MR and MC.

A firm may make either profit or loss in the short run. But in the long run the free entry and exit features of perfect competition see that these profits or losses will disappear altogether. If the industry earns profit new firms will be prompted to enter and compete with the already established firms. The resulting increase in demand for inputs may enhance their prices and raise costs. On the other hand, the increased product supply may result in a reduction in its market price. The result of this double pronged action will be that profit will be squeezed down towards zero or at least until no additional firms find it worth moving in.

Similarly, if there is initially a net loss to firms in the industry, the exit of firms, especially those who are not earning any profit, will raise profits and ultimately it will wipe out loss in the industry.

Figure 14.3a represents the short-run equilibrium position of a firm operating under perfect competition. Its profit maximizing output is OM where its marginal cost curve MC

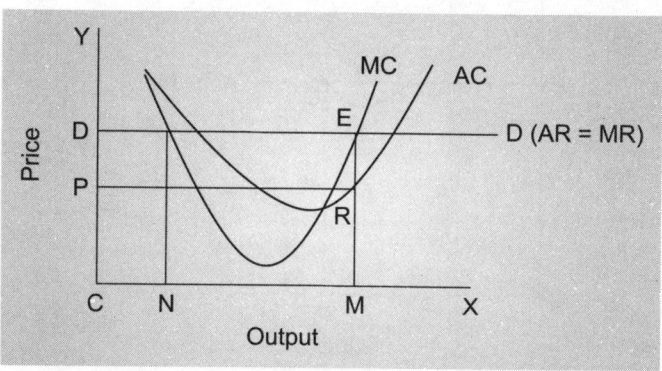

Fig. 14.3a

intersects the marginal revenue curve DD at E. At this point it is earning a profit PD = RE on each unit it produces (= unit revenue – unit cost). Thus its total profit (= unit profit multiplied by the number of units produced) is represented by ERPD. Note that output ON where also its marginal cost curve, MC intersects the marginal revenue (demand) curve DD is not the profit maximizing output. A careful examination of the Fig. 14.3a will make this point very clear. At output ON marginal cost has only just become equal to marginal revenue and has previously been greater. Beyond output ON, marginal cost is less than marginal revenue and this shows that it is profitable to produce more. The favourable situation continues up to OM where marginal revenue and marginal cost are equal. So if output is fixed at ON, the firm would be earning only minimum and not maximum profit. So here we may state that at the profit maximizing point the marginal cost curve must cut the marginal revenue curve from below. A firm can never earn maximum profits unless this happens. Fig. 14.3b represents a long run equilibrium situation. Here the average revenue curve (DD) is tangent to the average cost curve (AC). The reason is that if the unit costs were everywhere higher than price, every output would be unprofitable, and the firm

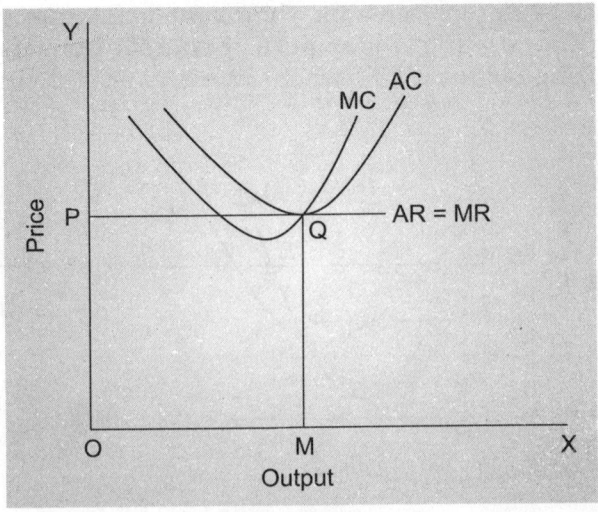

Fig. 14.3b

would leave the industry, thus shift the curves toward tangency by raising AR (price) and, possibly lowering the cost curves as well. Similarly, if the average cost curve were to intersect the demand curve, there would be some output at which profits could be earned and an influx of new firms would soon shift the cost and revenue curves sufficiently to wipe out those profits. Only when there is tangency will the "no profit, no loss" or "normal profit" position of long-run equilibrium be the best the firm can do , and no firm will be tempted to enter or leave the field if this is the typical situation of all firms in the industry.

Since the demand curve is horizontal, the point of tangency, Q, of the average revenue curve with the average cost curve must occur at an output at which the unit costs are at a minimum. For that reason the marginal cost curve will also intersect the average cost curve at that point. In short, at the point of equilibrium we have the impressive set of equalities, marginal cost = marginal revenue = average cost = average revenue = price.

$$(MC=MR=AC=AR=P)$$

It is to be noted that two essential conditions are to be fulfilled if there is to be equilibrium in the perfectly competitive industry. First, each and every individual firm must be in equilibrium. This will happen when each firm in the industry is earning maximum profits by equating marginal cost with marginal revenue. Second, the industry as a whole must be in equilibrium. This will occur when there is no tendency for firms either to enter or leave the industry, which will only happen when all the producers in the industry are earning enough to induce them to stay in the industry, and when no producer outside the industry thinks that he could earn enough money, were he to enter it, to make the move worthwhile.

The Equilibrium in the Competitive Industry

The equilibrium position of the industry under perfect competition can be depicted with the help of an industry supply and industry demand curve.

The supply curve can give an interpretation in terms of costs. In fact, in the long run it tends to approximate a curve, of average cost for the industry. This, as we know, is a consequence of the free-entry and free exit assumptions and its zero profit (normal profit) result. If the industry were to supply its commodity at a price which exceeds its average cost, some firms would be making a profit. But we know that the entry of new firms will wipe out that profit.

We must analyze the stability of the industry equilibrium in order to see whether this equilibrium point can be expected to be of direct relevance to any real market situations, i.e. whether there is any mechanism which pulls competitive prices and output into line with their equilibrium levels. It is neither feasible nor appropriate to go into a full dynamic analysis of this stability question. But we propose to examine the outlines of the mechanism which can work in the direction of stability. Figure 14.4a shows the usual supply and demand diagram for the competitive industry.

In Fig. 14.4a, the equilibrium occurs at the point of intersection of industry supply curve, SS' and industry demand curve

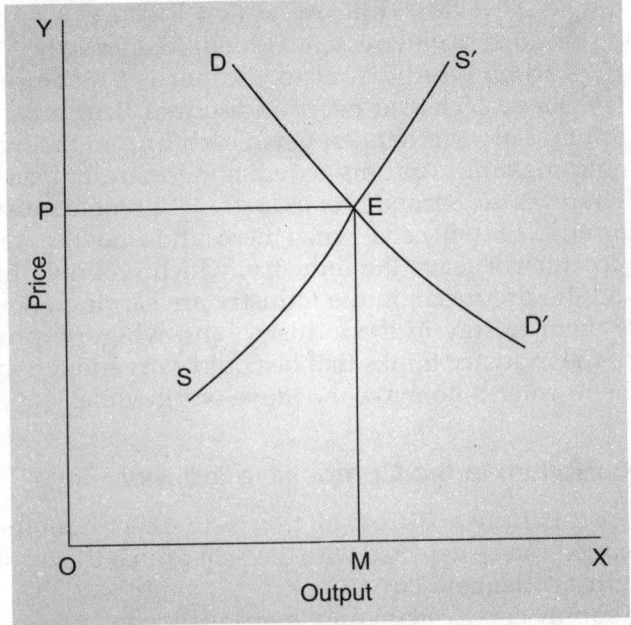

Fig. 14.4a

DD' at point E. At this point OP and OM constitute the equilibrium price-quantity combination of the industry.

Imagine now that, for one reason or another, the market price falls below the equilibrium price, say to OP' (Fig. 14.4(b). In this case the quantity demanded will exceed the quantity supplied by QR. In such a context we may expect the price to be pushed back toward the equilibrium price. Similarly a price OP'', which is above the equilibrium level, the quantity supplied will exceed the quantity demanded TN and so the price will be

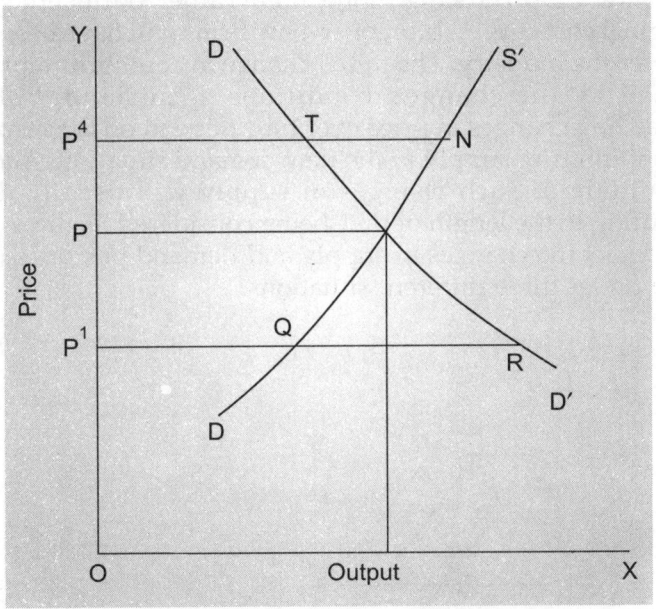

Fig. 14.4b

pushed down. In this situation, then, the equilibrium at least gives an appearance of stability which dynamic analysis can rationalize.

But it need not and often does not follow that the supply-demand equilibrium position will always be stable. On the other hand, it is easy to find a case where the system works in the wrong direction.

Equilibrium and Time

There is one other type of change in the demand and supply conditions which is important enough to merit special study. We know that, longer the period of time' we take into consideration, the greater the difference in the supply conditions. For instance, if demand suddenly increases, price is likely to rise sharply in the short-run because firms will be expanding output along fairly steep short-run marginal cost curves. But in the long-run, firms will be reorganized so as to produce the new and higher output more efficiently. For firms will now be producing along their rather flatter long-run marginal cost curves. Moreover, new firms will have been able to enter the industry. The initial change in equilibrium price is caused by the changed conditions of demand, but the succeeding changes in price over time depend on the response of conditions of supply to the new demand situation. And the magnitude of such changes in supply will usually differ according to the length of time being considered. Figures 14.5a to c depict the changes in supply and demand positions upon price under three different situations.

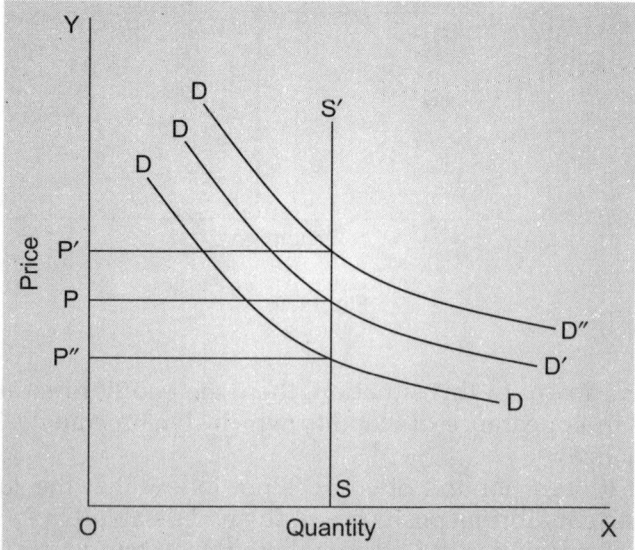

Fig. 14.5a

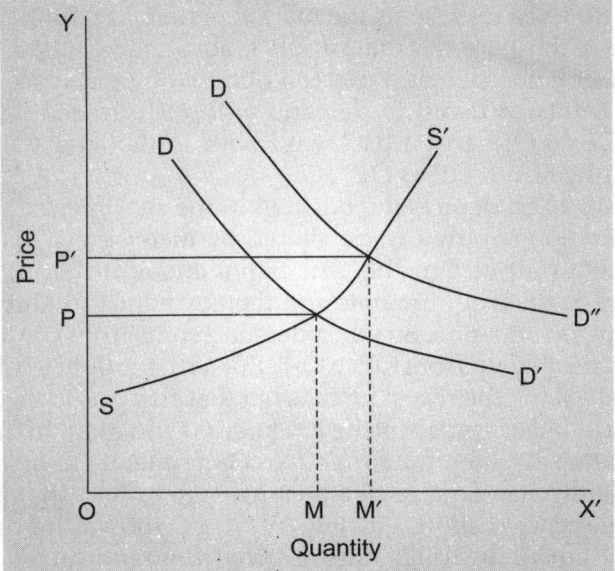

Fig. 14.5b

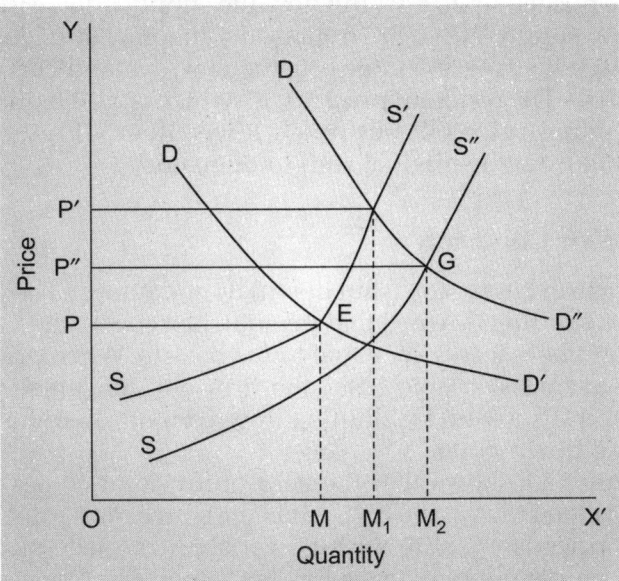

Fig. 14.5c

Figure 14.5a represents the market period. The fundamental feature of this period is that supply is absolutely limited. Under such a situation demand exerts a dominating influence on the price. A forward shift in demand will push the market price from OP to OP' and a backward shift in demand will push down price from OP to OP".

Figure 14.5b depicts the position in the short period. Under this situation supply can be altered by increases or decreases in current output. But the time is not enough to bring about changes in fixed equipments and thereby adjust production to the changed situation. So when demand shifts from DD' to DD" price is pushed up from OP to OP'. But as the supply is adjusted to some extent, the rise in price is not that sharp as in Fig. 14.5a.

Figure 14.5c represents the long period situation. In the long period there is time for firm's fixed equipments to be altered so that output is capable of adjusting itself fully to the changes in demand conditions. In Fig. 14.5c SS' shows the original supply curve and DD' the original demand curve. They intersect at point E and the resultant market price is given by OP. Now demand shifts from DD' to DD". Consequently the price is pushed up to OP'. But now the supply is increased and the new supply curve SS" represents the new situation. The new supply curve SS" intersects the new demand curve DD" at point G. The resultant price is OP" which is a bit higher than the original price OP but much lower than OP', the price resulting from the original shift in demand.

Shutdown Condition

When a firm has to stop (shut down) its operations? The golden rule for shutting down is that revenue just covers the variable costs or where losses are equal to fixed costs. When price falls below average variable costs, the firm will maximize profits (minimize its losses) by shutting down. Figure 14.6 shows the shutting down point.

Figure 14.6 shows that the zero profit point comes where price is equal to average cost, while the shut down point comes where price is equal to average variable cost. Therefore, the firm's supply curve is the solid rust line in the figure. It first goes up the vertical axis to the price corresponding to the shut

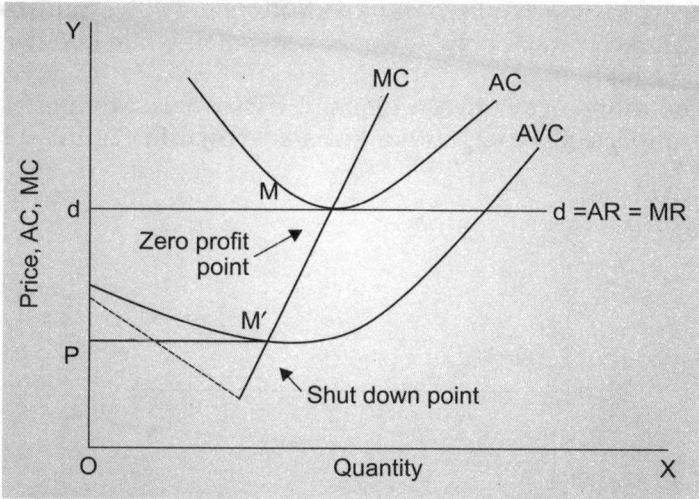

Fig. 14.6

down point at M′, where price equals the level of average variable cost (AVC) and then continues up the marginal cost curve (MC) for prices above the shut down price.

Imperfect Competition

Under imperfect competition we have different market situations such as monopoly, oligopoly and monopolistic competition. Prices will be higher and outputs lower under imperfect competition than under perfect competition. But imperfect competition has certain virtues along with these vices. Large firms under imperfect competition exploit economies of large scale production and are responsible for much of the innovations that propels long term economic growth.[2] If one has to understand how imperfectly competitive markets work, one will have a much deeper understanding of modern industrial economies.

Imperfect competition prevails when individual producers in an industry has some measure of control over the price of their output. But this doesn't mean that a firm under imperfect competition has absolute control over the price of its product. Moreover, the extent of discretion over price will differ from industry to industry. In some imperfectly competitive industries, the degree of monopoly power is very small while in others it may be high.

The difference between demand curves faced by perfectly and imperfectly competitive firms is shown in Figures 14.7a and b.

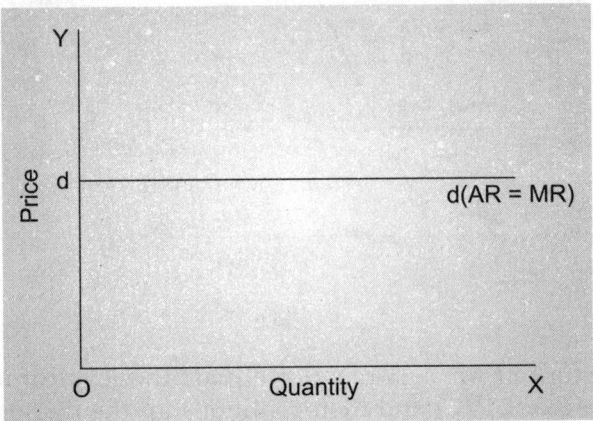

Fig. 14.7a

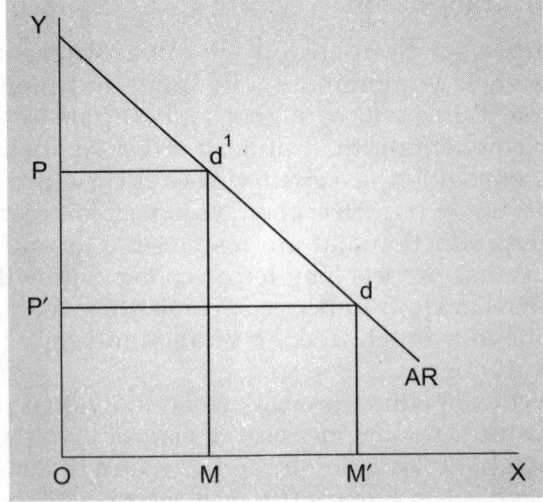

Fig. 14.7b

Figure 14.7a shows the demand curve faced by a firm under perfect competition. The demand curve in this case is a horizontal straight line indicating that it can sell as much as it wants at the going market price.

Figure 14.7b shows the demand curve facing a firm under imperfect competition. The demand curve in this case is a downward sloping curve which implies that if the firm wants to sell more it has to reduce its price.

We can also see the difference in price elasticities with respect to the two demand curves. *For a perfect competitor, demand is perfectly elastic while for an imperfect competitor the demand has finite elasticity.*

Monopoly

The extreme case of imperfect competition is monopoly. Monopoly is a case of single producer (seller) having complete control over the industry.

He is termed as the monopolist. The word monopolist is derived from the Greek words *mono* which means one and *polist* which means seller. It is the only firm in the industry and there is no industry producing a close substitute.

Pure monopolies are rare in the real market situation. Most monopolies exist because of some form of government regulation or protection. For example patent rights give monopoly control over the product for a number of years. Government also impose entry restrictions on many industries. In addition to government restrictions or legally imposed barriers, there can be economic barriers to entry. In addition, companies build up intangible forms of investment, and such investments might be very expensive for any new potential entrant to match. The software industry is an example in this case.

Another source of monopoly is the ignorance, laziness and the bias of the buyer, himself. Sometimes the producer convinces his consumers that his commodity is superior to the commodities produced by other producers and this gives him monopoly power. For maintaining this illusion the producer makes use of different types of advertisement and propaganda.

Pricing under Monopoly

As we already saw, unlike in perfect competition in monopoly price is deliberately fixed by the monopolist. He will fix that price at which the excess of gross receipts (revenue) over total costs will be the greatest. He can achieve this by regulating out put in such a way that the marginal revenue is equal to the marginal cost. "If he sold one unit less, he would lose more of revenue than he saved on cost, and if he produced one unit more, he would incur more cost than he gained of revenue." This situation is shown in Table 14.1.

Table. 14.1

Quantity Q	Price Rs.	Total revenue TR (Rs)	Total cost TC (Rs)	Total Profit TP (Rs)	Marginal revenue MR (Rs)	Marginal cost MC (Rs)
0	200	0	145	– 145	–	–
1	180	180	175	+ 5	+ 180	30
2	160	320	200	+ 120	+ 140	25
3	140	420	220	+ 200	+ 100	20
4	120	480	250	+ 230	+ 60	30
5	104	520	290	+ 230	+ 40	40
6	80	480	350	+ 130	– 40	60
7	60	420	420	+ 0	– 60	70

Table 14.1 shows that the most profitable output of the monopolist is 5 units when marginal revenue equals marginal cost.

In the case of pure or perfect monopoly the producer will be so powerful that he will be always able to take the whole of all consumers income whatever be the level of his output.[4] In the case of pure monopoly the elasticity of the average revenue curve for the monopolist will be unitary. In other words the total outlay on the firm's product will be the same at all prices and therefore the marginal revenue will always be zero. Hence the marginal revenue curve will coincide with the X-axis. This is shown in Fig. 14.8.

Under this situation all consumers spend all their income on the firm's product irrespective of high or low price it charges. But this does not mean that the "pure" monopolist can fix both

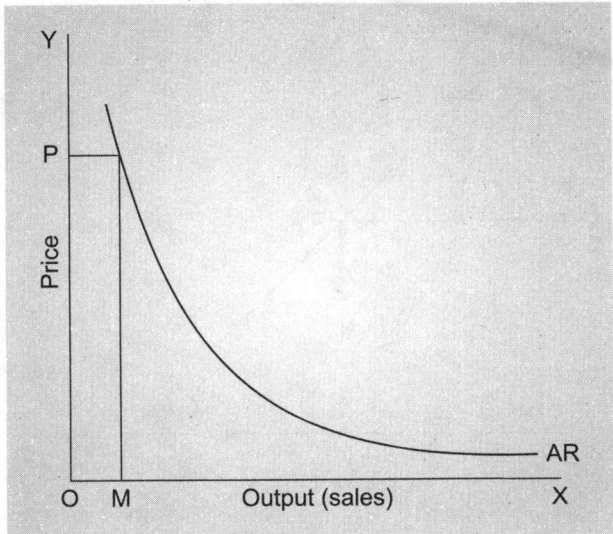

Fig. 14.8

the price and the output at the same time. When he fixes the price the quantity demanded will be decided by what the consumers will take at that price. On the other hand, when he fixes his output, the price will be decided by what his customers will pay for that much of output. The pure monopolist can fix either the price or the output; but not both at the same time. Anyhow, within these limitations his power is complete.

Monopoly Equilibrium in Graphs

First we analyze the situation where there is absolutely no cost of production. We take the case of a mineral spring. This situation is represented in Fig. 14.9.

The monopolist maximizes his profit when he equates his marginal revenue with the marginal cost. And this happens when he produces OM quantity of output and sells at the price of OP per unit (Fig. 14.9). Note that the elasticity of demand at the point R on the average revenue curve is equal to one and therefore at this point the total receipts will be the maximum. At this point marginal cost and marginal revenue are zero.

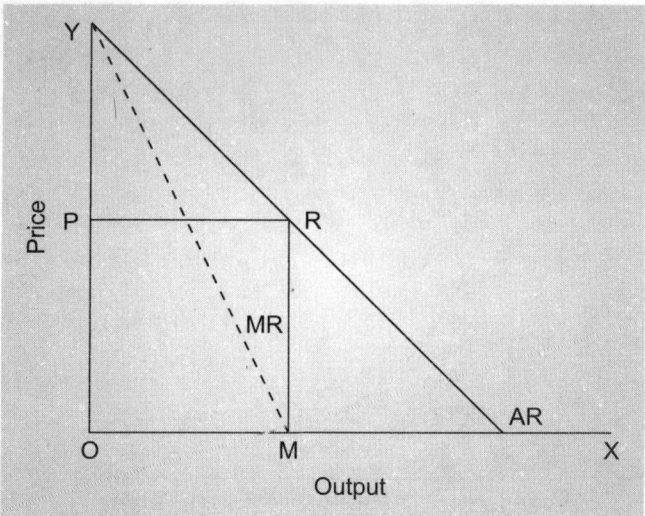

Fig. 14.9

Another situation is the one with positive marginal cost. This is a more real situation. To simplify the analysis we shall assume that the costs are constant (Fig. 14.10). Beyond point R on the average revenue curve in the figure the elasticity of demand is less than one and so the monopolist will not be interested beyond point R. (The monopolist will always try to fix his price where the elasticity on his revenue curve will be greater than one.) Between the points R and R' the average revenue curve's elasticity will be equal to one. And since the monopolist's marginal cost is positive, it will be better for the monopolist to reduce his output at least as far as R'. As is shown in Fig. 14.10, to the left of point R' it is likely that all monopolists will have ranges in their average revenue curves with elasticities of demand for their products greater than one. Thus the monopolist will produce up to OM quantity where marginal revenue equals marginal cost. At this point the elasticity of the average revenue curve will be greater than one.

Figure 14.11 shows the monopoly equilibrium when marginal cost is rising or under increasing cost. As already noted the monopolist's maximum-profit output point comes where he equates marginal cost with marginal revenue.

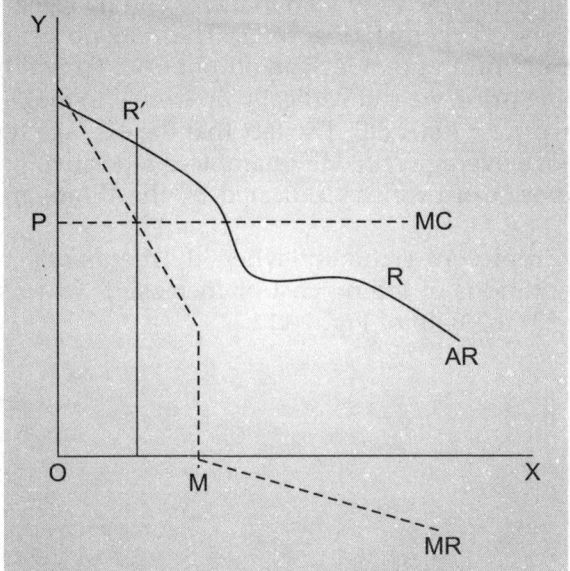

Fig. 14.10

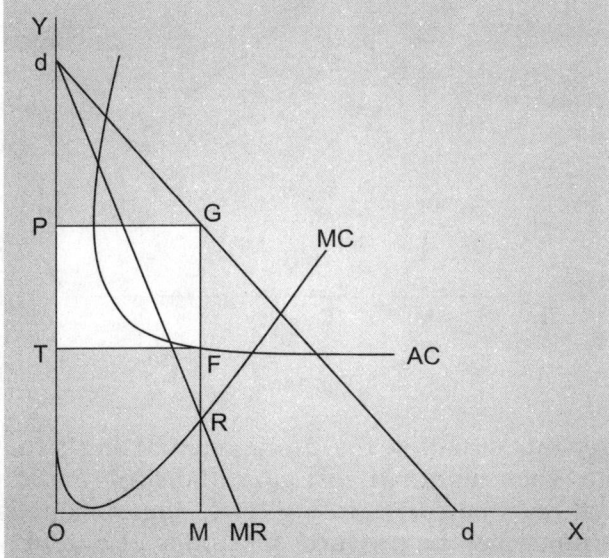

Fig. 14.11

This happens when the marginal cost and marginal revenue curves intersect at point R (Fig. 14.11). The monopoly equilibrium or maximum profit point is at an output OM. To find the profit maximizing price, we run vertically up from R to the *dd* curve at G, where price equals OP. The fact that the average revenue at G lies above average cost MF guarantees a positive profit. The actual amount of profit is indicated by the White area in the figure.

Now we represent a situation where the monopolist produces under conditions of falling cost or increasing returns. This is shown with the help of Fig. 14.12.

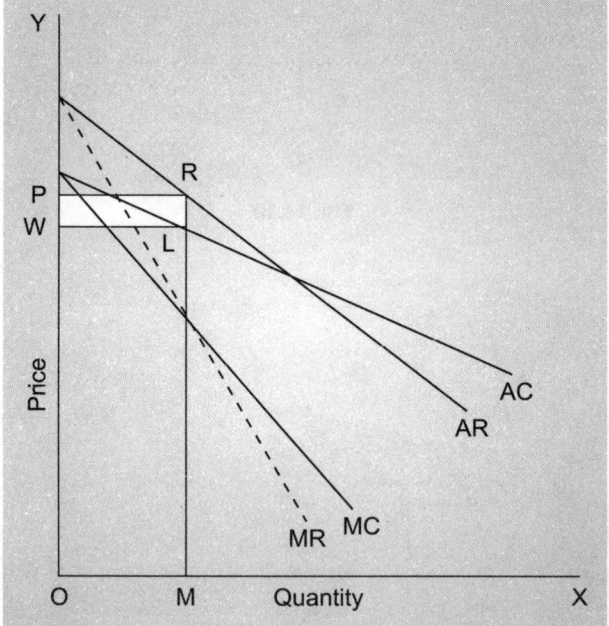

Fig. 14.12

Under this situation the profit maximizing situation is possible when marginal cost curve falls less rapidly than marginal revenue curve. In Fig. 14.12 the monopolist is in equilibrium when he produces OM units of output. At this output his marginal cost and marginal revenue are equal. The monopoly price is OP and the monopoly profit PRLW. If the marginal cost curve falls throughout more rapidly than the marginal revenue curve profit maximizing equilibrium will be impossible and this is the only situation under monopoly when profit maximizing equilibrium is impossible. On the other hand, for a firm under perfect competition equilibrium position can only occur when the marginal cost curve of the firm is rising at and near the point of equilibrium output.

Monopoly Equilibrium Under Constant Cost

Figure 14.13 shows the equilibrium of the monopolist under constant cost.

As per Fig. 14.13 the monopolist is in equilibrium when he produces OM units. At this output his MC and MR are equal. He charges a price of OP per unit and earns a total profit of PRQS.

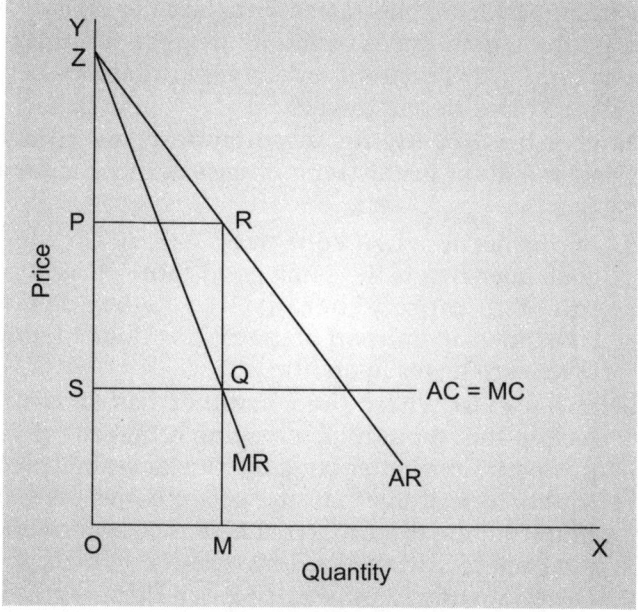

Fig. 14.13

Price Discrimination Under Monopoly

"Discriminating monopoly" or "price discrimination" occurs when a monopolist charges different prices for different units of a commodity, even though these units are in fact homogenous so far as their physical nature is concerned.[5] Depending on the nature of the circumstances the possible extent of discrimination will vary. There is a theoretical possibility that every individual unit is charged a different price that situation is called perfectly discriminating monopoly. But in practice discrimination between buyers is more common than between units of a homogenous product.

In the case of perfect competition price discrimination is not al all possible, because the customer who is charged more by one particular seller has got the opportunity of going to a different seller and buying from him. But even under monopoly it is not always possible to discriminate between different customers. The fundamental condition for price discrimination to take place is that there should not be any possibility of resale of the commodity from one customer to another. In case of the following [6] three main types of situations price discrimination can occur even if there is no fundamental difference between the goods sold to different buyers:

1. **Discrimination owing to consumers peculiarities:** "Discrimination in this type of case can occur for three reasons:

   i. It can occur when consumer A is not aware that consumer B gets the same good more cheaply. Or to put it in more generally, it can happen when consumers in one part of the market do not know that prices are lower in another.

   ii. It can exist where the consumer has an irrational feeling that though he is paying a higher price he is paying it for a better good. For instance, it is probably irrational to think that one gets a better view of the film from the front row of the Rs. 3.00 seats than from the back row of the Rs. 1.50 seats.

   iii. Discrimination can occur if price differences are so small that it does not seem worth worrying about them.[7]

2. **Discrimination based on the nature of the good:** This type of discrimination takes place when the commodities involved are direct services. Direct services cannot be resold and so differences can exist between their prices for different consumers, e.g. a lawyer's service or a doctor's service.

3. **Discrimination because of distances and frontier barriers:** Discrimination because of distances can be explained with the help of the following example: Suppose a commodity is sold for Rs.10 in one town and for Rs.15 in another. As long as the transport cost between the two towns is not less than Rs.5 per unit of the commodity no body can make profit by reselling the commodity and therefore discrimination is possible. There are also occasions when a monopolist sells in two different markets. Suppose one is a home market with a tariff and the other the world market without tariff. In this case the monopolist can charge a higher price in the home market.

Even in case of the same good different prices can be charged from the same consumer depending on the purpose for which it is used, e.g. different rates charged for electricity for different purposes such as domestic, Industrial and agricultural.

In the foregoing paragraphs we have analyzed the conditions when price discrimination is possible and profitable. For analyzing we can apply the equilibrium theory of the firm to a case where there are two markets. If the monopolist is to be in equilibrium the following conditions should be ful-filled: first of all, marginal revenue in both the markets must be equal. Moreover, marginal revenue should be equal to the marginal cost of producing the whole output. This situation is shown in Fig. 14.14.

In Fig. 14.14 the seller is a monopolist in market H, the home market where the elasticity of demand for his product is not very great. Therefore his average revenue curve AR^h and marginal revenue curve MR^h slope downwards. In the world market where there is perfect competition the demand curve is perfectly elastic. For the world market the average revenue curve AR^W and the marginal revenue curve MR^W coincide and that is a horizontal straight line. The curve MC represents the marginal cost. To determine the equilibrium output the meeting

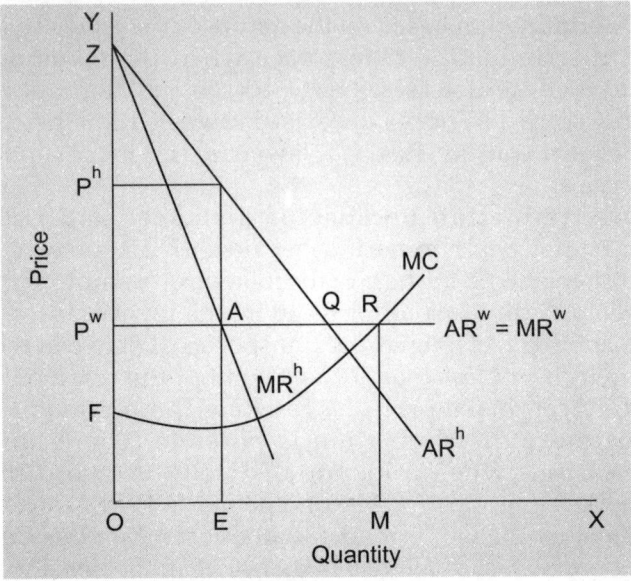

Fig. 14.14

point of marginal cost curve and the combined marginal revenue curve must be found. The total output should be allocated for the two different markets in such a way that the marginal revenues are equal in each market. The composite curve ZAQR represents the combined marginal revenue curve and the combined marginal revenue curve intersect at R. Thus OM is the equilibrium output. As is already mentioned equilibrium output is at that point where the marginal revenue of both the markets are equal and at the same time equate with the marginal cost. Therefore OE quantity should be sold in the home market at a price OP^h. At this price the marginal revenue is AE. The rest of the quantity EM can be sold in the world market at a price OP^w. Here the marginal revenue is MR which is equal to OP^w. MR and AE are equal. Thus the price OP^h in the monopolistic home market is higher than the price OP^w in the world market. The equilibrium profit, which is contributed to by both the markets is equal to the area ZAQRF.

Figures 14.15a to c show the monopolist's price output policy when both the markets are monopolistic.

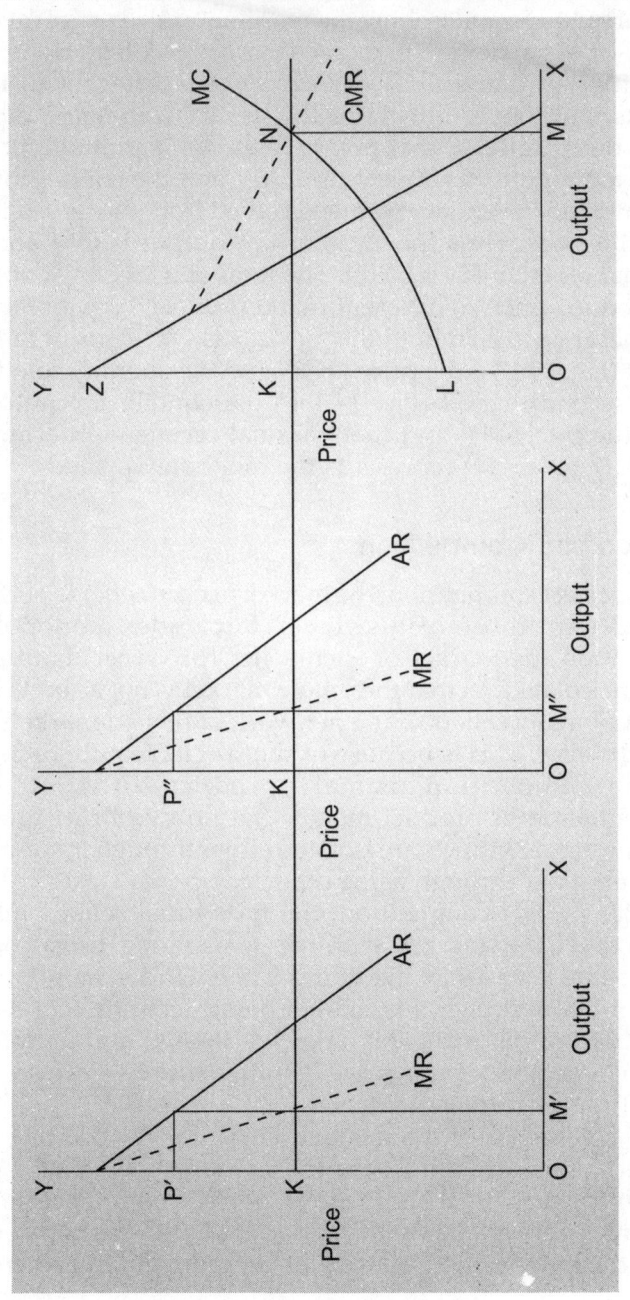

Fig. 14.15c

Fig. 14.15b

Fig. 14.15a

Figures 14.15a and b show the marginal and average revenue curves of a particular firm for two different markets. The elasticities of demand at each price are different in these markets. Fig. 14.15c illustrates the profit maximizing output. This is determined at that point where the marginal cost cure for the monopolist's whole output MC and the curve showing the combined marginal revenue received from the two markets CMR intersect. Thus the equilibrium output is OM and the marginal revenue is OK=MN. The total output OM should be allocated for the two different markets in such a way that the marginal revenues in both the markets is OK. Thus in the first market (Fig. 14.15a) the price is OP' and the quantity sold OM'. In the second market (Fig. 14.15b) the equilibrium output is OM",⁴the price OP" and the marginal revenue OK. The area ZNL in (Fig. 14.15c) represents the monopoly profit.

Monopolistic Competition

Under perfect competition, the market of each seller is perfectly merged with those of his rivals. But under monopolistic competition the market of each seller (producer) is in some measure isolated, so that the whole market is not a single large market of many sellers, but a net-work of related markets, one for each seller. This is because of the special feature of mono-polistic competition, namely product differentiation. Differentiation of product means that no two firms produce the same item. Products are isolated either through trade-marks or wrappers or through some other device.

Under perfect competition, the individual seller's market being completely merged with the general one, he can sell as much as he pleases at the going price. Under monopolistic competition, however, his market being separate to a degree from those of his rivals, his sales are limited and defined by three new factors: (i) his price, (ii) the nature of his product, and (iii) his advertising outlays.

The divergence of the demand curve for his product from the horizontal straight line imposes upon the seller a price problem which is absent under perfect competition. The problem is very similar to that associated with the monopolist. Depending upon the elasticity of the demand curve and its position relative to the cost curve for his products, profits may be increased, either by raising the price and selling less or by lowering the price and selling more. The decisions will be influenced by profit considerations.

The adjustment of his product similarly is a new problem imposed upon the seller by the fact of differentiation. The volume of his sales depends in part upon the manner in which his products differs from that of his competitors and in part upon the skill with which the good is distinguished from others and made to appeal to a particular group of buyers. Again, the seller may influence the volume of his sales by increasing advertisement expenditures. Such expenditures increase both the demand for his product, and his costs, and their prices will be adjusted, as are prices and "products" so as to render the profits of the enterprise a maximum. The advertisement expenditure is peculiar to monopolistic competition in the sense that it has no purpose to serve under perfect competition where any producer can sell as much as he wants without it. Gains from advertisements under monopolistic competition are possible on two accounts:

    i. Imperfect knowledge on the part of buyers to the means whereby wants may be most effectively satisfied, and

   ii. The possibility of altering wants by advertising or selling appeal.

Individual Equilibrium Under Monopolistic Competition

Under monopolistic competition the demand curve for the product of the firm may be expected to have negative slope, even though the firm is as small as one operating under conditions of perfect competition. This is because customers will have different degrees of loyalty to the firms from whom they make their purchases. A small reduction in one firm's price may only attract its competitors' most mercurial customers. But as larger and larger price reductions are initiated, it may acquire more and more customers from its rivals by drawing on customers who are less anxious to switch.

The equilibrium of the firm involves the usual conditions – marginal cost must be equal to marginal revenue. In the short run the firms may or may not earn a profit. Under monopolistic competition one can even expect something like freedom of entry. Since firms are small, relatively small very small amount of capital is required to setup business and turn out a product not quite the same as but still very like those already in the market.

The consequence is that, as under perfect competition, both profits and losses will tend to be eliminated in the long run. The two situations explained above i.e. equilibrium with profit and without profit are shown in Figs 14.16a and b respectively.

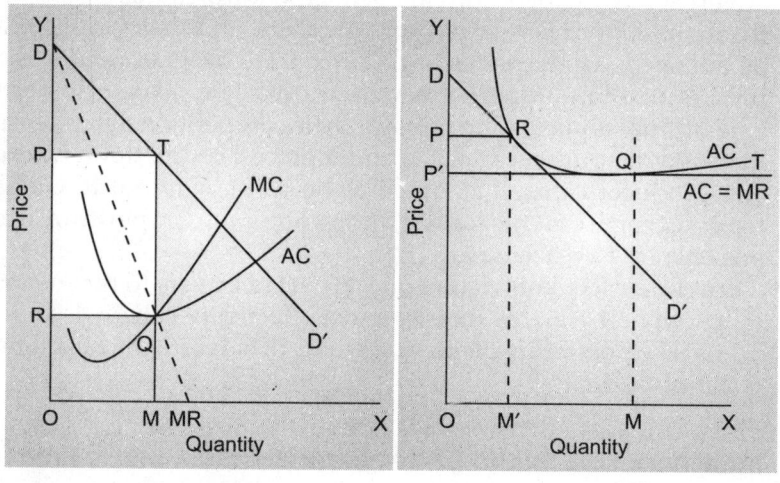

Fig. 14.16a   Fig. 14.16b

In Fig. 14.16a the firm is in equilibrium when it produces OM units. At this level of output the firm is equating marginal cost and marginal revenue and each unit is sold at a price OP and thereby earns a profit equal to the area represented by rectangle PTQR.

Figure 14.16b depicts a situation where the firm is not earning any profit. The equilibrium output here is attained by the tangency between the average cost curve and the negatively sloping demand curve DD'. It can be seen from this figure that at any other output, unit cost will be larger than price and so such an output will involve loss to the firm.

The average cost curve is generally taken to have the "U" shape indicated in the diagram (14.16a) on the assumption that both very small and very large output are difficult and expensive to produce. Even economies of large scale apply only up to a point, beyond which administrative costs and diminishing returns occur because of the presence of scarce (bottle-neck) inputs which raise the unit costs of production.

If this is valid, the point of tangency R between the U-shaped average cost curve (Fig. 14.16b) and the negatively sloping demand curve must be found somewhere to the left of the average minimum cost point Q. This is in direct contrast with the equilibrium of the competitive firms whose long run position is Q. Therefore the output of the firm under monopolistic competition must be smaller, and its unit cost and price higher than it would be under perfect competition.

Group Equilibrium with Price Competition

Group equilibrium under monopolistic competition with price competition is represented in Fig. 14.17. This relates a situation in which the "proper" or "optimal" number of firms is already in the product group.

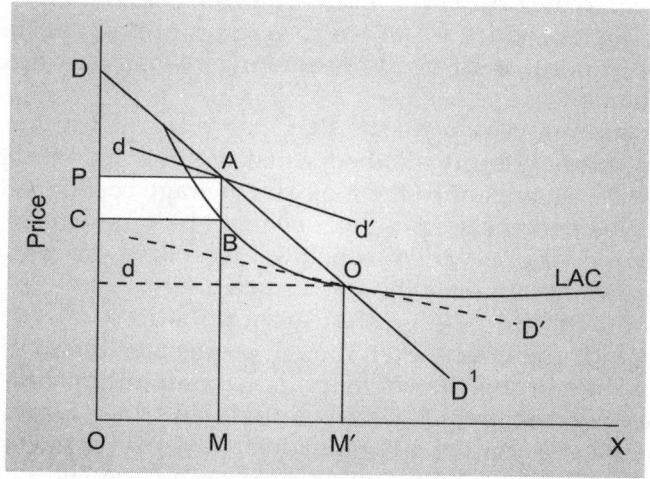

Fig. 14.17

In Fig. 14.17 DD' and *dd'* (Solid) represent two demand curves. *dd'* shows the increased sales any entrepreneur can expect to enjoy by lowering price, provided all other entrepreneurs maintain their original prices. DD' on the other hand, shows the actual sales to be gained as a general downward movement of price takes place. LAC is the long-run average cost curve for the typical firm in question. We assume an initial (short-run) equilibrium at point A, with output OM and price OP. Short-run profit is representted by PABC. Each entrepreneur, regarding *dd'* as his demand curve, realizes he can increase profit by reducing price and expanding output (according to the *elastic dd'*). Therefore each reduces price. But instead of moving along the *dd'* each in fact moves along DD'. In Chamberlin's terminology, *dd'* slides down along the DD' and becomes tangent to the LAC curve.

Despite the frustration of their initial plans' producers hold firm in their belief that *dd'* represents their demand curve. So they continue to reduce their price in an attempt to increase profit, and *dd'* continues to slide downward along DD'. The downward movement will continue until it comes to point Q, where it is shown as the broken curve. Of course, *dd'* might fall below the broken curve's position, in that case all entrepreneurs will incur loss and so price would be raised, shifting *dd'* upward. The position of long-run equilibrium is Q, where *dd'* becomes tangent to the LAC curve. Each firm, while having a monopoly of its own product, is pushed to zero profit point position by the competition of rivals producing readily substitutable products.

In summary we can state that long-run equilibrium under price competition is attained when the anticipated demand curve *dd'* is tangent to the long-run average cost curve. If *dd'* lies LAC curve, each producer believes he can increase profit by reducing price, if *dd'* is below LAC curve, price must be increased to eliminate the loss incurred.

Some critics believe that monopolistic competition is inherently inefficient, even though profits are zero in the long run. They argue that monopolistic competition breeds an excessive number of new products and that eliminating unnecessary product differentiation could really cut costs and lower prices. To understand this reasoning, see Fig. 14.18.

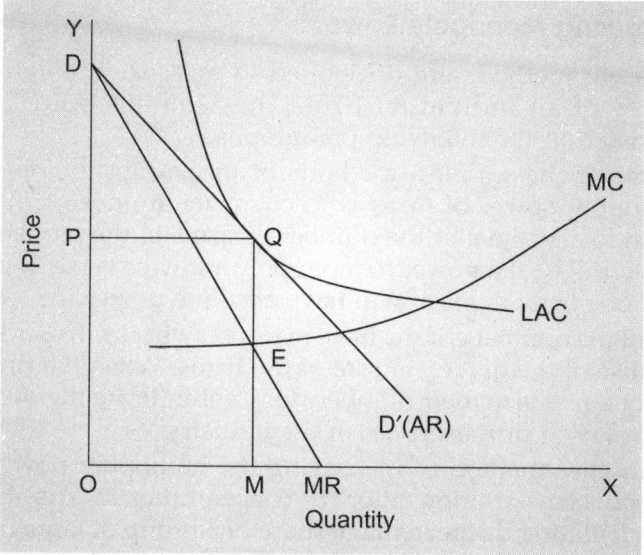

Fig. 14.18

In Fig. 14.18 at the long-run equilibrium price at Q, price is above marginal cost; hence output is reduced below the ideal competitive level.

The economic critique of monopolistic competition has considerable appeal, says Samuelson.[8] It takes real ingenuity to demonstrate the gains to human welfare from adding Elite bread to Modern bread and other varieties of breads. As Samuelson and Nordhous point out "It is sometimes hard to see the reason for gasoline stations on every corner of an inter-section. But there is logic to the great variety of goods and services produced by a modern market economy. Reducing the number of monopolistic competitors, while cutting costs, might well end up lowering consumer welfare as it will reduce the diversity of available products. Centrally planned economies tried to standardize output to a small number of goods – a standard uniform of blue cloths. But their consumers became highly dissatisfied when they looked at the variety available in market economies. People are ready to pay a premium to be free to choose."

Measuring Monopoly Power

Different methods are developed to measure the monopoly power of an individual firm. These methods are briefly discussed in the following paragraphs.

One of the simplest methods of measuring the degree of monopoly power of firms is to count the number of firms in the industry. Smaller the number of firms in the industry, the larger will be the power of monopoly and vice versa. If there is only one firm, the firm will have absolute power.

But the number criteria have many drawbacks. This is largely because of the divergent size of the firms. When the firms are of not equal size their number does not indicate the degree of control each firm exercises in the industry.

Another method of measuring the monopoly power is to find out concentration ratio. The concentration ratio is obtained by calculating the percentage share of a group of large firms in the total output of the industry.

But this method also has certain problems. First, the measure of concentration ratio involves statistical and conceptual problems. Production capacity may not be used fully and the value of assets invites valuation problems. Similarly, the measure of concentration ratio does not take into account the size of the market. The market may be local, national or international. Still another problem connected with this method is that it does not take into account competition from other industries. The degree of competition is measured by the elasticity of substitution which may be different under different classification of industries.

A third method bases excess profit criterion for measuring the monopoly power. Bain and others used excess profit (Profit in excess of opportunity cost) as a measure of monopoly power. They used the following formula for measuring monopoly power.

$$MP = \frac{R - O}{R}$$

Where MP = Monopoly Power
O = Opportunity Cost
R = Actual Profit.

If $\dfrac{R-O}{R} = 0$, there is no monopoly and if it is greater than

zero, there is monopoly. The higher the value of $\dfrac{R-O}{R}$, the greater the degree of monopoly.

The Lerner Index as a Measure of a Firm's Monopoly Power

The Lerner Index (L) measures the degree of a firm's monopoly power. L is given by the ratio of the difference between price (P) and marginal cost (MC) to price, or one over the absolute value of the price elasticity of demand e. i.e. MP = 1/e. (MP is monopoly power).The value of L can range from zero (for a perfect competitive firm) to 1 for a monopolist. (For example, if P=Rs.16 and MC=Rs.12 or e = 4, then L = (16 − 12)/16 = 0.25 or 1/e = ¼ = 0.25. On the other hand if P = 16 and MC = 8 or e = 2, then L = (16 − 8)/16 = 8/16 = 0.5 or ½ = 0.5. Now the firm has double the monopoly power compared with the previous case. For a perfectly competitive firm P = MC and e = alpha, L = 0. On the other hand, if MC is smaller in relation to P and the smaller is e the larger will be L and the degree of firm's monopoly power.

The Herfindahl Index as Measure of Monopoly Power

The Herfindahl index (H) is a measure of the monopoly power in an industry as a whole. H is given by the sum of the squared values of the market sales shares of all the firms in the industry. That is

$$H = S_1 + S_2 + S_3 + \dots + S_n$$

Where S_1 is the market sales share of the largest firm in the industry, S_2 the market sales share of the second largest firm in the industry, and so on, for all the N firms in the industry. In general, the greater is the value of H, the greater is the degree of monopoly power of the industry. For example, with monopoly or a single firm in the industry, so that its market share is 100%, H = 100 x100 = 10000. On the other hand, if there are 100 equal sized firms in the (competitive) industry, each with 1% of the market, H = 100. For an industry with 10 equal size firms, each with 10% market share, H = 1000.

Triffin's Cross-elasticity Criterion

Triffin considers cross elasticity as a measure of the degree of monopoly. The lower the cross-elasticity of the product of a firm, the greater will be the degree of its monopoly power.

Oligopoly

Oligopoly is another case of imperfect competition where a few sellers sell identical products or slightly differentiated products. When the products offered are similar or identical products, it is termed as pure or homogenous oligopoly and when the products are differentiated, differentiated oligopoly. The oligopoly situation (including the limiting case of duopoly) has one common feature on which most of the economist's attention has been centered. This is the interdependence in the decision-making of the various firms, an interdependence of which is recognized by all of them. In an industry which consists of a small number of large companies, each seller must be acutely conscious of the actions of his rivals and of their reaction to changes in his policies. This is because a major policy change on the part of one firm is likely to have obvious and immediate effect on the other firms which comprise the industry. In other words, there exists sufficient cross elasticity of demand so that each seller must take in his pricing decisions, the rival's reactions into account. As a result, the oligopolist has developed an armory of aggressive and defensive marketing weapons. For example, it is only under oligopoly that advertising comes fully into its own.

Oligopolistic interdependence has another consequence. That is under oligopolistic interdependence a very whole variety of behavior patterns becomes possible. Rivals may try to get together and operate in the pursuit of their objectives, at least as far as the law permits, or, at the other extreme, they may try to fight each other and perish. Even if they enter into agreement it may last or it may break down. And the agreements may follow a wide variety of patterns.

Because of this, the literature of oligopoly there is a variety of models, many of which describe, at most one particular arrangement – a price leadership agreement or some particular method of using freight charges as a means for sharing (dividing) market territories.

First we propose to discuss price rigidity under oligopoly which is represented by what is known as kinked demand curve. The kinked demand curve explains the question why once a price-quantity combination has been decided upon, it will not readily change.

Consider the impact on quantity demanded of a reduction in the price of a commodity. This is demonstrated by the demand curve for the product. Suppose, first, that the reduction in the price which is charged by one firm is matched by other competing firms. In that case the firm may expect to increase its sales slightly, but since it is not possible to get any customers away from its rivals in these circumstances, no large addition to its sales is to be expected. Its demand curve (DD' in Fig. 14.18) will be relatively inelastic.

Imagine, on the other hand, the firm in question is the only to reduce its price. If so, a much larger increase in its demand is to be anticipated. Thus, where no other firm follows its price moves, the firm in question is likely to have a relatively elastic demand curve such as *dd'*.

In Fig. 14.19 let point G represents the firm's current price-quantity combination. It has often been suggested that the large oligoplistic firm is likely to anticipate the following competitive reaction pattern to a price change:

1. *Price reductions*: If the firm in question reduces its price, its competitors will feel the drain on their customers quickly and so they will be forced to match this price reduction. In other words, for downward price movements from G, the relevant portion of the firm's demand curve will be GD' of the demand curve DD' (Fig. 14.19).

2. *Price hike*: If the firm increases its price, it may expect that its competitors will welcome the new customers which they gain from the price raising firm as a result, and they will have no inclination to match the price hike. Hence for price hikes the relevant part of the demand curve will be elastic segment dG.

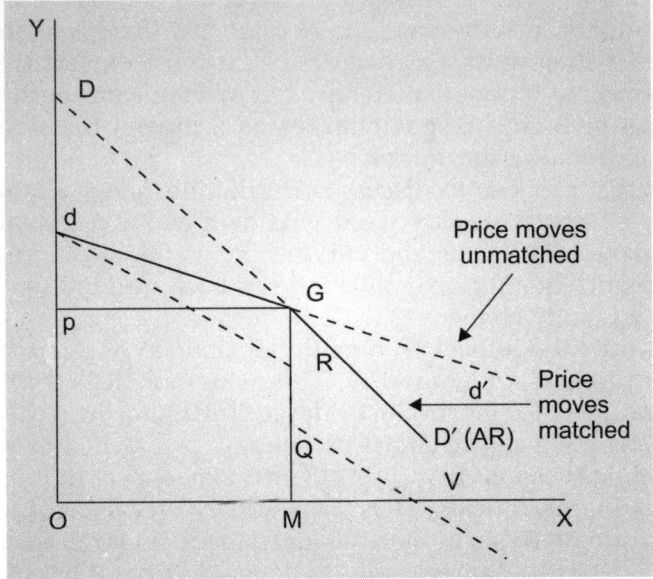

Fig. 14.19

In short, given this view of competitive reaction patterns the firm's demand curve will be composite demand curve dGD', characterized by a kink at the point G which represents the current price-output combination.

Now it is easy to visualize that a firm with such competitive response pattern will be extremely reluctant to vary its price. For a fall in its price will not bring about any substantial increase in its sales, while a price hike will result in a substantial cut in business, and neither of these is very attractive propositions.

It may be noted here that the kink in the demand curve causes a finite discontinuity (break) in the marginal revenue curve, which is given by the broken line dRQV. dR is the segment corresponding to the dG portion of the demand curve, QV corresponds to the less elastic GD' segment. At point G, there is a finite discontinuity represented by the segment RQ.

The chief feature is the absolutely vertical section RQ. If the marginal cost curve happens to pass through anywhere through the gap RQ in the marginal revenue curve, the profit maximizing firm will have no motivation to modify the current price, OP. Even if there is a sharp rise in costs, as long as the marginal cost curve does not rise above R it will lead to no price change.

George Stigler has questioned this proposition on empirical grounds.[9]

It seems evident that in an inflationary situation Oligopoly firms do often follow one another's price rises. However, as pointed out by Baumol the (Oligopoly) analysis does show how the Oligopolistic firm's view of competitive reaction patterns can affect the chargeability of whatever price it happens to be charging.

Game Theory

To analyze strategic interactions more carefully, economists rely upon game theory. This is the analysis of situations involving two or more interacting decision makers who have conflicting objectives. See the findings of game theorists in the area of imperfect competition:

- As the number of noncompetitive oligopolists becomes large, industry price and quantity tend toward the perfectly competitive outcome.
- If firms decide to collude rather than compete, the market price and quantity will be close to those generated by a monopoly. But experiments suggest that as the number of firms increases, collusive agreements become more difficult to police and the frequency of cheating and non-cooperative behavior increases.
- In many situations, there is no stable equilibrium for oligopoly. Strategic interplay may lead to unstable outcomes as firms threaten, bluff, start price wars, capitulate to stronger firms, punish weak opponents, signal their intentions, or simply exit from the market.[10]

Duopoly

Duopoly is a limited case of oligopoly. Under duopoly there will be only two sellers. A certain move, say price reduction, may be advantageous to one seller in view of his rival's present policy, i.e. assuming it not to change. But if rival is sure to make a counter move, there is no reason to assume that he will not; and the first seller to recognize the fact that his rival's policy is not a datum, but is determined in part by his own, cannot be construed as a negation of independence. It is simply to consider the indirect consequences of his own acts – the effect on himself of his own policy, mediated by that of his competitor. Of course, he may or may not take them into account, but he is equally independent in either case.[11]

If a seller determines upon his policy the assumption that his rivals are unaffected by what he does, we may say that he takes into account only the direct influence which he has upon the price. Since the problem of duopoly has usually been conceived of in this fashion, we shall analyze the results under such an assumption. Following this it will be argued that the only solution fully consistent with the central hypothesis that each seller seeks his maximum profit in one in which he does take into account the effect of his policy upon his rivals (and upon himself again). In this latter case we may say that he considers his total influence upon the price, indirect as well as direct.[12]

One more distinction is made before we analyze the problem, i.e. his rival's policy may remain fixed with respect to the amount he offers or the price at which he offers it. The solution will be different in the two cases.

First we give the solution offered by Curnot.[13] Here mutual dependence is ignored. Each seller assumes his rival's supply constant.

Curnot assumed that each seller determines the supply which is most profitable for him in the light of his rival's present offering which do not change. He gives the example of two mineral springs, exploited by two owners without any expenses of production and contributing to the same market. For simplicity it is assumed that the demand curve for the mineral water is a straight line, DQ. This is illustrated in Fig. 14.20.

In Fig. 14.20, OA=AQ = the daily output of each spring. The price is zero when the total possible output OQ is put upon the market. Suppose that initially there is only one seller in the market. To maximize his profit, he sells OA units of mineral water, for; at that level he equates his marginal revenue with the zero marginal cost.[14] Price is OP (= AC) per unit and profit

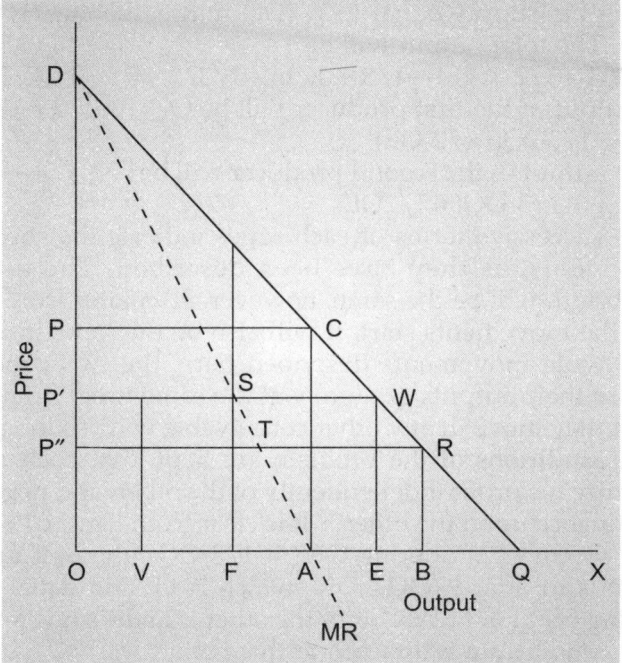

Fig. 14.20

is OACP. Now suppose that the second seller enters the market. Here comes Curnot's crucial assumption. To get an analytical solution of a duopoly situation one must make a behavioral assumption concerning each producer's expectations of his rival's policies. Curnot's assumption is that (as already stated) each entrepreneur expects his rival never change his output. So the best encroachment that his rival can make is to offer AB, rendering the total output OB and the price BR (the rectangular area ABRT, being the largest rectangle which can be drawn in the triangle AQC). The first producer now finds his profits reduced to OATP′. Thereupon he tries to increase them by reducing his output to ½ (OQ—AB). The process will continue, the first producer being forced gradually by the moves of the second to reduce his output, the second producer being able slowly to increase his share of the market until each one is contributing equally to the total market. In these adjustments, each producer will always find his maximum profit by making his supply equal to ½ (OQ minus the supply of the other). The total output will be

OQ(1—1/2 + 1/4—1/8 + 1/16—1/32...) = 2/3 OQ (= OE). The output of the first producer will be OQ(1—1/2—1/8—1/32...) = 1/3OQ(=1/2 OE)

The output of the second producer will be OQ(1/4 + 1/16 + 1/64...) = 1/3 OQ(= 1/2OE)

The successive terms of each series indicate the successive adjustments, as they have been described. The ultimate equilibrium will be the same, however, no matter from which point the movements start. It will also be the same if, instead of the wide movements described here, the two producers increase their outputs gradually at the same time, from ½ OA each if they move in any other conceivable way, so long as the initial conditions of the problem are kept, that each tries to maximize his profit independently of the other, and neglecting his influence upon the other.[15] It is clear from Fig. 14.19 that, if either producer is offering OF (= 1/3 OQ), the best his rival can do is to offer ½(OQ—OF), which is FE and equal to OF, securing profit of FEWS. Since the other is in the same position, stable equilibrium is attained at this point.

Similarly, it can be shown that if there were three producers the total supply would be ¾ OQ, each supplying 1/3 of this amount and so on for larger number. If there are 100 producers the supply would be 100/101OQ, and if the number is extremely large, it would be virtually OQ. When supply tends to OQ, price tends to zero. The addition of cost curves will not in any way affect the essential conclusion, which is that as the number of producers increase from one to infinity the price is continually lowered when what it would be under pure or perfect competition. The price is perfectly determinate irrespective of the number of sellers. The equilibrium price for any given number of sellers would be closer to the purely competitive price under diminishing cost than under constant cost, and closer under constant cost than under increasing cost.

Edgeworth's Solution

Edgeworth's analysis is based on Joseph Bertrand's criticism about Curnot's analysis. Curnot assumed as we have seen that each seller assumes his rival's supply constant. Bertrand, on the other hand, believed that a solution should be worked out on the assumption that entrepreneurs believe that their rivals maintain a constant price. This suggestion was developed by Edgeworth into duopoly solution.

Mutual dependence ignored: Each seller assumes his rival's price constant.

Edge worth's solution is illustrated in Fig. 14.21

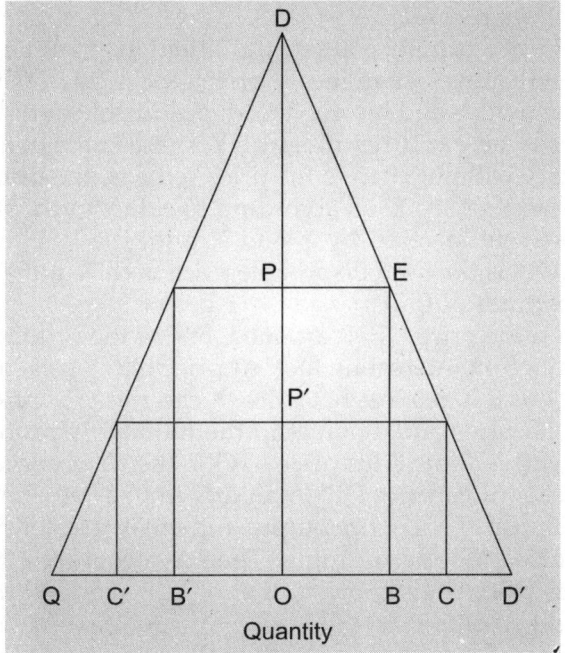

Fig. 14.21

As in Curnot's solution, let us suppose two firms situated side by side selling a homogenous product produced at zero marginal cost. The entire market is pictured as being divided equally between the two producers, X and Y. DD' is the demand curve facing producer X and DQ is the demand curve facing producer Y.

Each producer has a maximum achievable rate of output and, therefore, rate of sale. These maxima are represented by

OC for X and OC' for Y. Finally the ordinate OD is the price axis. By construction OB'=B'Q. If X enters the market first, he will produce and sell OB units, selling each unit at OP price. He will thus reap a maximum monopoly profit OBEP. Now Y enters the market under the assumption that X will not change his price. So he sets his price slightly below that of X (=OP') and sells his maximum producible output OC'. In other words Y's price being lower than that of X and their products being identical, Y sells as much as he can produce capturing a sizeable portion of X's market.

Now it is X's turn to evaluate the situation. Assuming (as he does) Y will never change his price, X can lower his price slightly below Y's and his maximum producible output OC. In the process he captures most of Y's market. Then, Y still assuming X will not change his price reduces the price below that of X and so on. Thus according to Edgeworth, price will be successively lowered by Y and X until the level of OP' is reached. OP' is the total disposable price both X and Y can sell their maximum outputs.

But once the price OP' is attained, one of the producers (say X) will notice an interesting fact. At price OP, Y sells his entire output. Thus if Y retains that price, X can raise his price to OP and sell OB units and again reap the monopoly profit OBEP. Consequently, X raises his price to OP. Then Y observes that if he raises his price from OP' to an amount slightly below OP, he can dispose of his entire output and enjoy greater profit. So he raises his price accordingly. Then X recognizes that if he lowers his price slightly below that of Y, he can sell his entire output and so on.

Consequently price move continually between OP and OP'. The duopoly situation, according to Edgeworth, is unsuitable and indeterminate. The Edgeworth case, just as the Curnot case, requires no comment because it is based upon the naïve assumption that is itself continually shown to be wrong by market results.

Chamberlin's Solution

Chamberlin's solution is based on the assumption of mutual dependence. Chamberlin's analysis is very similar to that of

Curnot except for the final result. Chamberlin's analysis is illustrated in Fig. 14.22.

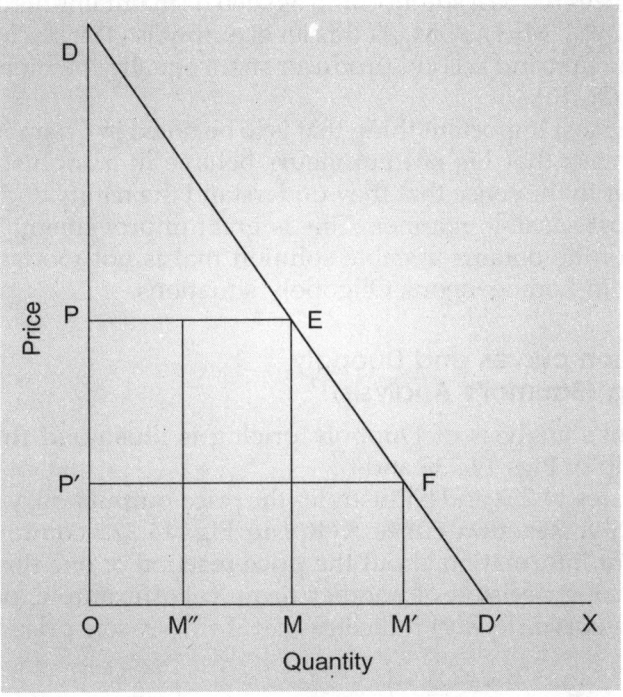

Fig. 14.22

In Fig. 14.22 DD′ represents the linear demand for mineral water. Initially the first producer (owner) enters the market and sells OM units at price OP, thereby reaping a monopoly profit OMEP. Now the second producer enters the market. Seeing that the first producer produces OM units, the second producer regards ED′ as his demand function. The best he can do is to sell OM′ units. Price falls to OP′ and total profit for both producers is given by OM′FP′.

The difference between Curnot's and Chamberlin's solutions is that according to Chamberlin the first producer will survey the market situation after the second producer's entry, recognize their mutual inter-dependence and recognize also that sharing monopoly profit OMEP is the best either the first or the second producer can do. Consequently the first producer reduces his output to OM″ = ½ OM. The second producer also recognizes the best solution and as such he maintains his output at MM′=M″M=1/2OM. At this level output is OM, price is OP, and the first and second producer share equally the monopoly profit OMEP.

The most important thing that is to be noted in Chamberlin's solution is that his entrepreneurs behave in a sophisticated manner in the sense that they understand the reality and act in the most sensible manner. This is great improvement; but in addition he obtains a stable solution that is not too far from reality in homogeneous Oligopoly situations.

Reaction curves and Duopoly Pricing (Baumol's Analysis)[17]

Baumol's analysis of Duopoly pricing is illustrated through the help of Figs 14.23a and b.

Figures 14.23a and b illustrates the price-output policy under Duopoly. Reaction curve RyR'y in Fig. 14.22a contains the relevant information about the price reaction of one firm Y to the pricing decision of another firm, X. For example, point P on this curve (RyR'y) indicates that if firm X sets price Px for

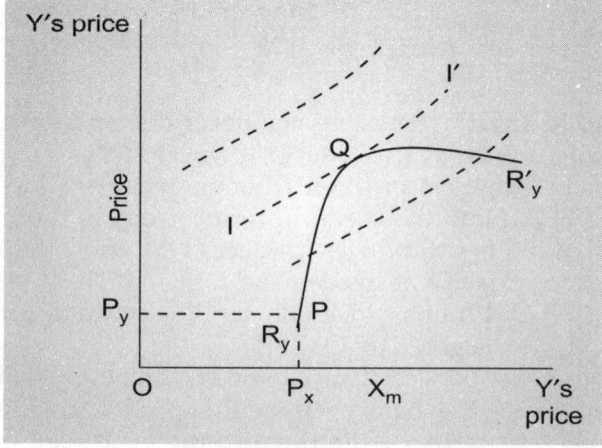

Fig. 14.23a

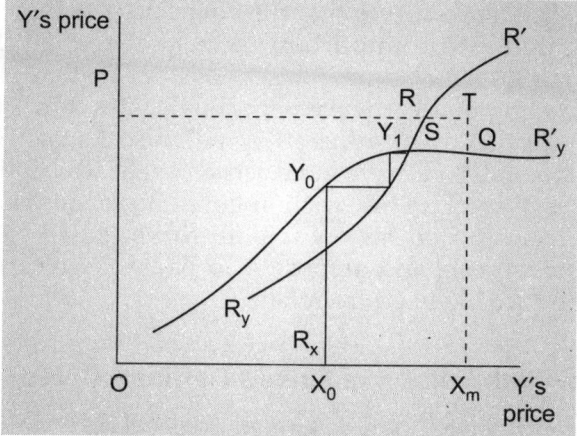

Fig. 14.23b

its product and if firm Y reacts in accordance with the
information by its reaction curve, the price of Y's product will
become OPy.

If Y sticks to this reaction pattern, X's optimal price decision
can be represented quite easily. The dotted curves in
Fig. 14.22a represents the indifference curves of X's objective
function, i.e. they are his iso-profit curves if X is a profit
maximiser.

Then the highest indifference curve which X can attain (the
highest indifference curve compatible with Y's reaction pattern)
is ll' which is tangent to Y's reaction curve at point Q. To get
this point, X must set price OXm and accordingly, this must be
his optimal price.

So far, so good. But unfortunately for the analysis, two can
play at optimization. Figure 14.22b contains, in addition to Y's
reaction curve RyR'y, which indicates the manner in which Y
expects X to react to his prices. Y, in turn, may now pick an
optimum point, say R, on X's reaction curve RxR'x, and thus
he will set his price at OP. But if both X and Y choose these
"optimal" prices they will end up neither on point Q nor on
point R. Rather the resulting point combination will be
represented by T, a point which lies on neither reaction curve.

The result will be that producers (both) will be surprised at
their earnings—they may either be pleasantly surprised (on

higher indifference curves that they expected) or they may be disappointed. More important, they will realize that the reaction curves have become falsehoods, for neither producer is now reacting in accordance with the dictates of his reaction curve. Once they realize this, they will also know that their optimality conditions have gone astray. What was optimal for X so far as Y stuck to his reaction curve no longer is optimal once Y strikes off on his own? Both firms must begin their calculations afresh, and according to Baumol we cannot say where they are likely go from here.

Hall and Hitch Version of Kinked Demand Curve

The Hall and Hitch model of kinked demand curve is based on an empirical survey conducted among well managed firms in UK. The survey was directed to know how firms in the real world determine price and output.

The major findings of their study are listed below:
   i. In the real world most manufacturing firms operate in oligopolistic markets.
  ii. Contrary to what is assumed by economic theory, in reality oligopolistic firms do not know their demand curve because of uncertainty regarding their rivals' reaction. They do not therefore know their marginal revenue curve. Since most of the large firms tend to be multi-product firms, they also do not know their marginal cost curve. Thus in the real world, firms cannot determine their equilibrium price and output by equating marginal cost and marginal revenue.
 iii. Oligopolistic firms in reality determine their price on the basis of the full cost principle. They charge a price which not only covers variable and fixed costs but also yields a fair profit margin. The full cost is the sum of average variable cost and average fixed cost at normal output level and a predetermined percentage of this sum added for fair or reasonable profit. In short, according to this principle, price = full cost at normal output + fair profits as a percentage of full cost.
  iv. The demand curve has a kink at the price which is equal to full cost price. If a firm charges higher than full cost,

its rivals will not follow suit but will keep their prices constant. Hence for prices higher than the full cost price, the demand curve of an oligopolist has high elasticity. If a firm charges less than the full cost price, its rivals will follow suit by lowering their prices. Hence, for prices less than the full cost price, the oligopolist's demand curve has relatively low elasticity.

v. Oligopolistic firms adopt full cost pricing rule because it not only covers average fixed cost at normal output but also earns a reasonable rate of profit. The objective of oligopolistic firms is to have long-run stable profits and a 'quite life' free from uncertainties. If profits exceed what is regarded as 'reasonable' or 'fair', it may attract new entrants and complaints or accusations of excessive profit from customers as well as distributors. Both these will cause instability of long-run profits and make life difficult for firm's decision makers. Similarly charging a price below full cost will be considered unethical by competitors and create a threat of price war. Also, it is difficult to raise price later to the full cost level. Thus, for oligopolistic firms, price tends to remain rigid or sticky at the full cost level, and short-run changes in costs and demand will not cause changes in the oligopolistic price.

The full cost version of the kinked demand curve is shown by Fig. 14.23c where OM = normal output, OP full cost price and DPiDi is the kinked demand curve. Elasticity e for DPi is greater than elasticity ei for PiDi.

The kink occurs at the full cost price. Thus unlike the Sweezy version, the Hall and Hitch version explains how the existing price is determined.

Game Theory

Game theory is connected with the choice of the optimum strategy in conflict situations. Specifically game theory can help an Oligopolist choose the course of action (for example, the best price to charge, the optimum degree of product differentiation, or the best level of advertising) that maximizes its benefit or profit after considering all possible reactions of

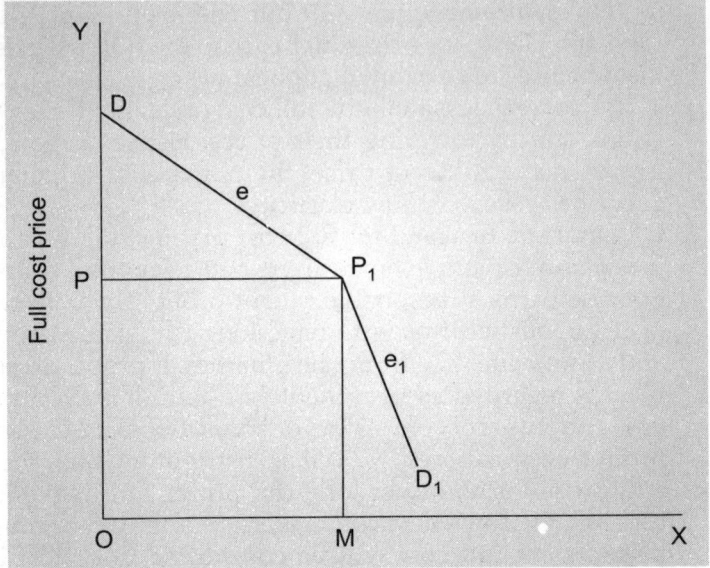

Fig. 14.23c

its competitors. For each strategy adopted by one firm there is usually a number of strategies open to the other firms. The outcome of each combination of strategies adopted by two firms is called the pay off. The pay off all the strategies is called the pay off matrix.

Contestable Market Theory

According to the contestable-market theory, even if an industry has only a single firm (Monopoly) or a few firms (Oligopoly), it would still operate as if it were perfectly competitive if entry is "absolutely free" (i.e. if other firms can enter the industry and face the same costs as the existing firms) and exit is "entirely costless" (i.e. if there are no sunk costs so that the firm can exit the industry without any loss of capital). In this case, the market is said to be contestable. Actual competition is then less important than potential competition and the firm or firms will charge a price that only cover average costs (and earn only zero or economic or normal profit).

Monopsony

Monopsony is a market situation where there will be only one buyer. In such a situation it is in the interest of the buyer to try at as low a cost (price) as possible, just as the monopolist tries to obtain as large a return as possible. Thus the monopsonist firm's output level will be chosen with an eye on the consequences for input prices of a change in its demand for inputs (William Baumol).

The optimizing buyer's demand curve will always be a marginal curve. The business firm facing an input whose price is fixed will buy inputs up to the point where the input's marginal revenue product is equal to its price. The firm's input demand curve is, therefore, a curve of marginal revenue product, i.e. for every possible quantity of input purchase it indicates the value of its marginal revenue product. Exactly through the same argument it can be shown that the optimizing consumer's demand curve must be a curve of marginal utility (with utility measured in money terms). That is, at any product quantity it shows the maximum money amount which the consumer would be willing to give up for an additional unit of the product.

The profit maximizing monopsonistic firm's equilibrium requires the normal marginal cost equals marginal revenue condition. This means that the monopsonist's input purchase must be at a level which the marginal revenue product of the input is equal to its marginal cost to the firm. A similar argument would apply to monopsonistic purchases of finished products.

Because of the above mentioned reasons the monopsonist's equilibrium point will be given by the intersection of his demand curve with the curve marginal to the supply curve of the input (the average input cost curve). (William Baumol).

Bilateral Monopoly

Bilateral monopoly can be explained by extending the concept of the indifference curve by interpreting the curve either as a curve of constant utility or a curve constant profitability (William Baumol). So any two points on such a curve are

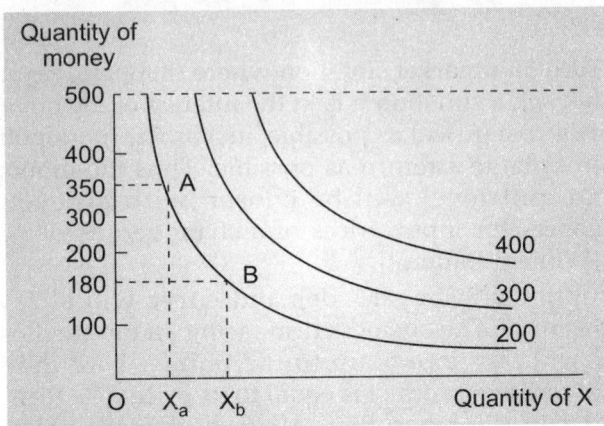

Fig. 14.24a

equally profitable. Here we take the case of two people who are exchanging two commodities. If one of the items exchanged is money, one of the bilateral monopolists (the money payer) may be identified as the buyer and the other as the seller. Assuming that the buyer is an input buyer and the seller an input supplier we may draw an indifference map between money and the quantity of the input sold for each of these persons. In Fig. 14.24a we have such an indifference map.

Here it is assumed that the buyer starts with Rs. 500 in money. In interpreting the indifference map we should read down the figure to determine the amount the buyer gives in exchange of the input. For example, at point A he ends up with OX units of X and Rs. 350 of his original supply of money (Rs. 500) left. This implies that he has spent Rs. 150 for buying OX of X.

Each such indifference curve is a locus of money – input purchase combinations which are equally profitable. All points on the lower curve (just in the case of indifference curve) yield lower profit compared with points on the higher curve.

We can draw a diagram to represent the circumstances of the supplier by measuring the maximum supply capacity level downward.

The profit indifference curve represents the locus of all

combinations of quantity supplied and revenue which yield him a fixed level of profit (after reducing the cost of production of that quantity of output from his total revenue at that point).

The two indifference curve maps can be combined in an ingenious rectangular diagram (Fig. 14.24b). One of the indifference curves maps is turned upside down and the ends of the axes joined. Thus the buyer's total money supply

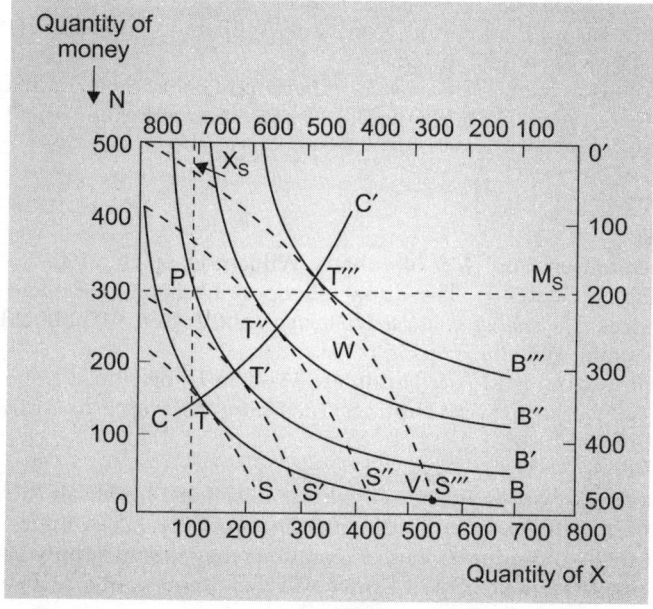

Fig. 14.24b

determines the length of the vertical axis, and the fixed output production capacity gives length of the horizontal axis. Now any point in the diagram may be interpreted as a trade. That is it shows simultaneously where both of the bilateral monopolists will end up after an exchange. For example point 'P' represents a trade in which the buyer ends up with 100 units of input and 300 units of money while the seller ends up with the balance— Rs. 200 (point M) on the right hand axis) and 700 units of X in the form of unused production capacity – point Xo on the top axis (Note that the sellers holdings are read downward and to the left from the upper right-hand corner of 'O' which is the origin of his upside-down indifference curve map. Any point thus automatically indicates the ending position of both the buyer and the seller.

References

1. Baumol, William J; *Economic Theory and Operations Analysis,* op.cit.p.335.
2. Samuelson, Paul A and Nordhaus, William D; *Economics* (18 ed); Tata McGraw Hill, p.166.
3. Robinson Joan; *The Economics of Imperfect Competition*; London, p.51.
4. Stonier, Alfred W & Hague Douglas C; *A Textbook of Economic Theory*; op.cit., p.106.
5. *Ibid; p.*172
6. *Ibid*; p.174
7. *Ibid*
8. Samuelson, Paul A & Nordhaus, William D; op.cit.p.190.
9. Stigler, George J; "The Kinky Oligopoly Demand Curve and Rigid Prices"; *Journal of Political Economy*, Vol.LV, Oct.1947; quoted from Baumol, William J; op.cit; p.356.
10. Samuelson, Paul A & Nordhaus, William D; op.cit.p.191.
11. Chamberlin, Edward Hastings; *The Theory of Monopolistic Competition*; 1965, p.31
12. *Ibid*; pp.31-32
13. *Recherches Surles Principes Mathematiques dela Theories des* Richesses, chapt. Vll; quoted from Chamberlin; op.cit. pp.221-223.
14. If the two producers were to combine, they would supply between them the amount OA at a price AC, their joint profit OACP, being a minimum at that price.
15. Chamberlin, Edward Hastings; op.cit.; p.33
16. *Ibid*; p.34
17. Baumol, William J; *Economic Theory and Operations Analysis*; op.cit., pp.356-357.
18. Schaum's outline of theory and problems —Macro Economic Theory; Third Edition.

15 Pricing Methods

Pricing Methods

Formulating pricing policies and setting the price is often a critical factor in the successful operation of business organizations. Even though the basic pricing ingredients are the same for all firms (costs, competition, demand and profit), the optimum mix of these factors varies according to the nature of products, markets and the overall objective of the firm. Thus, the job for the management is to develop and implement an appropriate pricing strategy that meets the needs of the company.

Here we propose to discuss at first the most widely used pricing methods adopted by firms. These include cost-plus or mark-up pricing, break-even pricing, variable cost pricing, peak-load pricing, going-rate pricing, product tailoring, cyclical pricing, and other related pricing techniques. The chapter concludes with a discussion on new product pricing and environmental pricing factors.

Practical Pricing Methods

Generally businessmen prefer a pricing procedure which is easy to implement and require only very few assumptions on demand. The simplest method which satisfies the above condition is known as cost-plus pricing or mark-up pricing.

Cost-Plus or Mark-Up Pricing

Two studies of pricing behaviour have been made in the United Kingdom, one by a group at Oxford University,[1] who interviewed business magnates, and another by Clive Saxton, who depended on a mail questionnaire. These studies revealed that a majority of businessmen set prices on the basis of cost-plus a 'fair' profit percentage. By cost they usually mean all allocated cost at current output and wage levels. By 'fair profit' is meant a fixed percentage mark-up which differs greatly among industries and firms. Some of this variation may be due to differences in cost base and some to differences in turnover rate and risk.

Evaluation of Cost-Plus Pricing

Does the use of rigid customary mark-up over cost make logical sense in the pricing of products? The answer is usually, no. Any pricing technique that ignores current demand elasticity in formulating prices is not likely to lead, except by chance, to the achievement of maximum profits, either in the short-run or in the long-run. As elasticity of demand changes, as it is likely to do seasonally, cyclically, or over the product life cycle, the optimum mark-up should also change. If mark-up remain a rigid percentage of the cost, then under ordinary conditions it would not lead to maximum profits.

Under special conditions it may be possible that a rigid mark-up at the right level may lead to optimum profits. The two conditions are that average (unit) costs must be fairly constant over the range of likely outputs and price elasticity must be constant for different points on the demand curve and over time.

In spite of the shortcomings mentioned above, cost-plus pricing or mark-up pricing continues to be popular with a sizeable population of the business community. The reasons for this popularity are:

i. There is less uncertainty about costs than about demand. So by relying on costs, pricing is simplified and the seller does not have to make frequent adjustments as demand conditions change.

ii. Where all firms in the industry use cost-plus pricing approach, their prices are similar. This helps to minimise price competition which would not be the case if firms paid attention to demand fluctuations when they priced.

iii. There is the feeling that cost-plus pricing is socially fairer to both the buyer and the seller. The seller does not take advantage of the buyer when his demand becomes acute; yet the seller earns a fair return on his investment.

iv. Cost-plus pricing is the safest though not the most profitable method of pricing.

In short, the popularity of a cost-oriented approach to pricing rests on considerations of administrative simplicity, competitive harmony and social fairness.[2]

Break-even Pricing

Break-even pricing indicates how many units must be sold at selected prices to regain the funds invested in a product. A break-even chart prepared for ABC Ltd is given below (Fig. 15.1). The figure assumes that production and selling of ABC's product involve annual fixed expense of Rs. 85000 and the variable production costs for direct labour materials, and factory overhead are Rs. 2 per unit. When the fixed and variable costs are added, total cost intersect the revenue-price curves at point A, B and C. These points show the volume needed to recover full costs at factory prices of Rs. 3; Rs. 3.60; and Rs. 4.60.

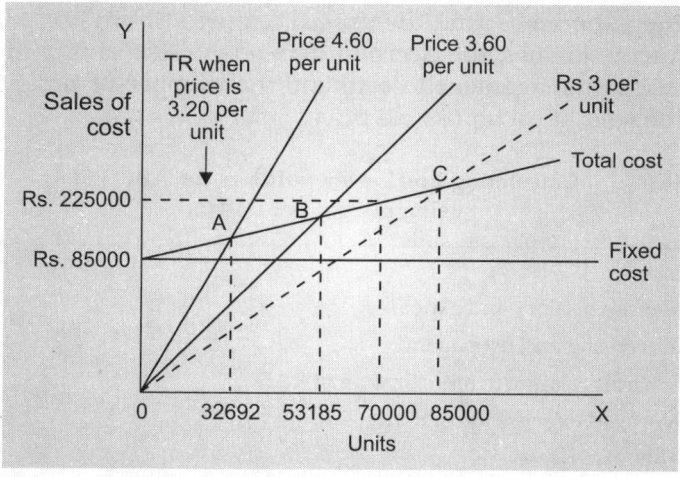

Fig. 15.1

Profits are generated when sales exceed break-even points and losses occur when sales fail to reach the break-even levels.

Although a break-even chart provides a visual representation, it lacks some of the details that can be included in a tabular analysis. Table 17.1 gives break-even volumes for six potential ABC prices by dividing the total fixed costs by the margin generated at each price. The table also indicates the final prices the consumer would pay when the wholesale and retail margins are added to ABC's selling prices. It may be pointed out that the price and the break-even volume are inversely related. A price of Rs. 2.60 requires sales of about 141,700 units to break-even while a price of Rs. 5 requires only 28300 units to be sold.

The most serious defect associated with break-even pricing is its inadequate treatment of demand. The relationship between the final retail price and the number of ABC's products that will be purchased by consumers is crucial to the selection of the optimum price is obvious. Breakeven diagrams, however, usually indicate total revenue as straight lines implying that larger volumes can be sold without lowering prices (see the break-even charts). This is rather unrealistic and the company management must consider which combination of price and break-even volume will lead to maximum profits. Some of the factors influencing this decision are rival's offerings, previous pricing experience, and the special features (if any) of ABC's products. Finally, the decision depends on the ability of the company management to estimate the number of units that will be sold at each possible price.

**Calculating break-even volumes for ABC Ltd
using margin per unit**

Rs.	
Sales force salary and expenses	25000
Advertising and propaganda	40000
Expenses relating to amortization of R&D	5000
Overhead expense allocation	10000
Other expenses	5000
Total	85000*

Contd...

Retail price (Rs. including wholesale & retail margins) possible manufacturing	5.42	6.25	7.50	8.33	9.58	10.42
Selling prices (Rs.)	2.60	3.00	3.60	4.00	4.60	5.00
Variable cost (Rs)	2.00	2.00	2.00	2.00	2.00	2.00
Margins (Rs.)	0.60	1.00	1.60	2.00	2.60	3.00
Break-even volume in 000 of units (Rs. 85000) mfg's margin	141.7	85.00	53.20	42.50	32.70	28.30

- The fixed costs could be increased to include a profit so that the break-even volumes would show the sales needed to return a planned profit.

Rate of Return Pricing

Pricing to achieve a planned rate of return on investment is popular among a number of business firms. It is also associated with the pricing policies of the public utility concerns.

The pricing procedure used in rate of return pricing can be illustrated by referring to ABC's Ltd, mentioned earlier. Here the management's first task is to estimate its total costs at various levels of output. The total cost curve is shown rising (Fig. 15.1) at a constant rate until capacity is approached. Management's next task is to estimate the percentage of capacity at which it is likely to operate in the coming period. Suppose that ABC's capacity is 100000 units and the total cost of producing this volume is Rs. 250000. Assume further that the firm expects to operate at 70 percent capacity. This means that it expects to sell 70000 units. The total cost of producing 70000 units, according to Fig. 17.1 is Rs. 225000 or about Rs. 3.21 per unit. Management's next task is to specify a target rate of return so that the planned rate of return on investment will be achieved. If ABC aspires for a 20 percent after-tax rate of return on its Rs. 250000 (0.20 × Rs. 250000 = Rs. 50000) and the tax rate is 50 percent, and then the price must be set to produce Rs. 100000 in total profits. Since ABC plans to sell 70000 units, a factory selling price of approximately Rs. 4.64 per unit will generate the desired profit and return on investment.

Rate-of-return pricing, however, has a major defect. Sales estimates are used to derive a price ignoring the fact that price is an important factor that influences sales. A price of Rs. 4.64 may be too high or too low to sell 70000 units. What is missing from the analysis is a demand function, indicating how many units ABC Ltd could expect to sell at different prices. With an estimate of the demand curve and with the requirement to earn 20 percent on costs, ABC Ltd could solve for those prices and volumes that would be compatible with each other. In this way, ABC Ltd would avoid setting at a price that failed to generate the estimated level of output.

Variable Cost Pricing

Variable cost pricing is often based on the idea that the recovery of full costs is not always realistic or necessary for the profitable running of business firms. Instead of using full costs or standard costs as the lowest possible price, this system suggests that variable cost or incremental cost represents the minimum price that can be charged. For instance, assume that company ABC Ltd's products have been marketed successfully through normal wholesale-retail channels and a total of 70000 units have been sold in the past year at a price of Rs. 4.64 per unit. This price covers full costs of Rs. 3.21 and allows company ABC Ltd a 20 percent after tax return on its investment of Rs. 250000. Company ABC Ltd is now approached by a new customer who wants to make a special purchase of 20000 units of its products at a price of Rs. 2.50 per unit. To evaluate this proposal company ABC Ltd must know how much it will cost to produce these 20000 units. If the variable cost per unit comes to Rs. 2 per unit; ABC Ltd could make a contribution of Rs. 10000 out of this order.

Under what circumstances Company ABC Ltd can accept this order is a big question. Some would suggest that the order can never be accepted as the price offered does not cover full costs. Others would point out that if company ABC Ltd were to cut prices for this particular customer, other customers would demand and equal cut in prices. This could result in losses because there would be no way for ABC Ltd to cover full expenses. While there is an element of truth in this line of argument, the crucial point is that the full cost of manufacturing each unit is not constant but, in reality, is quite sensitive to changes in volume. This is shown in Fig. 15.2 where unit costs decline as the fixed expenses are distributed over a larger volume. If we assume that ABC Ltd's variable costs are constant at Rs. 2 per unit, then 20000 units can be produced for Rs. 6.25 per unit and 70000 for Rs. 3.21 per unit. If volume could be expanded further to 170000, unit cost would be reduced to Rs. 2.50 offered by the new customer. This indicates that a very low price can cover full costs if volume of production expands sufficiently.

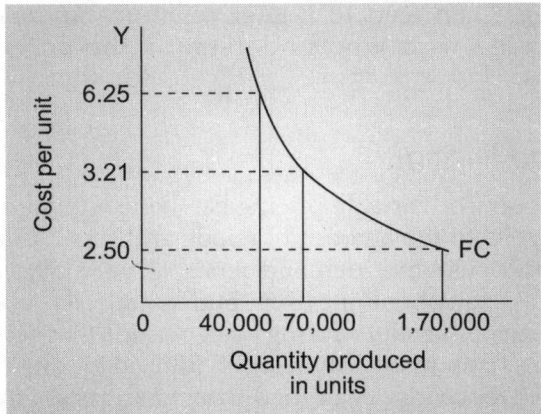

Fig. 15.2: Relationship between volume and unit cost for ABC Ltd

In the present situation, adding 20000 units to the current production of 70000 units lower estimated fixed costs per unit to Rs. 0.9444 (85000/90000) When fixed costs are added to variable costs of Rs. 2.00 (which is constant), total costs (Rs. 2.94) exceed the Rs. 2.50 offered by the new customer. Since the order will bring less than full costs, it is important to consider whether the two markets being served are really insulated. Whether the sales to the new customer will in any way reduce the existing sales? If the two markets are really separated, then the new order will look more attractive. Acceptance of the new order will also depend upon the availability of unused capacity.

Variable cost pricing is often encountered in situations where fixed costs make up a large production of total unit costs. The rail roads and airlines are two industries with high fixed costs that have made effective use of the volume generating aspects of variable cost pricing. The underlying idea is that it is better haul bulk commodities and special classes of travelers at low rates and make some contributions than not to have the business at all. Railways typically face a declining unit-cost curve except when volume approaches capacity and tracks and yards become congested. This means that more volume usually increases profits by reducing the average cost of hauling merchandise. The airlines have used variable cost pricing when they set fares for excursions or special groups of customers. Variable cost pricing is not a panacea for all products or for all firms, but it can lead to higher revenues and profits for sophisticated firm who understands the potential and limitations.[3]

Peak-Load Pricing

A special form of variable pricing can be used when there are definite limits to the amount of goods and services a firm can provide and customer demand tends to vary over time. For instance, the telephone industry builds capacity to satisfy 80 to 90 percent of its callers during peak periods that occur during week days. This results in a lot of unused phone circuits at night and weekends. Peak-load pricing suggests that phone rates should be raised above average costs during high demand periods and reduced towards variable costs during low demand periods and allows the phone industry to operate with below full capacity. Again, the very low off-peak rates may increase revenue by attracting some callers that normally do not use the phone for communication purposes.

This form of pricing is also adhered by telegraph departments, electricity undertakings, etc.

The most important advantage of peak-load pricing is that it depresses peak demands and thereby reduces the total resources needed to satisfy customer demand. Again, it stimulates off-peak consumption and allows more utilization of available (existing) facilities.

Going-Rate Pricing

The most popular form of competition-oriented pricing exists when a firm tries to keep its price at the average level charged by the industry. This form of pricing is known as going rate or imitative pricing. This system of pricing is popular for a number of reasons. Some of them are mentioned below.

i. Where costs are difficult to measure, it is felt that the pricing rate represents the collective wisdom of the industry concerning the price that would yield an attractive return.

ii. It is also felt that conforming to a going price would be least disruptive of industry harmony.

iii. The difficulty of knowing how buyers and competitors would react to price differentials compel the producers to adhere to the going rate-pricing.

Going-rate pricing primarily characterizes pricing practice in homogenous product markets, although the market structure itself may vary from pure competition to pure oligopoly.[4] Under pure or perfect competition a firm has actually no choice about the setting of its price. There is apt to be a market-determined price for the product which is not established by any single firm or group of firms but through the collective interaction of a multitude of knowledgeable buyers and sellers. The firm daring to charge more than the going rate will attract no customers. The firm need not charge less than the going rate as it can dispose of its entire output at the going rate. Thus, under highly competitive conditions in a homogenous product market the firm really has no pricing decision to make. The major challenge facing such a firm is good cost control.

In pure oligopoly also the firm tends to charge the same price as in competition, although for different reasons.[5]

Product Tailoring

Product tailoring refers to a policy of determining the selling price in advance and then working back to the design of the product. It is an inverted cost–price relationship in which the price of the product appears to determine its cost, instead of the other way round discussed so far. Product tailoring is directly applicable only when product design is fluid and when the target price is sharply defined by the economic situation in respect of substitutes and demand. This approach has the virtue of starting with market price realities; it looks at the problem from the view point of the buyer in terms of what he wants and what he will pay. This technique may profitably be employed in an aircraft industry.

Refusal Pricing

Refusal pricing is related to products that are designed to the specifications of a single buyer. Such products are priced on the basis of estimated incremental cost plus a gross margin equivalent to the opportunity cost. The producer's pricing is called refusal pricing because he is deciding whether or not to make the product at all; in other words, he has the option to refuse the order if he wants. But it may be noticed that even here cost sets only a floor for prices; otherwise, the seller might miss potential immediate profits and ignore the effects of price upon future business.

Cyclical Pricing

The pricing decisions of a firm have to take into account fluctuations in inventory, in capital outlays, in national income and in employment. It is of common knowledge that the prices of agricultural products and certain raw materials and manufactured goods have been predominantly flexible over the cycle. But the prices of certain other raw materials and the products of price leaders is relatively inflexible over the cycle. This is because of the fact that price leaders are reluctant to change their price frequently and they often try to limit price cuts in products of declining demand. They also refrain from major price increases in periods of rising demand. The main reasons for this type of price inflexibility can be grouped under four heads on the basis of cyclical changes in conditions of: (i) demand, (ii) competition, (iii) costs, and (iv) profits.

On the demand side, producers often believe that the demand for their products is highly inelastic and hence price changes will not lead to any appreciable change in demand. From the point of view of competition, it may be stated that much industrial pricing is done under oligopoly conditions and that even the price leader has to maintain a degree of price stability in order to ward off retaliation from others. This in effect freezes prices and delays changes, usually until other prices have started moving. On the cost side, variable cost per unit tends to remain relatively constant over long periods and widely differing outputs on account of the rigidity of prices of raw materials and labour. Fixed cost per unit, as reported in conventional accounts, varies inversely with volume and with cyclically sensitive material prices. Current full costs, therefore, appear cyclically rigid and the prevalence of cost-plus pricing imparts some of the cost rigidity to prices. On the side of profits, many firms, especially the price leaders who have considerable latitude in price-making, have generally as their goal a 'reasonable' profit rather than profit maximization. Hence they may not lower or raise prices appreciably during business cycles.

The main practical problems of cyclical pricing arise as to the degree, the timing and the pattern of cyclical price changes affected in net prices may take many forms of which the most important are:

   i. Changes in list prices,

  ii. Changes in product-mix and product-line differentials, and

 iii. Changes in the structure of discount and merchandising allowance. In formulating policy on cyclical pricing, a potential price leader or firm having substantial independence in price determination can consider several possible policies some of which are mentioned below:

1. Price rigidity
2. Price fluctuations that conform to cost changes
   a. Current full cost
   b. Standard full costs
   c. Incremental cost
3. Price fluctuations that conform to prices of substitutes
4. Price fluctuations that conform to changes in general price level
5. Price fluctuations that stabilize market share
6. Price fluctuations that conform to change in industry demand determinants.

These policies might be characterized more accurately as objectives, since some of them cannot be fully attained.

Price Rigidity

Absolute or approximate stability of the firm's price level over the course of the business cycle is a policy followed by some producers of industrial materials and equipment. It is largely based on two assumptions:

    i. that the wide cyclical fluctuations in demand are caused by basic economic changes (e.g. in incomes, profits, expectations) and

    ii. that changes in the firm's prices within the range of feasibility will be ineffective in altering these conditions or in tampering these cyclical fluctuations in demand.

Price Fluctuations that Conform to Cost Changes

Confining cyclical changes in price to changes in production costs is another popular price policy. This policy has several variants depending upon which of the cost concepts, viz. full cost, incremental cost, or some forms of standard cost, that are employed.

Price Fluctuations that Conform to Prices of Substitutes

The use of substitute products as a cyclical pricing guide is an appropriate price policy in many situations. By keeping the spread between the firm's product and substitute products stable, or by manipulating it to obtain specified volume objectives, this cyclical pricing policy can protect or improve the company's market position.[6] Such a policy may also help to stabilize the industry's share of the vast substitute market. Under conditions of homogenous oligopoly, where there is strong price leadership, the cyclical price policy followed by many price followers is of this type.

Conformity to Changes in Purchasing Power

Keeping the price in line with the declining purchasing power of money is a depression pricing standard that has strong appeal. But it may be pointed out that this kind of blanket index of purchasing power is an inferior pricing guide.

Price Fluctuations that Stabilize Market Share

Price is one important background determinant of the market share especially when products and services are dissimilar. Again, price policy has considerable effect upon the larger share of the substitute market. Market share can be a useful pricing guide for cyclical pricing. But the administration of such a policy presupposes moderately **accurate** and current information about what is happening to market positions. It also demands alertness and flexibility in pricing.

Price Fluctuations that Conform to Changes in Demand Determinants

It is a known fact that demand schedules, both of the industry and of the firm, shift continuously consequent upon changes in general business conditions and changes in special outside conditions that affect the product. If these shifts in demand are marked, they should be taken into account in formulating prices. In reality, they are often more important than the elasticity of demand.

Changing prices in relation to some appropriate index of shifts in demand for the product is a form of recession pricing policy. Sometimes it is possible to find a direct relationship between some index like disposable income and past fluctuations of the price of the product. This functional relationship can then provide a rough criterion of the appropriate price at any given or forecasted level of demand.[7]

The use of any such historical relationship as an absolute recession pricing criterion has severe limitations that destroy its usefulness in most industries.[8] This pricing method implicitly assumes that

  i. flexible rather than rigid prices are appropriate,
 ii. changes in the price in the past have adjusted for changes in demand correctly,
iii. past pricing objectives are today's objectives; and
 iv. cost behaviour and competitive reactions will be the same as in similar periods in the past.

So far we have been discussing the different pricing techniques that are popularly followed by business firms under different situations. Here we propose to start a discussion on new product pricing. In this discussion we focus attention on the specific plans and strategies needed each phase of the product life cycle to improve the competitive position of the firm.

All successful products follow a four-phase life cycle that includes introduction, growth, maturity and decline. These typical stages are illustrated for a hypothetical product in Fig. 15.3.

At the introductory stage products are not known to the consumers. So here the emphasis should be on promotional activities so as to acquaint consumers with the product and gain acceptance. The sales of the product rise slowly and if it 'catches on', follows a period of rapid growth in sales volume. This stage is characterized by increase in the number of competitors, major product improvements, line production methods, penetration of other market segments, etc. So during this phase emphasis should be given in opening new distribution channels and retail outlets. When the product reaches maturity, sales grow slowly or remain stable. Special promotions are needed to cope with such situation. Finally the product reaches a stage of prolonged or rapid sales decline. At this stage the product needs to be

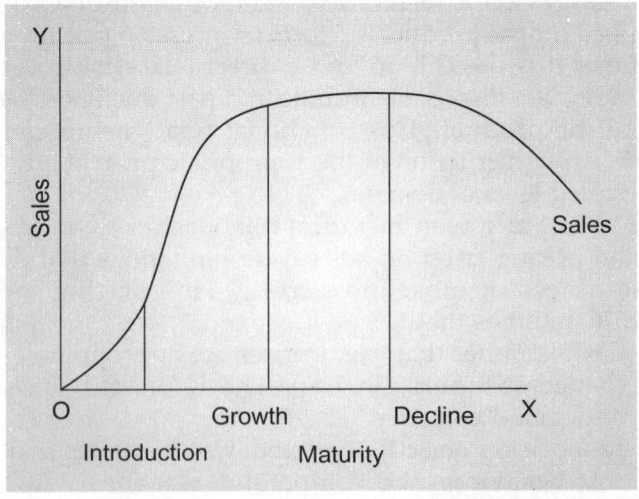

Fig. 15.3: Stages in the product life cycle

redesigned or the cost of production should be reduced so that they can continue to make some contribution to the company. When products become unprofitable, the firm must decide whether the product should be carried at a loss or phased out to make room for more profitable lines.

Product life cycle vary in length from few weeks for fashion goods to a number of years for appliances and food items. The length of time a product stays in any one stage of the life cycle depends on customer adoption rates and the extent of new product competition.

Three strategies that can be employed to stretch product markets are promotion of more frequent and varied usage among current users, finding new users for the product by expanding the market.[9]

Pricing a New Product

Formulating prices for new products is one of the most difficult problems faced by company management. These decisions are often complicated by lack of adequate information on both demand and costs. As the product has not sold before, price elasticity cannot be estimated from an analysis of past data. Even the simple expedient of following the competitor's price is not a practical alternative for new products. In spite of all these problems the firm must set a price that will help to the profits of the firm. A common approach to new product pricing is to make an intuitive appraisal of the product and to apply either a skimming or penetration price strategy.[10]

Skimming Price

The basic idea is to set a relatively high price that skim the cream of demand coupled with heavy promotional expenditure in the early stages of market development. The price is lowered at later stages. The objective of skimming price is to gain a premium from those buyers who always stand ready to pay a much higher price than others because the product, for one reason or another, has high present value for them.

The skimming price policy assumes that the demand for the product is likely to be more inelastic with respect to price in the early stages than when the product is full-grown. The situation is illustrated by the downward sloping curve DD in Fig. 15.4.

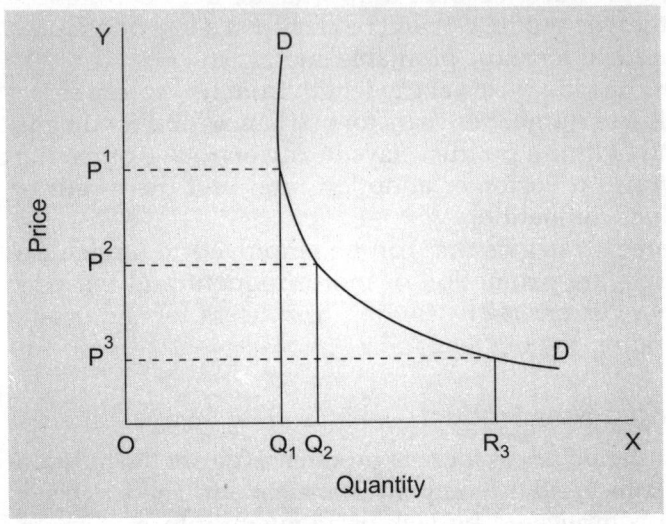

Fig. 15.4

The high initial price P^1 is designed to skim off the segment of the market that is insensitive to price, and subsequent price cuts $p^2 p^3$ broaden the market by tapping more elastic segments of the market. The logic of skimming price strategy is further supported by the assumption that many new products have no technical substitutes and price is not as significant as it is for traditional products.

The skimming pricing strategy has the advantage that it generates greater profit per unit than would be possible with lower prices. By setting a high initial price and then gradually lowering the price, the company is able to reap the maximum that each market segment is willing to pay for the product. Another advantage of a skimming price strategy is that it helps to restrict sales at a time when the firm may be unable to keep up with customers' orders. A policy of slowly lowering prices to expand sales makes it easier for the firm to increase production capacity to meet the growing demand.[11]

The strongest argument for adhering to the skimming price strategy is that it generally is the safest and the most conservative approach available. By starting with a high price the company can find out how many customers are willing to pay for the product while retaining the ability to lower the price if competitive conditions warrant such an action. If the company should accidentally set a price that is too high, it can always be reduced; whereas a price that is too low may be difficult to increase.

The most important disadvantage of the skimming price strategy is that the high margins associated with such a strategy attract competitors into the field. This suggests that the skimming price strategy can be best used when the product has patent protection or when there is barrier to entry such as technical know-how or high capital requirements.

Penetration Price

A penetration price is a relatively low price designed to stimulate the growth of the market and to capture a large share of it. The penetration price strategy is based on the following assumptions:

1. Demand for the product is highly elastic such as shown by the curve DD′ in Fig. 15.5

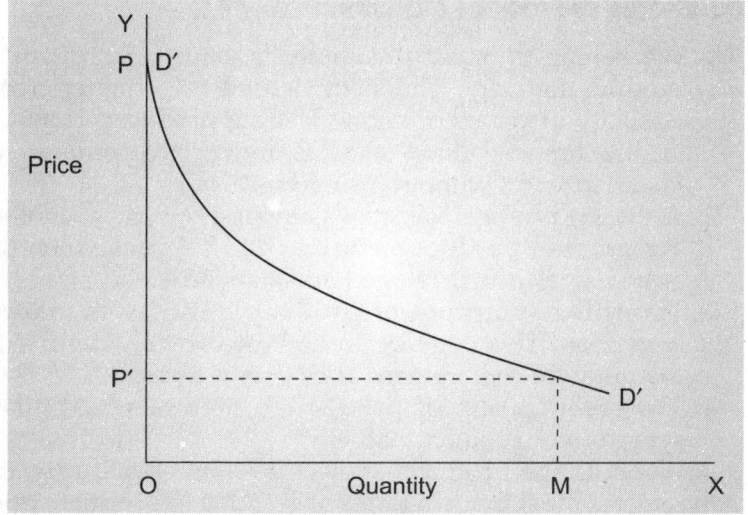

Fig. 15.5

2. There is no elite market that can be exploited with high initial prices. Under these conditions, a high price P' may actually result in zero sales.
3. The unit costs of production and distribution fall with increased output.
4. A low price would discourage actual and potential competition.

But it may be pointed out that penetration pricing is a high risk strategy that can lead to losses if sales do not live up to expectations. Another problem is the low margins which suggest that it will take longer time to recoup development expenses than it would with a skimming price policy.

Pricing in Maturity

The problem here is to determine a pricing policy for later stages of the cycle, i.e. after initiators have invaded the market of the once unique product. To formulate such a policy the producer must know when a product is approaching maturity. Hence we propose to list some of the symptoms of product maturity.

Symptoms of Product Maturity

1. Weakening in brand preference is the first symptom of product maturity. This is evidenced by a higher cross-elasticity of demand among leading products. Now the leading brand will not stand as much price premium, as it started with, without losing position.
2. Reducing physical variations among products is another symptom of product maturity. This happens when the best designs are developed and standardized.
3. The third symptom of product maturity is market saturation. This is generally indicated by an increase in the ration of replacement sales to new sales.
4. The stabilization of production methods is the last symptom of product maturity.

As soon as the products show the signs of maturity the management must think in terms of granting appropriate price reductions taking into account the cross elasticity of demand.

Environmental Pricing

So far we have been focusing our attention on the immediate demand and cost factors that influence pricing activities in mono product firms. There are, however, a number of other considerations that frequently influence pricing policies. These include the effects of multiple product lines, distributor's margins, competitive reactions, and legal restrictions imposed by governments. All these factors tend to influence profit and revenue maximizing prices derived from an analysis of demand and cost data.

Product Line Pricing

Since almost every firm has several items in its product line, product-line pricing becomes an important phase of price policy. The problems of product-line pricing are to find the proper relationship among prices of members of a product group.[12] Product-line pricing may refer to products physically the same but sold under difficult conditions. This gives the seller an opportunity to different prices. Thus differentials (e.g. hot coffee versus iced coffee), seasonal differentials (e.g. night flights or night telephone calls), and style-cycle differentials are all phases of product-line pricing. The rationale for this heterodox approach to pricing is that the essential economic feature of the product line is the cross-elasticity of demand that exists among parts of the seller's output.

General Approach to Product Line Pricing

The underlying principle in product-line pricing is that demand elasticities and competitive situations rather than cost should form base for determining the patterns of relative prices of the firm's products. And the role of cost should be confined to set lower limits for price and to help select the price-output combination that is most profitable. But in reality this principle is not widely employed in product-line pricing. Instead firms fix prices in such a way that they are proportional to full cost, (i.e. that produce the same percentage net profit margin for all products) or incremental cost (i.e. that produce the same contribution – over incremental costs for all products), or with profit margin that are proportional to conversion cost. Prices are also set in such a way that they produce contribution margins that depend upon elasticity of demand of deferent market segments or that are systematically related to the stage of market segments or that are systematically related to the stage of market and competitive development of individual members of the product line.

Demand Relationship in the Product Line

There are two demand relationships that are important in product-line pricing. The first is the interdependence of the demand for various items in the product-line. This interdependence may result from their nature as substitute or complementary products. The second demand characteristic is the importance of the products as instruments for market segmentation and price discrimination.

Product-line pricing has also to take account of competitive differences in respect of the different products in the line. The number of competitors, the extent of the firm's market share and the degree of substitutability of the competitor's product are symptoms with which the existing competition can be measured and the price adjusted accordingly.

The relevant concept of cost applicable in product-line pricing is incremental cost. Normally the incremental costs of each item of the product-line can be compared with its price. The margin between incremental costs and price will differ greatly from product to product depending on the demand conditions. Incremental cost set a floor below which the price should not go normally. Sometimes strategic considerations warrant the continuance of a product in a line even when its contribution to the profit margin is below average. Such a product may be "loss limiter" (i.e. it limits the losses from otherwise idle facilities) "line-filler" (i.e., it completes a product-line by offering a full range of colours, sizes, designs, etc.) or "price meter" (i.e. its role is to carry out the firm's policy of meeting every competitive price with some member of the product line).

Price Differentials

The two parts of a price are:
  i. the basic list price and
  ii. the net price actually charged. The difference between the two is due to the trade status of the buyer, the amount of his purchase, the location of the buyer, the promptness of payment, the time of purchase and the personal situation. The total returns realized by the manufacturer depend on the price charged on each section of the buyers and also the size of their purchase.

An important aspect of price differentials is price discrimination. By price discrimination is meant a policy of charging different prices for the same product; in other words, price discrimination exists when differences in prices charged by a seller do not exactly match differences in costs.[13] The relevant cost concept applicable in this context is marginal cost, though it has limitations when the plants do not function at full capacity and also when joint products involving common costs go into the product mix. From the welfare point of view, price discrimination often acts as an instrument for the equalization of the real burden. And even governments increasingly resort to various measures of price discrimination in the form of farm price support, subsidized low cost housing and food subsidy. The practical problem of price discrimination is to break the market into segments that differ in price elasticity of demand. Market segmentation can be justified only on the basis of the incremental concepts cost and revenue, i.e. only when the incremental revenue exceeds the incremental cost. The extreme form of price discrimination is practiced by media practitioners in whose case market segmentation may extent to the level of individual clients.

The manufacturer will have various goals in adopting differential prices for his products. Some of such goods are:
  i. *Implementation of a marketing strategy:* Differential price may be part of an overall strategy in order to reach particular sectors of the market.
  ii. Market differential price help in achieving profitable market segmentation when legal and competitive considerations permit price discrimination.

iii. *Market expansion:* Differential pricing that is designed to encourage new uses or to attract new customers is a common goal of product-line pricing, but it also extends to discount structure.

iv. *Competitive adaptation:* Differential prices are a major device for selective adjustment to competitive situations. When there are standardized products in the industry, differential prices help to achieve competitive parity with customers of different backgrounds.

v. *Reduction of production costs:* Seasonal discounts and the like reduce the overall production costs by encouraging off-season purchases.

Distribution Discounts

These are price deductions that systematically make the net price vary according to the buyer's position in the chain of distribution. They are also known as "trade channel discounts" and "functional discounts". They take different forms like functional discounts to buyers (e.g. wholesalers versus retailers), special price to manufacturers who incorporate the product in their own original product (e.g. spark plugs sold to automobile manufacturers), special prices to other member firms of the same industry (e.g. gasoline among petroleum companies) and special prices to government departments and other industrial buyers.

Quantity Discounts

There are deductions in the net price that are systematically related to the amount bought. They help to raise general efficiency of the economy though they do not encourage the development of small enterprises. Quantity discounts must be integrated into the general marketing strategy; the main management problem connected with these are what type of discount system should be chosen and how should the discount be for various sizes of purchase.

Cash Discount

Cash discount refers to reduction in the price, which depends upon promptness of payment. They promote prompt payment and are also a convenient way of identifying bad credit risks. They are, in fact an indirect collection cost.

So far we have been focusing our attention on trade discounts, quantity discounts and cash discounts. Now we turn to another aspect of the firm's system of price differentials, the geographical structure of prices.

The down to earth problem of deciding how a company's delivered price should be related to the geographical location of the buyer involves

    i. an examination of the various methods of geographical pricing; and

    ii. a survey of the factors that are significant in working out a policy on geographical pricing.

Geographical Pricing Methods

Geographical pricing methods may be categorized as follows:[14]

    i. Uniform delivered pricing methods

      a. Postage stamp pricing

      b. Zone pricing

    ii. Basing-point pricing method

      a. Single-basing point

      b. Multiple-basing point

      c. Full-freight equalization

    iii. FOB pricing methods

      a. Uniform FOB price with no freight absorption

      b. Regulated FOB price with freight absorption

      c. Unregulated FOB price with price absorption unrestricted.

Postage Stamp Pricing

Postage stamp pricing means delivered prices that are the same for all buyers regardless of location.[15] In this case the final retail price is the same every where. Examples are magazines, wrist watches, razor blades, etc. Normally, transportation costs are negligible in such cases.

Zone Pricing

Zone pricing means that delivered prices are uniform within specified zones and differ systematically among the zones mainly depending upon the transport costs.

Single-Basing-Point Pricing

Under this system, all plants, regardless of their location calculate the delivered price of the product by adding to a base price the cost of transportation from a single pricing point.

Multiple-Basing-Point Pricing

Under this system of pricing, a number of producing centres are designated as basing points and the delivered price is calculated by starting with the base price at the nearest basing point, and adding standard transportation cost from that basing point irrespective of the location of the plant from which the product is actually transported.

Freight Equalization Pricing

Under full-freight-equalization pricing system all plants form pricing points. Delivered price is figured as the factory price at the nearest plant, plus standard transport cost to the customer.

FOB Pricing

Under 'Free-on-board' pricing (FOB), products are priced at the sellers plant and the buyer pays the actual freight and selects the mode of transportation. Three variations of FOB pricing can be distinguished on the basis of price absorption. They are:

- Uniform mill-net (no freight absorption);
- Freight absorption limited by regulation; and
- Freight absorption unrestricted.

Selection of Geographical Price Structure

In deciding its policy on geographical pricing, a firm must take into account a number of problems such as:

    i. What is legal?

   ii. What do competitors do?

  iii. How standardized is the product?

  iv. Where are competitors located in relation to the location of important customers?

   v. How important are transportation costs?

  vi. What policy is to be adopted on re-sale price maintenance?

Legal Constraints in Pricing

There are certain constraints in pricing. In the case of certain commodities, firms are not allowed to fix a price more than what is statutorily fixed by the government. In India, statutory price fixation is done by the Tariff Commission and Special Committee appointed for this purpose. Thus prices of commodities such as motor cars, iron and steel, cotton textiles, sugar, paper pulp, matches, salt, heavy chemicals, plantation rubber, etc. have been fixed by the Tariff Commission at one time or the other. The Commission, in fixing the price of these commodities, generally followed the cost-plus basis.

Review Questions

  1. Define the following:

    a. Cost-plus pricing

    b. Break-even pricing

    c. Rate of return pricing

    d. Variable cost pricing

    e. Peak-load pricing

    f. Going-rate pricing

    g. Product tailoring

    h. Refusal pricing

    i. Cyclical pricing

    j. Skimming price

    k. Penetration price

    l. FOB pricing

    m. Postage stamp pricing

    n. Basing-point pricing

2. List the advantages and disadvantages of cost-plus pricing
3. Mention the symptoms of product maturity.

XYZ Ltd.

Early in 2006, the Sales Manager and Controller of XYZ Ltd met for preparing a joint pricing recommendation for item 345. After the Chairman approved their recommendation the price would be announced in letters to retail customers. In accordance with the company and industry practice, announced prices were adhered to for the year unless radical changes in market conditions occurred.

The XYZ Ltd was the largest company in its segment of the textile industry; its 2005 sales had exceeded Rs. 6 million. Company salesmen were on a straight salary basis, and each salesman sold the full line. Most of the XYZ Ltd's competitors were small. Usually they waited for the XYZ Ltd to announce prices before making out their own price lists.

Item 345 an expensive yet competitive fabric of the sole product of a department, whose facilities could not be utilized on other items in the product line. In January 2004, the XYZ Ltd had raised its price from Rs. 1.50 to Rs. 2 per yard. This has been done to bring the profit per yard on item 345 up to that of other products in the line. Although the company was in a strong position financially, considerable capital will be required in the next few years to finance a recently approved long term modernization programme. The 2004 pricing decision had been one of several changes advocated by the Directors in an attempt to strengthen the company's working capital position so as to ensure that adequate funds would be available for this programme.

Competitors of the XYZ Ltd had held their prices on products similar to item 345 at Rs. 1.50 during 2004 and 2005. The industry and the XYZ Ltd volume for item 345 for the years 2000 to 2005, as estimate by the Sales Manager, are shown in exhibit No.1. As shown by this exhibit the XYZ Ltd had lost a significant portion of its former market position. In the Sales Manager's opinion, a reasonable forecast of industry volume for 2006 was 700,000 yards. He was certain that the company could sell 25% of the 2006 industry total if the Rs. 1.50 price was adopted. He feared a further volume decline if the competitive price was not met. As many consumers were convinced of the superiority of the XYZ Ltd's product, the Sales Manager reasoned that sales of item 345 would probably not fall below 75000 yards even at Rs. 2.00 per yard.

During the pricing discussions the Controller and the Sales Manager had considered two other aspects of the problem. The Controller was concerned about the possibility that competitors would reduce their price below Rs. 1.50 if the XYZ Ltd announced a Rs. 1.50 per yard for item 345. The Sales Manager was confident that competitors would not go below Rs.1.50 because they all had higher costs and several of them were in tight financial straits.

The controller prepared the estimated costs of item 345 at various volumes of production (Exhibit-2). These estimated costs reflected current labour and material costs. They were based on past experience except for the estimates of 75000 and 100000 yards. The company had produced more than 100000 yards in each year since World War II and pre-war experience was not applicable due to equipment changes and increase in labour productivity.

Exhibit 1, XYZ Ltd
Prices and production 2003–2008, item 345
Physical volume of production (yards)

Year Ltd's	Industry Total	XYZ Ltd Item 345	Price charged by most competitor's	XYZ price
2003	610,000	213,000	Rs. 2.00	Rs. 2.00
2004	575,000	200,000	Rs. 2.00	Rs. 2.00
2005	430,000	150,000	Rs. 1.50	Rs. 1.50
2006	475,000	165,000	Rs. 1.50	Rs. 1.50
2007	500,000	150,000	Rs. 1.50	Rs. 2.00
2008	625,000	125,000	Rs. 1.50	Rs. 2.00

Exhibit 2, XYZ Ltd
Estimated cost of item 345 at various
volumes of production (per yard)

When production in (yards)	75000	100000	125000	150000	175000	200000
Direct labour	Rs. 0.40	Rs. 0.39	Rs. 0.38	Rs. 0.37	Rs. 0.38	Rs. 0.40
Material	Rs. 0.20	Rs. 0.20	Rs. 0.19	Rs. 0.19	Rs. 0.19	Rs. 0.20
Material Spoilage	Rs. 0.20	Rs. 0.20	Rs. 0.19	Rs. 0.19	Rs. 0.19	Rs. 0.20
Department expenses						
Direct*	Rs. 0.60	Rs. 0.56	Rs. 0.50	Rs. 0.50	Rs. 0.50	Rs. 050
Indirect**	Rs. 0.40	Rs. 0.30	Rs. 0.24	Rs. 0.20	Rs. 0.18	Rs. 0.15
General Overhead ***	Rs. 0.12	Rs. 0.117	Rs. 0.114	Rs. 0.111	Rs. 0.114	Rs. 0.120
Factory cost	Rs. 1.20	Rs. 1.083	Rs. 1.003	Rs. 0.950	Rs. 0.943	Rs. 0.940
Selling and administrative expenses #	Rs. 0.780	Rs. 0.704	Rs. 0.652	Rs. 0.618	Rs. 0.613	Rs. 0.611
	Rs. 1.980	Rs. 1.787	Rs. 1.655	Rs. 1.568	Rs. 1.556	Rs. 1.551

*Indirect labour, supplies, repairs, power, etc.
** Depreciation, supervision, etc.
*** 30% of direct labour.
# 65% of factory cost

Review Questions

1. How, if at all, did the company's financial condition relate to the pricing decision?
2. What price, i.e. Rs. 1.50 or Rs. 2.00 should have been recommended?

References

1. R.L.Hall and C.J Hitch, *Price Theory and Business Behaviour*, Oxford Economic Papers, 1939
2. Philip Kotler, *Marketing Management; op.cit. p.525*

3. Dalrymple, Douglas J, et al. *Marketing Management,* op.cit. p.349
4. Philip Kotler; *Marketing Management*; op.cit. p.529
5. See chapter 14 for a detailed discussion of this aspect.
6. Dean, Joel; *Managerial Economics*; op.cit. p.464
7. Ibid; p.465
8. Ibid.
9. Dalrymple, Douglas J, et al. *Marketing Management*; op.cit. p.304
10. Dean, Joel; "Pricing Policies for New Products"; *Harcard BusinessReview;* vol.28 (Nov–Dec.1950); pp.28–36. Also see Dean,Joel; op.cit. p.419
11. Dalrynple,Douglas J; et.al.; *Marketing Management*; op.cit. p.358
12. Dean, Joel; *Managerial Economics;* op.cit. p.471
13. For further details see Chapter 14
14. Deab, Joel; *Managerial Economics;* op.cit.pp.541–542
15. Ibid. p.542.

16 Theories of the Firm

A theory generally serves two purposes. First it must explain what exists and, second, it must enable us to predict what does not exist. The purpose of the theory of the firm is to provide models for the analysis of the decision-making in the firm under different market structures. A theory of the firm must be capable of explaining the whole range of price out-put decisions—how the firms set their prices under different market situations, decide their product line, advertisement expenditure and sales promotion effort. R&D expenses, entry decisions and strategic as well as tactical decisions.

Any theory regarding the firm is expected to have some degree of generality capable of explaining the behaviour of a group of firms instead of a particular firm. Of course, case studies with reference to individual firms are relevant and important, but several such studies are required before constructing a theoretical model capable of predicting the behaviour of firms.

It is to be borne in mind that several changes have occurred with respect to the size and complexity of the markets after the days of industrial revolution. These changes are also reflected in the size, structure, complexity and operations of the firms. Many of the firms today operate on a global level. In their attempts to approximate the real world situation, the theorists also developed their models at different levels of aggregation and sophistication depending upon the requirement. Consequently, today we have a number and variety of models capable of explaining and predicting, with different degrees of precision the behaviour of firms. The

334

available theories of the firm can be grouped under three categories. They are:

1. Economic theory of the firm
2. Behavioural theory of the firm, and
3. Managerial theory of the firm.

It is to be borne in mind that these theories are not absolute. New interpretations are given or new theories are formulated as context and conjuncture differ. In chapters 14 and 15 we have explained how firms take or make price-quantity decisions under various market and real situations.

The Economic Theory of the Firm

A firm is a transforming unit. It transforms inputs into output under different conjunctures and in different quantities. When firms transform inputs into outputs they generate some surplus value. If firms do not create any surplus value, economists believe, they have no right to exist. If clay is transformed into pots and if that doesn't create any surplus value, there is no meaning in doing so. The firms can add form utility or place utility and adding such utilities enhance the market value or surplus value. The surplus value the firms create either by transforming the inputs into usable outputs or creating place or time utility is termed as profit. The economists hold the view that firms exists for making profit and the acid test of a firm is how much profit it makes.

Economists also believe that firms not only make profit, but they also attempt maximize profit. This is because, they believe, the level of profit reflects the level of efficiency of a firm, the profit distributed as dividends satisfy the shareholders, undistributed profit or retained earnings is the source of internal finance necessary for the firm for expansion and replacement programme. Taking into account all these aspects, economists hold the view that larger the profit that a firm makes, better is for the firm, its survival and growth. So, all firms aim at maximizing profit.

Firms maximize profits by equating their marginal revenues with their marginal costs. Then the firms attain equilibrium positions. The industry attains equilibrium by equating average revenue with average cost.

Under perfect competition the firm will have complete knowledge about the market and the product. So, it decides its policies on this understanding. Under other situations the firm knows its objectives and constraints; and accordingly the firm follows the optimum decision rule to operate on the relevant variables. For example, under perfect competition the firm acts as a price taker and under imperfect competition, the acts as a price maker. If demand elasticities differ in different markets then the firm acts as a price discriminator. Firms also work as price leaders or price followers depending upon the market situation. Some times firms rely on non-price factors such as advertisement and selling cost or after sales services. The firms may also operate on physical or real variables such as quantity or quality of the product rather than price variable. The decision regarding operational variables ultimately depends on the nature of the market.

Thus the economists' theory of the firm explains the adjustment process of the decision variable of the firm. It helps in predicting the firm's behaviour under different assumptions.

The economist's theory of the firm is criticized by various writers on the subject. The noted critics of this theory are Popandreou, Rothschild, Fellnex, Reder, Cooper, Scitovsky, William Baumol, Willaimson, Marris, Stackleberg, Simon, Savage and Small, Margolis. Boulding, Hall and Hitch, Milton Friedman, Machlup and Horowitz.

Let us now see their criticisms. In order to understand the significance of their criticisms we must have some idea regarding the basic assumptions underlying the economists' theory of the firm, viz;

1. Motivational assumption, and
2. Cognitive assumptions.

The motivational assumption is that the driving force of a firm's activity is profit. This assumption has two sides. First the firm maximizes profit and no other decision variable. Second the firm maximizes profit and maximization of profit describes the behavioural intention of the firm.

The cognitive assumption is stated in the form of complete knowledge or certainty. The firm is assumed to have complete knowledge about its decision environment and that is why it can function rationally and operate on a decision variable as per the optimum decision rule. Complete knowledge about the environment in which the firm operates makes the actions of the firm risk free. When firms take decisions under conditions of risk-free situations, the outcomes can be predicted definitely and accurately.

But is this true in the real situation? Do firms really maximize profit? Whether firms only maximize profit?

Differing answers are proposed to these questions. In the real world situation, it is observed that profit is not the only variable in the objective function of a firm. The firms have different goals such as production, inventory, market share, consumer consciousness, social responsibility, brand image, and so on. Further the firms may not always 'maximize' and in several cases they only 'satisfies'. In consonance with this general observation and criticisms, a number of alternate hypotheses are formulated by writers on the subject whose names are already cited. According to Popandreou firms intend to maximize a general preference function considering the profit interest of different groups such as owners, shareholders, managers, workers, consumers, government, etc. and not a single variable profit function.

According to Rothschild, in view of long-term survival, firms aim at organizational stability and security rather than maximizing the single variable profit function.

Fellnex hold the view that firms are interested in safety margin particularly when market competition is confined among the few.

Reder believes that firms often sacrifice profit objective when there is financial control. In such situations firms resort to internal financing out of retained profits so that they can keep financial control over their operations.

Cooper, on the other hand, believes that business firms like banks attempt to keep liquidity reserve sufficient to assure a sound financial position and retention of control. Liquidity considerations are combined with safety and economy considerations.

According to Scitovsky firms often trade-off between profit and leisure. The more profit they have, the less leisure they have and, therefore, firms aim at an ideal combination of profit and leisure in view of organizational safety and security.

William Baumol points out that, firms are often found to maximize sales revenue subject to the constraint imposed by a target profit set exogenously.

In the dynamic context the firms aim at stable growth of revenue, and profits are then exogenously determined.

Williamson is of the view that firms do not maximize profit, they only maximize the utility involved in managerial discretionary power.

Marris is of opinion that firms aim at balanced growth subject to financial and managerial constraints they face.

Stackleberg points out that oligopoly firms are not interested to maxi mum profits, they are only interested in stable market shares and reasonable regular flow of profits. They may thus share profits and share markets so as to occupy slowly and gradually the position of a market leader.

Simon believes that firms' behaviour is often 'satisficing' rather than 'maximizing'—satisfaction depending on the match between their aspiration and actual performance.

There are several more hypotheses with respect to the theories of the firm.

It is sometimes observed that firms sacrifice their profits to serve their social responsibilities. Sometimes they are more concerned about customer service or mass welfare of the society or pollution control or self-sufficiency or autonomy, etc. This is all the more true with respect to our public sector concerns.

Now we turn our attention to the cognitive assumption. This assumption also is not tenable in the real world situation. Business decisions are often directed to cope with changes occurring on account of very many factors. In reality most of these changes are unknown. The order, direction and impact of changes can never be accurately known. So the decision environment is full of risk and uncertainty. To assume perfect knowledge under such situation is highly unrealistic and fraught with danger. Firms working on imperfect knowledge cannot work for maximum profit. Economists calculate profit as the difference between production cost plus selling cost and the sales revenue. They don't take into consideration the information collection cost and that cannot be justified as collection; processing, storing and retrieving information involve cost. Modern decision support system using computer cannot be cost free. In the light of this a number if new hypotheses were proposed. Some of them are highlighted below:

According to Savage and Small the theory of choice and the theory of search have become two essential part of the theory of business firm.

Gordon and Margolis hold the view that firms are 'deliberative' rather than maximizing in their attitude.

According to Kenneth E Boulding a theory which assumes knowledge of what cannot be known is clearly defective as a guide to actual behaviour of the firm.

Popendreou writes that in the absence of knowledge concerning entrepreneurial horizons and expectations, the profit-maximizing construction becomes an empirically irrelevant tautology.

Hall and Hitch hold the view that firms do not maximize profit; in fact, they do not know what the maximum to aim at is. In reality, they follow short-cuts and rules of thumb, rather than the marginal principle of profit maximization.

The opinions expressed by Boulding, Popandreou and Hall and Hitch constitute vehement attack on the economists' theory of the firm. Some economists have tried to overcome these criticisms. For example, Milton Friedman has argued that the test of a theory depends on its explanatory and predictive value. He further argued that the soundness and significance of a theory depends on its operational use, its underlying assumptions cannot be the relevant point of attack. Machlup tried to defend the economists' theory of the firm by holding the view that the profit maximization considerations do guide business decisions; it is a subjective consideration, not being capable of being measured objectively. The marginal principle, if necessary, can be modified by the more general principle of incrementalism. Incremental concept and reasoning often guide business decisions.

Horowitz, on the other hand, reconstructed the economic theory of the firm under uncertainty and showed that profit maximization hypothesis can be extended to take care of risk and uncertainty in the real world. Developments in game theory, econometric theory, theory of probability and decision-making models strengthened the traditional economists' theory of the firm. It can also be seen that the behavioural theories and the managerial theories only supplement the economists' theory of the firm rather than rejecting the economists' theory.

After acquiring some knowledge about the economists' theory of the firm and the criticisms levelled against it and the later defence of the theory by authorities like Milton Friedman and Machlup we propose to discuss the behavioural theories of the firm.

It was Simon who first proposed in 1955 an alternate model to explain the economic behaviour of the firm. According to Simon businessmen must always have imperfect knowledge on which to base decisions. Under such a situation decision-making will be too complex. Given this and other uncertainties surrounding decision-making in reality, businessmen can never know whether they are maximizing profit or not. So, according to Simon, businessmen only 'satisfies' and they do not 'maximize'. In other words businessmen aim merely at satisfactory profit.

According to Simon, organization behaviour and individual behaviour are comparable. Like individuals organizations have their own aspirations, achievements, successes and failures and their aspirations levels are set to work in view of their needs, drives and attainments of goals. Firms make periodic review of their goals. They may face three alternate situations:

1. The actual performance is less than the aspirations
2. The actual performance is equal to the aspirations
3. The actual performance is greater than the aspirations.

The first situation may be due to several reasons such as inadequate information about future, pitching the aspirations very high, fluctuations in the economy, qualitative deterioration in the performance level.

In the second case as performance and aspirations (targets) tally, the firm will be more or less satisfied. So, no action will be taken except to review that the aspirations or targets have not been pegged too low and that the firm's potential performance has been rightly estimated.

The third situation indicates the firm's commendable performance. The firm will be satisfied. But there is a need to ensure that the quantitative achievement is not the result of decreasing quality of performance. This line of reasoning is tantamount to questioning success. While questioning failure is normal, questioning success is rare.

In the circumstances explained above, the firms remain satisfied except under the first situation. In the first case the firm has to organize search activity and choose to improve information flow.

Some Observations about Simon's Model

Simon's theory of the firm is based on his analysis on the analogy between individual and organizational psychology. Since Simon's theory is consistent with psychological theories of motivation it seems plausible. Psychological theories of motivation hypothesize that human action stems from drives, and that these actions terminate once these drives are satisfied. It may be seen that Simon's theory envisages a marriage between economics and psychology. Simon's theory is also consistent with empirical observation of business behaviour such as the propensity of businessmen to set prices on the basis of cost-plus, a mark-up designed to generate 'reasonable profit' or the tendency of big companies to state their profit targets in terms of earning a satisfactory return on capital invested.

The major defect of the 'satisficing' theory is the difficulty of making an operational statement of what is to be regarded as a 'satisfactory' level of performance. According to some critics Simon's approach is less satisfying than the economists' profit maximizing model that suggests an optimum level of profit consequent upon the operation with the decision variables. Against the 'optimum level' there may be many 'satisfactory levels' depending upon the groups that takes interest in the firm's activity. In such a situation the operational value of Simon's model is nil or negligible.

A firm has to satisfy a number of stakeholders. Unless attractive dividends are paid the shareholders will be dissatisfied. If fair or living wage is not paid, the workers will not be satisfied. Similarly, if prices are moderate and quality good, consumers will not be satisfied, and if attractive returns are not available from investment, owners will not be satisfied. Unless attractive pay, perquisites and working conditions are not provided, the managers will be satisfied. If taxes are not paid, the government will not be satisfied. If environment is not protected, the environmentalists will not be satisfied. Therefore, the firm must choose a particular level of profit and rate of return on capital employed so as to satisfy all the stakeholders. But the question is whether this is operationally feasible under all circumstances?

Cyert and March Model

Cyert and March, in their book titled *A Behavioural Theory of the Firm* published in 1963, focused on the decision-making process of large multiple product firms under uncertainty in an imperfect market. In such big firms, ownership and management will be separate. In the case of such firms, Cyert and March bestow their interests more in the decision-making process than in the motivation, profit maximizing or satisficing.

One must be familiar with certain concepts in order to understand the Cyert and March model. Some of these concepts are listed below.

Firms, as an adaptive rational system has the following properties:

1. There exist a number of states of the system. At any point, the system in some sense 'prefers' some of these states to others.
2. There exists an external source of disturbance or 'shock' to the system. These disturbances or shocks cannot be controlled.
3. There exist a number of decision variables internal to the system. These variables are controlled according to some decision principle.
4. Each combination of 'external shock' and 'internal decision variable' changes in the state of the system. This means that a new state is decided by the existing shock from the external environment and by the decision taken and implemented from within the firm.
5. Any decision rule that leads to a preferred state is more likely to be used in future than it was in the past.

In the light of the above propositions, we can state that the rationality on the part of the firm's behaviour suggests that the firm, operating with its internal decision variables, adopts itself to changing external shocks or disturbances and consequently a new sate results and the system continues through changing states.

Firm as a Coalition

Another view of the firm is that it is a coalition of various interested groups such as owners, workers, managers, shareholders, consumers, suppliers, financiers, government, and so on. These different groups may be having different motives, some expressed and some hidden. This is very similar to coalitions of political parties in government. If the firm is operating successfully; that means the coalition groups with conflicting interests is working satisfactorily. It is this coalition within the organization that has to be maintained so that the firm services and grows eventually. The growth of the firms may strengthen or endanger the coalition depending upon how the different groups in the coalition remain satisfied.

Organization Goal

Organizational goal is shaped by the objectives of the firm. Organization, just like individuals, set their goals to direct their respective business activities. The coalition members collectively decide on the goal and the goal directed activities of the firm. Several points regarding the organizational goals can be noted. Some of them are:

1. Goals are decided after deliberations among the coalition members.
2. All resolutions of goals within the coalition are not made by money. Many side payments are made coalition partners in the form of policy commitments.
3. Some goals are stated in the form of normative dictum.
4. Some goals are stated in non-operational form.
5. Achievements and aspirations can be compared when goals are set or stated in operational form. Such comparisons enable the coalition to modify goals and review its aspiration level mechanism.
6. Firms generally have multiple goals rather than a single profit maximization goal.

Organizational Slack

A coalition will be viable only if the payments made to the various coalition members are adequate to keep them together in the organization. If adequate resources are available to meet all demands, the coalition will be a feasible one. But owing to friction or conflict in mutual adjustment of payments and demands, there can be disparity between the resources available to the organization and the payments required to maintain the coalition. The difference between available resources and required payments is termed as 'organizational slack'. When firms operate under conditions of imperfections several types of slack can exist.

Process of Decision-making in Cyert and March Model

The organizational goals set by the top management are to be achieved through a series of decisions. Decisions are made at various levels of hierarchy in an organization. We can distinguish two levels of decision- making in an organization – one at the top management level and the other at the lower level of administration.

At the Top Management Level

Given the organizational goal and the resources, the allocation of these resources to the various departments is decided by the top management and implemented through the budget. Every Department will be getting allocation and the allocation will basically be based on the urgency, the bargaining power and skill of the head of the departments. The bargaining power will largely depend on the past performance of the department. The top management may retain some funds for discretionary use. The top management examines and decides the project proposals mainly based on two criteria, viz; (i) budgetary or financial criterion, and (ii) improvement criterion.

Decisions are based on information and information is not cost-free. Search has to be made to locate and collect information. Search involves employment of resources and the allocation of resources for this purpose is not made on marginalistic rules or principles suggested by economic theory. Again, there can be many slips in the information flaws. It may be distorted, diluted, delayed depending on the channels of information flow. So the decisions taken by top management may not always depend on adequate and appropriate information.

At Lower Levels of Administration

The decision process at lower levels involves various degree of freedom of action. Each manager has considerable degree of discretion in spending once the budget is allocated. For instance, the allocation of sales force is decided by the sales manager, the allocation of labour at the shop-floor is decided by the production manager and so forth. There may be delegation of authority to simplify the process of adminis-tration. Personnel at the lower level administration learn things from experience, individual staff tries to adjust and adapt themselves in the context of developments within and outside the firm which itself is an adaptive rational system.

Cohen and Cyert Model of Behaviourism

Here we present a simple model used by Cyert and March as an illustration of decision-making process within a large corporation. This has reference to homogenous duopoly selling at a single price ultimately. No changes in inventory are accommodated in this model. The steps illustrated by Cyert and March are given below:

1. *Forecast of rival's reaction:* This is a straight forward extrapolation of the past observed reactions.
2. *Forecast of firm's demand:* This is an extrapolation of past sales.
3. *Estimation of costs:* The present or current costs are assumed to be constant (or same as the historical cost) with necessary adjustments of slack payments.
4. *Specification of goals:* Based on revenue and cost calculations the firm fixes its profit goal. The aspiration level of profits may be taken as some average of past profits.
5. Evaluation of achievements vis-à-vis targets (goals or aspirations). The actual performance is compared with aspired goals as translated in terms of the target variables

such as price and output. If achievement tallies with aspiration, the firm is satisfied and otherwise, the firm is not satisfied and starts a fresh decision-making process, sometimes improving the information system.

6. If the profit goal is not realized the firm re-examines the cost estimate as some costs in the form of slack expenditure under the direct control of the firm.

7. If the new solution with downward adjustments of costs leads to the achievement of target profits, it is adopted.

8. If cost adjustments fail to yield target profit, the firm re-examines the demand forecasts. An upward adjustment in initial demand demands a revision in sales strategy.

9. *Evaluation of new solution:* If new solution with adjusted demand and cost estimates attains the profit goal, it is adopted; otherwise the firm proceeds to the next step.

10. *Downward adjustment of aspirations:* The firm lowers its profit goal.

What all these analysis want to highlight is that in reality a firm has multiple goals. Profit goal is just only one among them. Other goals such as production, inventory, market share, etc. are also equally important. When a firm works with multiple goals, in a goal programming frame-work, it works as a 'satisfier' rather than a 'maximizer'. The goals change as time passes goals change depending on the past experience or future aspirations or demands of the coalition constituents, shocks and slacks in the system. Failures force firms to resort to search and search activity yields better market information which may be used for improving the firm's performance. Through information searches the firm tries to improve information and thereby tries to overcome market uncertainty. Uncertainty with respect to rival's reaction is overcome by creating 'negotiated environment'.

A Critique of Behavioural Theory

The behavioural theory has contributed much to the development of the theory of the firm. Its major contributions are:

1. It highlights the process of goal formations in firms. The view that a firm is a coalition of groups of conflicting

interests is extremely realistic. Attempts to resolve conflicts lead to formation of agreed goals for implementation through managerial decisions.

2. It provides a practical view of the decision-making process. Fixing targets in the context of multiple goals, selecting instruments to achieve targets, specifying the decision variables for operationalization of the decisions, evaluation of performance against targets, planning and organizing search activity for improving information flow for better performance— all these are elements in decision-making process and the behavioural theory has laced them together in a logical frame-work vis-à-vis reality.

3. It deals with the dynamic process of resource allocation inside the firm from behavioural angles that were left out by traditional economic theory.

4. The concept of 'slacks' and 'shocks' have significant operational use. Slack payments often play a stabilising role for the firm and its smooth functioning.

Though the behavioural theory of the firm has contributed much for the understanding of firm's behaviour, it is not free from criticisms. The major criticisms levelled against this theory are listed below:

1. The theory basically provides a simulation approach to the complexity of the mechanism of the modern multi-goal, multi-product corporation. But simulation is a predictive technique and that does not explain the behaviour of firms. It only predicts the behaviour of firms without explaining any specific action of firms.

2. The behavioural theory concentrates on short-run situation when search activity is organized on a selective basis in problem areas only. Such search activities cannot explain dynamic aspects of either invention or innovation that have long-run implications.

3. The behavioural theory does not deal with industrial equilibrium. It neither explains the interdependence and interactions of firms nor the way in which inter-relationship of firm's leads to stable equilibrium of price and output at the industry level. The theory does not say anything about the conditions of entry of new firms or

effect of threat of potential entry of firms on the behaviour of established firms.

4. The lowering of the aspiration level (target) whenever the aspiration levels are not attained deprives the theory any objective criterion of measuring or evaluating satisfactory performance of firms.

5. No precise prediction of the firms' behaviour can be made by the behavioural theory. The acceptance of 'satisficing' behaviour makes the theory a tautological structure. That is whatever the firms do can be rationalized on the lines of satisficing.

6. Cyert and March developed their theory on the basis of results obtained from four actual case studies and two experimental studies conducted with hypothetical firms. So the empirical base is weak to formulate theories.

Managerial Theories of the Firm

Under this category we propose to discuss only three theories. They are: Baumol's sales maximization theory, Marris' model of managerial enterprise, and Williamson's model of managerial discretion.

The managerial theories can be considered as a sub set of the behavioural theories as the basic hypotheses of these theories are the same. As in the case of the behavioural theory the starting point of the managerial theories is the same: the firm is a coalition of different groups with conflicting interests, but to be reconciled for the survival of the firm. It is further hypothesized that the top management is the most important constituent in the firm because of its power in decision-making and access to information. In modern corporations what we see is the divorce of ownership from management. The owners are promoters and shareholders whose power lies in appointing the Board of Directors who in turn appoints the top management. The top management takes strategic and tactical decisions with respect to the running of the firm and if they can produce a profit that is 'acceptable' to the owners and if they can declare dividends sufficient to keep the shareholders happy, the top management will have job security. The divorce of ownership from management gives freedom to top management to deviate from profit maximization and follow goals that will maximize their own utility subject to a satisficing profit constraint. With this background information let us first take up Baumol's model of sales maximization.

Baumol's Model of Sales Revenue Maximization

William Baumol, in his famous book *Business Behaviour, Value and Growth* published in 1959 postulated the sales maximization hypothesis as an alternative to the profit maximization hypothesis. He has two models: one a static single period model, and the second, a multi-period dynamic model. For each model, he has two versions: one without and the other with advertisement expenditure. Some empirical evidence is available to verify Baumol's hypothesis and thereby the predictions of Baumol's model.

Static Models

The static models are based on the following assumptions:
1. The time span of a firm is a single period.
2. The objective of the firm during this period is to maximize sales revenue (i.e. value and not volume).
3. The firm operates under the profit constraint: the critical minimum profit is exogenously determined by demand and expectations of shareholders and other members of the coalition.
4. Conventional U-shaped average cost curve and the downward sloping average revenue curve hold true.

Under the above assumptions four models are conceived. They are:
- A single-product model, without advertisement
- A single product model with advertisement
- A multi-product model without advertisement
- A multi-product model with advertisement.

A simple representation of Baumol's model of a sales maximizing firm without advertisement is explained with the help of Fig. 16.1.

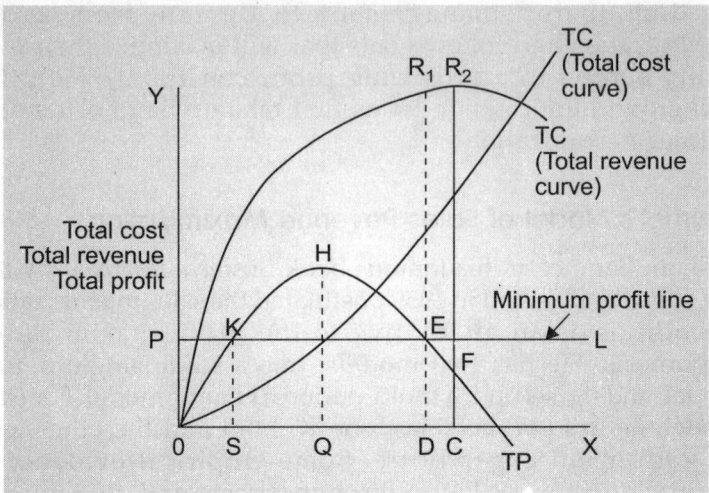

Fig. 16.1

TC, TR and TP curves in Fig. 16.1 show the Total Cost, Total Revenue and Total Profit of the firm respectively. The total revenue and the total profit curves of the firm rise up to a point and then decline.

The Total Cost Curve rises continuously. The horizontal straight line PL represents the minimum profit which the management expects from the operation of the firm. If the firm's objective is to maximize profit it would produce OQ as the highest point of the profit curve TP lies corresponding to this output. Since the firm wants to achieve sales maximization (Sales revenue maximization) it has to expand its operations up to a level at which the marginal revenue will be zero. This is attained when it produces OC level of output. (When total revenue is maximum, marginal revenue will be zero.) This output is larger than the profit maximizing output OQ. But the total profit at this level is only CE which is less than QH (the maximum profit the firm could earn). The sales maximizing profit is also less than the minimum profit (PL) that the management expects from the operation of the firm. The total profit that the firm should earn must be at least equal to OP and this is achieved when the firm operates at the level of OD output. At point E the total profit curve intersects the minimum profit line and so the sales maximizing firm will produce output OD. At output OD the firm will be having total revenue equal to DR_1 which is less than the maximum sales CR_2. But total revenue DR_1 is the maximum obtainable revenue to earn the minimum desirable profits PM. It may be noted that the firm can earn minimum profits DE even by producing SK output (minimum profit line PL also cuts the total profits curve TP at point K). Since the total revenue at output OS is much less than at output OD, the firm will not stop its operation at that level of output. Thus, in Baumol's model, oligopolistic firm will be in equilibrium at output OD and will earn a total profit equal to DE or OP. The price charged at this level will be equal to total revenue divided by total output that is, DR_1 divided by OD.

If the minimum profit expected is QH the firm will produce the profit maximising output OQ.

Sales Maximizing with Advertisement

Figure 16.2 represents this situation. In the figure TR represents the total revenue curve which represents change in total revenue as the firm raises its advertising expenditure, given the price of the product. Line OS represents the advertising cost. The line is drawn with 45° angle with X-axis. The rationale of this is that we have simply transferred the advertising outlay shown on the X-axis to the vertical axis. For example OC = CR. The other costs such as fixed and variable of the firm are taken to be independent of the advertising outlay. Therefore, by adding a fixed amount of other costs equal to OW to the advertising cost curve OS, we get the total cost curve WZ. Then taking out the difference between the total revenue curve TR and total cost curve WZ the total profit curve PQ is drawn.

It can be seen from the figure that if the firm wants to maximize profits, it has to incur advertising outlay equal to OH. At this level of advertisement outlay the profit curve reaches its maximum point T. If OL is the minimum profit constraint and the firm wants to maximize its total revenue with OL as the minimum profit constraint, it will incur OA on advertisement which is higher that OH. This implies that the objective of constrained revenue maximization leads to a greater level of advertisement outlay than the profit maximization. It may be noted here that there is no possibility of unconstrained sales or revenue maximum, as is there corresponding to output OD as in Fig. 16.1.

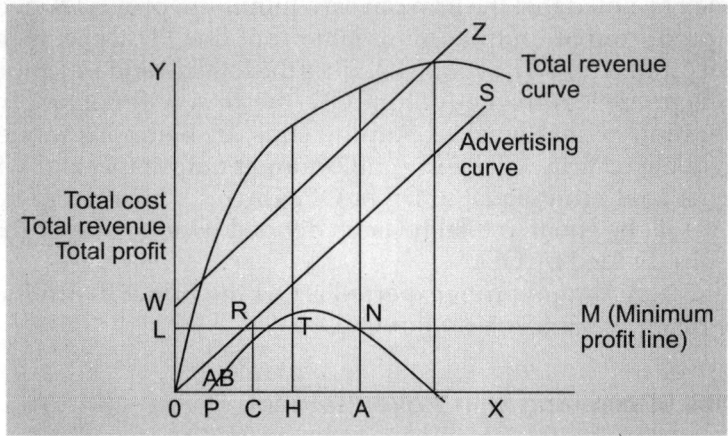

Fig. 16.2: Optimal advertising expenditure with sales maximization

The reason being, unlike a reduction in price, increase in advertisement outlay (by assumption) always raises total revenue or sales. So Baumol concludes that "It will always pay the sales maximiser to increase his advertising outlay until he is stopped by the profit constraint—until the profit have been reduced to the minimum acceptable level. This implies that the sales maximiser will normally advertise no less than, and usually more than, do the profit maximsers.

Sales Maximization Model: Pricing and Changes in Fixed Costs

An important implication derived from Baumol's sales maximization hypothesis is the effect of changes in fixed costs on prices of products. The traditional price theory based on profit maximization assumption asserts that so long as fixed costs do not vary with output the changes in them will not affect the prices of the products and nor even outputs produced of the products. But in reality it is seen that the changes in fixed costs do affect the prices and outputs. So, Baumol remarks

"This piece of received doctrine is certainly at variance with business practice where an increase in fixed costs is usually the occasion for a serious consideration for a price increase."

Based on his analysis Baumol asserts that sales maximization hypothesis with its minimum profit constraint can explain and rationalise the change in prices as a result of changes in overhead costs, whereas profit maximization, as explained above cannot account for it. If a firm chooses to maximise sales with a minimum acceptable profit constraint and is in equilibrium, then the rise in overhead costs would bring about increase in total costs and as a result the profit of the firm will fall below the minimum acceptable profit level. To prevent this fall in the profit level and to be in equilibrium again, the constrained sales maximizing firm will reduce the production of the product so as to raise the selling price of the product.

In Fig. 16.3 only profit curves are shown. At the initial stage let us assume that given certain cost and revenue total profit curve is PP_1. If OL is the minimum profit constraint, then, sales maximization firm with OL as the minimum profit constraint will be in equilibrium when it produces output OMi. On the other hand profit maximising firm will be in equilibrium when it produces OM output.

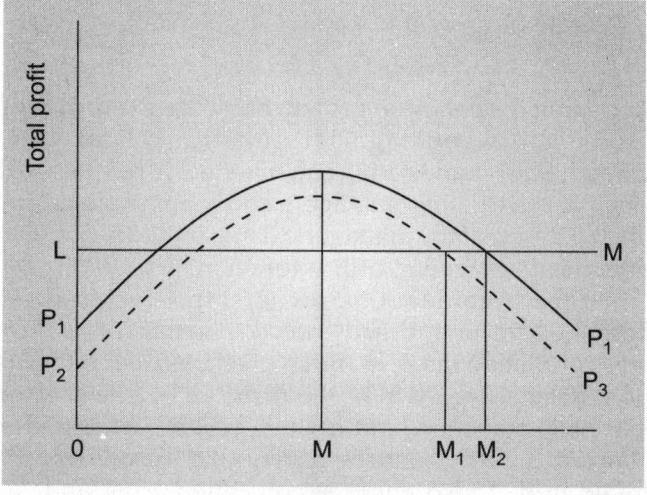

Fig. 16.3

We do not want to go into the details of the other models except to state that various studies have been conducted to test the veracity of Baumol's hypothesis. But empirical evidence is not conclusive either to prove or disprove the sales maximization hypothesis.

Marris Model of Managerial Enterprise

Marris' model is found in two of his significant works:
   i. An article entitled 'A Model of the Managerial Enterprise' published in the Journal of Economics in 1963, and
   ii. A book entitled *The Theory of Managerial Capitalism* published in 1964 (Macmillan).

Marris postulated a dynamic model of the firm stating vividly the objectives and constraints of the firm.

Objectives and Constraints

The objective of the firm is maximization of the balanced rate of growth (G). G depends on two factors:
   i. the rate of growth of the demand for the product of the firm (G_d), and
   ii. the rate of growth of capital supply (G_s).

$$\text{Thus } G = f\,(G_d, G_s)$$

In pursuing the balanced growth objective the firm confronts two constraints: managerial constraint and financial constraints. The managerial constrained is set by skill and efficiency of the existing managers and the financial constraint is set by the desire of the managers to maximize their own utility function and the owners' utility function.

In modern organizations ownership is separated from management. We have already noted that mangers and owners can have conflicting interests. But sometimes their interests may coincide. Balanced growth of the firm can be one such area of interest. Both managers and owners will be interested in this as balanced growth ensures fair return on owners' capital employed and it also ensures continued trust and faith in managers who were instrumental in achieving it. If the firm fails to attain balanced growth that may adversely affect managers' job just as owners' capital is at stake. Thus the goals of managers may coincide with the goals of owners. In other words, even though ownership and management are separate, owners and managers still may work together for a common cause – the balanced growth of the firm.

In such a context Marris specifies two different utility functions: one for the owner and the other for the managers. The utility function of the manager (U_m) includes variables such as salaries, power, status, job security. The utility function of the owner (U_o) includes variables such as profits, capital, output, market-share, public esteem. Most of these explanatory variables are finally related to the size and steady growth of the firm. Thus Marris states:

$$U_m = m(G_d, s)$$
$$U_o = 0(G_s)$$

Marris treats s as an exogenously determined constraint by assuming that there is a saturation level of job security. Above that level $(dU_m/d_s) = 0$, whereas below that level, $(dU_m/d_s$ =alpha. With this assumption the marginal utility function can be restated as

$$U_m = {}_m (G_d)s'$$

S = s' is the job security constraint.

Now we may have a second look at the constraints in this model. First is the managerial constraint. Marris adopts the thesis of Penrose that there exists a definite limit on the rate of managerial expansion such that managerial ceiling sets a limit to the managerial growth of a firm. Second is the financial constraint and that can also set a limit to the growth of a firm. This constraint originates in the job security considerations. Vis-a-vis job security; the managers become risk avoiders by choosing a judicious financial policy which consists of determining optimum levels of some critical financial ratios such as:

1. Leverage or debt ratio (Value of debts/total assets)
2. Liquidity ratio (Liquid assets/total assets)
3. Retention ratio (Retained profits/total profits)

These three ratios may be combined into a single parameter r to represent the financial security constraint.

To achieve balanced growth of Marris' firm, there are three instrumental variables.

$\bar{r}$ = the financial security co-efficient

d = the rate of product diversification

p = the average profit margin.

Taking into consideration the set of objectives, constraints and instruments, Marris' model in the complete form can be stated as under:

Structure of the model:

1. Demand growth equation = $G_d = D(p, d)$
2. Profit equation : $\pi = \pi (p, d)$
3. Supply of capital equation : $G_s = \bar{r} [\pi (p, d)]$
4. Security constraint : $\bar{r}$ less than or equal to r
5. Balanced growth equation : $G_d = G_s$

It may be seen that in this model the level of profit is endogenously determined, while the security constraint is exogenously determined by the risk attitude of the managers. Under this, the balanced growth of the firm is achieved through the operation of two instrumental variables, p and d. In balanced growth formulation, we have one equation in two unknown:

$$D (p, d) = \bar{r} [\pi (p, d)]$$

Williamson's Model of Managerial Discretion

Williamson, in his article 'Managerial Decision and Business Behaviour' published in American Economic Review in 1963, argued that mangers have discretion in pursuing policies which maximizes their own utility, rather than attempting the maximization of profits which maximize the utility of owner – shareholders.

Managerial utility function includes variables such as salary, security, power, status, prestige and professional excellence. Among these variables, only salary is measurable; the rest are non-pecuniary and non-operational; but they can be measured in terms of other variables. For example, manager's prestige and position is reflected in accordance with the amount of emoluments or slack they receive in the form of expense accounts, luxury offices, and company car, and so on.

We do not intent to present the technicalities of Willianson's model except to state that his model is a realistic one. He has tested his hypothesis that managerial discretion influences the expenditures for which managers have a strong expense preference (staff expenditure, emoluments, discretionary investment, etc.). Some of his experimental evidence supports the managerial discretion model:

1. Increase in staff and managerial emoluments(slacks) during boom and drastic cut in these expenditures during recessions.
2. Reaction of firms to changes in taxation.
3. Changes in staff expenditure, managerial emoluments and quantity in response to changes in fixed costs.
4. Drastic cut in staff expenditure by newly appointed top management, without affecting the productivity of the firm.

But it is often pointed out by critics that such evidence is not adequate for verification of a theory. More empirical research is needed to establish the propositions of these new theories.

In conclusion we may state that the managerial theories have some basic limitations. Such theories may be suitable in the case of large firms where there is scope for product diversification and discretionary investment. But in the case of small firms managerial decision is limited. Similarly, these theories fail to explain Oligopolistic interdependence in non-collusive markets. The theories also fail to explain how price is determined in the market. These theories focus output as a decision variable and the impact of output decisions on revenue, costs and profits. These theories also fail to capture all the constraints a firm faces. Williamson's model, for example, wishes away the role of many constraints in a very convenient manner. His model takes into consideration only two constraints, namely financial and managerial. Apart from this, in real life, firms face several other constraints such as social, political, cultural, environmental. Finally the managerial and the behavioural models do not really replace the traditional economic theory, but they only reinforce the profit maximization behaviour of a firm.

Review Question

1. Explain Baumol's sales maximizing theory of the firm.

References

1. Koutsoyiannis A (1979); *Modern Microeconomics* (2nd ed), Macmillan.
2. Wildsmith J.R; *Managerial Theories of the Firm*; 1972; Martin-Robertson.
3. Gilbert M(ed); *The Modern Business Enterprise*, Penguin; 1973
4. Baumol W.J (1967); *Business Behaviour, Value and Growth* (Revised edition) Harcourt Brace & World Inc.

17 Profit

A business firm is an organization designed to make profits, and profits are the primary measure of its success.

The above statement of Joel Dean brings to the fore the importance of profit in the context of managerial decision-making. Hence we propose to discuss in some detail the nature of profit, theories of profit and some managerial aspects of profit such as profit measurement, policy decisions on profit standards, profit goals and the use of profits for control purposes in a complex business organization.

Nature of Profit

Profit is the factor reward accruing to the entrepreneur for bringing together the other three factors of production, viz. land, labour and capital for producing some salable product or service. But who is an entrepreneur? Opinions differ. In the case of a modern corporation, for example, is it the equity share holders or paid managers that perform the entrepreneurial function? Vera Anstey, for example believes that the term should cover both these groups; and her suggestion seems a sensible one.

In a stationary economy in which everything turns out as expected and people know what their income will be, costs can be accurately imputed and the whole of the economic returns can be distributed as wages, interest and rent; so there remains no residual for profit. A firm can make agreements in advance to pay as costs these incomes to the factors of production. But in the world of reality incomes do not turn out as expected. Some one gets a bonus and some one else finds himself short. The resulting unexpected residuals could be shared equally by all factors of production through a profit-sharing plan, but they usually are not. Most people would rather be able to count on a limited income than depend on the uncertain chance of striking a bonanza. In practice, almost everyone gets a commitment from his employer to pay a definite income, and one or a few people (those who own the shares) agree to take what is left as profit.[1]

Profit thus is the revenue that is left after costs. But what to include as cost? There is difference of opinion on this point. There is no confusion regarding the outlays on raw material, on labour or interest on borrowed money. But problems arise when we consider the wages of management. Some economists are of the opinion that wages of management should be included in costs whereas certain others hold the view that they form part of profit. Again, certain non-cash items such as income that owner could earn if they work elsewhere, and interest that their funds could command if lent to others (what we call opportunity costs) do not appear in the books of accounts and, therefore, are excluded from conventional accounting of profit. Hence profits reported under accounting conventions lump interest return with reward for taking risks.[2] In other words what is by accounting convention, labelled net profits in the corporate income statement, is not profits as the economist typically views them. Instead, it is hybrid which includes elements of interest and perhaps wages and rent, as well as economic profit.[3]

Theories of Profit

We can classify the theories of profit under the following heads:
- Profit as an implicit return to any service/s or resource/s supplied by entrepreneurs to their own services.
- Profit as a return for risk bearing.
- Profit as a return for uncertainty bearing.
- Profit as the reward for enterprise and innovation, and
- Profit as a monopoly return.

We propose to discuss the above mentioned theories in some detail.

Profit as an Implicit Return

According to this view, profit represents nothing but a mixture of rent, interest and wages. The profits reported by a firm are the rewards that accrue to the owners of the firm for the factors of production that they supply in the form of personal work done by them, self owned natural resources made available to the firm, or the capital that the owners put therein. These different factor rewards cannot be easily spelt out as rent, wages or interest in separated categories; they are in fact implicit rent, implicit wages and implicit interest, all put together under the rubric of profit.

Among those who developed this type of thinking, mention may be made of FA Walker, an American economist. Walker regarded profit as nothing but rent of ability. Just as rent arises because of the differential advantage enjoyed by superior land over the marginal land, profit also is the reward for differential ability of the entrepreneur over the marginal entrepreneur. Profit is thus like rent, and like rent it does not enter into price.[4]

Another name which deserves mention in this context is that of FW Toussig. Taussig enunciated what is known as the wages theory of profit. According to him profits are merely wages for a special kind of labour.

Profit as a Return for Risk Bearing

The risk bearing theory of profit was advanced by FB Hawley. He was of the opinion that profit is the reward for risks and responsibilities that the entrepreneur subjects himself to. Peter Drucker identifies four kinds of risk: replacement, risk proper, uncertainty and obsolescence. A business risk is an eventuality which, though cannot be known in advance with precision, may nevertheless be anticipated in a rough and ready manner, and at least some of them are insurable. A risk should be distinguished from an uncertainty, the latter covers eventualities that are non-insurable. The major business risks and uncertainties are those arising from holding special purpose assets and fro price variations, technological changes and business cycles.

Profit as the Return for Uncertainty Bearing

Frank Knight, an American economist, has developed an important theory of profit. According to him all true profit is linked with uncertainty.[5] It is uncertainty, says Knight, bearing rather than risk taking which is the special function of the entrepreneur that leads to profit. As risks can generally be insured, says Knight, they involve little or no danger as contrasted with uncertainties which are non-insurable. Risks can, hence, be taken care of insurance companies. Uncertainties, on the contrary, cannot be known in advance with any degree of precision and hence they alone should count when profit is considered.

A similar but a bit different theory was advocated by JB Clark and his theory is popularly known as the dynamic theory of profits. In a dynamic business situation, says Clark, frequent changes take place; and those entrepreneurs who can foresee them will act wisely and reap the benefits of their action in the form of profits. In a static world there would be no profit but only "wages" of management. Hence profit represents the reward accorded to farsighted, clever and daring entrepreneurs for their wise response to changes taking place in the business world.

Profit as Reward for Enterprise and Innovation

Professor Joseph Schumpeter regarded profit as the reward accruing to the entrepreneur for the service of innovation. As in the risk theories, profit is thus a functional income, albeit risk plays no essential part in the innovation theory. According to Joel Dean, 'more than any other theory of profits, this one gets at the meaning of profits as the word is commonly used today, for it is hard to deny that innovation has been the backbone of business success'.[6]

Innovation refers broadly to any purposeful change in the production methods or consumer tastes that increases national output more than it increases costs.[7] Innovation includes the introduction of new commodities, new forms of organization, the opening up of new markets and the conquest of a new source of supply of raw materials.

Peter F. Drucker defines innovation as the entrepreneurial function of creating effectively and purposefully the new and the different.[8] He goes on to add that the business enterprise, its structure and organization, the way in which it integrates knowledge into work and work into performance—and the way in which it integrates enterprise with society and government—these are also areas of major innovative opportunity.[9] The measure of any innovation is on its impact on the environment. Innovation in a business enterprise must therefore always be market focused.[10]

Innovative opportunity exists where (i) there is glaring disparity between various levels of an economy or of a market and (ii) the exploitation of the consequences of events that have already happened but not yet had their economic impact.

An innovative strategy assumes that whatever exists is aging and will have to be changed or replaced. The governing device of a strategy for the ongoing business is: 'Better and More'. For the innovative strategy the device has to be: 'New and Different'.

The foundation of innovative strategy is planning and systematic sloughing of the old, the dying, and the obsolete. Improving organizations spend neither time not resources on defending yesterday. Systematic abandonment of yesterday alone can free the resources, and especially the scarcest resource of them all, capable people, for work on the new.[11]Again innovation efforts must aim high.

An innovation does not proceed in a nice linear progression. For a good long time, sometimes for years, there may be only effort and no result. Even more difficult to predict than the eventual success of the genuinely new is the speed wit h which it will establish itself. Examples are the computers, the antibiotics, the Xerox machine—all these are innovations that swept the market.

In the pure theory of innovation the key role is played by the entrepreneur who perceives the value of a new idea and is able to organize and carry out the job of turning it into cash. Generically the new idea is either a method to produce an existing product at less cost, to expand its sales at existing prices, or to make a new product that will sell at higher prices. The entrepreneur converts the idea into a net increase in national output by acting as organizer: he borrows capital at market interest rates, hires workers at current market wage rates and sets up the production and sales function into a going concern. Everyone employed is paid as much as he could earn elsewhere, and the entrepreneur pockets the surplus, if any, that is left out.

A point to be noted here is that risk and uncertainty are not necessary for the innovation theory. Innovation can strike and even shatter a stationary economy. In such a situation the innovator may be able to predict what his gain will be while other firms are blissfully ignorant of the obsolescence impending hanging over them.

Innovation theory thus, in a way points to the fact that profit is the reward for disturbing the *status quo*. Once the innovation hits the market there is bound to be a short or long period readjustment in which new firms climbs on to the bandwagon, labour shifts to the new industry, and obsolete products die out. If no other disturbance occurs; things will eventually reach equilibrium again, with a new set of prices, wages, producers and products. By this time profits might have been eliminated, for innovation profit exists only in times of dynamic change.

In innovation theory, says Dean, profits become an objective measure of the social value of ideas.[12] The concept of innovation becomes very broad in this theory, Dean adds, since it includes not only new products, but new organizations, new markets, new promotion and new materials. To an important degree, innovation has been built into competitive system complete with research laboratories and advertising staff. In many industries every one has to run fast to stay in the same place.[13]

Profits as a Monopoly Return

So far we have been concerned with a market structure characterized by perfect competition. But we know that the dream world of perfect competition is a far cry from the real world of business. Imperfections including those related to monopoly are the rule in the actual market situation. In the factor market, for example, two units of land seldom, if ever, show equality in fertility. Similarly two labourers of the same class are not likely to show the same efficiency. These examples indicate that the assumption of homogeneity under perfect competition has got only limited validity. Homogeneity in the factor market means that those units of a factor which are superior in quality to the rest can command a higher reward. They, in other words, will have a monopoly advantage over the others. Naturally, as per usual monopolistic practice, the supply of those units will be restricted artificially. The restriction of supply under monopoly conditions give rise to what is termed as 'contrived scarcities'.[14] And at least part are what is called profits is the reward for contrived scarcities. This reward can take the form of rent, wages or interest, depending upon the factor in question.

Contrived scarcities, whenever they exist, can distort the optimum allocation of resources. The earnings occurring as a result can be high or low depending upon the strength of the monopoly situation.

Having discussed the theories of profit, we now pass on to discuss the managerial aspects of profits. Initially we start with the problems associated with profit measurement.

Profit Measurement

The measurement of the amount of profit by a firm during a given period of time, say a year, is not an easy task. Several practical difficulties are involved here; some of them arise out of differences in definition of profits by accountants and economists and some others out of conceptual differences among them with reference to costs, income and valuation of assets.

Multiple meanings of the word 'profits', says Joel Dean, has always been troublesome. Economists are often unhappy about conventional accounting methods for measuring business income. Many consider them inadequate and sometimes misleading for penetrating analysis which often requires a complete reshaping of the conventional income statement.

The major points of difference between the economist's and accountant's approaches centre on: (i) the inclusiveness of costs; (ii) the meaning of depreciation; (iii) the treatment of capital gains and losses; and, perhaps more important, (iv) the price-level basis for valuation of assets.[15]

Inclusiveness of Costs

Here the problem is to decide what should be subtracted from revenue to get profit. The accountant will deduct the explicit or actual costs only from the revenue to determine profit. But the economist holds the view that in addition to the deduction of explicit costs, i.e. the costs that would have been incurred. In the absence of the employment of self-owned factors, should also be deducted. Examples are (i) entrepreneur's wages (which he could earn for working for someone else), (ii) rental income on self-owned land employed in the business and (iii) interest on self-owned capital. The profit arrived at by deducting imputed costs from accounting profit can be called as economic profit.

From the point of view of management, economic profit is more important than accounting profit. This is because economic profit alone reflects the true profitability of the business.

Even in accounting terms, measurement of profit is not easy. There are a number of accepted accounting concepts which provides for different methods of treatment for certain items of revenue or expenditure. Examples are (i) depreciation, (ii) valuation of assets, (iii) allocation of resources, over time periods, and (iv) capital gains and losses.

Depreciation

It is generally known that the equipment, machines and buildings get depleted with time and use. As time passes the equipment become useless from the point of view of business. This calls for some provision for the future replacement of the machinery and equipment. Accountants make periodic depreciation charges to income to recover the cost of equipment and machinery before their usefulness is exhausted. The procedure is to estimate the useful life in years and to make the annual charge just large enough to recover the original cost within the period. But the difficulty is that there is no single generally accepted method of depreciation and different companies use different methods[16] and this often vitiates the reporting of business profits.

For economists, there are two distinct types of depreciation charge. The first is the opportunity cost of the equipment and the second the exhaustion of a year's worth of limited valuable life.

The opportunity cost of equipment is the most profitable alternate use of it that is foregone by putting it to the present use. The alternative involved in using the asset for one year may be viewed as selling it at the beginning instead of the end of the year. The opportunity cost could then be measured by the fall in value of the equipment during the year.

The opportunity cost of depreciation depends upon the nature of the alternative.

The alternative may be to keep the equipment idle and save it for future years. Or there may be no alternative uses in other places or times, and thus no real cost of using it in its present function. A hydroelectric dam is perhaps an illustration of this kind of specialized and immobile sunk investment. The economic cost of using the equipment for one year, in any case, has nothing to do with original cost and nothing to do with the eventual disposal of the equipment—the two important factors in accounting depreciation.[17]

In the case of the dam, where there is no opportunity cost, the future useful life (which measures its unique value to the going concern) is nevertheless continuously running out. Tom preserve one's capital, enough of the dam's gross earnings must be saved and reinvested to shift capital out of the dam into equally profitable ventures, perhaps a replacement dam. The amount of this kind of economic depreciation is not determined by the historical cost of the equipment. It id better measured by the replacement value of equipment that will produce comparable earnings. This kind of depreciation is not cost; the cost was incurred when capital was originally frozen into the plant. Rather it is an act of saving and the amount to charge each year is a financial problem related to past, present and future patterns of gross earnings as well as price level expectations.

Both of these economic concepts of depreciation are important to management. The first, opportunity cost is needed for operating problems of profit making; the second, replacement of eroded earnings ability, is need for financial problems of preserving and administering capital. But in both cases the original cost does not play any role in estimates.

Treatment of Capital Gains and Losses

Capital gains and losses, or 'windfalls' are often defined as unanticipated changes in the values of property relative to other real goods. Conservative companies generally do not include capital gains until they are turned into cash by purchase or sale of assets, since it is never clear until then exactly how large they are in money terms. But at the same time they invariably decide to write off capital losses from the current profit of the year in which the loss occurs. There are companies that include capital gains in the profit of the year in which the capital gains may accrue even though they are not turned into cash by selling. This shows that there can be discrepancies in the profit reported by different companies because of the different approaches they adhere to in the treatment of capital gains and losses.

Current *vs* Historical Costs

In measuring income, accountants typically state costs in terms of the price level at the time of the purchase, by recording the historical outlay, rather than in terms of the current price level. Reasons such as (i) historical costs produce more accurate measurement of income; (ii) historical costs are more objective than the calculation of the present replacement value; (iii) the function of the accountant is to record history whether or not history has relevance for future business or economic problems, etc. are advanced by accountants in justifying their approach to income. But this approach has some defect in the sense that (a) the assets are undervalued in times of inflation and overvalued during periods of deflation, and (b) depreciation is understated and profit overstated during inflation and vice versa.

For many enterprises, says Joel Dean, contemporary (dollar) profits can be approximated by a combination of replacement value depreciation and LIFO (Last-in-first-out) costing of materials.[19] But a full correction of price level distortions requires separate deflation of all assets each year to dollars of constant purchasing power.

Policies on Profit Maximization

Although economic theory has all along advocated a policy of profit maximization as the basis of a firm's operations, there are very serious managerial problems connected with such a policy. A typical modern corporation need not necessarily aim at profit maximization. It rather sets standards or targets of reasonable profits only.

The policy problems in setting profit standards arise only in imperfect competition. When competition is perfect or near perfect prices have to be set close to the cost level, and only by trying to maximize profit can a firm stay solvent. But in the case of a firm which has substantial monopoly position, either short-run or permanent crucial policy decisions on profit standards become imperative. Here we propose discuss the conceptual ground-work for these decisions. The questions that we consider pertinent in such a situation are:

- What are the reasons for aiming at reasonable profit rather than maximum profit?
- What standards of reasonable profits are available?
- How can these standards be applied?

Reasons for Aiming at Reasonable Profit

The reasons for aiming at reasonable profits rather than maximum profit may be grouped as follows:

1. To discourage potential competitors entering the industry,
2. To project a favourable image of the firm to the public and to the government,
3. To restrain wage-hike demands by trade unions,
4. To maintain customer goodwill,
5. To keep internal control in tact, and
6. To maintain congenial working conditions.

There is a basic difference, says Joel Dean, between the first four reasons and the last two. The first four are reasons why the company (firm) as an entity wants to limit short-run profits in order to maximize profits in the long-run (or more strictly, to maximize the present value of the enterprise). The last two are reasons why the executives, as distinguished from the company, want to limit profit in order to maximize their own benefits (of whatever kind). Management's financial interest in modern corporations is typically small and is only one of many motives that keep executives going. Other motives which are just as important often run counter to the corporate financial interests and thus distinguish management clearly from stock holders, in whose eyes the company is essentially a financial, as opposed to a social, organization.[20]

Competitive Considerations

The reasons for profit restriction vary with the particular environment and the way the executives think about the problem. The classical economic reason is to restrain the entry of competitors in a weak monopoly situation. A 'weak' monopoly is one that has no protective barriers around strategic resources or markets, and that has little real patent protection.[21] In such a situation competitors can invade the market once they discover its profitability, find ways to skirt the patents, and make the necessary development outlays in product design, production plant, and technique and market penetration. To ward off such a contingency, firms adopt a policy of 'stay out' pricing subordinating short-run to long-run profit maximization.

To Protect a Favourable Image of the Firm to the Public and the Government

Profit restrained is sometimes exercised with a view to project a favourable image to the public and to the government. This is because of the awareness on the part of the management that public standards are framed more by ethical judgment than by the tenets of classical economics. So many firms set prices below maximum profit levels when a stigma attached to charging what buyers will pay. Again, for many firms a goal of 'reasonable' or 'socially acceptable' profit makes a better policy than maximizing profits during the time of inflation.

Restraining Wage Hike Demand by Trade Unions

Profit restraint is sometimes used as a defensive weapon when the management realizes the fact that any attempt to raise profit by raising prices would be further wage increases.

Maintain Customer Goodwill

Profit limiting is sometimes practiced to maintain congenial working conditions within the firm. Often the inadequacy of hired management's incentive to maximize profits is to make the 'public service' aspects of business leadership more interesting to executives. Again, there appears to be a growing awareness about the social responsibilities of management, i.e. increasing concern with the direct effect of management's decisions upon workers, consumers and the business cycle.

Standard of Reasonable Profit

There are several criteria for setting the most appropriate standard of profit for a firm. For example, Profit standards can be formulated in aggregate rupee terms, as a percentage of sales, or as a return on investment. They can be formulated for individual products or for the combined product line of the firm.

The form of profit standard most appropriate depends on its uses. For the purpose of discouraging potential competitors, return on investment is the relevant standard if new entrants have similar costs. Similarly, for soothing consumers or beating down suppliers, percentage margins over unit cost in relation to rupees they spend is usually appropriate.

Problems such as what it takes to attract outside capital, what earnings are needed to finance firm's development solely from retained profits and depreciation, what the company or comparable firms have normally earned may also be taken into consideration before setting the form of profit standard.

Profits for Control

The use of profit incentive and profit accounting in the measurement and control of executive performance in large business enterprises is another managerial aspect of profit.[22] "Bureaucratic deviationism" may sometimes act as a major internal threat to vitality in big corporations. According to Keith Powlison[23] three deviationist tendencies appears when the profit motive is attenuated. They are:

1. More energy is spent in expanding sales volume and product lines than in raising profitability, the valid company objective.
2. Subordinates spend too much time and money doing jobs to perfection regardless of cost and usefulness—this is

particularly common among staff men who don't understand or appreciate the insignificance of that last digit in their estimates and projections.

3. Lower management's insecurity feelings become barricaded by expensive overstocking and playing-safe-tactics, since there is no reward for imaginative ventures that can possibly offset the perils of making a mistake.

The above problems can be solved to a considerable extent by setting profit goals at individual executive levels.

Profit Forecasting

Forecasting, as we know, has got all the problems connected with the uncertain future. Profit forecasting is no exception. However, there are at least three important ways of formulating profit. They are:

1. Spot projections,
2. Environmental analysis, and
3. Break-even analysis.

Spot projections: This relates to projecting the entire profit and loss statements for a specified future period by forecasting each important element in the profit and loss statement. Profit is the difference between sales revenue and cost.

Environmental analysis: This relates to forecasting the firm's profit on the basis of the general economic trends that are likely to prevail in the economy during the relevant period. The data on general economic activity can be obtained from government publications and the like Break-even Analysis: The break-even analysis, as we have already noted, is a powerful tool for profit planning and management control. Of the three techniques, break-even analysis is the most important tool of profit forecasting.

Review Questions

1. Explain the various theories of profit.
2. Distinguish risk from uncertainty.
3. What do you mean by innovation?
4. What do you mean by depreciation?

5. List the reasons for aiming at only reasonable profit.
6. Distinguish accounting profit from economic profit.

References

1. Dean, Joel; Managerial Economics, op.cit. p.4
2. Ibid; p.5
3. Ibid; p.6
4. F.A. Walker closely follows David Ricardo's explanation of rent.
5. Frank H. Knight; Risk, Uncertainty and Profit, London School of Economics and Political Science, Series Reprints of Scarce Tracts, No.16, 1933.
6. Dean, Joel; Managerial Economics, p.8
7. The increase in net output is the profit that comes from innovation.
8. Drucker, Peter F, "The Innovation Organization", The American Review, Summer, 1977, p.3
9. Ibid, p.5
10. Ibid, P.8
11. Ibid, pp. 7–8
12. Dean, Joel, Managerial Economics, p.10
13. Ibid, pp.10–11
14. This enables the firm to establish high monopoly prices. The most widespread is the price agreement system when the firms dominant in a given branch agree to fix prices at a level, which other firms have to follow.
15. Dean, Joel, Managerial Economics, p.13.
16. Some companies use straight-line method, some others use declining balance method, while a third category use what is known as sum of the year's digits method.
17. Dean, Joel, Managerial Economics, p.17.
18. Ibid, pp. 17–18.
19. Ibid, p.22.
20. Ibid.
21. Ibid, pp.29–30.
22. Ibid, p.39.
23. Powlison, Keith; "The Profit Motive Compromised", Harvard Business Review, March 1950, p.102. Also see, Dean, Joel, op.cit; pp.39–40.

18 National Income

One of the most important achievements of economics in the twentieth century is the development of concepts and data relating to national income. It supplies the most valuable data we have about our economy. The national income provides a frame-work of data about output, spending and income which we can utilize for forecasting the level of economic activity in the next year or even beyond. Companies also can utilize these data for forecasting their level of activity in the next year and even beyond. Again, from the historical data in the national income accounts, we can determine how rapidly output has grown in the past, how is its growth compared with population or labour force growth, and what proportion of output has been devoted to growth stimulating investment. The national income concept has become an essential tool for thought and action with respect to economic affairs in the modern world.

In this chapter we propose to discuss national income, different concepts related to national income, measurement of national income, problems connected with the measurement of national income and the uses of national income studies.

National income can be interpreted in various ways, and there are at least six different variants which demand our consideration. They are:

1. Gross National Product (GNP)
2. Gross Domestic Product
3. Net National Product
4. National Income at Factor Cost
5. Personal Income, and
6. Disposable Income.

Gross National Product

Gross national product or in more extended form gross national product at market prices is the most comprehensive measure of national income. By gross national product we mean all the final goods and services produced in a country during a specified period of time, usually a year. The money value of this is called as the gross national income. The use of the word 'final' in the definition is important. Then gross national income does not include all the goods produced. Many goods that are produced are intermediary products that enter as raw materials, or semi-finished articles into the final goods product and whose costs form part of the cost of final goods.

The total volume of purchases and sales of all kinds made in a market in any one year exceeds by 10 to 12 times the volume of final goods and services produced. In the process of production there is a vast 'churning around' of raw materials and semi-finished products. The same raw material passes through many forms and is sold again and again before it finally reaches in finished form, to the ultimate consumer. But no product which enters into the making of a final product is included in the gross national income, only the final product is included in the computation of gross national income.

Gross Domestic Product

In the present day world almost all countries are involved in foreign trade. When countries are involved in foreign trade whatever they produce domestically may not be available for internal consumption. But in certain other cases they get more for internal consumption than they domestically produce. Whether the people of a country get more or less than what they produce domestically will depend on whether the country exports less or more than what it imports. So, gross domestic product can be termed as (GNP + imports) – exports. Another way of expressing GDP is

$$GDP = C + G + I + NX$$

Where C = All private consumption spending in the economy

G = Government spending

I = Total of country's business spending on capital

NX = Total net exports, calculated as total exports— total imports.

Gross Domestic Product is commonly used as an indicator of the economic health of a country, as well as to gauge a country's standard of living.

Real GDP and Nominal GDP

Real GDP is the inflation adjusted measure that reflects the value of all goods and services produced in a given year, expressed in base year prices, often referred as constant prices. It can account for changes in the price level, and hence provide a more accurate picture about the economy.

Unlike real GDP, nominal GDP is the Gross Domestic Product figure that has not been adjusted for price changes. It is also known as GDP at current prices.

As performance of a government is measured in terms of the scale of growth of the country and the growth with GDP scale, GDP has much relevance in the financial circles.

Net National Product

During the process of production depreciation takes place in the case of equipments, machinery, etc. This depreciation or fall in value of equipments and machinery, etc. is deducted from the gross national product to get net national product. In other words, while the gross national product includes in addition to final consumers' goods and services, all the new capital goods produced in the period in question without any deduction for the capital goods consumed in the process, the net national product includes only the final consumption goods and services plus the net addition to capital goods, account having been taken of the capital consumption. Thus, suppose that in the year 2008 the gross national product was Rs. 40 billion and the capital consumption involved in the production of the said amount was Rs. 1 billion. Then the net national income in 2008 is Rs. 39 billion only.

Net National Product = Gross National Product – Depreciation.

National Income at Factor Cost

National income at factor cost is commonly termed as national income. This nomenclature may seem to be rather unfortunate as all the six concepts represent a kind of national income. *National income at factor cost means the sum of all incomes earned by the factors of production through their involvement in the process of production of the net national product or net national income. In other words, national income at factor cost shows how much it costs to the society, in terms of economic resources, to produce net national product.* It is for national income at factor cost that we use the term national income. The difference between national income at factor cost and net national income arises from the fact that indirect taxes (such as excise, sales tax and other duties) and subsidies cause market prices of output to be different from the factor income resulting from it. Suppose that a yard of mill cloth sold for Rs. 125 includes an excise duty of Rs. 25. In this case while the market price of the cloth is Rs. 25 a yard, the factors engaged in the production and distribution would receive only Rs. 100 a yard. The value of cloth at factor cost would thus be equal to its value at market price minus the indirect taxes on it. On the other hand, a subsidy will cause the market price to be less than the factor cost. Suppose that handloom cloth is subsidized at the rate of Rs. 25 per yard and it sells at Rs. 100 per yard. Then while the consumer pays Rs. 100 per yard, the factors engaged in the production and distribution of such cloth will receive Rs. 125 per yard. The value of the handloom cloth would thus be equal to its market price plus the subsidy paid on it. It follows, therefore, that the national income at factor cost (NI) is equal to the net national product plus subsidies minus indirect taxes.

National Income at Factor Cost or National Income
= Net National Product + Subsidies − Indirect Taxes

Personal Income

In a sense personal income is likely to be regarded by the public as of primary significance, since it is the money income payments made to all individuals in the community.

National income (NI) is the income of the factors of production, but it is not the income that the individuals actually receive. On the one hand, part of national income is never paid out to individuals. Social security contribution, for example, is considered part of the factor income for labour, but labour actually does not receive this, it is directly paid to the government. In the same way corporate profit taxes are considered as part of the factor share of the owner of the business, but they are not received by the owners. Instead, they too are directly paid to the government. Also undistributed profits of corporations or companies are not actually paid out and individuals do not actually receive them, even though they are considered as part of the factor income that is allocated to the share holders of the corporation or companies. All these elements would have to be excluded to obtain the actual personal income that individuals receive. Conversely, individuals receive some income other than from factor payments. Both government and business firms make payments to individuals for reasons other than payments for services rendered. For example, the government pays old age pensions, unemployment compensation, relief payments, interest payments on the public debt, etc. and the business makes certain charitable contributions. These are all payments which individuals receive for reasons other than current services rendered. These non-factor payments are known as transfer payments and they must be included as part of personal income.

Personal income thus excludes those factor payments which are not received by individuals and includes all non-factor payments that are received by individuals. The resulting total shows the actual amount of income received by individuals in the economy. Thus

Personal Income = National income + transfer payments–(Social security contributions + Corporate income taxes+ undistributed corporate profits).

The interactions among all the national income measurements are given below:

GNP	NNP	National Income	Personal Income
Capital Consumption Allowance			
Indirect Tax and Non-Tax Liability	Indirect Tax and Non-Tax Liability		
Social Insurance Contribution	Social Insurance Contribution	Social Insurance Contribution	
Wages and Salaries	Wages and Salaries	Wages and Salaries	Wages and Salaries
Income of Unincorporated Enterprises	Income of Unincorporated Enterprises	Income of Unincorporated Enterprises	Income of Unincorporated Enterprises
Net Interst	Net Interest	Net Interest	Net Interest
Corporate Profits and Tax Liability	Corporate Profits and Tax Liability	Corporate Profits and Tax Liability	Dividends
Dividends	Dividends	Dividends	
Undistributed Profits	Undistributed Profits	Undistributed Profits	Non-factor Payments Received by Individuals

Disposable Income

By disposable income, we mean, the amount of money which individuals have at their disposal to save or spend. All personal income cannot be considered as disposable income as individuals have legal obligation to pay taxes to the government. Disposable income, therefore, means personal income minus personal taxes.

Measurement of National Income

We have defined gross national product as the total value of all the final goods and services produced in any given period, normally one year. "But literally hundreds of thousands of different kinds of goods and services make up the gross national product. How can we add automobiles with symphony concerts, frozen food with doctors' services, pencil sharpeners with vacation trips? The answer is given by the term 'value'. To each good or service we assign relative importance or value given by its price". Thus for example, an automobile sold for Rs. 3.5 lakh is counted in GNP as Rs. 3.5 lakh, a ticket for a symphony concert prices at Rs. 100, is counted in GNP as Rs. 100. In other words, each good or service is multiplied by its price and the resultant rupee value totals GNP.

It may be seen from the above fact that during the time of inflation the value of GNP increases simply because of the price rise. Therefore, in order to determine how much real output has changed, we must first adjust for the effect of changes in prices, so that any increase in GNP reflects a rise in output, not the rise in prices.

Measuring Output in a Private, Two-Sector Model

A private two-sector model consists of a business sector and a household sector. It is assumed that the business sector is the organizer of economic resources and produces all goods and services. It is further assumed that all economic resources are owned by households. The business sector hires the services of the factors of production from the households by paying remuneration. Labour is paid wages, capital, interest; land, rent and organization, profit. The households use this income to buy goods and services from the business sector. These activities taking place in a private two-sector model is represented in Diagram 18.1

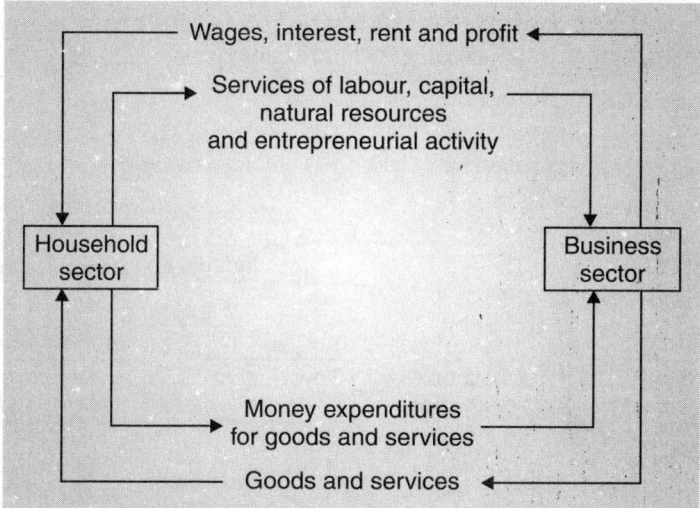

Fig. 18.1

The upper portion of diagram 18.1 traces the flow of services from households to business sector; the return flow consists of compensation(wages, interest, rent and profit) for these services. The lower portion of the diagram depicts households spending their income on goods and services with the return flow being the receipt of goods and services.

Measuring Output in a Three-and Four-Sector Model

The three-sector model comprises of private sector, government sector and business sector. This model has three spending sectors, viz.; household consumption (C), investment (I) (Net investment) and government expenditure (G). Part of the income generated from the production of goods and services is paid to households and part to government in the form of direct or indirect taxes. The household sector pays direct taxes to the government. Indirect taxes are imposed at the production level by the government upon goods produced. Thus the upper portion of the flow in diagram 18.2 shows the business sector paying households for the services of economic resources and indirect taxes to the government. Household income is used to pay direct taxes, consumption spending and saving. When the government budget is balanced, tax revenue equals government purchases of goods and services.

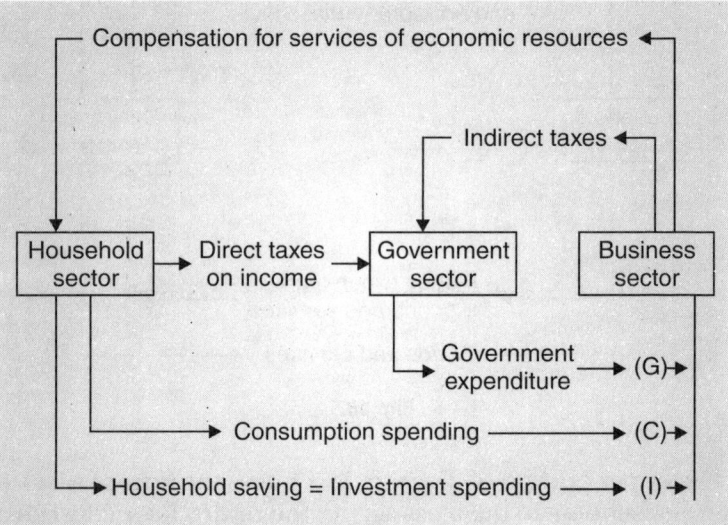

Fig. 18.2

The four-sector model adds international connections (Foreign Transactions) to the three-sector model. Goods and services available for domestic use include domestic production plus imports minus exports.

Computation of National Income

There are at least three methods of computation of national income. They are:
1. Product method,
2. Income method, and
3. Expenditure method.

Product Method

This method approaches national income from the output side. Under this method the economy is divided into different sectors such as agriculture, mining, manufacturing, commerce, communication, transport. Then the gross product is found out by adding the values of all final goods that have been produced in these different sectors during the period under reference. But the adding business is not that simple as one usually visualizes. Take for instance a loaf of bread that is priced at Rs. 5. To produce the loaf of bread, the baker purchased flour worth Rs. 2.75, baked it into bread and sold it for Rs. 5. The flour miller in turn purchased wheat for Rs. 1.50 and milled it into flour; selling it for Rs. 2.75. The farmer supplied wheat worth Rs. 1.50 to the miller and himself purchased fertilizer and seed worth Re. 0.50 from other industries. In estimating GNP should we add up the value of bread, flour, wheat, seed and fertilizer to a total of Rs. 9.75/. Surely not. If we do so, we will be committing the mistake of double counting because the value of wheat, flour, seed and fertilizer is already included in the price of bread. In order to avoid this mistake, we add only the value of the final product—the bread. Thus, the net values of all goods and services produced in different sectors of the economy will give us the gross national income. This method of calculating national income will enable us to trace the origin of the national income to the different sectors of the economy. Therefore, this method is also known as national income by industrial or sectoral origin.

This method of national income calculation can be followed when there is a census of production for the year. But in many developing countries figures of data regarding production with respect to several industries are not available. So this method is supplemented with other methods to measure national income. The main advantage of this method is that it reveals the relative importance of the different sectors of the economy by indicating their respective contribution to the national economy.

Income Method

This method approaches national income from income side (distribution side). In this method we add up the income generated at each stage in the production process. The income method of estimating national income has the great advantage of indicating the distribution of national income among different income groups such as landlords, capitalists, wage-earners.

Expenditure Method

This method approaches national income from expenditure side. If we add up all the expenditure made on goods and services by individuals, business and government we can get national income. In other words, national income is found out by adding up:
1. All personal consumption expenditure
2. Gross domestic private investment
3. Net foreign investment, and
4. Government expenditure.

After seeing the methods of computation of national income, let us see some of the difficulties connected with national income computation. They are listed below:
1. *Treatment of economic and non-economic activities:* The first problem relates to the treatment of economic activities. The major way to distinguish what is an economic activity from essentially a non-economic activity is to ask whether it goes through the market place or is it for sale. This is generally the criterion used in deciding whether or not a particular kind of activity is to be considered for inclusion in GNP. In order to confine GNP to measurement of economic output or activity, some such criterion is necessary. Even though the criterion of the market place is sensible, it some times leads to apparently strange results. For example if I spend my earnings for a year building a new room on the back of my house, the value of labour which I put into this effort is not considered for inclusion in the GNP, but the value of the jumper, nails and paint purchased from the local hardware dealer is counted. Those of us who are likely to hammer more thumbs than nails would have to have the whole job contracted if we wanted (and could afford!) a new room. In this case the entire value of the room, including the

wages and profits of the builder will be included in GNP, because the entire transaction was economic in nature. Similarly, the wages of domestic servants represent 'services' produced, and as such add to the GNP. But the same service performed 'non-economically' by the house-wife is not included in GNP. This anomaly prompted one eminent English economist to remark that the man who married his housekeeper would reduce the national income.

2. *The danger of double counting:* As the categories of finished goods and intermediate goods do not always remain the same, it may be that what is finished good at one time may be an intermediary good at another time. Hence extreme care should be taken to avoid double counting in such cases. Also services performed by one firm for another, including transport, insurance and banking should be offset properly.

3. *Difficulties of calculating depreciation:* Depreciation differs from item to item and is also difficult to aggregate.

4. *Calculation of foreign payments:* Great care has to be exercised in order to see that only the net income from abroad is included in the national income.

5. *Problems of inventory revaluation:* The term 'inventory' includes the value of stocks and work-in-progress at the end of the year, as indicated in a firm's balance sheet. In the trading account of the firm the opening and closing stocks are the inventories of the current and preceding years respectively. If prices rise during the year, gross profits on stocks held will increase, but the replacement cost of such stocks also will rise. Business profits include any such gains; but, for the purpose of national income computation, it is more useful to shoe this item separately and make the necessary adjustment.

6. *Changes in money value:* The value of money changes from time to time in accordance with changes in the general price level. National income for different years will not have any meaning unless the purchasing power of money for those years is known. Though index numbers of prices give an indication of the relative purchasing power of money for different years, they cannot give the exact

measure of the purchasing power. (Using consumer price index, national income at current prices and constant prices are computed.)

In the case of developing countries like India, there are some special difficulties in estimating national income. Firstly, the existence of a large non-monetised sector precludes a sizeable portion of the output from being accounted for in terms of money. For national income purposes, only rough estimates are possible in such cases. Secondly, illiteracy and the habit of not following proper accounting practices on the part of many producers make it difficult to get information on the output. Thirdly, because of the inadequate development of occupational specialization, an individual may receive income from a variety of sources which may be difficult to calculate precisely.

The Significance of National Income

1. National income estimates serve as the most important economic indicators in a country. Alfred Marshall who was the first among modern economists to point out the significance of national income studies, considered national income a more suitable measure of economic progress than wealth. Nobel laureate JR Hicks has also expressed the same view by saying that 'when the national income has been converted to real terms it is the best single measure of the nation's well-being or economic progress.' The per capita income of a country is the principal determinant of the people's standard of living there.

   Also, international comparison of the standard of living is often made on the basis of the national income and the per capita income of the different countries concerned.

2. National income makes it possible to know the extent of the volume of production as such within a country. Such production data for different years can be compared and the trend of production assessed. Per capita production of the different important items for different years shows the relative change in the standard of living of the people.

3. National income figures enable one to know the rate of growth of an economy over a period of time. They show

whether the economy is growing, declining or remaining stagnant. The national income of India is said to have remained more or less stagnant during the seventies and eighties of the last century.

4. Through national income estimates it is possible to know the contribution made by the different sectors of the economy to the total income. In a mature economy, the predominant share of national income originates in the manufacturing sector, whereas in a developing economy the agricultural sector is likely to account for the major share.

5. It is possible to know from the national income estimates the relative contribution made to the national income by the various factors of production. An approximate idea about the level of inequality prevailing in the economy will be available from the relative proportion of wages on the one hand (i.e. the share of the working class) and rent and profit on the other (i.e. share of the owners of property).

6. Figures relating to consumption, savings and investment are available from the national income estimates. These figures are very useful for the purpose of planning and economic development.

7. National income estimates serve as a reliable guide to economic policy. With the aid of these estimates the government can have an idea of the weak spots in the economy and can undertake suitable remedial measures in the context of economic planning, regulation and control.

National Income Accounts

Table 18.1: Presents national income accounts

Gross national product	Rs. 4880.6 million
Minus depreciation allowance	Rs. 513.6 million
Net national income	Rs. 4367.1 million
Minus indirect business taxes	Rs. 594.5 million
National income	Rs. 3972.6 million

Real National Income: When we express national income in terms of the base year price index, we get real national income or national income at constant prices, i.e.:

Real National income =

$$\text{National income for the current year} \times \frac{\text{Base year price index}}{\text{Current year price index}}$$

Review Questions

1. Define national income
2. What are the different concepts of national income?
3. Explain the different methods of computing national income.
4. Explain the difficulties in computing national income.
5. Explain the uses of national income studies.
6. From the following data, calculate national income, net national income, gross national income, personal income, personal disposable income and personal saving.

Capital consumption allowance	Rs. 3564
Compensation of employees	Rs. 18663
Business interest payments	Rs. 2649
Indirect business taxes	Rs. 2663
Rental income of persons	Rs. 341
Corporate profits	Rs. 1648
Proprietor's income	Rs. 1203
Corporate dividends	Rs. 664
Social security contributions	Rs. 2530
Personal taxes	Rs. 4021
Interest paid by consumers	Rs. 644
Interest paid by government	Rs. 1051
Government and business transfers	Rs. 3745
Personal consumption expenditure	Rs. 19919

19 Business Cycles

Depression of trade and the economic distress associated therewith are almost as old as business history. But the character and intensity of economic fluctuations have indeed changed with changes in the methods of production and in the institutions of society.

Earlier writers on economics did not use the term 'crises' to denote the recurring upheavals which characterized the last half of the 18th century and the first half of the 19th, especially in England. The notion of regularity of occurrence (periodicity) and the use of the term crisis came relatively late. For instance, neither Henry Thornton[1] (1802) nor David Ricardo[2] (1817) used the term crisis to explain great commercial distress or revulsions of trade. The same is the case with Lauderdale[3] (1804) and Malthus[4] (1820). But Sismondi used the term 'commercial crises in 1819.

It was Willard Philips in his Manual of Political Economy (1828) who conceived a cyclical movement in business. He not only used the term 'crisis' but also suggested a wavelike movement in business. In 1833 John Wage used terms such as 'commercial cycle' and 'periods of prosperity and depression'. By 1848 the use of terms 'commercial crisis' and also the concept of periodicity of these crises appear to have come more or less into common use. John Stuart Mill in his book "Political Economy" (1848) referred to 'commercial crises' and to the almost periodical recurrence of these 'fits of speculation.'

In 1860 Clement Juglar referred to the periodicity of commercial crises. He also used the term 'cycle' and developed the idea of succession of phases in economic fluctuations.

He divided the cycle into three phases, viz; (i) prosperity, (ii) crisis, and (iii) liquidation. He considered them always following one another in the same order. He also emphasized the influence of bank credit on the development of crisis.

WS Jevons held the view that 'great vintage years' recur every ten or eleven years, and it seems probable that commercial crises are commenced with a periodic variation of weather affecting all parts of the earth, and probably arising from increased waves of heat received from sun at average intervals of ten years and a fraction.[5] John Mills in 1867 spoke of credit cycles and commercial panics. Mills divided the credit cycle into four phases, viz; declining trade. Increasing trade, over excited trade and crisis. He held the view that the life history of the credit cycle was governed by 'moral causes' and insisted that the 'malady of commercial crises is not, in essence, a matter of the purse but of the mind.'

Alfred Marshall regarded the crisis as related to reckless inflation of credit. The depression which followed was regarded as a state of commercial disorganization. 'The chief cause of the evil', according to Marshall, 'is a want of confidence. The greater part of it could be removed almost in an instant if confidence could return, touch all industries with her magic wand, and make them continue their production, and their demand for the wares of others.'

As the close of the 19th century two great books appeared which marked a new epoch in business cycle theory. These books were:

  i. Tugan Barnowsky's "The Industrial Crisis in England in 1894 and

 ii. Wicksell's "Interest and Prices" appeared in 1898. Though Wicksell was not directly concerned with depressions and cycles, his analysis became starting point for the modern theory relating to saving and investment. The first modern scientific work devoted entirely to business cycles was that of Tugan Burnowsky.

So far we have been dealing with the genesis of business cycle. Now we propose to discuss some of the major theories of business cycle. In our discussion we include the theories enunciated by Wesley C. Mitchell, RG Hawtray, Joseph Schumpeter, JM Keynes and JR Hicks.

Wesley C. Mitchell's Theory

The quest for profits, says Mitchell, is the central factor controlling economic activity. Hence any discussion about business cycles must centre on the prospects of profits.

Thus any factor which affects profits comes within the sweep of Mitchell's analysis. The factors of chief significance are:

   i. the prices which constitute business receipts,

   ii. the prices which constitute business expenses,

   iii. volume of sales

   iv. currency to make payment and

   v. availability of bank credit. Mitchell holds that we must know what fluctuations these factors undergo and we must follow their interactions to see how they affect the prospects of profits.

A typical business cycle, says Mitchell, consists of four phases. They are:

   i. The revival phase

   ii. The expansion phase

   iii. The recession phase

   iv. The contraction phase.

The four phases of the business cycle are shown in diagram 19.1.

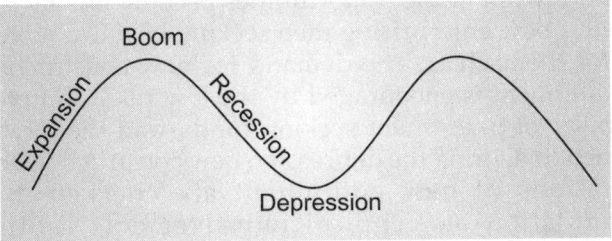

Fig. 19.1

The Revival Phase

Mitchell's explanation starts with the upswing phase of the cycle. The "very conditions of business depression beget a revival of activity". The revival can be attributed to processes necessarily unfolding in the period of depression, which breed favourable conditions. The favourable effects of a period of hard times are listed as follows:

  i. a reduction of cost, both prime and supplementary,
  ii. reduction in inventory stocks,
  iii. low rates of interest,
  iv. strong lending position of banks, and
  v. growth of investment-seeking funds. These conditions emerge out of the depressions, and each contributes to an environment favourable to revival.

Once disinvestment ceases, current prices of retailers and whole-salers increase even though there may be no change in current consumer purchases. Dealers no longer sell from stocks. Orders to manufacturers are therefore increased. Similarly families' stocks of clothing and furnishings are gradually worn out and discarded. It becomes necessary to buy new articles if money can be found for the purpose. The continued growth of population tends to influence the aggregate volume of consumers' demand. The "Development of new tastes among consumers, the appearance of new materials and the introduction of new processes, do not come to a standstill even in times of depression." New men seeking business openings can for a time by the old enterprises on favourable terms (owing to bankruptcies and reorganizations caused by the depression) but after a while these opportunities become less favourable. Thereafter new enterprising men seeking business adventures build for themselves. The demand for new construction and new equipment is encouraged by the low rate of interest, the availability of investment seeking funds, and the low cost of construction. During the depression new construction and new installations of new equipment are checked, but the "accumulation of technical improvements continues." Accordingly, there develops an increasing inducement to invest in new equipment.

Under the combined pressures of these various forces there occurs a marked increase in consumers' and producers' demand. This expansion in demand raises the physical volume of business. The reduction in prime costs and fixed charges combined with this increase in physical volume raises current and prospective profits.

The interrelation of costs and selling prices unfolds in a manner to widen the profit margin. This process, combined with the greater physical volume, increases profits. And since the 'quest of profits is the driving force of the money economy' the cumulative process is reinforced.

The Upper Turning Point Prosperity does not continue indefinitely. Unfavourable events do occur and they accumulate within the system and finally disrupt the business system. For example, during seasons of high prosperity fixed charges such as interest rates, rentals, depreciation charges, etc. rise. Obsolete equipments are brought back into use in view of unfilled orders and heavy demand. Wage rates rise, less efficient labour is employed and overall labour efficiency declines in periods of prosperity. The cost of materials rises. Rising interest on short-term loans is a matter of some importance, especially to the mercantile classes. Business management itself is over burdened and losses its grip on economic administration. All these increasing costs threaten to encroach upon profits. This results in the downswing. Depression Inevitably Follows Booms.

Once the downswing has started, the cumulative process drives the economy from crisis into depression. Workmen are discharged, with a resulting decline in consumers' demand. Merchants sell from left-over stocks. While existing factories stand idle there is little inducement to install new equipment. The prospect of a further fall in prices induces the postponement of new projects. These processes are cumulative in effect. Each reduction in employment and in consumers' demand causes further decline.

Under the pressure of hard times, costs are reduced, money becomes redundant, accumulated stocks are gradually used up, new products and new processes are developed, and so depression prepares the way once again for revival.

RG Hawtrey's Theory

Hawtrey holds the view that there is an inherent tendency toward fluctuations in the money economy, with its existing banking institutions and practices. So long as credit is regulated with reference to reserve proportions, the trade cycle is bound to occur.

Hawtrey's argument runs somewhat on the following lines. Most of the business is carried on with borrowed money. When business prospects are bright, the banks extend credit facilities without much difficulty. This enables businessmen to expand their business. A huge superstructure of credit is built up. This super- structure can be maintained by the continuance of cheap money conditions. Bankers do not realize that they have over-expanded until this drain of cash from the banks severely reduces bank reserves. At this point bankers conclude that the amount of credit money in existence is more than they think prudent, having regard to their holdings of cash applies the brake, raises the discount rate, curbs further expansion of credit, and begins to call back advances: This sudden suspension of credit facilities proves a bombshell to the business community.

The first affected in this process is the dealer. A moderate rise in the cost of borrowing will make the carrying of costs appreciably less attractive to him. He will buy less and sell more, and this will result in a fall in prices.

A fall in prices forces the producer either to reduce output or to reduce the cost of production. If he chooses the first horn of the dilemma, unemployment ensues; and so business depression; if he chooses the second, wages, salaries, interest, rent and profits must be lowered. Interest on borrowed funds is a fixed charge, and it cannot be reduced unless the business actually becomes insolvent. Profits will likely to be the first to be encroached upon. But if the margin of profit is narrow, there is no recourse, except lower the wages or dismiss some of the employees. If wages are lowered sufficiently, production might be maintained, but the consequent redistribution of the national income would at least entail a necessary shift in production. However, wages cannot in point of fact be lowered except by the pressure of distress. Thus unemployment being the inevitable whip by which labour is forced to accept lower wages, the readjustment to a lower price level cannot be accomplished except by passing through a period of depression. Nor can the fixed charges be curtailed except by the pressure of insolvency. If the habits of the people could be adapted without delay to the change, the production of wealth might continue unabated in spite of a fall in prices. But customary wages, rents, interest and profits exert such profound influence upon men's minds that the readjustment can in point of fact not be made except under the pressure of such distress as is experienced in periods of depression.

Schumpeter's Theory

Economic development in a capitalist system is propelled by the force of 'innovation'. Innovation necessarily wells up in a great tidal wave, and then recedes. Business cycle consists in essence in the ebb and flow of innovation, together with the repercussions resulting in the reform.

Schumpeter starts with a closed commercially organized system in which private property, division of labour and free competition prevails. Then he proceeds to describe a system of stationery equilibrium in which the demand of the consumers determines what would be produced, and the supply creates its own demand. The system has been constructed on Walrasian technique of general equilibrium in which the production function is given and is invariant in form. This is designated as circular flow of economic life which reproduces itself with the same magnitude of economic quantities.[6]

The circular flow is broken through the introduction of innovations by a set of far-sighted business men who are willing to take the necessary risk to improve their profit situation. Schumpeter indicates at one point that in a narrow sense an innovation is defined as the setting up of a new production function. However, he also indicates that a new production function covers not only new techniques, but also the introduction of new commodities, new forms of organization, the opening up of new markets and the conquest of a new source of supply of raw materials.

Innovations do not remain isolated events, and are not evenly distributed over time. They tend to "cluster" to come in "bunches", simply because "first some, and then most, follow in the wake of successful innovation".

We must distinguish, says Schumpeter, between innovation possibilities and the practical realization of these possibilities. Prosperity does not really as a result of innovations or discoveries. It waits upon the actual development of innovations, which is the driving power of the period of prosperity. Only a few leaders have the intelligence and energy to find new undertakings, to develop new possibilities. While only a few can lead, many can follow. Once some one has gone ahead, it is not difficult to imitate him. Few are capable of securing financial backing for a new venture of which bankers and investors are skeptical; but once one such new establishment is a going concern; others can easily secure credit for similar undertakings. If a new process is put into successful operation, others can simply copy. In other words the success of the innovators will produce a swarm of innovators. Hence the process of expansion is not simply a process of cumulation but proceeds by "rushes".

The "swarm like appearance of new enterprises" is intensified by the cumulative process – the secondary waves which spread all over the business sphere. The errors of optimism may intensify the boom. But here we want to stress the fact that the process of introducing innovation is the essence of the boom.

The peak of the expansion is characterized by the innovators ceasing to innovate. In this sense all the new techniques have now established, the new market has penetrated, and all the new products that are going to appear have appeared. In other words, there are no new forces to emulate. The recession is now at hand, the most difficult phase of which is the 'adaptive' period, during which the old and new firms and new firms and products compete and the laggards in emulating the new change lose ground or even be forced out of the industry entirely. This is a period of retrenchment and a reevaluation of the current market before innovating future activity is begun.

Simon Kuznuts sums up this phase in the following words:

At the turn, the rate of innovation slackens and a period of readjustment ensues in which entrepreneurs take stock and the economy reduces to a new equilibrium level which both growth and innovations make higher than that from which the expansion started. During this period of recession credit volume, prices and interest rates decline but total output is likely to average larger than in the preceding prosperity.[7]

Schumpeter's theory of trade cycle can be summarized in the following words:

Cyclical movements are movements away from neighbourhoods of equilibrium and back again. It is the process of innovation which drives the system away from equilibrium into a boom of capital investment. This is the phase of "prosperity", and it is followed by "recession"—the struggle back to equilibrium. But as the depressive forces gather momentum the system usually upturns also this neighbourhood of equilibrium and thus plunges beyond the "depression excursion". From here the recuperative forces of adjustment, bit by bit promote "revival" and gradually pull the economy back again toward equilibrium. From here a new swarm of innovations starts the economy on a new cycle. Starting from the neighbourhood of equilibrium, the innovational surge drives the economy on into the next phase of "prosperity". Innovations supply the propelling force which generates a new cycle. Combining the first and the second waves gives us a four phase cycle. We have expansion, recession, depression and revival.

Keynes's Theory of Trade Cycle

John Maynard Keynes holds the view that "the succession of boom and slump can be described and analysed in terms of the fluctuations of the marginal efficiency of capital relatively to the rate of interest."[8] He argues that the trade cycle is occasioned mainly by a cyclical change in the marginal efficiency of capital, though complicated and often aggravated by associated changes in the other significant short-term variables of the economic system such as the liquidity preference and the propensity to consume.

The schedule of the marginal efficiency of capital is of fundamental importance because it is mainly through this factor that the expectations of the future influences the present.[9] Now the marginal efficiency of capital depends upon two factors, (i) the prospective of annual yields (that is R1+ R2 + R3 + ...Rn) from investment in a new capital good, and (ii) the cost of capital (that is Cr). Fluctuations in the rate of investment are mainly due to the changes in the R1 series and in Cr. A sudden decline in R1 series – the prospective annual yields from fixed capital goods – is the primary cause of the fall in the marginal efficiency of capital, though rising costs also may play a part. The explanation of the downturn is, then, "not primarily a rise in the rate of interest, but a sudden collapse in the marginal efficiency of capital".[10]

Expectations of future yields (i.e. the R1 series) rest in part on the abundance of capital goods in relation to other factors of production and in part upon the pessimism or optimism of entrepreneurs. Toward the end of a boom, excessive optimism may be strong enough to offset (i) the tendency toward diminishing marginal returns (the R1 series) due to the growing "abundance" of fixed capital goods (ii) the rising cost of capital goods, and (iii) the rise in the rate of interest.[11] Reasonable estimates of the 'future yields of capital assets' are swept aside by an overoptimistic market.

It is highly improbable, opines Keynes, that fluctuations in the marginal efficiency of capital are necessarily of a cyclical character.[12] But, he suggests that there are 'certain definite reasons' why in the nineteenth century environment, fluctuations 'in the marginal efficiency of capital should have had cyclical characteristics'. [13]

As the boom progresses, two hard facts press increasing for recognition. They are (i) the growing abundance of capital goods and (ii) rising costs of production of capital goods. Both of these push down the marginal efficiency of capital. Nevertheless, the later stages of the boom are characterized by optimistic expectations as to their future yield sufficiently strong to offset their rising costs, and probably also the rise in the rate of interest. The expectations exceed a 'reasonable estimate of the future yield of capital assets'.[14] Doubts arise with respect to the probability of the prospective yield (R1 series) as the stock of newly produced durable goods steadily increases. When disillusion falls, it may fall 'with sudden and even catastrophic force'. The ensuing collapse in the marginal efficiency of capital precipitates a sharp increase in the liquidity preference—and hence a rise in the rate of interest.[15] Thus a collapse in the marginal efficiency of capital tends to be associated with a rise in the rate of interest, and this aggravates the decline in investment. But the essence of the situation is the fall in the marginal efficiency of capital.

"Later on, a decline in the rate of interest will be a great aid to recovery and, probably, a necessary condition of it. But, for the moment the collapse in the marginal efficiency of capital may be so complete that no practical reduction in the rate of interest will be enough."[16] It is this which renders the slump so intractable. "If a reduction in the rate of interest was capable of proving an effective remedy by itself, it might be possible to achieve a recovery without the collapse of any considerable interval of time and by means more or less directly under the control of the monetary authority.[17] But it is no easy matter to revive the marginal efficiency of capital, 'determined as it is by the uncontrollable and disobedient psychology of the business world'. It is the 'return of the confidence' which is so insusceptible to control.[18]

Time-Element in Trade Cycle

The explanation of the time-element in trade cycle is to be sought in the influence which governs the recovery of the marginal efficiency of capital. The influences which govern the recovery of marginal efficiency of capital are: (i) the length of durable assets in relation to the normal rate of growth and (ii) the period required to absorb the surplus stocks of inventories which continue to accumulate in the first phase of the downturn. The carrying cost of surplus stocks force their absorption within a certain period. Now the process of absorbing the stocks represents negative investment. During the downswing, moreover, there is also a reduction in working capital. Thus the initial decline in fixed capital investment exerts a strong cumulative influence operating through the disinvestment of stocks and the disinvestment of working capital.

A serious fall in the marginal efficiency of capital affects adversely the propensity to consume. This is all the more true in the case of the class which takes active interest in the stock market. This group's readiness to spend is directly influenced by the rise and fall in the market value of their financial investments. The propensity to consume luxury goods fluctuates with fluctuations in the stock market. Thus, the depression, if started, feeds on itself, and cumulates; and is the same with respect to recovery.

When the stock of real capital has reached the appropriate level (end of investment boom), no further investment may be needed for some time. In such a situation saturation has been reached, but not necessarily excess capacity. Still the investment spurt is likely to be overplayed, and so condition of overinvestment may be reached.

Overinvestment may mean two things: (i) It may refer to investments which are destined to disappoint the expectations which prompted them or for which there is no use in conditions of severe unemployment, (ii) It may indicate a state of affairs where every kind of capital goods is so abundant that there is no new investment which is expected, even in conditions of full employment, to earn in the course of its life more than its replacement cost.[19] In Keynes' view, it is only in the former sense that the boom can be said to be characterized by overinvestment.

Errors of optimism are in fact important for Keynes' theory of the boom. This can be seen from the following statement:

"The boom which is destined to end in a slump is caused, therefore, by the combination of a rate of interest, which in a correct state of expectation would be too high for full employment, with a misguided state of expectation which, so long as it lasts, prevents this rate of interest from being in the deterrent. A boom is a situation in which over-optimism triumphs over a rate of interest which, in a cooler light, would be seen to be excessive."[20]

Keynes opposed the view that the way to manage the cycle is to choke off the boom; rather, he would try "to enable the so called boom to last". To this end he favoured a lower rate of interest.[21]

Hicks' Theory

Hicks, in his book *A Contribution to the Theory of Trade Cycle* considers cyclical fluctuations as movements of the system above and below the rising line of tend or growth. Stated simply it means that the growth path of the economy is characterized by cyclical fluctuations. The long-run equilibrium growth path of the system is determined by the growth rate of autonomous investment. The ratio of the equilibrium income to autonomous investment depends on the size of the accelerator and multiplier. Hicks had built up his theory around the interaction of multiplier and accelerator. To him 'the theory of the multiplier' and 'the theory of the accelerator' are the two sides of the theory of fluctuations, just as the theory of demand and the theory of supply are the two sides of theory of value.[22]

In Hicks' theory of trade cycle the theory of the multiplier, the accelerator and warranted rate of growth of income[23] play a significant role. The warranted rate of growth of income is consistent with the saving-investment equilibrium. The system is said to be growing at a warranted rate of growth, when the real investment is taking place at the same rate at which the real saving is taking place in the economic system. The interaction between the multiplier and the accelerator weaves the path of movements of income around the warranted rate of growth which is the equilibrium output path. Basic to Hicks' cycle model are consumption function and an induced investment function with a fixed accelerator.

Starting with the required rate of growth, equilibrium can be upset by a change in autonomous investment, yielding a subsequent situation in which aggregate investment is either greater or less than savings and triggering a departure from equilibrium output. When there is no change in the autonomous factor, disequilibrium output. When there is no change in the autonomous factor, dis-equilibrium can result from the change in the ratio of induced investment. It is hardly conceivable that a system could hit upon the exact delicate balance that is required or that, having done so, it could maintain it for any length of time. In reality the economy does not adjust smoothly along its equilibrium path, but adjust in the form of cyclical interruptions. When the Hicksian model is used, our approach shifts from Figs 19.2 to 19.4.

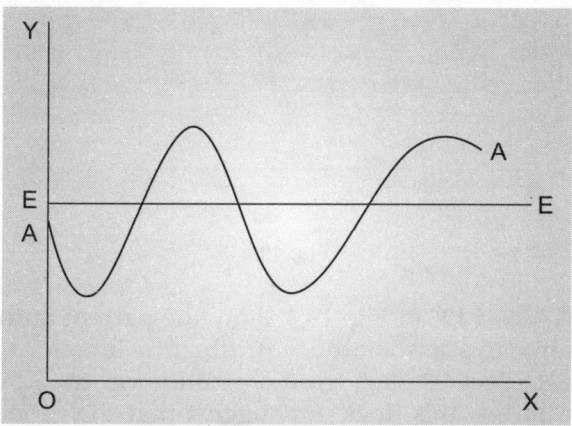

Fig. 19.2

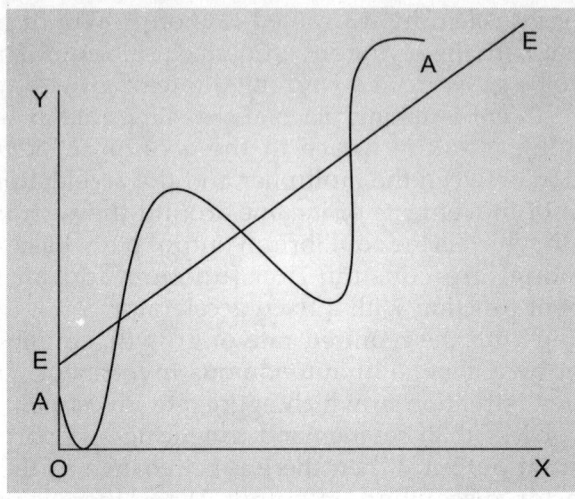

Fig. 19.3

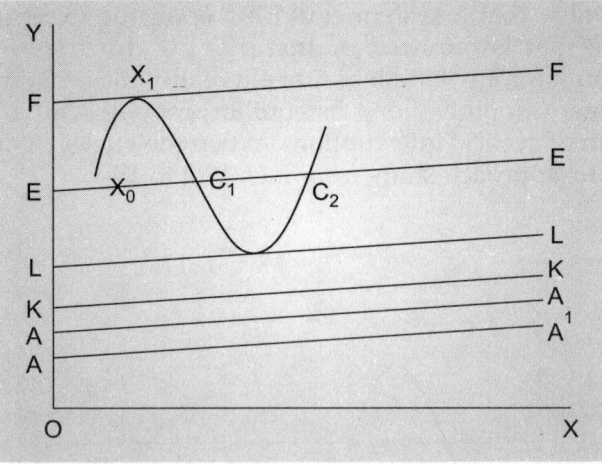

Fig. 19.4

Line AA and EE in Fig. 19.4 show the path of autonomous investment and associated equilibrium levels of output, respectively. Let us start from a position on the EE line. As Hicks indicates, this does not suggest that the economy has ever been on such a path, but only that the causal forces for the path of the cycle that we wish to indicate are most vividly seen if we begin from a cycle less situation. At Xo there is an up kick in equilibrium level as a result of an increase in the rate of autonomous investment, which therefore will return to its original level. The autonomous factor itself is sufficient cause to disturb the system EE, but this disturbance or displacement will in turn induce a higher level of investment, through the action of the accelerator. In other words, once displaced, the economy relentlessly pulls away from equilibrium, propelled by the multiplier and accelerator, and no longer needs the impetus of the autonomous factor. We can consider the change in autonomous investment as the triggering device. The rate of output growth along the expansion phase XoXi, clearly exceeds the growth rate along EE.

Line FF shows the 'limit' to the increase in real output brought on by full employment and full utilization of industrial capacity. It may be pointed out here that the above situation does not mean that at any point of time every firm is straining at capacity and that absolutely no further increase in employment or output is possible. This 'ceiling' only implies that beyond some level of output, the emergence of declining profit ratios is in general restrictive to further increase in output. For instance, Hicks states: "I shall follow Keynes in assuming that there is some point at which input becomes inelastic in response to and increase in effective demand". Such a point will reflect the factors—bottlenecks of supply, a growing scarcity of resources and in general rapidly increasing costs of doing business—that are characteristic of the peak of the business cycle, although cycles may peak before such ceiling conditions are present. Note that the FF line slopes upward and is parallel to the EE line, indicating that a growing economy means an increasing ceiling level of output, with the rate of growth of ceiling output being equal to that of equilibrium output. Furthermore, there is the possibility that the level of investment is such as to produce an EE path, which is identical to the ceiling.[24]

Returning to the cycle, we find that the expansion must ultimately reach the ceiling output Xi because of the combined effect of a larger autonomous investment plus the induced rise in consumption (the multiplier) plus the induced increase in investment (the accelerator). But once the peak level is attained, autonomous investment declines to its normal pace. So the only force that now sustains this higher output level along FF is the higher induced investment together with the lower autonomous investment. This total investment is not sufficient enough to sustain the increases in output that are necessary to maintain the economy at the ceiling level. So it must fall. In other words, it is the total 'smoothing-out of the increase in autonomous investment that finally precipitates the contraction.

When the economy contracts, it must do so until it touches the EE line. The EE line represents the growth rate commensurate with the normal pace of growth in autonomous investment. But the explosiveness of the forces that now work in reverse may plummet the economy past the equilibrium position. Let us note the forces that are at work at point C_i, at which output has declined to EE line.

The output changes that affect current investment decisions are either the declining output along path X_iC_i, the more distant output changes along the ceiling, or the farthest influence of the output growth along X_oX_i. Now, if the lag in investment change is more, the more will be the decline in induced investment. We can very well assume some sort of distributed lag with declining coefficients the longer the period, and we can consider the distribution over a sufficiently long period, and we can consider the distribution over a sufficiently long period, so that decisions to contract orders will to some degree be influenced by the experience of the previous expansion. The induced investment based on the ceiling rate of output will be sufficient to maintain output growth along EE. But the lower level of induced investment that results from contraction path is insufficient. The accelerator effect is powerful enough to force the reduction in investment to drive income below equilibrium levels.[25]

If the accelerator works as well during the downturn as it does during the upturn, the decline cannot be stopped until it reaches an output equal to that produced by the application of the multiplier to autonomous investment–point C on the KK line. But disinvestment ceases to depend on the decline in output even before income is pushed to this low level. The accelerator, as already pointed out, does not work as well during the downturn. If the decline starts out severely the pace of reaching zero gross investment is hastened. From here on, the accelerator ceases to work. Investment is not negative, being equal to depreciation factor. Hence the total level of investment is really equal to the autonomous factor minus depreciation or line AiAi. Now the multiplier effect of the autonomous factor, combined with the decline in the level of income in the absence of the reverse accelerator, will be sufficient to lift output to a level at which some induced investment is called for. This is point C2 on line LL. The level of output on line LL must lie above that of KK, since the multiplier effects start from higher income base, and it is less than the output on EE. This is so because it does not include any induced investment effects. The floor to the contraction is the LL line, resulting from the limitation to induced investment and rising autonomous investment. Once C2 is turned, the presence of induced investment indicates that the full effect of the accelerator has been triggered. Output must, therefore, be growing at a faster rate than does on LL, the economy has moved upward in the direction of EE. However, in doing so it is generating a rate of growth of output that is faster than if output were on EE line, therefore, the upward movement plunges through the equilibrium path, only to be constrained once again upon encountering the ceiling.[26]

It may be noted here that it is possible that at C2 the system will be faced with excess capacity as incomes begin to rise, thus preventing the appearance of an accelerator effect strong enough to lift the economy off the floor.

It is possible that the accelerator becomes non-linear around the turning points, so that the cycle is turned gradually rather than being bounced of the ceiling and the floor.[27]

Review Questions

1. Explain business cycles.
2. Analyze the various theories of business cycle.
3. Discuss the various phases of business cycle.
4. Explain the role of expectations in business cycle.

References

1. Henry Thornton in his book '*An Enquiry into the Effects of the Paper Credit of Great Britain*' (1802) refers to great commercial distress. See Hansen, Alvin H: B*usiness Cycle & National Income*, George Allen & Unwin, London, 1968.
2. David Ricardo speaks of 'revulsions of trade'.
   3&4 Both were concerned with the problems of depression and inadequate aggregate demand.
5. W.S. Jevons: *Investigation in Currency and Finance*, MacMillan & Co.Ltd, London, 1884. Also see Hansen, Alvin H, op.cit., p.219.
6. Khan, M.S.:*India's Economic Development and International Economic Relations*, Asia Publishing House, Bombay, Second Revised Edition 1966; p.27
7. Kuznets, Simon; '*Schumpeter's Business Cycles; in his compilation of Essays entitled Economic Change;* W.W.Norton Co., New York, 1953, p.107
8. Keynes, J.M.: *The General Theory of Employment, Interest and Money;* MacMillan & Co.Ltd; London, 1936, p.144
9. Ibid; p.145
10. Ibid; p.315
11. Ibid
12. Ibid; p.314
13. Ibid
14. Ibid; p.310
15. Ibid; p.316
16. Ibid; p.316
17. Ibid. p.317
18. Ibid
19. Ibid; pp.320–321
20. Ibid; p.322
21. Ibid
22. Hicks, J.R; *A Contribution to the Theory of Trade Cycle (1950);* p.38
23. The rate of growth which maintains itself over time.
24. Bobber, Stanley: *The Economics of Cycles and Growth;* Wiley Eastern private Ltd; New Delhi, 1968, p.217.
25. Ibid; pp.218–19
26. Ibid; pp.219–20
27. For further details see Hicks J.R; op.cit. and Hansen Alvin H op.cit pp.483–84.

20 Contra-Cyclical Policies

Till 1930s experts saw little scope for governmental intervention of any kind for economic management. The economic system was thought to be largely self-regulating and more likely to prosper under free competition than through the exertions of government departments. But after the great depression of the 1930s it is increasingly realized that everything cannot be left to anonymous market forces. The recent sub-prime crisis in the American economy and the consequent global financial melt down have fortified the belief that the market forces that operate have to be regulated by government as it cannot afford to allow the workings of the economic system to reflect exclusively and imperfectly the spending habits of individuals in their private capacity with all the instability, inequality and short-sightedness that this would imply. But it will be always profitable to remember that this does not justify capricious interference in the affairs of individual business where no general interest is at stake. Nor does it justify an extension of government control in every instance where a good case can be made for it. Where ever a choice is to be made, the government should seek to exercise control in ways that do least damage to individual freedom, making use of mechanisms that operate predominantly to the public advantage, and seeking to improve the ways in which these mechanisms function rather than replace them by a heavier layer of bureaucracy.[1] In other words, the government should not go for unlimited control and there are good reasons why it should have more than is necessary. There is a limit to the advantage that control confers on a government and this is as valid in economics as in politics. Beyond the limit, control becomes self-defeating because it squeezes out initiative and discretion and all the scope for the necessary urge to innovate that lies behind economic growth and development.

Another important factor to be remembered at this juncture is that the simple point on which John Maynard Keynes and others fastened attention was that the fluctuations that took place in the economy were primarily fluctuations in demand and purchasing power. Stabilization in this context, therefore, meant efforts to stabilize demand and this did not necessarily call for extensive detailed interference by the government in the economy. But it can be seen that there has always been an effort by governments to use regulatory measures for many different purposes. Today we should say that most of these devices were designed to promote more rapid growth or to secure greater equality and protect the weak. Stability has to be reconciled with these other objects of policy, economic development and growth, a better distribution of income and industrial and regional policy aimed at encouraging economic activity of particular types or in particular places. These objectives are not necessarily compatible with greater stability of indeed with one another.[2]

The fact that there are other objectives which have somehow to be reconciled with greater stability implies that control can never be a purely technical matter. It may be true that management of demand has become so complex that it must be left largely to experts. But the experts have a choice of instruments and the methods that they elect to use have different effects on particular outputs, the distribution of income, economic growth and so on. In the following paragraphs we propose to discuss questions such as:

    i. What they actually do to manage demand?

    ii. What instruments are at their disposal?

Generally governments take recourse to monetary policy, fiscal policy and a variety of administrative controls either separately or in combination to manage demand. Here we propose to discuss the policy measures directed to manage demand in some detail. First we deal with monetary policy.

Monetary Policy

The term 'monetary policy' signifies the policy of the monetary authority to regulate the ebb and flow of money in the economy.

The monetary policy is implemented to achieve the following objectives, namely (i) price stability, (ii) exchange stability, and (iii) full employment. The monetary policy is operated through the central bank. In essence monetary policy means credit policy pursued by the central bank with the above stated objectives. Monetary policy has a much longer history as an instrument of economic control. A proper understanding of the manner in which the central bank shapes monetary policy presupposes some knowledge about the nature and functions of the central bank. Here we may briefly touch upon them.

Nature and Functions of the Central Bank

The concept of central bank is of recent origin even though the banking system in its modern form originated about two centuries ago. The central bank of a country constitutes the apex of its monetary and banking structure. As such, it is the most important banking institution in the country. In the modern context, especially since the 1930s, it has come to play a dominant role not only in the limited sphere of monetary policy but in the broader field of economic policy at large. Unlike the commercial banks, the central bank does not operate under the profit motive; also it deserves special mention that central bank generally stands above political and ideological considerations on questions of policy. Again, the central bank does not deal with the public directly but only through the commercial banks and the money market.

Functions of Central Bank

The central bank functions as
1. The Bank of Note Issue
2. The Government's Banker, Agent and Advisor
3. The Custodian of the Cash Reserves of the Commercial Banks
4. Custodian of the Nation's Reserves of International Currency
5. The Bank for Rediscount and the Lender of Last Resort
6. The Bank of Central Clearance, Settlement and Transfer
7. The Controller of Credit.

Since we are more concerned with demand management and the instruments through which demand is managed, we do not want to go into the details of the functions of the central bank.[3]

To get a clear picture about the manner in which the central bank controls the money supply and thereby manage demand, we must have some idea about the supply of money. So here we propose to discuss in some detail the components of money supply.

The supply of money Ms has two components—Mo which includes paper money and coins and Md the demand deposit component—the checking amounts which the public has in commercial banks. On the basis of this, we can define money supply as

$$Ms = Mo + Md \qquad \qquad ...1$$

For simplicity we shall assume here that the currency component of the money supply is constant, i.e the amount of currency in the hands of the public does not change. This assumption means that changes in the money supply occur only as a result of changes in the demand deposit component. For if Mo is constant,

$$dMo = 0$$

and

$$dMs = d\ Md \qquad \qquad ...2$$

Stated in another way, this means that a change in the demand deposit component brings about an equal change in the money supply—Ms.

Demand Deposits, Reserves and Reserve Ratio

Having assumed that Ms changes only when Md changes, we now wish to show what determines the size of Md to change and the amount by which Md can change.

In the banking system commercial banks are required by law to have reserves R in the form of either deposits at the central bank or currency in their own vaults. The amount of reserves they should have depends upon the demand deposits the public has in their banks and the required or legal reserve ratio r. The required Reserve ratio is a percentage set by the central bank. It is the percentage of demand deposits which commercial banks must have in reserve.[4] Thus we can write reserves required by law as a function of the demand deposits of commercial banks and the required reserve ratio.

$$R = rMd \qquad \qquad \dots 3$$

For example, if commercial banks have demand deposits of Rs.1000 and the required reserve ratio is 10 percent, the required reserve would be 10 percent of Rs. 1000 or Rs. 100.

When we are interested in knowing what determines the maximum size of Md in the economy, a more useful form of equation 3 is found by dividing both sides of the equation by r

$$\frac{rM_d}{r} = \frac{R}{r}$$

$$M_d = \frac{R}{r} \qquad \qquad \dots 4$$

Equation 4 tells us that the amount of demand deposits in the economy may equal as much as the reserves of the commercial banks divided by the required reserve ratio. If commercial banks have Rs. 100 as reserves and the required reserve ratio is 10 percent, the demand deposits in the economy could (at most) be Rs. 100 divided by 10 percent, or Rs. 1000. In using equation 4, we shall assume that demand deposits are always as large as allowed by the reserves and the required reserve ratio. This means that we assume that commercial banks never have an excess reserve.

In summary, we assume that the demand deposits of an economy equals the reserves held by commercial banks divided by the required reserve ratio set by the central bank.

Changes in the Reserves and the Required Reserve Ratio

If demand deposits in the economy depend upon the reserves of commercial banks and the required reserve ratio, then a change in either reserves or the reserve ratio will bring about a change in demand deposits (and in the money supply). Let us see first how a change in the reserve ratio changes demand deposits.

Changes in Reserves

When reserves change by dR, demand deposits change by dMd. Using equation 4 above we can write

$$Md + dMd = \frac{R + dR}{r} \qquad \ldots 5$$

From equation 5 we subtract equation 4 and obtain

$$dMd = \frac{dR}{r} \text{ Or } (dR \frac{1}{r}) \qquad \ldots 6$$

The change in demand deposits and in the money supply equals the change in reserves divided by the required reserve ratio (or the change in reserves multiplied by the reciprocal of the reserve ratio). Note that the sign dR/r is positive. This implies that when reserves increase, demand deposits will increase; and when R decreases, Md also decreases.

Suppose, for instance, that r is 10 percent and R increases by Rs. 100, then Md can increase by an amount equal to Rs. 100 times $1/0.10$ = Rs. 100 times 10, or Rs. 1000. If r is 20 percent and R increases by Rs. 100, the Md could decrease by Rs. 100 times $1/0.20$ = Rs. 100 times 5, or Rs. 500.

The reciprocal of the required reserve ratio is often called the deposit multiplier. In the two examples above, the reciprocal of 10 percent and the deposit multiplier is 10 and the reciprocal of 20 percent and the deposit multiplier is 5. The change in demand deposits that accompanies a change in the reserves of commercial banks is equal to the change in reserves times the deposit multiplier. We should note that the smaller the required reserve ratio, the larger the deposit multiplier and vice versa. (The Reserve Bank of India uses two types of reserves –statutory liquidity ratio and cash reserve ratio.)

Why and how do the reserves of commercial banks change? They change primarily because the central bank wants them to change in order to bring about changes in the demand deposits and the money supply. The central bank alters reserves by two principal means. It may lower or raise the discount rate, the rate at which commercial banks can borrow from the central bank, to expand or contract the reserves of commercial banks. (Please note, the recent actions of the Reserve Bank of India in this respect.)

The central banks may also buy or sell government securities in the open market because these securities increase or decrease commercial banks' reserves. The details of these two methods of changing commercial bank reserves are discussed later.

The Modus Operandi of Bank Rate

The bank rate is the rate at which the central bank discounts first class bills presented to it by the member banks. It is assumed that there is a strong customary connection between bank rate and most other rates for short-term funds. When bank rate is raised these rates move up more or less automatically, and as a rule, to a corresponding extent. So by changing the bank rate the central bank can indirectly control the volume of credit in the economy. When the central bank feels, for example, the inflationary conditions should be checked, it raises the bank rate as a result of which the commercial banks, on their part, have to raise their lending rates. It is possible that an increase in the cost of bank credit might be sufficient by itself to induce merchants and others to reduce the level of their stocks and those acts of disinvestment would provide an effective check on business expansion and thereby inflation is held in check.

A second *modus operandi* is through long-term rates. A change in bank rate, and the accompanying changes in other short rates, has effects in the security market, sought or unsought. If the connection is a close one, it can be argued that changes in bank rates sooner or later work through to the long end or the market and check or encourage interest-sensitive form of investment. The Macmillan Committee, which developed this line of argument, drew attention to the role of the banks in mediating between the two parts of the market. If fall in bank rate were backed up by open market operations, this would encourage the credit base and put the banks in a position to buy government securities. Their purchases, together with those made by the central bank in carrying out open market operations, will give a lift to the guilt-edged market and thus would encourage their buying. The movement would spread to other parts of the market and would improve the cost of long-term borrowing by other first class borrowers until, with the revival of the new issue market, real investment would also recover.[5]

The theory underlying the use of the discount rate as the chief instrument of credit control under the gold standard was that changes in the discount rate of the central bank would bring about more or less corresponding changes in local money rates generally, and that such changes in money rates would, through their operation on the supply of and demand for money and credit and on the international flow of capital, have the effect of readjusting the domestic levels of prices, costs, production and trade, and correcting any disequilibrium in the balance of payments.[6]

But it may be noted here that the successful applications of the discount rate policy requires that

i. the discount rate of the central bank should have a prompt and decisive influence on money rates and credit condition within its area of operation, particularly when it was desired to raise money rates and contract credit;

ii. there should be a substantial measure of elasticity in the economic structure in order that price, wages, rents, production and trade might respond to changes in money rates and credit condition;

iii. the international flow of capital should not be hampered by any arbitrary restrictions and artificial obstacles; and

iv. there should be a well-developed money market.

While it is obvious that under present day conditions of economic rigidity and complexity as well as monetary liquidity, there is less scope for an effective discount rate policy than was formerly the case, the discount rate of the central bank has, nevertheless, a useful function to perform in certain circumstances and in conjunction with other measures of control. In short, changes in discount and interest rates can be employed as a necessary instrument contributing towards the restoration of equilibrium, since they operate in various ways to correct wrong trends, namely, through their influence on the supply of and demand for money and credit, or on the rate of investment and speculation, or human psychology in general.[7]

Prior to 1914 the central bank (the Bank of England especially) relied upon bank rate as the primary instrument of credit control. At various times, however, owing to large foreign balances, or for other reasons, the bank experienced great difficulty in making its rates effective and felt the need for some method which would enable it to reduce the liquidity of the market whenever it desired to raise money rates generally.

The method which was evolved in earlier days aiming at the desired expansion or contraction of money and credit and of general economic activity was termed as open market operations. It was designed to have a direct and immediate effect on the volume of money and credit as well as money and interest rate generally. The theory behind open market operations is that purchases or sales of securities by the central bank tend directly and immediately to increase or decrease the quantity of money in circulation and the cash reserves of the commercial banks; that an increase or decrease in the supply of bank cash and, therefore, in the credit creating capacity of the commercial banks, tends still further to increase or decrease the quantity of money; and that changes in the quantity of money tend to bring about relative changes in money rates and credit conditions, which in turn tend to bring about the desired adjustments in the domestic level of prices, cost, production and trade.[8]

An important feature of open market operations is that the buying of securities by the central bank makes the monetary position liquid in a different manner from what rediscount does. In some countries the commercial banks have traditionally shown a tendency towards greater caution whenever they are indebted to the central bank, even though the latter openly desires expansion of credit at the time, and for this reason, does not raise its discount and interest rates. Thus, there is more chance for the central bank's policy of expansion being implemented under open market operations than under rediscount.[9]

Scope of Open Market Operations

The question as to how far the open market operations of a central bank can be adjusted for the purpose of counter acting the effects of disturbing factors has attracted a great deal of attention from certain economists. Hawtrey,[10] for example, admits emphatically, the connection with an increase in the credit base resulting from open market operations, that an addition to the outstanding quantity of money, 'unspent margin' in itself accomplishes nothing, since the supply of money, in the only sense in which markets feel it, is the flow of money spent in exchange for commodities,' and since 'the release of cash by trade in an indispensable condition of an increase in the consumer's income'. He also admits that 'the release or absorption of cash is not rigidly dependent upon the increase or decrease of lending by banks, and that 'there may be other causes affecting the amount of balances people are willing to hold'; but be maintains that 'these other causes must be taken into account by the authorities regarding credit', and that they must endeavour so as to adjust their measures that the resultant enlargement or compression of the consumers' income and outlay will be just what is required.

For the effective carrying out of a comprehensive open market policy it is essential not only that there should be broad and active markets in the short-term and long-term government securities, if not also other securities, but also the obviously gilt-edged securities in respect of which open market operations are conducted should represent the central and sensitive part of the financial structure as a whole.

In addition to the two methods explained above, central banks employ certain other measures such as moral suasion, publicity, credit rationing, inspection, license cancelling, consumer credit regulation and reserve variation.

Moral suasion implies issuing of persuasive instructions by the central bank to the member banks requesting them to follow particular lines of credit policy depending on the nature of the situation. At a time of inflation, for example, the member banks could be persuaded to refrain from increasing their loans for speculative or non-essential activities. This method, however, can succeed only when the central bank commands adequate respect from the member banks. It may be pointed out here that the Reserve Bank of India has been successfully applying this method during the last couple of decades.

The central bank can resort to publicity of different types to have the member banks and the public to follow particular courses of action. Generally these take the form of warnings supported by, or supplemented with, statistical data and statements made through highly respected intermediaries. Central banks also resort to credit rationing for controlling credit. Credit rationing means restrictions imposed on demand for financial accommodation made on the central bank by member banks during the time of monetary stringency. The available funds are rationed out among the applicants on the basis of pre-determined criteria. But we are of the opinion that this method can be justified only under exceptional circumstances because of the likelihood of its misuse.

Again, it is possible for the central banks to have inspection of member banks to check that its policies are being carried out by them in accordance with the need of the hour. If the central bank finds that certain member banks are not working in conformity with the guidelines given, then it may cancel the licenses of such defaulting member banks. Consumer credit can be modified by properly reformulating the terms and conditions under which credit is repayable in instalments with reference to purchase of consumer durables. The central bank may, if the situation warrants, change the legal reserve ratio in order to regulate credit in the country. The Reserve Bank of India has applied this method after the banking sector reforms were introduced on the basis of Narasimham Committee's recommendations.

The Advantages of Monetary Instruments

The most important advantage of monetary instruments, according to Cairncross,[11] is acceptability. A large section of informed opinion is willing to endorse policies of dear money or cheap money in the right set of circumstances when it might hesitate to accept budgetary changes or direct controls. It may be as professor Kahn has argued,[12] that dear money is more acceptable than cheap, and the choice tends to be biased towards monetary measures on the restrictive tack and the other methods on the expansionist tack. It is certainly true as he points out, that there is greater disposition to persevere with monetary restriction and apply another turn of the screw if the initial effects are disappointing than to continue with monetary expansion and rely exclusively on cheap money when a recovery is slow in coming. But there is nothing sinister about this: it merely reflects the greater power of high interest rates to check investment than of low interest rates to encourage it.

Secondly, monetary measures are acceptable than others because of their anonymity. They operate through market mechanism on the whole range of borrowing and lending transactions and do not single out some group of individuals or some particular forms of demand for control or regulation. But it may be noted here that a general restriction of purchasing power may be ineffective as a means of aligning the pattern of demand with the pattern of economic activity and it may be necessary to impose selective checks where excess demand is the greatest. The need will be most evident where industrial mobility is slow and where producers are least inhibited in raising their prices when they have full order books. If bottlenecks appear only in isolate industries, they can usually be quickly removed without creating any great strain in the structure of costs or starting of wage inflation.

Another factor that favours monetary policy is its flexibility. It can be used as and when it becomes necessary. No parliamentary sanction is required for the application of monetary weapons.

Monetary policy was used frequently by the Reserve Bank of India after the reforms was implemented in the financial sector on the basis of the Narasimham Committee Report.

Limitations of the Monetary Policy

Against the advantages of monetary policy mentioned in the foregoing paragraphs, monetary policy has certain limitations. Firstly and most obviously, the expansion of the public sector extends the possibilities of direct action and limits the response to monetary measures.

Secondly, the fact that monetary policy operates on a broad front, without regard to the bottlenecks or shortages, puts in certain circumstances, at a disadvantage.

Thirdly, although monetary measures, given adequate time, do exercise an influence on fixed investment, this influence may be harmful if it is used in order to bring about sharp changes in industrial and commercial investment.

Fourthly, monetary policy tends to have strong directional effects. It tends to operate by cutting off or seriously curtailing the flow of credit to particular types of borrowers.[13] It has always been accepted that smaller firms, with few alternative sources of finance outside the banking system, are more affected than larger firms with access to a wider range of facilities. Precisely because any particular business is affected by monetary measures, firms have to keep asking themselves not just whether the government will act and whether it will use monetary measures but what monetary measure/s it will use. It becomes difficult as time goes on to draw a clear line between broad measures operating on the level of purchasing power and specific intervention affecting an identifiable group of firms. The professedly unintentional outcome of demand management may come very close to direct discrimination against particular business.

Fifthly, fluctuations are often communicated from abroad and not domestic in origin. Efforts to control a single national economy may be thwarted by compulsions of situations in other countries. Export markets, for example, may suddenly fall off (as happened during 2008–09 fiscal year) or credit restrictions in some important financial centre may initiate an outflow of funds and push up interest rates. Those mysterious influences which lie concealed in the balances of payments may swarm out of their bottle like a genie in the Arabian Nights and knock the economy out of balance. It may then be necessary to take steps to de-stabilise domestic activity in order to restore external balances.

The Radcliffe Committee was of opinion that there was a limited role for monetary policy in the traditional sense. It had nothing to say about short-term rates and concentrated its attention on long-term rates. These, the Committee thought, should not be held stable in face of major changes in the incentive to capital development; neither should they be made to fluctuate widely in order to make them bite deeply. To follow the first course would be to destroy all control over liquidity in the economy by making government securities as liquid as bank deposits, it would also make for a useful use of capital. To follow the second course would be to spoil the market for government paper securities and embark on sales and purchases that might prove very difficult to carry out or oversee without disastrous side effects. The Committee preferred an intermediate solution with long rates moving from 'middle' to 'high' gear in periods of sustained pressure on the supply of new capital and from 'middle' to 'low' when the demand for new capital remained continuously low. It wanted these changes of gear to be an object of deliberate policy, not accidental by products of action on discount rates.[14]

If interest rates—or at least long-term rates –have to be kept fairly stable in times of boom or recession, other more direct, means can still be used to control lending to the private sector. Bank credit has a special importance not only because of the banks have larger total assets than any other group of financial institutions but also because the power to obtain bank finance often plays a critical, 'bringing' role in the early stages of business investment. If the government is unable to carry out funding operations on the scale necessary to limit the liquidity of the banks, it may be necessary to apply a break to bank lending by imposing higher liquidity ratios or by obliging each bank to add to its deposits with the central bank. This form of control does not necessarily force the banks to cut down their loans to the private sector, which is, or should be, the main purpose of the control; on the other hand, it may well push the banks into selling government investments—that is, into very transactions in the gilt-edged market in which the authorities conceive it to be out of their power to engage.[15]

Fiscal Policy

The classical economists almost universally held that the budget aught to be kept in balance in all circumstances and unbalanced budgets were inherently wrong. In view of the proneness of governments to overspend, this has been no bad rule in ordinary situations especially at a time when the state was relatively a small element in the economy. So long as the economy is in balance, there is no need to unbalance the budget and indeed to have done so would have been to unbalance the economy. But under conditions of prosperity and depression, when the economy is out of gear, the budget offered a means of reshaping the balance of private spending and saving. Note that such an idea was advocated at a time when the very existence of trade cycle had yet to be discovered, and economic fluctuations were still thought of in terms of panics and crises. But even if fiscal weapons had been used to stabilize economic activity, they might well have been comparatively ineffective so long as the flow of government revenue and expenditure remained a very negligible fraction of GNP, as was the case in peace time in the 19th century. The smaller the size of the budget, the bigger must be the variation in the flow of revenue or expenditure to offset a given swing in the pressure on resources generated by private demand.

Whatever may have been true under 19th century conditions when it would have been natural to rely mainly on monetary policy as an economic stabilizer, the expanding role of the government after the great depression of the 1930s and the acceptance of the concept of welfare state by modern governments after the publication of the Beveridge Report made the use of fiscal weapons indispensable since the budget is the natural means for harmonising the spending plans of public authorities and private business.

Fiscal policy comprises of three elements, viz; public revenue, public expenditure and public debt management. The instruments of fiscal policy are being increasingly used in modern times as important levers influencing aggregate outlay, employment and the level of prices in the economy. The significance of fiscal policy has become so evident especially after the great depression of the 1930s and the recent global financial melt down.

As in the case of monetary policy the fiscal policy also have three major objectives. They are (i) achievement of full employment, (ii) achievement of price stability, and (iii) achievement of exchange stability.

Let us first deal with the component of public revenue. The major source of public revenue is taxation. Several economists have enunciated different principles with respect to taxation. The most important among them is that put forward by Adam Smith. He enunciated four maxims of taxation. They are principle of ability (equity), the principle of certainty the principle of convenience, and the principle of economy.

It is often said that Smith introduced ability and benefit considerations in taxation. Following Smith the classical economists postulated principle of taxation on the criterion of benefit. But later it was accepted that there is no *quid pro quo* in taxation. Hence the ability to pay principle got sway over the benefit principle.

The ability-to-pay approach has led to different interpretations about taxation based on different assumptions. Three types of ability-to-pay approaches are distinguished. The first view addresses itself to the distribution of tax as a subject of welfare economics. According to this view taxes should be imposed and distributed as to minimize the total sacrifice involved.

The welfare approach to tax grew out of the equity view. According to John Stuart Mill equity is to be defined in terms of equal sacrifice of the tax payers. As the neo-classical economists developed the concept of marginal analysis, equal sacrifice came to be defined as equal marginal sacrifice.

The third view retained the welfare approach. Thus it came to be looked as a more or less general plan to maximize welfare.

Concept of Equal Sacrifice

Cohen Stuart and Edgeworth advocated three concepts of equal sacrifice. They are equal absolute sacrifice, equal proportional sacrifice and equal marginal sacrifice (or least aggregate sacrifice).[16]

Different types of taxes were advocated depending on the assumptions regarding marginal utility of money. Table 20.1 indicates the types of taxes that will help to achieve the desired goals under the different assumptions.

Table 20.1

	Equal marginal sacrifice	Equal proportional sacrifice	Equal absolute sacrifice
Marginal utility declines over the entire range	Progressive tax with exemption at lower level	Progressive tax	Proportional tax
Marginal utility of money remains constant over the entire range	Any tax	Proportional tax	Progressive tax
Marginal utility of money increases	Progressive/ Regressive	Progressive/ regressive	Progressive/ regressive

Source: Richard, A. Musgrave: The Theory of Public Finance; Mc Graw Hill Book Co.

The above principles of taxation relate to personal taxes. In the early days this was the common form of tax that existed. Later a variety of taxes were introduced. The major among them is commodity taxes. Commodity taxes are regressive taxes. The burden of such tax falls heavily on the low income group. Smith's second maxim of taxation is certainty. According to Smith:

The tax each individual is to pay ought to be certain, and not arbitrary. The time of payment, the manner of payment, the quantity to be paid, ought all to be clear and plain to the contributor and to every other person. Where it is otherwise, every person subject to the tax is put more or less in the power of the tax gatherer who can either aggravate the tax upon any obnoxious contributor, or extort, by the terror of such aggravation, some present or perquisite to himself. The uncertainty of taxation encourages the insolence and favours corruption of an order of men who are naturally unpopular, even where they are neither insolent nor corrupt. The certainty of what each individual ought to pay is, in taxation, a matter of so great importance, that a very considerable degree of inequality, it appears, I believe, from the experience of all nations, is not so great an evil as a small degree of uncertainty.[17]

The third maxim of Smith with respect to taxation relates to convenience of payment. Every tax, says Smith, Ought to be levied at the time or the manner, in which it is most likely to be convenient to the contributor to pay it. A tax upon the rent of land or of houses, payable at the same term when it is most likely to be convenient for the contributor, to pay, or when he is most likely to have wherewithal to pay. Taxes upon such consumable goods as are articles of luxury, are all finally paid by the consumer, and generally in a manner that is very convenient for him. He pays them little and little, as he has occasion to buy the goods. As he is at liberty too, either to buy, as he pleases it must be his own fault if he ever suffers any considerable inconvenience from such taxes. [18]

The fourth maxim of tax advocated by Adam Smith relates to economy in collection. This maxim states that no tax should be imposed if the collection charges are more than the revenue realized from the tax.

Public Expenditure

The second component of fiscal policy is public expenditure. Pursuing the line of reasoning advocated in Schaffle's principle of proportional satisfaction of public and private wants, Pigou and subsequently Dalton proposed two principles of budget policy.[19] The first principle states that resources should be distributed among different public uses so as to equalize the marginal return of satisfaction for each type of outlay. The second principle states that expenditure should be pushed to the point where the satisfaction obtained from the last dollar (rupee) expended is equal to the satisfaction lost from the last dollar (rupee) taken in taxes. This approach is represented in Fig. 20.1.

In Fig. 20.1 the size of the budget is measured horizontally, and the marginal utility or disutility is measured vertically. Suppose that the marginal utility of successive rupees of public expenditure, allocated optimally between different public uses, is shown by the line 'ee'; and that the marginal disutility of taxes, imposed so as to cause least total sacrifice, is shown by line 'tt'.

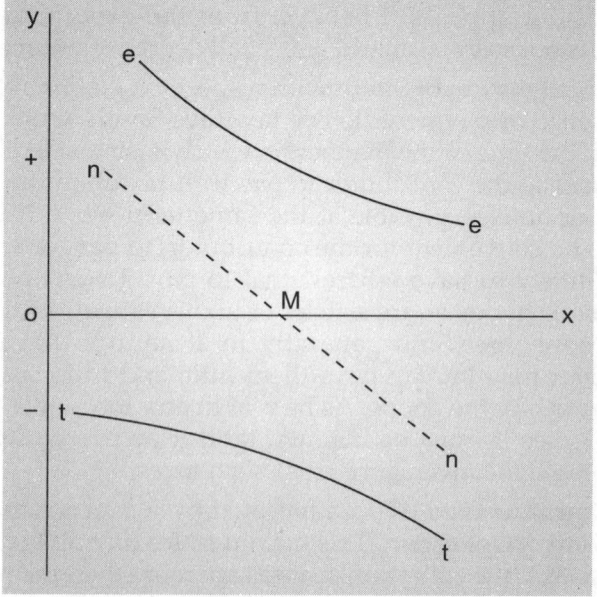

Fig. 20.1: Attainment of maximum welfare through the budget

Since the marginal utility of both public and private outlays declines with successive increments, both schedules fall from the left to the right. The line 'nn' is obtained by deducting 'tt' from 'ee', and measures the net benefit. The optimum size of the budget is determined at OM, where marginal net benefits are zero. In this way the minimum sacrifice approach to the allocation of taxes is matched by a maximum benefit approach to the determination of public expenditures, and the two are combined in a general theory of budget planning.[20]

The classical economists considered saving as a virtue and spending as a vice. According to the classical economists savings lead to capital formation that is necessary for economic growth and development. But after the great depression of the nineteen thirties and especially after the publication of the 'General Theory' the Keynesians romanticized public expenditure. According to Keynesians saving is a vice and expenditure a virtue. For attaining full employment expenditure is to be increased. If revenue receipts are not adequate, expenditure is to be increased by resorting to deficit financing or through public borrowing or by both. Figure 20.2 explains the current situation and Fig. 20.3 explains how full employment can be attained through increase in expenditure.

In Fig. 20.2 X-axis represents the level of employment and Y-axis, the level of income. Line Pi represents private

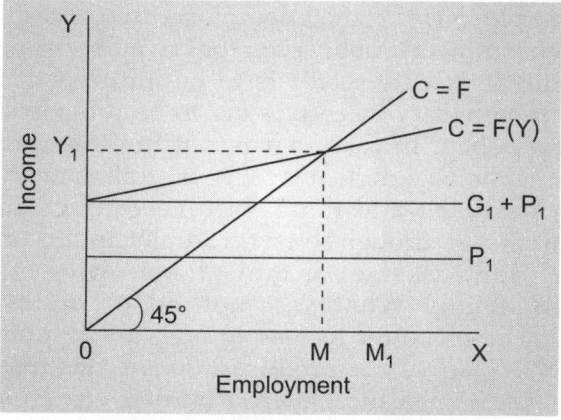

Fig. 20.2: The existing situation

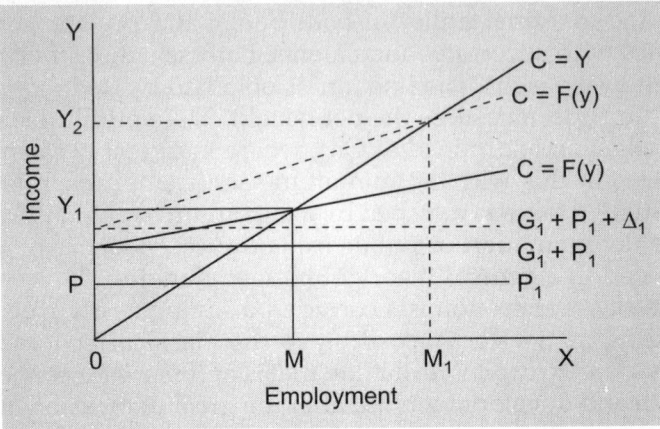

Fig. 20.3

investment Gi + Pi represent government and public investment put together. Under the given situation Line C = Y represents the 45 degrees line. A movement along this line consumption will be equal to income. (But generally there will be some discrepancy between consumption and income.) Line C = f(Y) represents consumption and consumption is a function of income. At the given level of consumption, employment is OM and income OY. Actual resources available in the economy, is OMi which shows that MMi resources are remaining unemployed. Fiscal policy management should be directed to provide employment to the unemployed resources. This can be either government (Public sector) or Private sector increasing investment. If private sector is to be induced to increase investment, necessary incentives are to be provided through budgetary policy. In case that is not the intention of the government, the government is to incur additional investment either by realizing additional income through imposing additional taxes or through better tax administration or through imposing additional taxes or through borrowing or through deficit financing. Whatever method or methods, the government resort to for increasing expenditure and thereby realizing the objective may produce different consequences like price rise, fiscal imbalance, interest burden, etc. To minimize such adverse impacts a lot of care and ingenuity is required on the part of those who manage the fiscal policy. Fig. 20.3 represents the new situation when investment is increased.

Fig. 20.3 shows that when investment goes to the new heights, income in the economy will be increased. That will shift the consumption line C = f(Y) upwards and will help to attain equilibrium under full employment. But in practice this will not be that simple.

A given change—increase or decrease—in the aggregate government expenditure causes change–increase or decrease– in the aggregate demand thereby increasing or decreasing factor incomes. Government expenditure incurred on wages and salaries of its employees, interest paid on government debt, social security and old age pension payments—all tend to increase the personal disposable income as a consequence of which aggregate demand for consumer goods increases. Thus an increase in the total expenditure of government tends to expand the aggregate economic activity in the economy. A point to be noted here is that expenditure often operates with magnified effect. The force of each rupee spends turn out to have a considerable leverage. This leverage may operate in one or two directions. Expenditure may have secondary effects (a) upon consumption expenditures and (b) upon private investment. The secondary effects of a given expenditure[21] upon consumption are generally discussed under the term 'multiplier principle', while the secondary effects upon private investment are referred to under the term 'acceleration principle'. This terminology is quite arbitrary, since the initial expenditures may be regarded as having raised the national income by a 'multiplier' or may be thought of as having an 'accelerated effect' on income. To avoid confusion, the coefficient which must be attached to the initial increment of expenditure in order to raise this increment to the incremental increase in the national income may be called the 'leverage'. The leverage coefficient, therefore, in itself indicates nothing with respect to whether the secondary effects operate through consumption or through investment. It may measure the effect of the multiplier principle, or the effect of the acceleration principle, or a combination of both. Where it is desired to segregate the two, the terms 'multiplier leverage' and 'acceleration leverage' may be used.

The Multiplier Principle

The multiplier principle, applied to fiscal policy, relates an increment of governmental expenditures to a consequent increment of consumption expenditures. [22] Let us assume that Rs. 10 million is expended on public works. The Rs.10 million of new funds pumped into the community is received by the contractors, who in turn pay out a part in wages and salaries, a part in dividends, a part in the purchase of materials from manufacturers, and a part in the purchase of materials from raw material producers. These in turn similarly pay out a part in wages and salaries, a part in dividends, and a part in finished and semi-finished goods and raw materials. The multiplier principle is, however, concerned exclusively with the effect of the initial expenditure on consumption, and is, therefore, peculiarly concerned with the effect of such expenditures upon the receipt of wages, salaries and dividends. It is evident that it is highly improbable that the full Rs. 10 million spent by the government will materialize down through the various stages in a Rs. 10 million of wages, salaries, or dividends. The reason for this is that many entrepreneurs in the various links in the productive chain will supply the goods sold from stock, will convert inventories into idle cash balances, or pay off bank loans and other debt obligations. Even if they supply their sales from current production, they will use a part of their profits not to pay dividends, but to accumulate cash or to pay off debts. Thus it is evident that the Rs. 10 million spent by the government on public works does not all materialize in income for individuals whether wage-earners, salaried employees, or stock holders. A part of the fund is diverted from becoming a part of the income stream by being drained off into idle balances or debt cancellation.

Similarly, the enlarged income of individuals flowing from the governmental expenditure and public works – the increased income in wages, salaries and dividends is not all used for consumption expenditures. The part that is not spent on consumption is saved. Such savings may be used either to pay off debt, hold in idle balances, or used for financial investment in mortgages, securities, life insurance policies, etc. It may be true that in some cases the individual will directly spend his savings on real investment, in a house, farm equipment or other investment goods. In this latter case it will be seen that such an individual is performing a dual function. On the one side, he is saving a part of the income, and on the other side, he is simultaneously making a purchase of real investment goods. As far as the multiplier principle is involved, we are concerned only with the consumption function, and we shall regard his real investment purchase as quite independent as though they are performed by another individual.

To repeat, the original Rs. 10 million of government expenditure on public works does not all result in consumption expenditures. A part is drained of directly by the entrepreneurial units engaged in the productive process in debt payments and idle balances, and a part of that paid out to wage earners, salaried employees, and dividend recipients is saved. Thus leakages—in the form of debt cancellation, hoarding of idle balances and financial investment—occur down the line of business units and individuals engaged in the private investment or public works project. The intensity of these leakages determines, in the ultimate analysis, what the secondary effects of the initial expenditures will be upon the volume of consumption expenditures.

The final effects of the Rs. 10 million on public works expenditure on consumption do not stop at the stage we have reached in our analysis. The individuals participating in the public works project decide to spend a portion of the new income they have received in consumption purchases. Thus we have reached the first stage in tracing the secondary consequences of public works expenditure upon consumption. The expenditure made on consumption goods now set in motion a new productive process necessary to supply these consumption goods. The funds thus expended again seep down through an entire productive process. Again, a part is not paid, as before, to wage and salary earners or dividend recipients, but is leaked out in the form of debt cancellation, idle balances, etc.; and, again, a part of the income received by wage and salary earners and dividend recipients is shunted off into savings and utilized for repayment of debts, held in idle balances, or used for financial investment.

This process continues indefinitely into the future. What leakages actually occur in any situation can be determined only by statistical investigation. But it is possible to state that multiplier will be high if the magnitude of the leakage is low and vice versa. If the leakages are zero, the multiplier is infinity, and if the leakages are 100 percent, the multiplier is unity. Often the magnitude of the multiplier is stated in terms of the marginal propensity to save, or conversely the marginal propensity to consume. The magnitude of the leakages is determined by the portion of the marginal income which is not used for consumption expenditures, or in other words, is saved. Thus, if the percentage saved is zero, the multiplier is infinity. If the fraction which is saved is one-tenth, the multiplier is 10, if one-fifth, five, and so on. The multiplier is thus the reciprocal of the marginal propensity to save, which determines the ratio of marginal saving to marginal income received. The multiplier can also be stated in terms of marginal propensity to consume. The multiplier (K) stated in terms of marginal propensity to consume dc/dy gives the multiplier.

$$K = \frac{1}{1 - \dfrac{dc}{dy}}$$

The Acceleration Principle

The multiplier principle concerns exclusively the effect of governmental expenditure upon subsequent net additions. The acceleration principle concerns exclusively the effect of a net increase in consumption expenditures upon induced investment expenditures. If we are to measure the full effect of governmental expenditure as income we must take account of both the multiplier and the acceleration principles. We must measure not only the effect of these initial expenditures upon subsequent consumption, but also the effect of subsequent consumption, but also the effect of the subsequent increases in consumption upon investment induced by increase in consumption expenditures. The volume of replacement investment expenditures is determined by the volume of consumption expenditures. In the event that consumption expenditures remain constant, no new investment expenditures are induced, but only a given volume of replacement. In the event, however, consumption expenditures go up, the net investment of consumption may prompt a given volume of additional investment. This will occur even before existing equipment is fully utilized. If we start from the bottom of a depression, a rise in consumptions expenditures is likely to prompt a larger volume of replacement expenditures in the old, established industries. This follows from the fact that during depression depreciation allowances are not fully expended, and recovery tends to restore replacement to a normal level. If the increases in consumption expenditure occur in new lines, a given volume of new investment will take place, even when the industry is still depressed. Thus it is by no means easy to determine exactly in what degree a rise of consumption expenditure from the bottom of the depression affects, on the one side, new investment expenditures, and, on the other side, new investment expenditure. Statistical enquiry by Kuznets did reveal that a rise in consumption expenditures from the bottom of the depression brings about a very smooth rise in gross investment, and there appears to be no point in the upswing at which one can clearly pinpoint replacement investment expenditure from new investment expenditures; nor is there any sharp break in the gross investment expenditure curve, such as might be implied from an over-emphasis on the effect of reasonably full utilization of existing equipment upon new investment, as consumption expenditures continue to rise.

The magnitude of the acceleration will depend upon the concrete nature of the new consumption. Certain types of consumption entail in their production virtually no capital requirement, while others require a very high ratio of capital to each unit of output. Thus, the acceleration leverage cannot be determined on *a priori* grounds, but must be determined by empirical studies regarding the actual character of the new consumption.

Acceleration principle states that the demand for capital goods varies directly with the changes in the level of output and the magnitude of the change depends upon the capital output ratio and the change in the level of output. Since the change in the level of output, as we have already noted, depends upon the change in the level of aggregate expenditure or demand which itself equals the change in the level of income in equilibrium, we might say that total investment in any given period of time depends upon the change in the level of aggregate demand which, in equilibrium, equals national income plus the replacement investment which is often assumed constant. Thus gross investment in any given any time period t will be equal to the increase in national income during that time period times the capital output ratio (K/O) plus the replacement of capital consumed in production. Designating the capital output ratio or capital coefficient by v, income period t, t—1 as Yt and Yt-1 and replacement investment as R, the gross investment in time period t(1t) will be

$$1t = v(Yt - Yt-1) + R \qquad \qquad ...1$$
$$= vdYt + R \qquad \qquad ...2$$

The capital output ratio v (= K/O) is called the accelerator.

The interaction of multiplier and accelerator results in a much higher income than what is initially spent by the government.

Impact of Fiscal Policy on Resource Allocation

Taxation, if wisely conceived and skilfully used, can become a very effective instrument of policy. As part of a general programme of development, taxation may be used to accomplish the following objectives:

a. Restraining or curtailing consumption and thus transferring resources from consumption to investment;
b. Increasing the incentive to save and invest;
c. Transferring resources from the hands of the public to the hands of the state to make profitable public investment;
d. Modifying the pattern of investment; and
e. Mitigating economic inequalities.

All these objectives, it will be seen, are related to the ultimate goals of rapid increase in national income and of improvement in the distribution. The problem is to design a structure of taxation that will be conducive to the accomplishment of these objectives.

Through an appropriate tax polity, for example, government can, to a large extent, check excess consumption and speculative investment. The tax net should be deepened and widened by raising old taxes and imposing new ones. Since at the time of inflation there is need to reduce aggregate demand at the strategic points each particular tax should aim to attack aggregate effective demand at each particular strategic point.

Public Debt

To the extend public borrowing leaves less purchasing power in the hands of the people it is anti-inflationary. The government should launch a mass scale program of borrowing with a view to controlling inflation. The public should be encouraged to save by offering the inducement of high interest rates. The most effective form of public borrowing is the scheme of compulsory saving (compulsory deposit as it was practised under the C.D. Act 1974).

Administrative Controls

The objectives of demand management may sometimes be better achieved by weapons other than monetary and fiscal policies or may be beyond the reach of such policies. There are alternative weapons in the possible use of administrative controls such as were widely introduced in war time, for the most part progressively abandoned by industrial countries after the war, but still in use all parts of the world in one form or the other, usually for balance of payments reasons. These controls include consumer rationing, building licensing and quantitative restrictions of exports. Controls imposed by the government on the financial system, such as exchange control, control over capital issues or even ceilings on bank credit, might also qualify for inclusion instead of being treated as monetary and fiscal weapons.[23]

Blending Fiscal and Monetary Policies

Monetary and fiscal policies are complementary. While monetary policy is operated by the central bank with the objective of affecting income and spending—particularly in the private sector—through influencing the money stock and the cost of borrowing it, fiscal policy is implemented through the budget and is directed to affect income and spending through its effect upon the amount, character, and timing of government spending and revenue. In a period of inflation economic stability can be achieved more quickly by combining the policy of surplus budgeting with dear money policy. Conversely, in a period of depression recovery can be initiated more quickly by reinforcing the policy of deficit budgeting supported by a cheap money policy. Thus, in the interest of achieving economic stability quickly it is necessary to coordinate effectively the two stability tools. The importance of fiscal and monetary policies in achieving economic stability is clearly stated by J. Cameron Thomson of the Committee for Economic Development in his testimony before Douglas Committee in the following words:

Fiscal, monetary and debt policies are appropriate means for attacking the problem of instability in a free society. The problem of instability is essentially a problem of broad forces affecting the overall magnitudes of the economy. The problem arises when millions of workers are simultaneously unemployed, or when there is a general, although probably uneven, rise of most prices. The advantage of fiscal, monetary and debt policies is that they allow the government to influence the over all forces—especially the level of aggregate demand—that determine the stability of the economy without necessarily involving the government in detailed control of the particulars of the economy. These overall measures will, of course, affect different individuals and business differently. But the differences are determined by the market process, not by government decisions.[24]

Thus monetary and fiscal policies are essential for any stabilisation policy. They can also be used to canalize resources to desired activities or check resources going to undesirable activities.

References

1. Cairncross, Sir Alec; *Essays in Economic Management*, George Allen & Unwin Ltd., London; 1971; p.22.
2. Ibid; pp.49–50.
3. Those who are interested to know more details about the functions of the Central Bank may please read: *Central Banking* by DeKock, M.H; London, 1969.

4. Commercial banks in India have to comply with cash reserve ratio and statutory liquidity ratio.

5. Report of the Commission on Finance and Industry (1931), quoted from Cairncross, Sir Alec; op.cit. p.94

6. DeKock, M.H; *Central Banking;* op.cit., pp.151–152

7. Ibid; p.175.

8. Ibid; pp.183–184

9. Ibid; p.184.

10. Hawtrey, R.G; *The Art of Central Banking;* pp.145–148

11. Cairncross, Sir Alec; op.cit. p.97

12. Memorandum of Evidence to the Committee on the Working of the Monetary System, para.7 (Memorandum, vol.3. p.130) Quoted from Cairncross, Sir Alec; op.cit. pp.97-98.

13. For example in 1975-76 it was very apparent in India that constructional activity was particularly vulnerable to tight money policy.

14. Cairncross; Sir Alec; op.cit pp.100–102.

15. Ibid; p.102

16. Richard, A. Musgrave; The Theory of Public Finance; Mc Graw Hill Co.; New York; p.95

17. Adam Smith; The Wealth of Nations, p.778

18. Ibid

19. Richard, A.Musgrave; op.cit

20. I bid, pp.113–114

21. What is true of public expenditure is also true of private expenditure.

22. Hansen, Alvin H.; *Fiscal Policy and Business Cycles;* W.W.Norton & Company, INC; New York; 1960; p.205.

23. Cairncross, Sir Alec; op.cit., pp.107–108.

24. Quoted from Vaish, M.C. *Monetary Theory;* Ratan Prakashan Mandir; Agra; 1968; p.279.

21 Balance of Payments

Several institutions as well as individuals have defined the term 'Balance of Payments'. According to the Reserve Bank of India balance of payments is a statistical statement that systematically summarises, for a specific time period, the economic transactions of an economy with the rest of the world.

According to IMF Balance of Payments Manual, the balance of payments is a statistical statement for a given period which shows:

1. Transactions in goods and services and income between economy and the rest of the world.
2. Changes in ownership and other changes in that country's Monetary gold, Special Drawing Rights, and claims on and liabilities to the rest of the world, and
3. Unrequited transfers and counterpart entries that are need to balance, in the accounting sense, any entries in the foregoing transactions and changes which are not mutually offsetting.

" The balance of payments of a country" says Kindleberger, "is a systematic record of all economic transactions between its residents and residents of foreign countries" To Benham "The balance of payments of a country is a record of the monetary transactions over a period with the rest of the world." According to Sodersten "The balance of payments is merely a way of listing receipts and payments in international transactions for a country."

From the above definitions we can list the main features of balance of payments. They are:

1. It is a systematic record of receipts and payments of a country with other countries.
2. It is a statement of accounts for a fixed period of time (Normally one year).
3. It includes all transactions coming under visible, invisible and capital transfers.
4. The record is prepared on the basis of double entry system
5. Double entry system keeps the debit and credit sides of the accounts in balance.
6. Whenever there is any difference in actual total receipts and payments, necessary adjustments are made.

Balance of Trade and Balance of Payments

Two often used terms with reference to international trade are balance of trade and balance of payments. Balance of trade represents only transactions (exports and imports) connected with visible items (goods). It does not include items transacted that fall under invisible category (services). For example, services rendered by shipping, insurance and banking, interest and dividend payments, expenditure of tourists, expenditure incurred by Embassies, cultural exchange programmes, visits of various functionaries of the government, capital transfers, external assistance, lending and borrowing.

Balance of payments account represents transactions falling under visible as well as invisible items. So balance of payments is a broader concept vis-à-vis Balance of trade. So balance of payments is a better indicator in assessing the economic strength of a country.

Favourable Balance of Trade

A country is said to have favourable balance of trade when the total value of the goods exported by it is more than the total value of goods imported by it.

Unfavourable Balance of Trade

A country is said to have unfavourable balance of trade when the value of the country's imports is more than the value of that country's exports.

Equilibrium in Balance of Trade

A country's balance of trade is said to be in equilibrium when the value of the country's imports and exports is equal.

The Format of the Balance of Payments

The Balance of Payments is prepared on the principle of double entry system. The credit (total receipts) and debit (total payments or obligations) entries in the balance sheet are generally grouped under four heads. They are:
   i. Current account
   ii. Capital account
   iii. Unilateral payments account
   iv. Official reserves asset account.

Current Account

Under Current Account all items of imports (visible as well as invisible) and exports (visible and invisible) will be recorded.

Capital Account

Both short-term and long-term capital transactions will be recorded under Capital Account. Capital outflow will be recorded as debit and capital inflow as credit.

Payment of interest, loans and interest will be recorded in the Current Account as they are really payments for the services of capital. For example, interest on loans taken from foreigners, dividend on foreign investments (i.e. for foreigners) will be entered under the head debit and interest received on loans given to foreigners and dividends on investments made in foreign countries will be recorded under credit.

Unilateral Transfers Account

Gifts, private remittances, government grants, reparation and disaster payments received by the country or citizens of the country will be recorded under credit and gifts, private remittances, government grants, reparations and disaster payments paid to foreigners by citizens or government will be recorded under debit.

Official Reserves Account

Official reserves represent the holdings by the government or official agencies of the means of payment that are generally accepted for the settlement of international claims.

Methods of Measuring Balance of Payments

There are different methods of measuring the Balance of Payments. They are:

1. *Basic balance:* This includes the Current Account Balance of payments and long-term Capital Balance of Payments. The Current Account Balance of Payments shows the difference in values of the flows of goods, services, income and gifts between the home country and foreign countries. When there is a surplus under this category, the current balance is said to be positive and when there is deficit under this category, the Current Account is said to be negative. Similarly, when there is surplus in long-term capital receipts, Capital Balance of Payments is said to be positive and when there is deficit, Capital Balance of payments is said to be negative.

2. *Net liquidity balance:* It comprises of basic balance and short period private liquid capital balance.

3. *Official settlement balance:* This comprises of gross liquid balance and short period private liquid capital balance.

On the above discussion we can derive a formula for preparing the Balance of Payments Statement.

Balance of Trade = import – export	= a
(+) Transfer Balance of Payments	= b
(=) Current Balance of Payments	= c = (a+b)
(+) Long period capital balance	= d
(=) Basic balance	= B = (c+d)
(+) Short period illiquid capital balance	= f
(+) SDR disbursement	= s
(+) Errors and omissions	= e
(=) Net liquid balance	= I = (c + f + s + e)
(+) Short period private liquid capital balance	= j
(+) official settlement balance	= k = (I + j)

Based on the above information let us prepare a Balance of Payments Statement on double entry principle.

Balance of Payments Statement

Receipts (Credit)	*Payments (Debit)*

Items of Current Account

1. Export of goods	1. Import of goods
2. Export of services	2. Import of services
a. Services rendered by domestic commercial companies	a. Services rendered by foreign companies
b. Services of domestic experts	b. Services of foreign experts
3. Expenditure by foreign tourists	3. Expenditure of country's tourists abroad.
4. Receipts from transportation services rendered in foreign countries	4. Payments for domestic use of foreign transportation.
5. Income from foreign investments	5. Income to foreigners for investment made at home.
6. Income from expenditure of of foreign governments	6. Government's expenses in foreign countries.
7. Grants, donations and other payments received from foreign countries.	7. Grants, donations and other payments made to foreigners.
8. Miscellaneous expenditure by foreigners.	8. Miscellaneous expenses in foreign countries.

Items of Capital Expenditure

9. Foreign private debit	9. Recovery of private debit from foreigners
10. Inflow of banking capital	10. Outflow of banking capital
11. Debit received by the government	11. Payment of debit by government sector
12. Reserves and Monetary gold inflow	12. Payment of reserves and monetary gold outflow
13. International sale of gold	13. Purchase of gold from international market
14. Capital receipts	14. Capital payments

India's Balance of Payments: Summary (US $.million)

Sl. No	Items	2003-04	2004-05	2005-06	2006-07	2007-08 (PR)
1.	Exports	66285	85206	105152	128888	166163
2.	Imports	80003	118908	157056	190670	257789
3.	Trade balance	-13718	-33702	-51904	-61782	-91696
4.	Invisible (net)	27801	31232	42002	52217	74592
	Non-factor services	10144	15426	23170	29469	37565
	Income	-4505	-4979	-5855	-7331	-4917
	Pvt. transfers	21608	20525	24493	29825	41705
5.	Goods and services balance	-3574	-18276	-28734	-32313	-54061
6.	Current account balance	14083	-2470	-9902	-9565	-17034
7.	External assistance (net)	-2858	1923	1702	1775	2114
8.	Commercial borrowing (net)	-2925	5194	2508	16103	22633
9.	Non-resident deposits (net)	3642	-964	2789	4321	179
10.	Foreign investment (net) of which	13744	13000	15528	14753	44957
	i. FDI (net)	2388	3713	3034	7693	15401
	ii. Portfolio	11356	9287	12494	7060	29556
11.	Other flows (net)*	5735	9476	2427	9219	39315
12.	Capital account total (net)	17338	28629	24954	46171	109198
13.	Reserves (increase (-)/decrease (+)	-31421	-26159	-15052	-36606	-92164

Source: Economic Survey 2008 = 09 PR: Partially Revised

- Includes, among others delayed export receipts and errors and omissions, Balance of Payment's Disequilibrium.

The balance of payments of a country will be in equilibrium when that country's demand for foreign exchange is exactly equal to its supply of it. Balance of payments of a country is said to be in disequilibrium when it shows either a deficit or surplus in its foreign exchange. There will be a deficit in the balance of payments if the country's demand for foreign exchange exceeds its supply and vice versa. A number of factors are responsible for disequilibrium in balance of payments. These factors can be grouped under the following heads; viz;

    i. Economic factors,

    ii. Political factors, and

    iii. Sociological factors.

Economic Factors

Economic factors that cause disequilibrium in Balance of Payments themselves vary. The types of disequilibrium that they cause can be discussed under four heads. They are:

    i. Development disequilibrium,

    ii. Cyclical disequilibrium,

    iii. Secular disequilibrium, and

    iv. Structural disequilibrium.

Development Disequilibrium

Development needs (such as foreign capital and technology) necessitate large scale imports. Again large scale development expenditure within the country increases the income and purchasing power of the people. Both these result in large scale imports and that lead to balance of payments disequilibrium.

Cyclical Disequilibrium

Occurrence of trade cycles may lead to cyclical disequilibrium. As pointed out by Lawrence W. Towels depression always brings about a drastic shrinkage in world trade, while prosperity stimulates it. The shrinkage in world trade during 2008 due to the global financial meltdown vividly clarifies this.

Secular Disequilibrium

In the case of certain countries balance of payments disequilibrium persists for long periods owing to certain secular trends. Disequilibrium in balance of payments due to secular trends is termed as secular disequilibrium.

Structural Disequilibrium

Structural changes that occur in a country due to planning or extra effort on development activities may cause disequilibrium in balance of payments. Disequilibrium in balance of payments due to structural changes is known as structural disequilibrium.

Political Factors

Political factors such as instability of government and the consequent unpredictability of the policies of the governments may sometimes result in large scale flight of capital and that may adversely affect investment and production. Wars, disruptive activities, changes in trade routes, government's expenditure on Embassies and foreign missions, partition or unification of a country—All the above factors may lead to disequilibrium in balance of payments.

Social Factors

Social factors such as population explosion, changes in social values, tastes, preferences, fashion, education, etc. may result in disequilibrium in balance of payments.

Results of Adverse Balance of Payments

Unfavourable balance of payments situation of a country may create problems such as depletion of foreign exchange reserves, flight of foreign capital, lowering of credit rating, political and economic dependency.

Measures to Correct Balance of Payments Disequilibrium

Countries adopt different methods to correct their balance of payments disequilibrium. These measures can be classified under two broad categories. They are automatic measures and deliberate measures.

Automatic Correction

This worked well under the metallic currency (gold or silver) system. It was believed that if free play of market forces is permitted disequilibrium in balance of payments will be automatically corrected in course of time. For example, if there is any deficit in the balance of payments the demand for foreign exchange exceeds its supply and these results in an increase in the exchange rate and a reduction in the exchange value of the domestic currency. This makes the exports from the country cheaper and imports to the country dearer than what it was before. This increases exports and decreases imports and that helps to restore balance of payments equilibrium.

Under the fixed exchange system, the automatic adjustments of the balance of payments occur via changes in the adjustment variables –price, interest, income and capital flows.

Price Adjustments

Under the gold or silver standard, there will be an outflow of gold or silver as the case may be from a deficit country to a surplus country. This results in a fall in the supply of money in the deficit country and an increase in the money supply in the surplus country. This will result in a rise in prices in the surplus country and vice versa. The rise in prices in the surplus country will discourage exports and encourage imports from the deficit country where prices have fallen. This will restore balance of payments equilibrium.

Balance of Payments Statement

Under the paper currency system also a fall or rise in foreign exchange reserves consequent on a reduction or surplus in the balance of payments can cause similar change.

Interest Rate Adjustments

Apart from its impact on prices balance of payments surplus or deficit can have impact on the short-term interest rates. The decrease or increase in money supply due to balance of payments deficit or surplus can lead to rise or fall in the interest rates. This will stimulate investment in the deficit country where the interest rate has risen. This can happen in two ways: (i) By withdrawing their deposits from the surplus country where the interest has fallen, and (ii) the fall in the interest rate in the surplus country will prompt foreigners to withdraw their deposits from the surplus country and channel that to the deficit country. Such actions will help to restore equilibrium in balance of payments.

Income Adjustments

The classical economists really neglected adjustments in income to correct balance of payments disequilibrium. It was John Maynard Keynes who first exhorted that under the fixed exchange system adjustments in income will help to restore balance of payments equilibrium automatically.

A nation with persistent payments surplus will experience rising income from increasing exports. The opposite will happen in the deficit country. The increase in income in the surplus country will increase the purchasing power of the people and that will prompt them to demand more foreign goods. The reverse will take place in the deficit country. Ultimately this is expected to restore the balance of payments equilibrium between the surplus and deficit country.

Capital Flows

As already explained, changes in the interest rates in the surplus and deficit countries due to balance of payments disequilibrium will encourage capital inflows to the deficit country and capital outflows from the surplus country due to the interest impact and that will help to restore equilibrium in balance of payments.

Deliberate Measures

Automatic correction in balance of payments disequilibrium may become a long and drawn out process. Hence deliberate measures are initiated by governments to correct the balance of payments disequilibrium. The deliberate measures implemented to correct balance of payments disequilibrium can be classified under three heads, viz;

    i. Monetary measures,

   ii. Trade measures, and

  iii. Miscellaneous measures.

Monetary Measures

The important monetary measures implemented to correct the balance of payments disequilibrium are:
   a. Expansion or contraction of money supply,
   b. Devaluation, and
   c. Exchange control.

Expansion or Contraction of Money Supply

Domestic price level and through that aggregate demand for imports and exports can be influenced by expansion or contraction of money supply. When money supply is increased in the surplus country, ecteris *paribus*, price level will rise and this will dissuade foreigners to buy from that country where the price level has gone up and this will result in decrease in exports. When money supply is reduced in the deficit country price level will fall and that will prompt foreigners to buy more from the country where prices has fallen. This will encourage exports. Thus the fall in imports in the deficit country and fall in exports in the surplus country will help to correct the balance of payments disequilibrium.

Devaluation

Devaluation is the process of reducing the official exchange rate of the currency. (i.e. the rate at which the domestic currency is exchanged for a foreign country's currency.) A country which has a fundamental disequilibrium in the balance of payments may devalue its currency in order to push up exports and pull down imports. Devaluation makes export of goods cheaper and imports, dearer. This is expected to help to correct the balance of payments disequilibrium.

Exchange Control

Exchange control is another measure generally adopted by deficit countries to correct the balance of payments disequilibrium. Under exchange control the government or the Central Bank of the country assumes complete control over the foreign exchange reserves of the country. The government or the Central Bank of the country, as the case may be, direct all the recipients of foreign exchange to surrender such foreign exchange to the government or the Central Bank in exchange for domestic currency. By virtue of its control over the use of foreign exchange, the government can control imports. Under this system only license holders are permitted to import. Some times quota for different items of imports is fixed. These measures are expected to correct the disequilibrium in balance of payments.

Trade Measures

Trade measures relate policies directed to promote exports and reduce imports. Export promotion measures include reduction or abolition of export duties, providing export finance and subsidy, providing incentives, organising trade fairs, providing infrastructural facilities. Imports can be restricted through imposition of tariffs, quotas, licensing or even by prohibition.

Miscellaneous Measures

In addition to the measures mentioned above there are several other measures that governments can use to correct balance of payments disequilibrium. Some of such measures are:

a. Taking assistance from foreign governments or agencies
b. Attracting more tourists
c. Through liberal industrial policies
d. Reducing expenditure on embassies and consulates
e. Encouraging NRI deposits
f. Awakening the national spirit as at the time of freedom movement
g. Encouraging foreign investment
h. Using foreign exchange reserves, etc.

The list mentioned above is not exhaustive, but only indicative.

22 Theories of Exchange Rate Determination

Exchange Rate–Meaning

Exchange rate is the price at which a unit of one country's currency is exchanged for one unit of another country's currency. Like all prices, when flexible, the exchange rate is expected to keep a country's balance of payments in equilibrium with all other countries.

Exchange Rate Determinants

There are a number of theories of exchange rate determination. Under the metallic standard (gold or silver) the exchange rate of two currencies was determined on the basis of the metallic content in the respective currencies. This is popularly known as *mint parity rate.* For example, if an American dollar contained 10 grams of gold and an Indian rupee 5 grams of gold, the exchange rate between the Indian rupee and the American dollar will be two rupees equal to one dollar. Under this system the exchange rate can fluctuate only within limits and the limit is determined by what is termed as import or export point. That is the cost of importing or exporting the metal which is used for coinage. In case the exchange rate fluctuate more than the import or export point, then the account can be settled either by importing or exporting the metal concerned.

Fixed Exchange Rate or Pegged Rate

Under the IMF regime countries pegged the value of their currencies to gold or a major currency (dollar) or a basket of currencies. Under this system the exchange rates were allowed to fluctuate within a narrow margin of at most ± 1 percent around the central rate. This is popularly known as the snake. If the exchange rate fluctuates more than the 'snake', the country concerned can approach the IMF with a request to re-fix the exchange rate and in such cases the IMF normally permitted the country concerned to devalue its currency. Under the pegged rate the monetary authority used to ensure fixed parity through intervention.

Pegged Exchange Rate within Horizontal Bands

Under this arrangement the value of the currency is maintained within margins of fluctuations around a formal or *de facto* fixed rate that are wider than ± one percent around a central rate.

Crawling Peg and Crawling Band

The value of the currency is adjusted periodically in small amounts at a pre-announced rate allowing the parity (and therefore the band), to crawl in response to selective quantitative indicators. The degree of flexibility dependent on the width of the band and the commitment to maintain the exchange rate within the band imposes constraints on the monetary policy.

Purchasing Power Parity Theory

Under the paper currency system, the exchange rate between two currencies is determined by the relative purchasing power of the currencies. Purchasing power of currencies is reflected in the general price level. In case price level increases, purchasing power will fall and vice versa. Purchasing power parity theory states that nominal (spot) exchange rate (NER) will rise as the domestic price index rises relative to foreign country's price index. This, in effect, causes the domestic currency loses its value (depreciate). This can be expressed as

$$NER = p/p^*$$

Where p denotes the domestic price and p^* foreign country's price index respectively.

There is extensive literature that documents that purchasing power parity doesn't hold except perhaps in the very long run.

The purchasing Power Parity model in the short run may be modified by incorporating variables other than prices such as interest rates, investment rates, terms of trade (balance of payments position), fiscal deficits, foreign capital inflows.

Floating Exchange Rate

Genesis of floating: The American dollar was convertible up to 1971. After the Second World War, America spent millions of dollars in other countries, some for good purposes (like the reconstruction of economies which were shattered during the war), and some for bad purposes. When Mr. Nixon was the President of the United States of America a large part of this dollar which is popularly known as Euro dollar bounced back. America found it difficult to convert this dollar into gold. So President Nixon declared that America is withdrawing the provision of convertibility and decided to float the dollar to fix the price of dollar on the basis of market forces. This forced other countries also to float their currencies. This led a new method of exchange rate fixation which is popularly known as the floating rate.

Managed Floating

Under managed floating the monetary authorities influence the movements of exchange rate through active intervention in the foreign exchange market without specifying or pre-committing to, a pre-announced path of exchange rate. They announce no parity or band, but they typically worry if the rate depreciates a lot, and they intervene, or change interest rates, or sometimes seek to influence the flow of capital, with a view to having an impact on the exchange rate. They may also worry about the exchange rate appreciating so much as to threaten the country's trade competitiveness. The managed floating has become quite common in recent years and that is now followed in India.

Demand and Supply Theory

According to Dunlup the exchange rate is determined on the forces of demand for and supply of currencies.

A country's choice as to which currency regime it should follow reflects the national priorities about all facets of the macro economy, including inflation, unemployment, interest rate levels, trade balances and economic growth. Economists generally believe that a country cannot simultaneously have a fixed exchange rate, free international flow of capital and independent monetary policy. Milton Friedman preferred monetary rules and floating exchange rate while Robert A. Mundell, the supply-side economist was a fan of fixed exchange rate.

Overshooting Model

Rudiger Dornbusch (1976) developed a monetary model by relaxing the assumption of short-run purchasing power parity. This model assumes that in the short run the exchange rate can overshoot its long-run value as a result of a change in the fundamentals, but eventually, however, the exchange rate returns to the long-run value.

Random Walk Models

The random walk hypothesis of Engel and West (2005) suggests that the exchange rate follows a random walk with little or no drift. This implies that the exchange rate is unpredictable and the best predictor of tomorrows exchange rate is today's exchange rate itself. This is based on the Efficient Market Hypothesis of Eugene Fama (1991). Even though this is not fully supported by empirical evidence, it is generally found that exchange rates are non-stationary following a random walk under a system of fully floating exchange rate and normal inflationary conditions (Meese and Rogoff (1983), Somanath (1986), Imad Moosa (1998).

Portfolio Balance Model

The Portfolio Balance Model states that the exchange rate is determined by trade and capital flows as recorded on the balance of payments (Sabastian Edwards, 1994). In this model, the exchange rate is determined by the forces of demand for and supply of foreign currency.

Supply and demand are determined by several important factors as growth of relative income levels, relative price levels, interest rate differential, foreign exchange reserves, current account balances, net flow of foreign capital, etc. in the host country. The portfolio balance model assumes that the ratio of domestic assets to foreign assets is determined by their relative returns defined as the sum of interest rate differential and the expected change in the exchange rate. In an economy, given the relative rates of return and the degree of sustainability between domestic and foreign assets, market agents strive to achieve a portfolio balance.

Rational Expectations Theory

Economists have found that exchange rates do not seem to be affected by economic fundamentals in the short-run. When the fundamentals are combined with market expectations of future exchange rates, the model yields the value of the current exchange rate. Future economic fundamentals also matter because they determine the market's expectations about the future exchange rate. If the market expects the rupee price of dollar to become higher in the future than it is today, the dollar will tend to be high today against the rupee. But if the market expects the price to be lower in the future than it is today, the price of dollar will tend to be low today. Though largely associated with the free market, the rational expectations revolution has been far more wide reaching. In a world of fast clearing asset markets, exchange rate overshooting might be a rational response to monetary shocks.

Two of the most distinguished rational expectations economists, viz; Robert Lucas and Tom Sargent have made extensive studies and developed sophisticated models. They have gone beyond the simple context of the new classical world of perfect markets with instant market clearing and have considered the role of rational expectations when markets are distorted.

According to George Shackle (1958), each individual constructs in his imagination different scenarios or possible outcomes following on the different actions he is contemplating. Based on this, Shackle regards economic decisions as entirely subjective and so not predictable. However, econometric models assert that economic behaviour is predictable and regular. The corner stone of econometrics is the implicit assertion that in the mass, individual decisions exhibit regularity even though each individual decision will be quite unpredictable. Individuals when aggregated in a large sample will behave like many typical individuals, to a certain extent supported by central limit theorem, i.e. large samples tend to follow normal distribution.

The exchange rate is often sensitive to all of the influences that typically affect trade and investment decisions and expectations about future asset prices.

Index

Reader's Notes

Reader's Notes